The Puerto Ricans

THE
PUERTO RICANS

A DOCUMENTARY HISTORY

Updated and Expanded 2020 Edition

EDITED BY

Kal Wagenheim
Olga Jiménez de Wagenheim

AND

Luis Martínez-Fernández

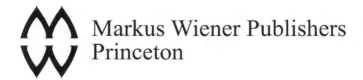

Markus Wiener Publishers
Princeton

Library of Congress Cataloging-in-Publication Data

Names: Wagenheim, Kal, editor. | Jiménez, Olga, editor. |
  Martínez-Fernández, Luis, 1960- editor.
Title: The Puerto Ricans : a documentary history / edited by Kal Wagenheim,
  Olga Jiménez de Wagenheim, and Luis Martínez-Fernández.
Description: Sixth Markus Wiener Publishers edition, updated and expanded.
  | Princeton : Markus Wiener Publishers, 2020. | Includes bibliographical
  references and index. | Summary: "This book covers five hundred years of
  history, providing a kaleidoscopic view of the island's past. This new
  edition covers the debt crisis, Hurricane Maria and its aftermath, and
  the Revolt of 2019."— Provided by publisher.
Identifiers: LCCN 2019049484
ISBN 9781558766433 (pbk : alk. paper) | ISBN 9781558766426 (hc : alk. paper)
Subjects: LCSH: Puerto Rico—History. | Puerto Ricans—United
  States—History. | Nationalism—Puerto Rico—History.
Classification: LCC F1971 .P79 2020 | DDC 972.95--dc23
LC record available at https://lccn.loc.gov/2019049484

Markus Wiener Publishers books are printed in the United States
of America on acid-free paper, and meet the guidelines for
permanence and durability of the Committee on Production
Guidelines for Book Longevity of the Council on Library Resources

CONTENTS

PREFACE

First published in 1973, Kal Wagenheim and Olga Jiménez de Wagenheim's *The Puerto Rican's: A Documentary History* has long been a classic in the field of Puerto Rican studies. It has been widely used in hundreds of History of Puerto Rico courses and has helped provide a deeper understanding of the island's history to generations of students. I have put this book to good use in my own courses as required text for over fifteen years.

I was honored to receive an invitation from the Wagenheims and publisher Markus Wiener to update and expand *The Puerto Ricans* for its sixth Markus Wiener Publishers edition. Last updated in 2013, the book's new edition includes an entire new section (Part XI): "Puerto Rico in Crisis".

The section includes an introduction and thirteen new readings, a combination of primary documents, journalistic articles, and scholarly essays that touch upon some of the most important developments since 2006. Among these are: the economically damaging phase out of Section 936 of the US Internal Revenue Service Code, the financial crisis that exploded in 2015, the imposition, since 2016, of the Financial Oversight and Management Board for Puerto Rico, Hurricane Maria (2017) and its aftermath, the peaceful revolt of July 2019 that forced Governor Ricardo Roselló to resign in shame, and the unending political status debate.

As the new section's contents indicate, the period has been a combination of human-made calamities and natural disasters that have sunk the island into what is arguably its deepest crisis ever—the Great Depression included. The last three readings, however, strike some positive notes, namely the determination, resilience, and creativity with which hundreds of thousands of Puerto Ricans have stood up to corrupt, inept and immoral politicians, bond-speculators and their agents, and the fury of hurricanes.

We can only hope that future expanded editions will contain better news.

Luis Martínez-Fernández, Ph.D.
Orlando, Florida, November 6, 2019

INTRODUCTION

In the summer of 1898, when American troops first raised the Stars and Stripes on Puerto Rico's southern shore, their commanding general promised the natives the "advantages and blessings of enlightened civilization."

Three decades later, American historian Hubert Herring observed, "We were not invited by the Puerto Ricans, nor did we ask their consent. . . . Viewed in the light of the rosy promises made by those who took the island . . . our record has not been brilliant."

Subsequent years have confirmed the emptiness of the general's promises. The invasion of Puerto Rico ended four centuries of oppressive Spanish colonial rule, only to replace it with a more subtle brand of colonialism that still endures.

This book of readings spans more than five hundred years in the history of the Puerto Rican people, from their ethnic origins to their present dilemma as members of a nation without nationhood—a people whose collective future is shrouded by uncertainty.

There are, in fact, two Puerto Ricos. The first is a small Caribbean island, densely populated by nearly 4 million Spanish-speaking people. That Puerto Rico, *la patria,* contains all the ingredients of any nation: there are impoverished rural folk and urban slum dwellers, but there are also politicians, and poets, teachers and students, bankers and clerks, factory workers, farmers, doctors, musicians, lawyers, judges, journalists, computer programmers, bus drivers, policemen—and enough thieves to keep the police busy.

The second Puerto Rico began as a small offshoot of the first: an amorphous mass of people, mainly rural, who from the end of World War II migrated to the United States to seek jobs that they could not find in *la patria.* The inhabitants of the second Puerto Rico were scattered throughout the fifty states of the Union, in fragmented, embryonic communities, forming part of a poor, silent, and polychromatic minority, in an affluent nation torn by racial strife. They were the heirs to the crumbling tenements of the inner city, and the dirty jobs that pay the lowest wages; they had few leaders to champion their cause; in some U.S. cities, their children could spend twelve years in school without ever hearing Spanish spoken in a classroom, without ever hearing their names pronounced correctly.

Today, decades later, serious problems of socioeconomic inequality remain. The level of poverty among Puerto Rican families is substantially higher than the U.S. average (in 2010, about 10% of non-Hispanic white families were below the poverty line, compared with more than 26% of Hispanic and black families).

But there has also been substantial change. The number of Puerto Ricans in the United States has soared to 4.6 million, far exceeding the island's population of 3.9 million. In 2010, they formed part of a U.S. Hispanic population of 50.5 million (vs. 35.3 million in 2000) that is a large, growing political and economic force. Many second- and third-generation Puerto Ricans have moved into the U.S. middle class and reside in suburbia. Many have intermarried with members of other ethnic groups. Many have won elections to the U.S. Congress, state legislatures, and city councils. In major U.S. cities such as New York, Chicago, and Philadelphia, bilingual Puerto Rican teachers, social workers, and other professionals are helping to pave the way for the latest wave of Hispanic immigrants from Mexico, the Caribbean, and Central America.

Despite the gradual process of assimilation that is taking place, ties to the island patria remain strong. The best proof of that is the difficulty one encounters in finding a seat on the many airline flights between Puerto Rico and the continental United States, particularly during the holidays. San Juan's international airport is among the busiest in the world, due to the constant back and forth flow of Puerto Ricans between the patria and the continental United States.

While Puerto Ricans share a great deal with earlier European immigrants, and with blacks, they are unique in several respects. To begin with, the political status of their homeland is in limbo, and its destiny is still ivery much in doubt. Thus, one often sees the bewildering phenomenon of Puerto Rican activists on the mainland demanding their full rights as U.S. citizens and moments later shouting vivas for the island's independence. This tug-of-war of apparently contradictory goals is just one of several factors that slow the impetus of Puerto Rican entry into the mainstream of American life. Another factor is the "tentative" status of many immigrants, who dream of returning to Puerto Rico as soon as they have enough money to buy a home; this dream is far more realistic today, when a Puerto Rican can hop a jet and be in San Juan three hours later, than it was among the European immigrants earlier in the century, who severed their ancient bonds, and spent days packed together in the holds of ships.

But—before I get carried away—this is not a book about the Puerto Rican migration, the history of which is still being acted out in America's streets. In this book, I have tried to offer a collection of readings that describe the history and social culture of Puerto Rico, with marked emphasis on this century, a period largely neglected by historians. My main purposes have been to make available in English a substantial body of knowledge for the benefit of thousands of Puerto Rican students on the mainland, who have been cut off from their national heritage, and to help North American readers to appreciate this important ethnic group. The idea for this book emerged shortly after I finished writing *Puerto Rico: A Profile* (Praeger, 1971), an introductory survey of the island. I realized then that the book's brief chapter on history barely scratched the surface of so vast a subject, and I hoped that a companion volume of readings, such as this one, would enable the interested reader to probe more deeply.

Even this book, in its attempt to cover five hundred years of history, is little more than a collage of events and impressions. But, in providing this kaleidoscopic view of the island's past, I have chosen carefully from a broad variety of sources: Spanish clergy and colonial governors, men of letters, farmers, slum dwellers, politicians (Puerto Rican and American), and journalists of varying opinion. Whenever possible, I have used contemporary accounts, to capture the heat and flavor of the moment. Also, I have given preference to the writings of Puerto Ricans, who have too often been spoken for by others. In most cases where I have used the writings of Americans, I have done so because they treat a vital topic in a unique way or illustrate the cultural bias of a foreigner (I leave to the reader the fun of deciding which does which).

I have no doubt that a book such as this—and others like it—is necessary. During a visit to a small Puerto Rican community in Syracuse, New York, I was impressed by the intense curiosity of Puerto Rican students toward their island's history, and I was saddened to see how desperately they were searching for their own identity. My memory of one college student is especially vivid. After struggling to speak Spanish, he lost patience and said, in perfect English, "Look, we know that we Puerto Ricans are a colonial, exploited people. We don't have to study to know that. We see it every day in the lives of our parents, in our homes, on the streets. Now we want the lowdown; it's like walking backwards, to learn the 'why' of what we already know."

Puerto Rican scholar Frank Bonilla has said: "If we choose to go beyond survival as a community, then our creativity must be fed by a collective vision that reaches out to Puerto Ricans everywhere. When people ask in what way Puerto Ricans differ from earlier migrants, we must be ready with the true answer, which is that we are a displaced offshoot of a people and a land that have yet to be liberated, and whose freedom is our own."

* * *

For her help with this book, I offer my deepest gratitude to my wife—and colleague—Olga Jiménez de Wagenheim, a distinguished historian whose suggestions and guidance were essential. I also offer special thanks to two men who have since passed away: Pedro Juan Soto, the noted novelist, whose diligence and generosity were always an example and inspiration; and Leon King, my editor when the book was first published in 1973 and for decades after that a valued friend.

It is most gratifying to see that this book remains of interest more than three decades after its original publication. Since that time, some things have changed in Puerto Rico. These changes include the growing urbanization and diversification of the economy and the rapid growth of the Puerto Rican community in the United States. But much remains the same. For example, the perennial debate over the island's political status continues. The reasons for change and continuity can be found in a careful study of the island's history. I trust that the reader will find some of the answers among these pages.

Millburn, New Jersey
August 2012

PART I

DISCOVERY AND CONQUEST

We proceeded along the coast the greater part of that day, and on the evening of the next we discovered another island called Boriquén. . . . All the islands are very beautiful and possess a most luxuriant soil, but this last island appeared to exceed all others in beauty.

—Translated from a letter by Dr. Diego Alvarez Chanca,
who accompanied Christopher Columbus on his second voyage
to the New World in 1493

In 1493, during his second voyage to the New World, Christopher Columbus discovered a "very beautiful" island that possessed a "most luxuriant soil." He named the island San Juan, in honor of Saint John the Baptist. A few years later, the island would be renamed Puerto Rico—meaning "rich port"—because of its great potential, and the capital city would come to be known as San Juan.

Not long after Spain's settlers established themselves in Puerto Rico and the nearby Caribbean islands, they overwhelmed the weaker Indian societies that had lived there since earliest times. The following selections describe those first few years. They include an account of the sighting of Puerto Rico from Columbus's ship in 1493; a description of the way of life of the Tafno Indians who inhabited the island; Juan Ponce de León's official report on how he founded the first European settlement in Puerto Rico; an edict from Spain's Queen Isabella that established the *encomienda* system, which was a thinly disguised form of Indian slavery; an outraged account by Washington Irving of how the greedy Spanish settlers oppressed the Indians; and a history of the brief, abortive Indian rebellion in Puerto Rico—the last struggle of a vanquished people.

BORIQUEN

Because the existence of the New World was already a certainty, Columbus's second voyage in 1493 was ambitious and well supported. Seventeen ships bore 1,200 men, including astronomers, cartographers, soldiers, artisans, laborers, and pardoned criminals. The fleet left Cádiz on September 25 and reached the Caribbean on November 3. Although Columbus kept diaries of his first trip, the best-known eyewitness account of Puerto Rico's discovery is that by Diego Alvarez Chanca, the Admiral's physician. The doctor's brief notes were soon augmented by historians of the period; one of the best accounts of that brief first glimpse of Puerto Rico is the following, written by Fray Bartolomé de las Casas in 1527.

T he next Sunday, the 10th of November, he [Columbus] ordered the anchor raised and the sails spread, and he cruised the coast of the island of Guadeloupe . . . in search of Hispaniola, and he reached a very high island, which he called Monserrate, because it seemed to have the shape of the boulders of Monserrate, and from there he discovered a certain island which was very round, and very steep everywhere, and without ladders or ropes appeared impossible to scale, which is why he gave it the name of Sancta María la Redonda (Saint Mary the Round); another island he called Sancta María del Antigua, which had a coastline of some 15 or 20 leagues; there appeared many other islands to the North, all very high and heavily forested; he stopped at one which he called Sant Martin, and, when they raised anchor, pieces of coral were stuck to the anchor, it seemed. . . .

On Thursday, the 14th of November, the Admiral stopped at another island which he called Sancta Cruz [St. Croix, today]; and he sent men ashore to capture some natives, and thus learn their language. They seized four women and two children, and, as they were returning in the rowboat, they encountered a canoe, which contained four Indians and an Indian woman; when the Indians realized that they could not flee, they, including the woman, began to defend themselves; they began to fire arrows, and they wounded two Christians, and the woman even pierced a shield with her arrow; the sailors crashed their boat into the canoe and overturned it; one of the Indians, who had not lost his bow, swam and fired his arrows with almost the same vigor as if he had been ashore. They saw that one of the Indians had his generative instrument cut off; the

---

Translated from Fray Bartolomé de las Casas, *Historia de las Indias* (Mexico: Fondo de Cultura Económica, 1951), pp. 352-55.

Christians believed it was so that he would grow fatter, like a capon, and then the Caribs would eat him. From there, the Admiral continued his voyage towards Hispaniola, and saw many islands grouped together; they seemed to be beyond counting; the largest of them he called Sancta Ursula, and all the others he called the Eleven Thousand Virgins; from there, he reached another large island, which he called Sant Juan Baptista, which we now call Sant Juan, and which, as we mentioned before, was called Boriquén by the Indians, in a bay of this island toward the west, where all the ships caught many kinds of fish. . . .

Several Christians went ashore, and walked to some houses that were very artfully made, although all were of straw and wood; and there was a plaza, with a road reaching from it to the sea, very clean and straight, made like a street; and the walls were of crossed or woven cane; and above, beautiful gardens, as if they were vineyards or orchards of orange or citron trees, such as there are in Valencia or in Barcelona; and next to the sea there was a high watchtower, where ten or twelve people could fit, also well made; it was probably the pleasure house of the lord of that island, or of that part of that island. The Admiral does not mention having seen any people there; they must have fled in fright when they saw the ships.

THE INDIAN WAY OF LIFE

Ramón Pané was a Catalonian friar who, by order of Christopher Columbus, came to the New World to learn the language and customs of the Indians and to convert them to Christianity. His famous *Relación Sobre Las Antigüedades de los Indios* (*Account of the Antiquities—or Customs—of the Indians*), written in 1505, is probably the first anthropological study made in the New World.

Pané wrote of Hispaniola, just across the narrow Mona Passage from Puerto Rico. Early historians, such as Gonzalo Fernández de Oviedo and Fray Bartolomé de las Casas, affirm that there was no substantial difference between the Indians of Hispaniola and those of Puerto Rico, except—as Oviedo points out—the Puerto Rican tribes "were skilled bowmen and more warlike." Eugenio Fernández Méndez, one of Puerto Rico's leading present-day historians, includes Fray Ramón's account in his historical anthology on these grounds, and because "archeological evidence also confirms the fundamental unity of

---

The Spanish version appears in Eugenio Fernández Méndez (Ed.), *Crónicas de Puerto Rico: 1493-1797,* (San Juan: Ediciones Estado Libre Asociado, 1957), Vol. I, pp. 13-32. English version appears in Edward Gaylord Bourne, "Columbus, Ramón Pané, and the Beginnings of American Anthropology," *American Antiquarian Society,* April, 1906, pp. 318-39.

religion and beliefs" of both groups. The original Latin manuscript of this account has been lost. An admittedly marred Italian translation was later rendered into Spanish. The following segment has been translated by the editor, from the Spanish, after referring to a previous English translation.

Through the mist of translation, of Fray Ramón's pro-Christian bias, and of his obvious disdain for the Indians' religion, there emerges a fascinating portrait of their religious mythology; with more time, he might well have been able to construct an Indian counterpart of the Christian Bible, for his spare story has all the ingredients: a supreme being, saint figures (*cemíes*), an account of the creation of the sea (a great flood), a belief in the afterlife of the dead and a place where they reside, and so forth.

His is one of the first accounts of the use of tobacco [*cogioba*] for mystical and medicinal purposes. The friar also passes along to us the ominous prediction made by one of the Indian chieftains, who had learned from a *cemí* idol that one day their tribes would be vanquished and enslaved by a "clothed race"; this prediction accounts, at least partially, for the awe and the respect with which the Indians regarded Columbus and his men.

Finally, there is Fray Ramón's determination—surely reflecting that of all the conquerors—to "convert" the Indians, to Christianize them, to devalue the Indians' long-cherished life-styles, and, when necessary, to accomplish this by force.

I, Fray Ramón, a poor hermit of the Order of Saint Jerome, by command of the illustrious lord, the Admiral and Viceroy and governor of the Islands and of the mainland of the Indies, write this, which I have been able to learn and know of the belief and idolatry of the Indians and how they worship their gods. . . .

Each one, in praying to the idols that he has in his house, which are called by them *cemíes,* worships in his own fashion and superstition.

They hold that he is immortal in heaven, and that no one can see him, and that he has a mother, but he had no beginning. This god they call Yocahu Vagua Maorocotí, and his mother they call by four names: Atabex, Yermaoguacar, Apito, and Zuimaco. . . .

Likewise, they know from where they came, and whence the sun and the moon had their origins, and how the sea was made, and where the dead go. And they believe that the dead appear on the trails when one walks alone, and that when many go together they do not appear. All this those who have gone before have made them believe, because these people know not how to read or to count beyond ten.

Chapter I

From what direction the Indians came, and in what manner: Española has a province called Caonao, in which there is a mountain called Canta, with two caves: one called Cacibayagua, the other Amayauba. From the first cave came forth the larger part of the people who settled the island. When they dwelled in these caves, a man named Marocael kept watch by night. One day, he tarried in returning to the door, and the sun carried him off. When the people saw this, they closed the door, and he was converted into stone near the door. Later, they say, others who went off to fish were seized by the sun and became trees, which were called by them *Jobos* [a common fruit tree in the Antilles—ed.]. . . .

Chapter II

How the men were divided from the women: It came to pass that a man named Guaguyona said to another called Yadruvava that he should gather an herb called *digo,* used to cleanse the body when they wash themselves. He left before daybreak, but the sun seized him on the way and he became a bird which sings in the morning like the nightingale, and is called Yahuba Bayael. When Guaguyona saw that the man sent to gather *digo* did not return, he resolved to leave the cave.

Chapter III

. . . he said to the women, "Leave your husbands, and let us go into other lands. Leave your sons, and we will take only the herbs with us, and we will return for them."

Chapter IV

He set forth with all the women, in search of other lands, and came to Matinino [usually identified with Martinique—ed.], where he left the women, and went into another region called *Guanín.* The women had left the small children near a brook. When hunger began to torment them, they wailed and called upon their absent mothers; and the fathers could not help the children, who made sounds like "mama," as if to speak, but were really asking for the breast. Wailing in this fashion, as one who desires something with great longing, they were changed into little animals, after the fashion of frogs. . . . In this way, all the men were left without women.

Chapter V

. . . When Guaguyona carried away all the women, he likewise took with him the woman of his cacique, whose name was Anacacuya, deceiving him as he deceived the others; and, moreover, a brother-in-law of his went off with him by sea. And Guaguyona said to his brother-in-law, when they were in the canoe, "See what a fine *cobo* [sea snail] there is in the water," and when he peered into the water, Guaguyona seized him by the feet and cast him into the sea, taking all the women for himself, and he left them at Matinino, where it is said there are only women today. . . .

Chapter VI

Guaguyona returned to where he had taken the women. They say he had left one woman in the sea, and that he was greatly pleased with her, and straightway sought to wash himself, being full of those sores which we call the French disease. [This could be syphilis, indicating that this disease may have existed in the West Indies before the Spaniards arrived—ed.] She then put him in a place apart; and so he was healed. Then she asked permission to go on her way, and he granted it. This woman was named Guabonito, and Guaguyona changed his name to Biberoci Gua-hayona. The woman Guabonito gave him many *guaníns* [golden ornaments], and many *cibas* [beads] to wear around his arms. In those countries, *cibas* are of marblelike stone, and they wear them tied on the arms and neck, and they wear the *guaníns* in their ears, which they pierce when they are children. . . .

Chapter VII

How there were women again on the island of Aití, which is now called Española: They say that one day the men went off to bathe, and, while in the water, it rained heavily, and they were very desirous of having women. Oftentimes, when it rained, they went to search for their women, but without success. That day, they saw fall down from some trees, and hiding in the branches, a certain kind of persons who were neither men nor women, nor did they have the natural male or female parts. They tried to seize them, but they fled, as if they were eels. Wherefore, they called upon their cacique . . . for men who were *caracaracol,* men whose hands were rough, and could grasp the slippery creatures. They told the cacique that there were four of them, and he sent four men who were *caracaracoli.* This is a disease that causes scabs, and makes the body very rough. After they had caught the creatures, they gathered to discuss what they could do to make them women, since they did not have the natural parts of male or female.

Chapter VIII

How they found a device to make them women: They searched for a bird called Inriri, which bores trees, and in our language is called a woodpecker *[pico]*. They took these creatures, and bound their feet and hands, and took the bird, and bound him to the body. Thinking they were logs, the bird began to peck and bore where the natural parts of the women are wont to be. In this fashion, the Indian elders say that they had women. . . .

Chapter IX

How they say the sea was made: There was a man called Yaya, and his son was called Yayael, which means son of Yaya. Wishing to slay his father, the son sent him into exile, where he remained four months, but then the father slew him and placed his bones in a gourd, and fastened it to the roof of his cabin. One day, Yaya, longing to see his son, said to his wife, "I want to see Yayael." She was pleased at that, and he took down the gourd and turned it over to see the bones of his son, and from it came forth many fishes, large and small. . . . One day, when Yaya went to his fields, there came four sons of a woman whose name was Itiba Tahuvava, all from one womb; when this woman died in labor, they opened her and drew out these four sons, and the first they drew out was Caracaracol, which means scabby [or The Mangy One, or The Syphilitic]. The others had no name.

Chapter X

When the four sons, all born together, went to take hold of the gourd, none of them ventured to lay hands on it except Caracaracol who took it from its place, and all filled themselves with fish. While they were eating, they saw Yaya returning from the fields; trying in haste to replace the gourd, they let it fall to the ground, where it broke open. They say that so great was the mass of water that came from the gourd that it filled the whole earth, and with it issued forth many fish, and from this, they say, the sea had its beginning. . . .

Chapter XI

. . . and further, they say that the sun and the moon came from a cave which is situated in the country of a cacique named Maucia Tivuel, and the name of the cave is Yovovava, and they hold it in great regard; it is all painted in their fashion, without any figures, but with many leaves and other things of that sort, and in this cave there are two small *cemíes,* of stone, about a foot high, with their hands tied, and they appear to be sweating. They hold these *cemíes* in great regard, and, when it did not rain, they went to visit them, and suddenly it rained. . . .

Chapter XII

What they think as to how the dead wander about, and what manner of folk they are, and what they do: They believe that there is a place whither the dead go, called Coaybay, which lies in a part of the island called Soraya [which means "west," according to some scholars—ed.]. The first man in Coaybay was, they say, one called Maquetaurie Guayava, who was the lord of the dwelling place of the dead.

Chapter XIII

Of the shape which they say the dead are: They say that during the . . . night they go out to walk; and they eat of a certain fruit called *guannaba* [perhaps the guanabana —ed.], which has the flavor of the quince, . . . and they have feasts and walk with the living, and to know them one must touch their bellies, and, if one does not find the navel, they say that he is *operito,* which means dead. Because they say the dead have no navel. Sometimes men are deceived, and they lie with women from Coaybay, and when they think they have them in their arms, they have nothing, because they disappear in a trice. If the person is alive, they call the spirit Goeiz, and after death they call it Opia. They say the Goeiz appears often, both in the form of a man and a woman, and that a man once wished to contend with it, and when he clinched it, it disappeared, and the man thrust out his arms in another direction, over some trees, to which he hung. And this they all believe, both small and large, and that the dead appear to them in the form of a father, or mother, or brothers, or parents, and in other forms. . . . These dead do not appear to them in the daytime, but always by night, and with much fear do they venture forth alone at night.

Chapter XIV

Whence they derive this and who keeps it in such credit: There are some men called *bohutís* who practice among them, and try to make them believe that they converse with spirits, and know their secrets, and that when the Indians are ill they can take away the evil. . . . I have seen some of this with my own eyes, although of the other things I shall relate only what I have heard, especially from the principal men . . . because they believe such fables more firmly than the others; like the Moors, they have their laws reduced to ancient songs, by which they are ruled, as the Moors are, by their scriptures. And, when they wish to sing their songs, they play upon a certain drum instrument called the *mayohavau*, which is hollowed from wood and strongly made, and very thin, an ell long and half an ell in breadth, and the part where it is played is made in the shape of the pincers of a farrier, and the other part is like a club. It looks like a gourd with a long neck. . . . This instrument . . . has so loud a sound that it is heard a league and a half. To this sound, they sing the songs which they know by heart; and the principal men play it; they have learned from childhood to sound it, and to sing according to their custom. . . .

Chapter XV

The observances of these Indian *bohutís,* and how they practice medicine and teach the people, and in their cures, are oftentimes themselves taken in: All, or the majority, of the people of Española have many cemíes of different kinds. One has the bones of his father and his mother, and kindred and ancestors; others are made of stone or wood. Many have them of both kinds; some which speak, and others which make the things grow that they eat; and others which bring rain; and others which make the winds blow. These simple-minded, ignorant people believe in the idols, or to speak more fittingly, the devils, since they do not have knowledge of our holy faith. When one is sick, they take the *bohutí* to him as one would to a physician. The *bohutí* is obliged to abstain from food, like the sick man himself, and to play the part of the sick man. He must purge himself, like the sick man, sniffing a powder called *cogioba* [tobacco], which intoxicates them, so they do not know what they are doing, and in this condition they speak incoherently, and claim that they are talking with the *cemíes,* which tell them the cause of the sickness.

Chapter XVI

What these *bohutís* do: Before they set out from their lodging to visit a sick man, they take soot from pots, or pounded charcoal, and blacken their faces, to make the sick man believe whatever they feel is his ailment; then they take small bones and a little flesh, wrap it together in something so that it won't drop, and put it in their mouth. The physician then enters the lodging of the sick man—who has already been purged with the powder—and sits down, and all are silent; if there are children, they put them out, so that they may not hinder the *bohutí* in his duties; nor does anyone remain in the cabin, except one or two of the principal men.

And thus, being alone, they take some leaves of the *gueyo,* which are broad; and another plant, wrapped in an onion skin; and, crumbling it with their hands, they make a paste of it, and put it in their mouths at night to vomit up what they have eaten, in order that it may not harm them; then they begin to sing. And, lighting a torch, they drink that juice. After waiting somewhat, the *bohutí* rises and goes to the sick man, who is seated in the middle of his dwelling, and turns him over twice. Then he stands before him, and takes him by the legs, feeling his thighs, and running his hands down to his feet; then he tugs him hard, as if he wished to pull something out of him; then he goes to the door of the dwelling, closes it, and says, "Begone to the mountains, or to the sea, or whither thou wilt," and blows as though he were blowing away a straw. He turns around again, and puts his hands together, and closes his mouth; his hands shake, as if he were very cold, and he blows on his hands, and then draws his breath in again, like one who sucks the marrow from a bone; and he sucks the sick man's neck, stomach, shoulders, jaws, breasts, belly, and many other parts of his body. This done, he begins to cough and grimace, as if he had eaten something bitter, and he spits into his hand and draws out that which he had put in his mouth before coming there, either a stone, or meat, or a bone. And if it is anything edible, he says to the sick man, "Take notice! You have eaten something which has brought on this illness from which you suffer. See how I have taken from your body what your *cemí* had put there, because you did not pray to him, or did not build him some temple, or give him something of your possessions." And, if it is a stone, he says, "Keep it safe." Sometimes they are convinced that these stones are good, and that they help women in labor, and they keep it very carefully wrapped in cotton in little baskets, and give them of their own food to eat, and they do the same to the *cemíes* which they keep in their lodgings. On holy days, when they bring out much to eat—either fish, meat, or bread, or anything else—they put everything in the lodging of the *cemí,* so that the idol may eat.

The next day, they take all this food to their own lodgings, after the *cemí* has eaten. And so may God help them if the *cemí* eats of that, or of anything else, since it is a dead thing made of stone or wood.

Chapter XVII

How sometimes these physicians are deceived: When they have done what was described, and still the sick man dies, if the dead man has many relatives, or was lord of a village, and can resist the *bohutí* (because those with little power do not venture to contend with these physicians), he who wishes to harm him does so. Wanting to know if the sick man died through the fault of the physician, or whether he did not do what was prescribed, they take an herb called *gueyo*, which has leaves like basil. . . . They take the juice of this leaf, and cut the nails of the dead man, and cut hair from his forehead, and they make a powder between two stones, mixing it with the juice. They pour it into the dead man's mouth or nose, and ask him if the physician was the cause of his death, and if he had followed the regimen. They ask him this several times, until he speaks as plainly as if he were alive, . . . and the physician asks him if he is alive, or how it is that he speaks so plainly; and he replies that he is dead. When they have learned what they want, they return him to his grave. They also proceed in another way. . . . They take the dead man and build a big fire . . . and, when the wood has become live coals, they place the body into this great fiery mass, and then cover it with earth . . . and here they let it lie as long as they please. As it lies there, they ask questions, and the dead man replies that he knows nothing, and they ask him this ten times, and then he speaks no more.

Chapter XVIII

How the relatives of the dead man take vengeance: The relatives of the dead man get together and wait for the *bohutí,* and beat him with clubs till they break his legs, his arms, and his head, so that they fairly pulverize him, as in a mortar, and they leave him in that condition, believing that they have killed him. They say that, by night, there come many snakes of different kinds, which lick the face and body of this physician, who has been left for dead, and who remains so for two or three days. While he stays there, they say that the bones of his legs and arms unite and knit together, and he arises and walks leisurely in the direction of his lodging. Those who see him ask, "Were you not dead?" and he answers that the *cemíes* came to his aid, in the form of snakes. The relatives of the dead man, greatly enraged, because they thought they had avenged his death, grow desperate, and try to lay hands on him; if they do, they gouge out his eyes and crush his testicles, because they say that the *bohutís* will not die, no matter how much they are beaten, unless their testicles are destroyed. . . .

Chapter XIX

How they make and house *cemíes* of wood or stone: When someone is going along on a journey, and he sees a tree with moving roots, the man, in a great fright, stops and asks, "Who is it?" It replies, "Call the *bohutí,* and he will tell you who I am." The Indian goes to the physician, who runs immediately to see the tree, and sits down by it. The wizard goes to the tree, prepares *cogioba,* and tells the tree all his titles, as though he were some great lord, and he asks, "Tell me who you are, what you are doing here, and what you want of me, and why you have had me called. Tell me if you want me to cut you down, or if you want to come with me, and how you want me to carry you, and I will build you a house with land around it." Then the tree, or *cemí,* becomes an idol or devil, and replies to him. The wizard cuts it in the shape it has directed; builds a house for it; and many times a year makes *cogioba* for it. This *cogioba* is to pray to it, and please it, and to ask and learn things from the *cemí,* either evil or good, and to ask it for wealth. And, when they want to know if they will be victorious over their enemies, they go into a lodging where only the principal men of the tribe may enter; and their chief is the first to make *cogioba,* and none of them speak until the chief is finished; but when he has concluded his prayer, he stands a while with his head bowed and his arms on his knees; then he lifts his head towards the sky, and speaks. Then they all answer him in a loud voice, and, when they have given thanks, he relates the vision he has seen with the *cogioba,* which he has inhaled through his nose into his head. He says that he has talked with the cemíes, and that they are to enjoy a victory, that their enemies shall flee; or that there shall be great loss of life, or wars, or famine, or other things which occur to him. Consider what a state their brains are in, because they say the lodging seems to be turned upside down, and that the men seem to be walking with their feet in the air. . . .

Chapter XXV

Of the things they say were uttered by two of the leading caciques of Española: one named Cazivaquel, father of Guarionel; the other Gamanacoel: And that great lord, who they say is in heaven, commanded Cazivaquel to make a fast which all of them keep together; they are shut up six or seven days without eating anything, except the juice of herbs, with which they also wash themselves. Then they eat something which gives them nourishment. In the time that they have been without food, through the weakness which they feel in the body and in the head, they say they have seen something, perhaps desired by them, for they all keep this fast in honor of the *cemí*. . . . And they say that this cacique affirmed he had spoken with the *cemí* Yiocavugama, who told him that whoever remained alive after his death would rule over them only a short time, because they would see in their country a clothed people who were to rule them, and slay them, and they would die of hunger. At first, they thought these would be the Caribs, but reflecting that the Caribs only plundered and fled, they believed that it must be another people. Wherefore, they now believe it was the Admiral [Columbus] and the people he brought with him. . . .

In the province of Magdalena, it pleased God to enlighten with the light of the Holy Catholic Faith a whole household of the principal people. This province was [formerly] called Macorix, and the lord of it was called Guavaoconel. In the aforesaid house were his servants and favorites. . . . They were, in all, sixteen persons, all relatives, and among them five brothers. Of these, one died, and the other four received the water of holy baptism. I believe that they died martyrs, for so it appeared in their death and in their constancy. The first who received the water of holy baptism was an Indian called Guaticavá, who then received the name of Juan. This was the first Christian who suffered a cruel death; and, surely, it seems to me that he died the death of a martyr. I have heard from some who were present at his death that he said *"Dios naboria daca,"* which is to say, "I am a servant of God." And, in like manner, died his brother Antony, and with him another, saying the same thing. . . . Those that were left alive, and are living today, are Christians . . . and now, the Christians are many more in number through the grace of God. . . .

The Lord Admiral [then] told me that. . . I should go and reside with another principal cacique named Guarionex, lord of a numerous people, whose language was understood everywhere in the land [there was a cacique Guarionex in Hispaniola, and another of the same name in Puerto Rico—ed.]. . . .

We were with cacique Guarionex for almost two years, giving him instruction all the time in our holy faith, and the customs of Christians. In the beginning, he showed a good will and gave us hopes that he would do everything we wished, and of desiring to be a Christian, asking us to teach him the Lord's Prayer, the *Ave María,* and the Credo, and all the other prayers . . . and many of his household learned the same. Every morning, he said his prayers, and made his household recite them twice a day. But, later, he became offended and gave up that good plan, through the fault of some other principal men of that country, who blamed him, because he was willing to give heed to the Christian law, since the Christians were bad men and took possession of their land by force. They advised him. . . to conspire together to slay the Christians. For this reason, he broke off from his good intention, and we resolved to depart thence and go where we might be more successful in teaching the Indians, and instructing them in the matters of our faith. And so, we went to another principal cacique called Mauiatue, who showed us good will, saying he wished to become a Christian. . . .

The day after we departed, Guarionex . . . ordered six of his servants to carry off the holy images we had left in a house, where the Christians were to kneel, and pray, and console themselves. . . .

Chapter XXVI

What became of the images, and the miracle God wrought to show his power: When they came out of the house of prayer, these Indians threw the images down to the ground, and covered them with dirt, and urinated upon them, saying, "Now your fruits shall be good and great." In mockery, they buried the images in a tilled field. When the boys in charge of the house of prayer saw this, they ran to their elders and told them that the men of Guarionex had torn the images to tatters and mocked them. . . . The elders left their work, and ran crying out to give an account to Don Bartholomew Columbus, who was then governor, in place of the Admiral, his brother, who had gone to Castile. The offenders were tried, and, the truth being known, they were publicly burnt. This did not deter Guarionex and his subjects from their evil design of slaying the Christians, on the day appointed for bringing in the tribute. Their conspiracy was discovered, but . . . still they persisted, and killed four men, and Juan Mateo, chief clerk and his brother, Antonio, who had received Holy Baptism. Then they ran to where they had hidden the images, and broke them in pieces. Some days later, the owner of that field went to dig *ajíes,* which are roots like turnips or radishes, and in the place where the images had been buried, two or three *ajíes*[1] had grown, one through the middle of the other, in the form of a cross. It was not likely that anyone would find this cross, but the mother of Guarionex found it, and said, "This miracle has been shown by God where the images were found. God knows why." . . .

Truly, the island has great need of people to punish the chiefs when they will

---

1. Fray Ramón seems to have confused the *ají*—a chili pepper that grows above ground—with either the *ñame,* the yucca, or some other starchy root.

not urge their people to hear the things of the Holy Catholic Faith. . . . The first Christians . . . converted as soon as they understood that there is one God, who has made all things, and created heaven and earth, without any further arguments or controversy, because they easily believe. But, with others, both force and intelligence must be used, because we are not all alike. Because, if some begin well and end even better, others will begin well and later will laugh at what has been taught them. For these, force and punishment are necessary. . . .

THE FIRST SETTLERS

Boriquén was ignored for fifteen years after its discovery, as Columbus crossed the Mona Passage westward and founded the seat of Spain's New World government in nearby Hispaniola. It was not until the middle of 1508, when Nicolás de Ovando, Governor General of the Indies, agreed that Juan Ponce de León should found the first European settlement on nearby Boriquén. Ponce de León had fought in Europe against the Moors, and he had helped Columbus to quell Indian uprisings in Hispaniola during the Admiral's second voyage to America.

Ponce de León founded the first Spanish settlement in Puerto Rico at Caparra, near the southern shore of San Juan Bay, where he lived with his wife and children. Although he left a few years later and discovered Florida during his quest for the fabled Fountain of Youth, Ponce de León was Puerto Rico's first governor. Today, his remains lie beneath a marble slab in San Juan Cathedral, across the bay from the tiny settlement that he founded more than four centuries ago. The following account, a formal report to Governor de Ovando, details his first trip, in 1509, to the island of San Juan, which came to be known as Puerto Rico in 1521.

S eñor: What I, Juan Ponce de León, have done on my voyage to the island of San Juan, where I went to comply with the orders that your grace, in the name of His Royal Highness, sent me to do, is as follows:

First, I left the villa of Santo Domingo to go to San Juan on the twelfth day of July, year one thousand five hundred and eight: I went to Salvaleón in the caravel to seek supplies and the people who accompanied me, who were forty-two persons and eight sailors, fifty in all, and while we were in the port of

Translated from "Report to Fray Nicolás de Ovando," Juan Ponce de León, May 1, 1509, Cayetano Coll y Toste, ed., *Boletín Histórico de Puerto Rico,* Vol.1, 1914, pp. 119-21.

Yuma, on the third of August, there was such a storm that the caravel ran aground on some reefs, whereupon I freed it, but lost a good part of our supplies.

Item: After the storm, I continued my voyage and reached the island of Mona, where I found the caciques and Indians of the southern part of said island of San Juan, on the twelfth day of August. I landed near the beach that is in the land of the chief Agüeybana, and I went to his house and spoke to him on behalf of your grace, and told him to plant a field for His Royal Highness, and he said he would. Afterwards, they told me he had done it, but I have not been able to learn its size, nor have I been able to go see it, due to the many tasks which occupy me. While the caravel was anchored, on the sixteenth of August, there came another storm, which pulled the vessel aground, and it cost me great effort to free it.

Item: After the caravel was freed, I traveled around the island, talking with the caciques along the coast, and with the Caribs whom I found there, and giving them jewels [or presents] in order to win their confidence. Then I reached the bay, near which is now the house and site [of government]. From the sea, the port and island looked exceedingly good; I entered the bay and circled it, thinking that I would find water and a site, but I did not. From there, I sailed eight leagues down the coast, where I found a river called the Ana. The vessel was able to enter, and there I anchored and unloaded on land all that we carried, and I had *bohíos* [Indian style huts] built, and I sent the ship to Mona island in search of cassava bread.

Item: After one month, being displeased with the port and the water, I went by land in search of a large river, called the Toa, where I stopped with all the people, and the ship brought all our supplies. But, due to some difficulties, I returned to the bay and sought another site, and since I could not find it, I went back to the River Ana.

At the River Ana, I built a site, and a dock, and roads, and sent the vessel for supplies, but then the sea grew rough and flooded the port, and I was forced to leave with fifteen men in search of the bay, to build a site there. I had all the people and supplies brought there by ship, and there I built the site, and made a large *bohío,* a road, and a pavement to the seaside dock; afterwards, since the site was so humid, and for other difficulties, I moved from there half a league inland, where the house is now located, which is closer to the mining areas.

Item: I built a medium-sized house with its terrace, and railing, and tall battlements, and barricade before the gate, all metal within and with-out. . . .

Item: I had a crew gather some gold, but could not get more since I had no food to give to the people, and since none of the Indians of this island would help me; but the crew gathered eight hundred thirty six pesos worth of gold.

Item: I had two pieces of land prepared, one of them next to the town . . . for the colonizers; the other, four leagues from the River Toa, was for me, and in these lands we shall work for His Royal Highness, because, until now, we have been only able to tell the Indian caciques to work their own lands for His Royal Highness; there are five caciques whom I have ordered to work their lands for His Royal Highness. This is all I have been able to do so far, because I have been required to move the settlement so many times, and for lack of food, and because I have not been able to take advantage of the labor of the Indians, as should be done. . . .

QUEEN ISABELLA'S ORDER

The Spaniards who settled the West Indies were greedy for gold, and direly in need of food to sustain themselves. But they lacked the men to perform such arduous tasks as mining and farming, and the Indians were unwilling to volunteer assistance. This prompted an edict from Queen Isabella to resolve the problem. As Benjamin Keen comments in *Readings in Latin-American Civilization* (Boston: Houghton Mifflin, 1955), "The Indians were to be forced to labor, but as free men." Isabella's order of December 20, 1503, which follows, set the foundation for the *encomienda* system.

We are informed that because of the excessive liberty enjoyed by said Indians they avoid contact . . . with the Spaniards to such an extent that they will not even work for wages, but wander about idle, and cannot be had by the Christians to convert to the Holy Catholic Faith; and in order that the Christians of said island . . . may not lack people to work their holdings for their maintenance, and may be able to take out what gold there is on the island . . . and because we desire that the said Indians be converted to our Holy Catholic Faith and taught its doctrines; and because this can better be done by having the Indians living in community with the Christians of the island, and by having them go among them and associate with them, by which means they will help each other to cultivate and settle and increase the fruits of the island and take the gold which may be there and bring profit to my kingdom and subjects:

Cited in Lesley B. Simpson, *The Encomienda in New Spain* (Berkeley: University of California Press, 1929), pp. 30-31. Reprinted by permission of the University of California Press.

. . . I command you, our said Governor, that beginning from the day you receive my letter you will *compel* and *force* the said Indians to associate with the Christians of the island and to work on their buildings, and to gather and mine the gold and other metals, and to till the fields and produce food for the Christian inhabitants and dwellers of the said island; and you are to have each one paid on the day he works the wage and maintenance which you think he should have . . . and you are to order each cacique to take charge of a certain number of Indians so that you may make them work wherever necessary, and so that on feast days and such days as you think proper they may be gathered together to hear and be taught in matters of the Faith. . . . This the Indians shall perform as free people, which they are, and not as slaves. And see to it that the said Indians are well treated, those who become Christians better than the others, and do not consent or allow that any person do them any harm or oppress them.

I, The Queen.

"THE GRASPING AVARICE OF THE WHITE MEN"

Queen Isabella's order gave official sanction to the Spanish settlers to force the Indians to labor under a thinly veiled system of slavery that lent itself to many abuses. Washington Irving, born in New York City in 1783, is best known for his stories, notably "Rip Van Winkle" and "The Legend of Sleepy Hollow," but he was also an accomplished historian. In 1826, while attached to the American embassy in Madrid, he worked on a biography of Columbus. His account of the oppression of the Indians, which often cites Fray Bartolomé de las Casas, describes events in Hispaniola, which was the seat of government. But, as Las Casas himself relates in his famous *Brevísima Relación de la Destrucción de las Indias*, the same tragic situation prevailed in the islands of San Juan and Jamaica: "[They] look'd like fruitful gardens, [but, in the year 1509,] they were possessed by the Spaniards, with the same bloody intentions as the others were: for there they also exercised their accustomed cruelties, killing, burning, roasting men, and throwing them to the dogs, as also by oppressing them with sundry and various torments in the Gold Mines as if they had come to rid the earth of these innocent and harmless creatures. . . . So lavish were the Spanish swords of the blood of these poor souls, scarce two hundred more remaining; the rest perished without the least knowledge of God."

From Washington Irving, *The Life and Voyages of Christopher Columbus* (New York: United States Book Co., 1828, Vol. II), pp. 586–90.

Before relating the return of Columbus to Hispaniola, it is proper to notice some of the principal occurrences which took place in that island under the government of Ovando. A great crowd of adventurers of various ranks had thronged his fleet—eager speculators, credulous dreamers, and broken-down gentlemen of desperate fortunes; all expecting to enrich themselves suddenly in an island where gold was to be picked up from the surface of the soil or gathered from the mountain brooks. They had scarcely landed, says Las Casas, who accompanied the expedition, when they all hurried off to the mines, about eight leagues' distance. The roads swarmed like ant-hills, with adventurers of all classes. Every one had his knapsack stored with biscuit or flour, and his mining implements on his shoulders. Those hidalgos, or gentlemen, who had no servants to carry their burdens, bore them on their own backs, and lucky was he who had a horse for the journey; he would be able to bring back the greater load of treasure. They all set out in high spirits, eager who should first reach the golden land; thinking they had but to arrive at the mines and collect riches; "for they fancied," says Las Casas, "that gold was to be gathered as easily and readily as fruit from the trees." When they arrived, however, they discovered, to their dismay, that it was necessary to dig painfully into the bowels of the earth—a labor to which most of them had never been accustomed; that it required experience and sagacity to detect the veins of ore; that, in fact, the whole process of mining was exceedingly toilsome, demanded vast patience and much experience, and, after all, was full of uncertainty. They digged eagerly for a time, but found no ore. They grew hungry, threw by their implements, sat down to eat, and then returned to work. It was all in vain. "Their labor," says Las Casas, "gave them a keen appetite and quick digestion, but no gold." They soon consumed their provisions, exhausted their patience, cursed their infatuation, and in eight days set off drearily on their return along the roads they had lately trod so exultingly. They arrived at San Domingo without an ounce of gold, half-famished, downcast, and despairing. . . .

Poverty soon fell upon these misguided men. They exhausted the little property brought from Spain. Many suffered extremely from hunger, and were obliged to exchange even their apparel for bread. Some formed connections with the old settlers of the island; but the greater part were like men lost and bewildered, and just awakened from a dream. The miseries of the mind, as usual, heightened the sufferings of the body. Some wasted away and died broken-hearted; others were hurried off by raging fevers, so that there soon perished upward of a thousand men. . . .

It will be recollected that when Columbus was in a manner compelled to assign lands to the rebellious followers of Francisco Roldán, in 1499, he had made an arrangement that the caciques in their vicinity should, in lieu of tribute, furnish a number of their subjects to assist them in cultivating their estates. This, as has been observed, was the commencement of the disastrous system of repartimientos, or distributions of Indians. When Bobadilla administered the government, he constrained the caciques to furnish a certain number of Indians to each Spaniard, for the purpose of working the mines, where they were employed like beasts of burden. He made an enumeration of the natives, to prevent evasion; reduced them into classes, and distributed them among the Spanish inhabitants. The enormous oppressions which ensued have been noticed. They roused the indignation of Isabella; and when Ovando was sent out to supersede Bobadilla, in 1502, the natives were pronounced free; they immediately refused to labor in the mines.

Ovando represented to the Spanish sovereigns, in 1503, that ruinous consequences resulted to the colony from this entire liberty granted to the Indians. He stated that the tribute could not be collected, for the Indians were lazy and improvident; that they could only be kept from vices and irregularities by occupation; that they now kept aloof from the Spaniards, and from all instruction in the Christian faith.

The last representation had an influence with Isabella, and drew a letter from the sovereigns to Ovando, in 150J, in which he was ordered to spare no pains to attach the natives to the Spanish nation and the Catholic religion. To make them labor moderately, if absolutely essential to their own good; but to temper authority with persuasion and kindness. To pay them regularly and fairly for their labor, and to have them instructed in religion on certain days.

Ovando availed himself of the powers given him by this letter to their fullest extent. He assigned to each Castilian a certain number of Indians, according to the quality of the applicant, the nature of the application, or his own pleasure. It was arranged in the form of an order on a cacique for a certain number of Indians, who were to be paid by their employer, and instructed in the Catholic faith. The pay was so small as to be little better than nominal; the instruction was little more than the mere ceremony of baptism; and the term of labor was at first six months, and then eight months in the year. Under cover of this hired labor, intended for the good both of their bodies and their souls, more intolerable toil was exacted from them, and more horrible cruelties were inflicted, than in the worst days of Bobadilla. They were separated often the distance of several days' journey from their wives and children, and doomed to intolerable labor of all kinds, extorted by the cruel infliction of the lash. For food they had the cassava bread, an unsubstantial support for men obliged to labor; sometimes a scanty portion of pork was distributed among a great number of them, scarce a mouthful to each. When the Spaniards who superintended the mines were at their repast, says Las Casas, the famished Indians scrambled under the table, like dogs, for any bone thrown to them. After they had gnawed and sucked it, they pounded it between stones and mixed it with their cassava bread, that nothing of so precious a morsel might be lost. As to those who labored in the fields, they never tasted either flesh or fish; a little cassava bread and a few roots were their support. While the Spaniards thus withheld the nourishment necessary to sustain their health and strength, they exacted a degree of labor sufficient to break down the most vigorous man. If the Indians fled from this incessant toil and barbarous coercion, and took refuge in the mountains, they were hunted out like wild beasts, scourged in the most inhuman manner, and laden with chains to prevent a second escape. Many perished long before their term of labor had expired. Those who survived their term of six or eight months were permitted to return to their homes until the next term commenced. But their homes were often forty, sixty, and eighty leagues distant. They had nothing to sustain them through the journey but a few roots or agi peppers, or a little cassava bread. Worn down by long toil and cruel hardships, which their feeble constitutions were incapable of sustaining, many had not strength to perform the journey, but sank down and died by the way; some by the side of a brook, others under the shade of a tree, where they had crawled for shelter from the sun. "I have found many dead in the road," says Las Casas, "others gasping under the trees, and others in the pangs of death, faintly crying Hunger! Hunger!" Those who reached their homes most commonly found them desolate. During the eight months they had been absent, their wives and children had either perished or wandered away; the fields on which they depended for food were overrun with weeds, and nothing was left them but to lie down, exhausted and despairing, and die at the threshold of their habitations.

It is impossible to pursue any farther the picture drawn by the venerable Las Casas, not of what he had heard, but of what he had seen; nature and humanity revolt at the details. Suffice it to say, that, so intolerable were the toils and sufferings inflicted upon this weak and unoffending race, that they sank under them, dissolving, as it were, from the face of the earth. Many killed themselves in despair, and even mothers overcame the powerful instinct of nature, and destroyed the infants at their breasts, to spare them a life of wretchedness. Twelve years had not elapsed since the discovery of the island, and several hundred thousand of its native inhabitants had perished, miserable victims to the grasping avarice of the white men.

THE INDIANS REBEL

By the time the Indians of Puerto Rico and other Caribbean islands realized that it was impossible to coexist peacefully with the Spaniards, it was too late. Some of the Indian chieftains tried to resist the Spanish conquerors, but they were soon overcome. The final major Spanish-Indian battle in Puerto Rico is described here by Ricardo E. Alegría, executive director of the Institute of Puerto Rican Culture in San Juan. His text is based on earlier works by Puerto Rican historians, particularly Salvador Brau and Cayetano Coll y Toste. This battle marked the final chapter of Indian civilization on the island. From then on, the Indians would constitute a tiny, isolated minority, whose way of life would soon fade. Remnants of the Indian culture have survived, however, in many important ways: Numerous Indian words were absorbed by the Spanish language; the Europeans learned many lessons of survival that enabled them to live in the New World; and intermarriage between Spaniards and Indians left a striking racial imprint that is still visible on many of the people of the Caribbean.

As each day passed, the Indians of Puerto Rico felt unhappier with the treatment accorded them by the Spaniards, who had stolen their lands and their women, and deprived them of their freedom.

When the elder cacique Agueybana died, and he was replaced by his nephew Agueybana II (or Agueybana the Brave), Indian-Spanish relations worsened. The younger Agueybana,[1] a valiant warrior, had been assigned under the *encomienda* system to Cristobal de Sotomayor, and the treatment afforded the Indian chieftain by the young Spanish nobleman soured relations even further. Only the naive belief prevailing among the Indians that the Spaniards were immortal prevented them from taking up arms. Finally, in desperation, they decided to test the Spaniards' immortality.

An old cacique named Urayoán, whose village was on the island's west coast near the Guaorabo River,[2] decided to make the test. The opportunity arose in November, 1510, when Diego Salcedo, a young Spaniard, who was passing through the region, asked Urayoán to provide him with some Indians to carry

---

Translated from Ricardo E. Alegría, *Descubrimiento, Conquista y Colonización de Puerto Rico: 1493-1599* (San Juan: Colección de Estudios Puertorriqueños, 1969), pp. 51-69. Reprinted by permission.

1. All subsequent mentions of Agueybana refer to the young chief, not his uncle.
2. Near the present site of the town of Anasco.

his baggage across the river. Urayoán appeared willing to comply with the request, but secretly told the Indians what they must do. Upon reaching the river, the unsuspecting Salcedo allowed the Indians to carry him. When they reached the deepest part, they halted, dropped him in the water, and held him submerged for several hours. They carried him ashore and, still fearing that he might be alive, begged his pardon. After watching over him for a day, and convincing themselves beyond doubt that the Spaniard was indeed dead, they hastened to give the news to their cacique, Urayoán.

Finally, the Indians knew that the Spaniards, like themselves, were mortal. The news spread quickly, and was received with joy by the Indians.

Soon, the acts of rebellion began. Indians of cacique Aymamón, who reigned in the region of Aymaco [today Aguadilla], captured young Diego Suárez and took him to their chieftain, who offered him up as a trophy in a ballgame. Luckily for Suárez, a young Indian who served as a scout ran with the news to the Spaniards. En route, he met Captain Diego de Salazar. Guided by the Indian youth, Salazar reached Aymamón's village just as the Indians were watching the ballgame. He untied young Suárez from a tree, handed him a sword, and told him, "Do as you will." Then he commenced to slash at the Indians with his own sword. The Indians were astonished at Salazar's sudden brave attack. Aymamón himself confronted Salazar, but he was disabled by a swipe of the Spaniard's sword. Taking advantage of the confusion, Salazar, young Suárez, and their Indian aide fled the village and went to Sotomayor's settlement. They had not gone far when a group of Indians caught up to them and called to Salazar, begging him to stop because the cacique, Aymamón, wished to speak to him. Believing it was a trap, Suárez implored Salazar not to return. But Salazar did not want the Indians to think him a coward. When he returned to the village, he found a badly wounded cacique Aymamón, who praised him for his valor and begged that he be permitted to use his name. The cacique, like all the Indians, believed that names had magical powers, and that by taking on the brave Spaniard's name he would acquire his skill and valor in combat. Salazar agreed, but said that first he would have to be baptized by a priest. The captain returned with Suárez to Sotomayor's settlement, and Salazar's name was from that day on a source of fear among the Indians, since they considered him to be the bravest warrior on the island.

Young Agueybana, tired of the humiliations and abuses suffered by his people, and heartened by the news of the Spaniard's mortality, decided to convene the principal caciques of the island in an *areyto* [meeting] at his village. . . . There, the caciques agreed to wage a war to the death. But the accord reached at the *areyto* was witnessed by Juan González, a young Spanish scout, who had painted his body like an Indian, and knew their language. He hurried to Sotomayor's plantation near Guánica, to warn him. Sotomayor had already been told of impending danger by Guanina, cacique Agueybana's sister, who was the concubine of the Spanish conquistador.

Sotomayor decided to return to his village, accompanied by his nephew, his Spanish servants, and by the interpreter, Juan González. However, he recklessly asked Agueybana to send him some Indians to help carry the baggage. The cacique did so, but had already decided not to allow his hated nemesis to escape. Suspecting an attack, Juan González straggled behind, but he was surprised by a group of Indians who were commanded by Agueybana himself.

Severely wounded, González saved his life when he offered to become the cacique's slave. Agueybana left him there, and led an attack against Sotomayor's group, killing them all. They headed back to finish off González, but the interpreter hid in a treetop. At night, when the Indians returned to their village to celebrate Sotomayor's death, González climbed down from the tree and—despite his many wounds—began a long painful trek, crossing the island's central mountain range, until he reached the plantations of Toa, where he asked that the news of the Indian uprising be forwarded to Ponce de León in Caparra.

Meanwhile . . . Guarionex, cacique of the Otuao region, led his warriors in an attack upon Sotomayor's settlement, burning it, and killing several of its inhabitants. Only the courage of Captain Salazar, who directed the retreat, saved the Spanish families, who reached Caparra safely, although many were wounded.

Other colonizers, who lived on isolated plantations near the mines, were also slaughtered by the Indians, who were now engaged in an islandwide revolt to regain their freedom.

In Caparra, when Ponce de León heard the news, he organized his forces, and decided to attack. With the 120 men that remained, he formed three companies, under the command of Captains Diego de Salazar, Luis de Añasco, and Miguel de Toro. The defense of Caparra was assigned to Salazar and his men, almost all of whom had been wounded in combat at Sotomayor's village. With the remaining men, and without waiting for the reinforcements he had requested from Hispaniola, Ponce de León set out to fight Agueybana II on his own territory.

After crossing the mountains, and reaching the Coayuco River, Ponce de León learned that the Indians in Agueybana's village were celebrating their victories with a huge *areyto*. Knowing that it was their custom to celebrate, and drink a strong liquor fermented with maize. Ponce de León decided to wait until nightfall. When the Indians were drunk and exhausted, Ponce de León and his men launched a surprise attack. The Indians believed that all the slain Spaniards had risen from the dead, and they offered little resistance. Brandishing swords and spears, the Spaniards killed hundreds of Indians, and took others as prisoners, whereupon they returned to Caparra before the Indians could regroup.

Days later, the Indians renewed their attacks upon the Spanish plantations. Ponce de León decided to attack Agueybana once more. He was told that in the region of Yagueca, cacique Mabodamaca, commanding 600 warriors, was seeking combat, and daring Salazar to fight with him. When Salazar learned of this, he received Ponce de León's permission to fight the cacique; in the ensuing struggle, the Spaniards defeated the cacique and his men.

Soon afterwards, Ponce de León received warnings that Agueybana was approaching to attack, with a large contingent of Indians. An experienced soldier, Ponce de León decided to choose the battle site; he deployed his men in a protected area, where they could only be attacked frontally. Using tree trunks, stones, and earth, he fashioned a parapet to protect his men from Indian arrows, and then he waited. Among Ponce de León's men were Juan de León, armed with an harquebus, as well as two soldiers with crossbows. Each time the Indians attacked the parapet, the harquebus and crossbows inflicted many wounds. When the Indians attacked once more, the harquebusier noticed an Indian chief marching at the front, who wore around his neck a golden disc—or *guanín*—the emblem of the caciques. He took aim and fired, killing the man instantly. It was Agueybana himself. The warriors ran to recover him and retreated in disorder. . . .

Taking advantage of the Indians' confusion. Ponce de León returned to Caparra with his men. Knowing that the Indian resistance had received a fatal blow, he offered amnesty to those caciques who would make peace. Only two accepted the offer: Caguax, cacique of the Turabo region; and another cacique from the Utuao area, who would later be called *don* Alonso, when he was baptized by Bishop Alonso Manso.

The other caciques continued to resist. Many of them fell back to the mountains of the Sierra Luquillo, while others fled to neighboring islands, where they joined with their old enemies, the Caribs, in the common struggle against the Spaniards. The native rebellion had been squashed: the Indians' primitive weapons were no match for the steel swords, crossbows, and firearms of the Spaniards.

Concerned over the Indian emigration to the Lesser Antilles, Ponce de León asked the King for a brigantine to pursue and capture them, to prevent the island of San Juan from being left without people to work the mines. From then on, the struggle moved to those islands, and was directed mainly against the Caribs. . . .

PART II

THE COLONIZATION

The population of the island is so scattered that we find houses everywhere we go. There is a great abundance of bananas, and fish are plentiful in the rivers and along the coast; there is a great supply of fruits, sweet potatoes, beans, corn, and rice in the hills. Cow's milk is abundant. Household furniture . . . usually consists of only a hammock and a kettle. . . . A machete is the only instrument used in their work. With it, they cut the sticks, vines, and palm leaves to build their houses, and also clear the ground and plant and cultivate their crops.

—*Translated from Fray Inigo Abbad,* Noticias de la Historia Geográfica, Civil y Política de Puerto Rico, *Madrid, 1788*

During the first three centuries of Spanish rule, Puerto Rico was a stagnant, sparsely populated colony. The mother country held absolute control over the political, economic, and religious life of its Caribbean possession. The island seemed rich in natural resources—its soil was fertile, and its mountains promised gold and other minerals—but the Indians had fled or were killed, and the fortune-seeking settlers were not fit for arduous labor. In 1579, the Bishop of San Juan, Fray Diego de Salamanca, reported to the king that

The main reason for the deterioration and stagnation of this island is the lack of slaves, for planting the sugar and mining the gold as before, when it was in such great abundance. . . . There is no lack of gold, but there are no slaves to mine it, and if a number of them were brought here it would do much good for the Royal Treasury, and this poor island would truly recover the title of Puerto Rico [Rich Port].*

---

*Translated from Luis M. Díaz Soler, *Historia de la Esclavitud Negra en Puerto Rico* (San Juan: University of Puerto Rico, *1965),* p. 69.

But the gold mines had little more to give, and a small boom in sugar cane cultivation soon waned. Spain's fortune seekers shifted their eyes to other, more promising regions of the vast New World.

For military and commercial reasons, however, the island had strategic value; it was one of the relay ports for the treasure fleets that sailed between Europe and the Western Hemisphere. To protect this port, Spain converted the island into a military stronghold. By 1539, slaves and convicts were building El Morro fortress at the mouth of San Juan Bay. Because the island economy produced too little to underwrite this military enterprise, the *situado,* a subsidy fund, was sent from Mexico.

With its central location, Puerto Rico was viewed enviously by other European powers. Sir Francis Drake attacked the island in 1595 and was driven back in a hard-fought battle. George Clifford, Earl of Cumberland, took San Juan two years later, but tropical disease decimated his troops, and he retreated. The Dutch briefly seized and burned the capital two decades later, but also withdrew. The last major attack—by the British—was repelled in 1797. There had been sustained British interest. In 1706, Daniel Parke, Governor of the Windward Islands, reported, "If we had Porto Rico, the land is so good . . . in seven years we would make sugar so cheap as to be able to undersell the French . . . if we had that island, we should draw numbers of people from the barren land of New England."

At that time, the inhabitants of Puerto Rico lived in small, scattered settlements, where they farmed just enough to keep their stomachs full. Because Spain had outlawed trade with foreign countries, some islanders turned to smuggling with the nearby Dutch, French, and English colonies. Pirate ships roamed the waters of the Caribbean and nested near Puerto Rico's deserted beaches. In San Juan, there was a tiny governing elite that consisted of the military, the church, and a few well-to-do Spanish merchants.

But, as the nineteenth century began, Puerto Rico was stirred by new currents of change. It was not until 1807 that the first printing press came to the island. In the first two decades of the century, wealthy merchants and planters sought asylum from the wars of independence in South America and the slave rebellions in Haiti.

The *criollos* (native-born Puerto Ricans) soon came to resent the immigrants, and this feeling, together with Spain's inflexible system of rule, prompted demands for independence or autonomy. Many of the immigrants received land grants via a Spanish royal decree known as the *cédula de gratia.*

But most of the newcomers were Spanish loyalists, and their conservative influence dampened much of the "nativist" sentiment. Spain, having lost its foothold in South America, focused its strength on the liberal elements in Cuba and Puerto Rico and often used these islands as bases from which it harassed the new Latin American republics.

To maintain the *status quo,* Spain prohibited non-Catholics from settling in Puerto Rico, censured books with the slightest liberal bent, and restricted travel between the island's small, isolated communities.

Within these limits, the islanders were neglected, and allowed to pursue their own innocuous interests; the rural peasantry was free to prosper, or to perish.

THE COSTLY COLONY

With its meager gold deposits long depleted, and after a short-lived prosperity from sugar cane, Puerto Rico's small fanners raised cattle, ginger, tobacco, and subsistence crops. Spain's strict trade laws discouraged commerce between Europe and San Juan, so the enterprising *criollos* developed a flourishing contraband trade with nearby islands. Government officials looked the other way, or shared in the smuggling business, and precious little revenue found its way into the royal treasury. Governor Juan José Colomo, in 1744, referred to "public scandals without number . . . minor offices sold to the highest bidders; and soldiers . . . two-thirds of whom are married to *mulatas,* which explains why there is no need of barracks at present." Actually, Puerto Rico was enjoying one of the few periods in its history when the colonial power derived little or no benefit from its Caribbean possession. The people were poor and neglected but lived independently and in peace. There were many small farmers, and freemen outnumbered slaves by eight to one. Spain's apathy had permitted the growth of a type of blissful anarchy: Puerto Ricans, left to their own devices, were pursuing their own interests. This, of course, meant that virtually no profits or taxes flowed to the seat of empire in Spain. During the reign of Carlos III (1759-88), officials were sent to all of Spain's colonies to prepare reports that would lead to a thorough administrative reform of the empire. The King, in 1765, sent to Puerto Rico a no-nonsense "efficiency expert," Field Marshal Alejandro O'Reilly. Puerto Rico's governor at the time was a hedonistic fellow named Ambrosio de Benavides, who was known to invite the pretty *mulatas* of the region to frolic in La Fortaleza palace, after discreetly

---

Translated from *Memoria de D. Alejandro O'Reylly, Sobre la Isla de Puerto Rico, Año 1765.* From A. Tapia, *Biblioteca Histórica de Puerto Rico* (San Juan: Ed. Institute de Literatura, 1945), pp. 526-55. Also in Eugenio Fernández Méndez, ed., *Crónicas de Puerto Rico, 1491-1797* (San Juan: Ediciones del Gobierno, Estado Libre Asociado de Puerto Rico, 1957), Vol. I, pp. 239-49.

removing the King's somber portrait from the wall. O'Reilly undertook a major fact-finding study, when it turned out that Benavides knew little of the island he supposedly governed. His report launched a number of reforms designed to generate more revenue for the Spanish crown.

T he conquest, population, spiritual guidance, administration of justice, fortification . . . and troops for the defense of the island of Puerto Rico have cost the King, in the 255 years of his possession, many people and an immense fortune. Expenses from the Royal Exchequer still continue; more than 80,000 pesos per year come from Mexico for the costs of this island, and the amount must be increased considerably in the near future.

Who could predict that after so many years, and so much money squandered, that the yearly tribute would amount to only 10,804 pesos and 3 *reales?* Especially when one realizes that this island has 39,846 free persons and 5,037 slaves, that the climate is mild, and as healthy for Europeans as it is for the natives, that the island is bathed by many rivers, where good fish abound, and there is never lack of water in the hills, that the flatlands have beautiful plains, that one can harvest corn, rice, tobacco, and other fruits from two to three times a year; that the sugar cane is the thickest, juiciest and sweetest in the Americas; that cotton, indigo, coffee . . . cacao, nutmeg . . . are found in good quality; that the only reason for the poor quality of tobacco is the avarice of the planters, who pick it before it is ripe, in order that it have more juice and weigh more; that except for coffee, tobacco, and sugar cane, the other fruits grow wild in the mountains; that the *palo de Mora*—very much in demand by foreigners, for its yellow dye— is abundant, as is the *Guayacán,* a very good wood for blocks, furniture, and medicinal teas. The Dutch and British take a considerable amount of both each year . . . the island has a great abundance of excellent wood for buildings, ships, and charcoal. Near Guayama, I have seen saltpeter. There are enough salt beds to satisfy all needs; and an infinite number of herbs, roots, and medicinal plants, which could represent a considerable sector of commerce. . . .

The principal reason for the minuscule progress in Puerto Rico is that there is no governmental policy conducive to it. It was populated by soldiers far too accustomed to bearing arms to lower themselves to field work; add to these a number of stowaways, cabin boys, and sailors who deserted from each ship that touched port there. These people, quite indolent by nature, and undisciplined by government regulation, spread out into the fields and forests, where they built miserable shacks. With the few plantains that they planted, the fruits they found growing wild, and the cows that soon abounded in the mountains, they had milk, vegetables, fruit, and some meat; thus, they survived, and they still do. These lazy, aimless men, without tools or aptness in agriculture, nor anyone to help them clear the fields—what could be expected of them? The gentle climate encouraged their casual manner, since no formal attire was needed. They settled for a simple linen shirt, and long trousers. And since all lived alike, there was no cause for envy among them; also contributing were the fertility of the earth, and the abundance of wild fruits. With five days of work, a family has plantains for the entire year. With these, milk from the cows, yucca, and fruit, they are extremely content. For beds, they fashion hammocks from the bark of a tree called the *majagua*. For the bit of clothing they require, they trade with foreigners: cows, wood, horses, mules, coffee, tobacco, or some other item whose cultivation requires little toil. . . . I must add, however, that the inhabitants are very loyal to the King, and display an innocence and candor which I have neither seen nor heard of elsewhere in America. . . .

In all the island, there are only two schools for children; outside of Puerto Rico [San Juan] and the villa of San Germán, few know how to read. They count time by epochs of government, hurricanes, visits of the Bishop, arrivals of ships, or of funds from Mexico. They do not understand what a league's measure is; each man counts distance according to the length or speed of his stride. They walk barefoot in the countryside. Whites feel no repugnance when they mix with the darks. All of the towns, except for Puerto Rico [San Juan], have no more permanent population than that of the priest. The others are always in the countryside, except on Sundays, when those near the church come to mass, or during the three days of Easter, when almost all the parishioners attend. For those days, they erect houses which appear to be palm groves, made upon wooden piles; these houses consist of a pair of rooms; they are open day and night, and have neither windows nor doors. So little furniture have they, that they can move in an instant; the houses in the countryside are built the same way, and are barely more sturdy.

The distinguished persons of the island are few, the only difference among them being that they have a bit more fortune, or they may be officers in the militia.

The governors who knew of these problems tried to solve them by allotting land to the poor, who made enthusiastic offers to cultivate the land. The governors, full of zeal, believed them, without realizing that they could never comply with their promises. *La corte* [the Royal Court in Madrid], unable, at such a great distance, to discern anything except the optimistic picture painted by the island's governors, embraced the system. The result was to spread out the population, which gravely damaged the spiritual and physical development of the people, made schooling impossible, made it difficult to maintain a strong defense, and created less and less incentives for work and culture. . . .

What advantages have resulted? None. Before the allotment of lands, there was more than enough for the people's sustenance; today, they produce the same amount. All the citizens are laborers, and since each possesses the same crops, there is no market, or interior commerce, or reciprocal dependence; not one-twentieth of the land that was distributed has been cleared. . . .

Thus far, there is not even a market in the plaza of Puerto Rico [San Juan]; at times, canoes used to come to the docks with vegetables, eggs, and chickens; some days they sold little, others nothing. . . .

There is an open contraband trade throughout the island; foreign ships come most often to the south and west coasts; without even bothering to disguise their intentions, they drop anchor at any port, send their launch or canoe ashore, the inhabitants flock to the beach, and there the business is done. . . . The illicit trade is carried out with the Dutch of Curacao and St. Eustatius, the Danes of St. Thomas and St. Croix, and the English of the nearby islands. . . . The Dutch take most of the tobacco, the British take the wood, and the Danes take the food-stuff and coffee. All of them take cattle, and as many mules as they can get.

Via this contraband traffic, the citizens can order any item they want from England or Holland, and those involved in the business are very punctual. . . .

There are, on this island, 4,579 small farms, and 269 ranches for cattle. A number of mills supply all the island's needs for sugar and honey; some is used for making *aguardiente* [cheap rum], but that of the foreigners is even cheaper, and they supply the entire south coast; a profit they would lose entirely, if more sugar mills were developed. . . .

The soldiers of the permanent battalion of Puerto Rico [San Juan] are almost all of them married, with many children. [They] . . . live apart in their own, or rented, huts. . . . The captains would advance the soldiers the money they needed to maintain themselves and their families, and receive in return a good part of their salaries, . . . charging 10 to 15 per cent interest. The two companies sent to Puerto Rico when the last war broke out, to reinforce the garrison, soon followed this example. They had barracks, but each soldier went off to live with some negress or *mulata,* whom he called his housekeeper; he gave her all four of the pesos he received monthly; and, from this money, the soldier, the woman, and their children—if they had any—maintained themselves. What strength can such a poorly fed soldier have? . . . How much honor, zeal, or application to serve can one expect from someone who lives in such spiritual and temporal abandon?

All the veteran troops of Puerto Rico were without any uniforms whatsoever: each man bought and wore what he wanted; many, when not on duty, wore straw sombreros on the streets, and almost all wore broad trousers that reached to their shins. Drills were equally ignored; no one knew how to drill. . . . This was the only defense Your Majesty had for the conservation of the loveliest island in America, upon whose fortification, troops, and other obligations many millions have already been spent. . . .

The importance of the situation of Puerto Rico, the goodness of its port, the fertility, rich products, and population, the advantages that it should produce for our commerce, and the irreparable harm that would occur if foreigners possessed it, demand, it seems to me, the most serious and prompt attention by the King and his ministers. . . . In a few years, with proper regulation, it could be of relief to the Royal Treasury, and one of the finest jewels of the Crown. . . .

"CRIOLLOS" AND "BLANCOS"

Nearly two decades after O'Reilly's report. Fray Iñigo Abbad y Lasierra published the first comprehensive history of Puerto Rico, offering a rich chronicle of the people and their way of life. By this time, there was a distinct Puerto Rican identity. The *criollos*, or native-born Puerto Ricans, were neither Spaniards nor the children of Spaniards; their family lineage went back for several generations on the island. In this excerpt from his work, Fray Iñigo testifies to the creation of a new nationality: the Puerto Rican.

The Europeans of different nations who have settled on this island, the mixture of these with Indians and Negroes, and the effects of the climate, have produced different kinds of people, who are different in color, physiognomy, and personality. . . .

The first Spaniards who settled here partly changed the nature of the Indians, but, at the same time, they acquired the Indians' way of life, and habits of food and dwelling. . . .

Those who are born here, no matter from what breed or mixture, are called

---

Translated from Fray Iñigo Abbad y Lasierra, *Noticias de la Historia Geográfica, Civil y Política de la Isla de San Juan Bautista de Puerto Rico* (Madrid: 1788). A large excerpt is contained in the more recent Eugenio Fernández Méndez, ed., *Crónicas de Puerto Rico: 1493-1797*, Vol. I, pp. 313-25.

criollos. The Europeans are called *blancos* [whites], or *hombres de la otra banda* [men of the other band]. These cannot avoid the effect of the climate; they commonly fall sick, lose some of the liveliness of their color, and of their blood. With all this, they generally maintain their nature, and are more industrious than the *criollos.* The *criollos* are well-built; one barely ever sees a cripple. Their constitution is delicate, and their limbs are loose and slender, which is proper for a warm climate; but they are also lazy, and the climate makes them look so pale as to appear sick; they are deliberate, taciturn, and always observant; but they have a lively talent for imitating whatever they see; they love freedom, are unselfish, and very hospitable to strangers; but they are also vain and inconstant in their tastes.

They have an inclination for feats of honor and brilliancy: They have proved brave in war, and are good soldiers for short campaigns, since they are accustomed to a sedentary life, and dislike leaving it for long; they are more inclined to naval expeditions, and devote themselves to piracy and contraband with zeal and valor; they know how to resist hunger. . . .

They are wearied by the ardor and liveliness of the Europeans, but they receive them openly in their homes, feed them with pleasure, and glory in the fact that they descend from them. The women love the Spaniards more than the *criollos;* they are of good disposition, but the salty air of the sea consumes their teeth and deprives them of the agreeable color found in women of other countries; the heat makes them indolent and slovenly; they marry very young, and are fecund; they love dancing and horse racing, which they perform with extraordinary skill and abandon.

The *mulatos,* who form the largest part of the population, are the children of white men and negresses. Their color is dark, disagreeable, . . . they are tall and well formed, stronger, and more accustomed to work than the white *criollos,* who treat them with disdain. Among this class of people are many . . . who have distinguished themselves for their actions, and they are ambitious for honor.

Of the *Negros* on this island, some were brought from the coasts of Africa, others are *criollos;* the former are sold as slaves; of the latter, many are free. With all this, there is nothing more ignominious on this island than to be black, or to be descended from them; a white man insults any of them, with impunity, and in the most contemptible language; some masters treat them with unjust rigor, . . . resulting in disloyalty, desertion, and suicide. Others regard the slaves with great affection . . . employing them only in household service, but the slaves suffer the rigors of slavery when the master dies and they pass to another. . . .

Since the slaves come from different provinces, they are also of different inclinations; nevertheless, one can say that their ways are formed to a great degree
by their masters; if the slaves are loved and treated with affection, they respond,
even with heroism; but if masters are too harsh, the slave knows how to suffer
and hide his feelings until the time for revenge, which is performed by poison-
ing the cattle, or other slaves, or the master himself. Some slaves, especially
those from *Mina,* take their own lives, since they are convinced that they
shall be reborn in their homeland, which they believe to be the best in the world.
. . .

There is no doubt that the enslavement and lowliness of the blacks, and other
colored people, creates in the Spaniards of America a certain fantasy: From infancy, they are surrounded by servants who are supposed to guess their every
whim. . . . On the other hand, unaccustomed to finding any obstacles or resistance to their whims, or to receiving any form of punishment, they are raised
with a presumptuous spirit. They are raised without work and without contradiction, somewhat like Princes who have never known adversity. They are generally frugal, lively, and clear-sighted, but they are also ambitious for glory,
which could be useful in terms of politics, if this fact can be utilized by the
governors, to whom they display complete submission and respect. . . .

The favorite diversion of these *isleños* [islanders] is dancing: They organize
a dance for no other reason than to pass the time. . . . When someone gives a
dance, the news travels throughout the territory, and hundreds of persons come
from everywhere, without being invited. Since the houses are small, most guests
stay outside, until they wish to dance. To begin the dance, the guests stand at
the foot of the stairs with their timbrels, gourds, maracas, and small guitars;
and sing a song honoring the owner of the house. When the owner appears at
the entrance, he welcomes the guests, and urges them to come up; then they
embrace and exchange greetings, as though they had not seen each other for
years. The women sit on benches or hammocks; the men remain standing, or
crouch down upon their heels. . . .

They come out to dance one by one, or two by two; when a man invites a
woman to dance, if she has no slippers—as most of them do not—she borrows
a pair, and begins to dance around the parlor with exceptional speed. . . . The
man who dances remains in a corner of the parlor, his sombrero tipped sideways
on his head, holding his cutlass behind his back; he does not move from this
spot, but raises and lowers his feet with much speed and force. . . . When a man
wishes to show affection for a woman who is dancing, he removes his hat and
puts it on her head. Sometimes she has so many that she must carry them in
her hands and under her arms; when she tires of dancing, she returns the hats

to the men, each of whom gives her half a *real;* this is called *dar la gala* [giving the prize]. If one of the bystanders wishes to dance with a woman who is already dancing with someone else, he must ask the man's permission. This has caused some strong feuds, and, since all of them believe that might makes right, the dance usually ends in a clash of knives.

During the dance, a few slave women [he is obviously describing a dance on a farm large enough to have slaves, not that of subsistence farmers—ed.] serve bowls of breadstuffs with milk and honey, bottles of *aguardiente,* and cigars. Those who grow tired go to sleep in the hammocks, or enter the inner room to rest. . . . others retire to their homes, and return the next day, because these dances tend to last for a whole week. . . .

These dances are more common at Easter time, or before Ash Wednesday *[Carriestolandas],* or at the time of a wedding, whose celebration begins two months previous. The birth or death of a child is also celebrated with a dance, which lasts until the guests can no longer stand the foul odor of the corpse. . . .

Being a *compadre* to these islanders is a very important relationship. Nothing is denied a *compadre;* he enjoys full satisfaction and liberty in the home of his *compadres,* and makes use of their friendship, and comforts, as though he were in his own home. If a man accompanies a brother or sister to their wedding, or attends the confirmation or baptism of a child, he is no longer considered a brother; the treatment between *compadres* is always preferred, because it is more affectionate and expressive of intimate friendship.

Important fiestas are also celebrated with horse races. . . . No one misses these, not even the tiniest child, who is carried in the saddle. In each town, there are races for the most solemn holidays. In the capital, there are the days of San Juan, San Pedro, and San Mateo. The day before San Juan, at sunrise, a great multitude of riders arrive from all the towns of the island to show their horses; at the stroke of noon, men and women of all ages and classes emerge from their homes, all mounted on horses that are decorated to the utmost. Many have saddles that are lined with velvet or trimmed with gold, with spurs of silver, and some add breastplates with bells of the same metal. . . . Those who cannot spend so much adorn their horses with a great variety of ribbons and laces, and do not hesitate to pawn or sell the best items in their household to look good for the *corrida* [race].

There is no order at all: At the stroke of twelve, they race along the streets, generally in groups of friends or relatives; they gallop around the city, without stopping or resting the entire night, until the horses give out. Then, they take other horses, and continue with such vehemence that the entire population of the town seems to be on horseback, riding frantically in every direction.

Despite the confusion, there is rarely an accident, and if there is, the victim is usually some Spaniard who has turned the corner and, faced by a platoon of riders, cannot avoid the horses with the same skill as the *criollos*. Even when the horse is racing full speed, the *criollos* leave the reins loose upon the saddle, cross their arms, and while smoking a cigar, voice their compliments to the ladies in the windows, and to those who are racing. . . .

The entire *corrida* is not so tumultuous. At nine in the morning, out comes the banner of the city, accompanied by the municipal officials, the noblemen, and the officers, two companies of cavalry, and the troops, all presided over by the Governor. This *paseo* is performed with great pomp and order. . . . It proceeds through the main streets of the city, after which the banner is carried to the Cathedral. . . . After mass, it is returned to the city hall, with all the ostentation possible, while in the other streets, there are races, shouting, and merry-making, as the people express their joy and wild passion, which reign that day.

The many rivers, channels, lagoons, and swamps of the island, and the distance the people live from each other and from the churches, cause them to use their horses frequently. If they must go to mass, or a dance, or to visit a friend, or on any other errand, it is indispensable to travel by horse; when it rains, they would not go by foot for even a hundred paces. . . . This custom makes all of them fine horsemen, who travel by day or night, full speed, crossing rivers or swamps . . . without tiring. . . .

With the same facility, they travel by canoe to islands 40 or 50 leagues distant, taking with them a cluster of plantains for food. They go to deserted islands, catch shellfish, make a fire, gather water, and then proceed to another island, until they reach their destination. There is not a single inn throughout the island, but travelers are received in any household; they only seek shelter in case of rain. If it rains while they are en route, a large *yagua* leaf protects them from any shower. If they must cross a deep river, they remove their shirt and trousers and proceed without hesitation. . . . Wherever the night catches them, they dismount, and allow the horse to feed, since there is pasture everywhere. They then hang up their hammock, and fall asleep. The next day, they continue their trip, eat some provision, or satisfy their hunger in any plantain grove. They are not great hunters, nor are there many four-legged animals on the island, except for wild or runaway dogs, which cause great damage to the livestock, but the thickness of the woods makes it impossible to kill them with a rifle. For the same reason, they take little advantage of the hens, guineas, parrots, parrakeets, ravens, and other good-tasting birds; but, in recompense, they fish in the rivers and sea with great skill.

They have an abundance of domestic birds; common hens, guineas, turkeys, and ducks of many kinds; but they only kill them when in need; they usually keep them to sell in the capital city, or in the ports, to the ships that arrive, and this is the industry they most apply themselves to, without any cost or work. . . .

Although the towns are generally deserted, except for the priest, on Sundays and holidays they come to hear mass. They usually arrive at eight in the morning, mounted on horseback, . . . and then return to their haciendas, leaving the town as solitary as before. When they are sick, they advise the priest, who mounts a horse. . . . He confesses the patient, administers the holy sacraments, and returns to town. . . .

They bring the dead to be buried by the church, unless the man has died of some epidemic; then he is buried on his own hacienda, at the foot of a tree. A year or two later, his bones are removed from the earth and taken to the church, where all honors are paid, according to the stature of the person.

These islanders are very devoted to Our Lord: All carry the rosary around their necks, and pray to it at least twice a day. All families begin with this saintly exercise, some repeat it at noon, without forgetting the evening; but the youth are a cause of great ignorance, since most of them are not very well acquainted with Christian Doctrine, because they do not live close to the towns.

. . . . Without doubt, this would be one of the happiest places, if its inhabitants were more industrious. Until they are, they shall live in poverty and obscurity, . . . although this island could be one of the richest possessions of the Spanish Monarchy.

THE XIVAROS

By the early nineteenth century, Puerto Rico's economy was thriving, and the island's population had soared to nearly 400,000—including 45,000 slaves. In those days, it was widely assumed that only African slaves could withstand the rigors of tropical weather in the fields, but the case of Puerto Rico showed that this was not true.

Colonel George Dawson Flinter, son-in-law of one of the wealthiest landed proprietors of Caracas, came to Puerto Rico after Venezuela gained its independence, and for several years he commanded the island's Spanish regi-

From *The Edinburgh Review,* LX (1835), p. 328.

ment. He later produced a book—*An Account of the Present State of the Island of Porto Rico* (London: Longman Press, 1834).

The following book review includes the author's compelling description of Puerto Rico's "Xivaro"—an archaic way of spelling *jíbaro*—the white rural peasantry who "are proverbial for their hospitality, and . . . ever ready to fight on the slightest provocation." The reviewer also compares Puerto Rico with its neighboring islands, where slavery was more predominant. Free men, he pointed out, produce far more than slaves, and the "vice" and "tyranny" of slavery are avoided. The fact that the great majority of Puerto Rico's workers, whether white or black, were free made for a more desirable society than those on islands such as Cuba or Jamaica, where a large part of the population was in bondage. Most impressive is the reviewer's prediction that the social fabric of the island would erode once the small family farms were conglomerated into vast sugar estates. This would occur not during the era of slavery but later, in the early years of the U.S. occupation.

T he early history of Puerto Rico affords few features of interest. Although one of the oldest colonies of the Spanish crown, it
• • • served for three centuries only as a convict station; and its free population presented, until a few years ago, a marked specimen of the besotted indolence which characterized a Spanish settlement of the old times. The military and civil expenses were defrayed by remittances from Mexico; and it was not until the revolution caused these remittances to cease in 1810, that the island, owing to the extreme embarrassment of its financial condition, began to attract the notice of the mother country. In 1815 a decree was published in its behalf . . . [which] whilst it greatly encouraged free industry, unfortunately at the same time gave an impulse to the employment of slave labour, which had hitherto been unused, rather from indolence and want of capital than from motives of humanity. Colonists were invited to the island on the most liberal terms—lands were allotted gratis—the settlers were freed from direct taxes, and, for a certain number of years, from the tithes and alcabala; as well as from the exportation duties, which formed one of the most impolitic features of the old Spanish system.

From the period of this decree, the advance of Puerto Rico in wealth and population has been unexampled, even in the virgin regions of America. A great additional impulse was given by the arrival of capitalists, driven by civil war from the Spanish Main;—men distinguished in the more prosperous times of South America for their steady regularity and probity in the transaction of business. . . . [Puerto Rico is] next to Brazil and Cuba the most formidable rival with which our colonies have to contend in the production of their staple articles, and at the same time a granary competent to supply all the ordinary wants of her abundant population.

The island appears to be one of the most lovely of all those regions of loveliness which are washed by the Caribbean Sea. . . . The sugar-cane, notwithstanding the drought, thrives abundantly, and most of the chief plantations of the island are formed on this [the south] coast. This inestimable benefit of moisture Puerto Rico derives from its forests, which as yet clothe a large portion of the interior; the thick cover at once attracting the rain and preventing evaporation. . . .

[Puerto Rico's] inhabitants . . . seem to enjoy a more than ordinary exemption from the evils which afflict humanity in these sickly regions. The mortality, according to our author's tables, does not exceed that which prevails in some of the healthier countries of Europe. A still more singular characteristic appears to distinguish this island from its neighbors, namely, the great deficiency of native animals of every sort; and especially the entire absence . . . of those noxious reptiles and insects which seem to inhabit the rest of the West Indies as their peculiar possession. . . .

The population of Puerto Rico amounted, according to the Spanish census of 1830, to 323,858; of which 127,287 were free people of colour, and 34,240 only, slaves. But . . . our author calculates, apparently on good grounds, the whole number at 400,000, and the slaves at 45,000; or nearly 180 inhabitants to the square mile.

Here, then, we have a free white population of 200,000 souls, or half the entire amount of inhabitants. What causes can have produced a result so utterly different from that which exists in all the West India islands, except those of Spain? Whence arises this numerous and prosperous Creole yeomanry, (for we shall see that a great proportion of them are owners or occupiers of land), whilst other colonies are divided between a few white proprietors, and a degraded multitude of slaves, with hardly a vestige of an intermediate class? Such was not always the state of our own islands. . . . We have abundant evidence that Antigua, St. Kitts, Dominica, and other colonies, possessed, a hundred years ago, a multitude of English settlers; who have gradually dwindled away, by intemperance, by their own misconduct, and above all through the extension of the sugar cultivation, and of its companion the slave trade, to the small remnant which now exists. We believe, that if any causes should arise to give a sudden impulse to the colonial industry of this now happy Spanish island, it would soon follow—as Cuba is already following—the baneful course of our own settlements, and purchase wealth at the expense of happiness. . . .

Of the free inhabitants of Puerto Rico, a very small proportion is settled in the towns: indeed, the capital, San Juan, with about 8000 souls, is the only place which seems to merit such a title. Some of the best, in point of connexions and respectability, are the descendants of military men, who, during the long period when the island was a mere garrison, formed alliances and settled within it. These people maintain the pride of their descent with all the stateliness of grandees; and some of them are opulent. Wealthy merchants and planters (many of whom are foreigners) form the next class; but the latter, fortunately for the happiness if not for the riches of the island, form altogether but a small, and not now a very thriving class. The number of sugar estates is about 300; chiefly situated on the southern coast. They hardly pay at present, according to our author, the expenses of cultivation. But there are, in addition, some 1,300 small plantations belonging to poor cultivators, who, growing only an acre or two of cane, devote their attention chiefly to the raising of provisions. There are 148 coffee estates; but in this branch of cultivation, as well as that of sugar, the larger capitalists have been gradually losing money and abandoning their estates; whilst the small farmer who pursues various lines of industry on his little tract of land, has been able, in this way, to increase his comforts.

It is this class which forms the distinctive feature of the population. A numerous race of cultivators—brave, for their courage was largely tried in the exigencies of the South American wars—of white blood, and Spanish feelings, opinions, and prejudices,—is something so widely different from what is to be found in our own islands or those of France—that we are almost tempted to abandon the principles of political economy, and to feel grateful for the want of enterprise, and slothful contentment, which undoubtedly have prevented the conversion of the island into one wide sugar factory, with white overseers and negro labourers. Our author gives the extraordinary number of 19,000 proprietors of land in perpetuity: nearly 18,000 of these are small occupiers, raising provisions and herding cattle. The Xivaros—as the white country population are called—are, it cannot be denied, an indolent race; who seem to multiply under an easy condition of existence, without adding much to the commercial wealth or social refinement of their country.

"Like the peasantry of Ireland, they are proverbial for their hospitality: and, like them, they are ever ready to fight on the slightest provocation. They swing themselves to and fro in their hammocks all day long, smoking their cigars, and scraping a guitar. The plantain grove which surrounds their houses, and the coffee-tree, which grows almost without cultivation, afford them a frugal subsistence. . . . The cabins are thatched with the leaves of the palm-tree; the sides are often open, or merely constructed of the same sort of leaves as the roof— such is the mildness of the climate. Some cabins have doors, others have none.

There is nothing to dread from robbers, and if there were banditti, their poverty would protect them from violence. A few calabash shells, and earthen pots—one or two hammocks made of the bark of the palm-tree— two or three game-cocks, and a machete—form the extent of their moveable property. A few coffee-trees and plantains, a cow and a horse, an acre of land in corn or sweet potatoes, constitute the property of what would be denominated a comfortable Xivaro—who, mounted on his meagre and hardworked horse, with his long sword protruding from his baskets, dressed in a broad-brimmed straw-hat, cotton jacket, clean shirt, and check pantaloons, sallies forth from his cabin to mass, to a cockfight, or to a dance, thinking himself the most independent and happy being in existence."—pp. 76-78.

"Riding out one afternoon in the country, I was overtaken by one of those sudden showers of rain so common in tropical climates. I fled for shelter to the nearest house, which happened to be the cottage of a poor Xivaro. It was on the slope of a little hill, surrounded by plantain trees, which did not appear to be carefully cultivated, and a large patch of potatoes was close by. I placed my horse without ceremony under the projecting roof. I entered the humble dwelling with the usual salute, which is the same as in Ireland, 'God save all here,' which was courteously answered by the man of the house, who seemed to be about forty years of age. He was dressed in a check shirt and wide linen drawers. He was coiled up in a hammock of such small dimensions, that his body was actually doubled in two; one foot rested on the ground, with which he propelled the hammock to and fro; and at intervals with his great toe he turned a large sweet potato, which was roasting on a few embers, placed on a flag on the ground close to him, and which no doubt was intended for his evening meal. He had a guitar in his hand, from which he produced sounds which appeared to me discordant, but seemed to please him exceedingly. On my entrance he turned on his side, and offered me the hammock, which of course I refused to accept. Two small children, perfectly naked, were swinging to and fro in another small hammock, and greedily devouring large roasted plantains. The woman of the house was squatted on the floor, feeding four game-cocks, which were lodged in the best part of the house, while the husband every now and then would warn her not to give them too much corn or too much water. They received me with an urbanity unknown to the peasantry of Northern Europe. They placed a large leaf of the palm-tree over my saddle to protect it from the rain; and pressed me to sit down in the kindest manner. The host was very communicative; he gave me the whole pedigree of his game-cocks, and enumerated the battles they had won. He pointed out one to me which he said was 'a most delicate bird,' an expression made use of by the

Xivaros to denote its great value; and he concluded by offering it to me as a present. Indeed a Xivaro would form a very poor opinion of a person who could not discuss the merits of a game-cock. In going away they offered me their cabin with as much politeness as if it had been a palace, and hoped to see me again. I was forcibly struck with the native courtesy of these people, and it gratified me to observe the content and happiness they enjoy, without a thought for the present or a care for the future—without wants, without wishes, without ambition."—p. 80.

. . . It is quite clear, that the spread of these tropical backwoodsmen over the virgin soil of the island, has prevented it thus far from falling into the hands of the sugar monopolist; and it furnishes a sufficient answer to those who imagine that a European race, living by its own labour, cannot exist, where 80 degrees is the average height of Fahrenheit's thermometer. With the gradual diffusion of education, of which our author admits that there is a lamentable deficiency, much of the grosser parts of their character may be progressively removed. . . .

The free coloured inhabitants of Puerto Rico are by far more numerous than in any other West India island; and this fact alone,—when we consider the ineradicable prejudice attaching to colour, which has brought such infinite misery, and social discomfort, over a great part of the world,—speaks more than any eulogy in favor of its people and their government. The whole British West Indies contained, before 1834, not more than 80,000 free coloured inhabitants, in a population of ten times that amount; of these, sixteen thousand were to be found in Trinidad alone,—an island which had long been governed by Spanish laws. Although white blood is, in Puerto Rico, as everywhere else beyond the Atlantic, a patent of nobility, yet the Xivaro no more treats with contempt and contumely his inferior in caste than the grandee of Old Spain, his inferior in station. . . .

In 1823, Jamaica, with 340,000 slaves, exported 1,400,000 quintals of sugar. Puerto Rico, with 45,000 slaves, produces about 410,000. The French colony of Guadaloupe, with twice as many slaves as Puerto Rico, produces an equal crop of sugar. The soil of the latter is far more fertile than that of the other islands, already in great measure exhausted. But, on the other hand, capital and industry form essential elements of the manufacture, in the British and French isles, while the Spaniards are far behind in all pursuits requiring either. From these premises our author concludes, not unreasonably, that a large proportion (which elsewhere, however, he calculates at one-fifth only) of this crop of sugar is raised by free labour.

But it must be remembered, that, besides the greater estates, there are in

Puerto Rico some 1,200 or 1,300 small sugar plantations, the property of the Xivaros of the interior, who live cheaply and work lazily, but who contrive to raise a small quantity of this valuable article, together with provisions and cattle. If such rough cultivation as this succeeds at all, it can only be in consequence of the vast productiveness of the soil, cleared of its forests only within the last twenty years, which gives the planter the same advantage over his brethren to windward and leeward, as the settler of Illinois has over the cultivator of the worn out "old fields" of the Atlantic coast. Such production can in the nature of things be only temporary. On the other hand, the great sugar estates, which must form the main sources of this commodity, are evidently cultivated here as elsewhere by slaves; and although at present the cultivation of sugar on a large scale is extremely unprofitable, a rise in its price would undoubtedly cause at once an increased importation of slaves, and the application of more capital and ingenuity to the business, until the small farmers would be driven from the market by the slave-owning capitalists. . . .

At present the question of the future destiny of this beautiful and happy island may be said to remain undecided. But it soon must call for a final adjustment. Slave labour, reinforced by the slave trade, cannot long coexist with the industry of a free race of cultivators. Puerto Rico, long neglected and unknown, now called into unexampled prosperity by the same causes which once raised cities and established small commonwealths in the windward islands, is fast reaching the same crisis in her fate which they reached; and it is in the power of the Spanish Government, by abolishing the slave trade, to enable her to pass that crisis in safety. The island is only preserved from presenting a spectacle similar to theirs, by a concurrence of circumstances which render the cultivation of sugar at present a disadvantageous investment of capital; and by its yet unexhausted soil, which affords an ample return of other colonial produce to such labour as her free husbandmen are inclined to bestow upon it. Remove that obstacle, and let capital flow into the island, together with an unrestricted slave trade, and Puerto Rico will follow the fortunes of Cuba. That island, when visited by Humboldt, thirty years ago, was chiefly tilled by the labour of freemen. But at the close of the war, the baleful influence of African importation began. One hundred and eighty-five thousand slaves were landed at Havana alone in fourteen years; a peaceful and industrious people became contaminated with vice and disorder of every kind; the slaves already exceed in numbers the white free population; and the old Spanish kindness and loyalty between master and slave has so far disappeared, and tyranny has so far begun its usual work, that the planters openly confess that one of the reasons for the importation of fresh slaves is, to supply the masters with a guard of mamelukes against the discontented negroes of the colony. If the colonists of Puerto Rico will not follow the example, which Antigua alone of all the West Indian Islands has yet proclaimed, by setting her negroes free on the day when statutory emancipation began, without apprenticeship, or education from freedom of any kind, it is at least in the power of the crown of Spain, without injustice to any one, to cause the greater evil of the slave trade to cease; and to rescue one fair island,—one loyal and gallant people,—from the insidious advances of ruin. . . .

SLAVERY LAWS

As in the case of the Indians—who were exterminated—Spain promulgated laws to guarantee decent treatment of the African slaves. But the laws were often broken. Historian Luis M. Díaz Soler describes how "for the master, the negro represented an investment and a valuable instrument of production, but for the overseer he was a poor soul who must obey blindly, and who would be punished rigorously if he did not obey orders. Little did it matter to the overseer if the slave were killed or crippled."

Some masters had little regard for the investment value of their slaves. In his autobiography* (Alejandro Tapia y Rivera, *Mis Memorias, 1826-1882* [New York: Laisne & Rossboro. 1928], pp. 15-17, 76-84) nineteenth-century playwright Alejandro Tapia y Rivera—a militant abolitionist—recalls how some slaves grew so desperate over their plight that they "agreed to kill each other, including mothers and children." He recounts the case of one hacienda owner "who had the teeth yanked out from one of his servants, who used to chew on the sugar cane"; another, who "buried a slave woman alive"; and a third, "who once frankly complained that he had been unable to prevent the escape of his slave, despite the fact that he had forced him to eat human excrement."

The following is an excerpt from the "Regulation on Education, Treatment and Occupations Which the Masters of This Island Should Give to Their Slaves," issued in 1826 by Governor don Miguel de la Torre. The regulation reflects some degree of concern for the treatment of the slaves but also— to perhaps a greater degree—a fear of possible uprising if vigilance were relaxed.

Selections in this chapter:
1. Translated from Cayetano Coll y Toste, ed., *Historia de la Esclavitud en Puerto Rico,* compiled by Isabel Cuchi Coll (San Juan: Sociedad de Autores Puertorriqueños, 1969), pp. 27-40.
2. Ibid, pp. 79-S2.
3. Ibid, pp. 90-91.

*Translated from Luis M. Díaz Soler, *Historia de la Esclavitud Negra en Puerto Rico* (San Juan: University of Puerto Rico, 1965), p. 153.

Chapter II

Of the Christian and Civil Education the Masters Should Give their Slaves
. . . they should instruct them in the principles of the Catholic religion, and in those truths needed for them to be baptized within one year of their residence. . . . This instruction will be every night, after prayer hour. . . . On Sundays and holidays, those slaves already baptized should hear Mass. . . . Unbaptized negroes who are ill should be administered the Holy Sacraments of Baptism . . . so that they do not perish as Pagans. . . . The masters shall make every effort to make the slaves understand the obedience they must lend to established authority; the obligation they owe to revere the priests; to respect whites; to behave moderately with free coloreds, and affably with their equals. . . .

Chapter IV

Of the work and occupations of the slaves . . . they shall work nine useful hours a day . . . but during harvest-time . . . they shall work thirteen hours, so that the slave has at least 11 hours of rest daily. . . .

Chapter V

On where the tools shall be kept: On all the haciendas there shall be a room, with a good lock, where the tools are kept. This shall be in the exclusive care of the master, or his foreman, and not entrusted to any slave . . . at the beginning of work, each slave shall be given the tool that he will use, and it shall be returned when he has stopped working. . . . No slave shall ever leave the hacienda with any tool, much less any type of arms, unless he is accompanied by his master, foreman, or their families, whereupon he may carry his work machete. . . .

Chapter VI

Prohibition of slaves meeting with those of other haciendas. . . . No slave will be permitted to receive visits of slaves from other haciendas; and when they must leave their own hacienda, they should carry a written permission, with the date, saying where they are going, and why. . . .

Chapter VII

On Diversion. Masters will permit their slaves to have honest enjoyment and recreation on holidays (after hearing Mass, and attending the explanation of the Christian Doctrine) inside the hacienda, without mixing with slaves from other haciendas, and in a place open to the view of their owners, or foremen. . . . These diversions shall last from three in the afternoon until sunset, or the prayer hour, no more. . . . Owners and foremen are particularly warned not to permit mixing of the two sexes, excess drinking, nor the introduction of slaves or freemen from outside. . . .

Chapter VIII

Masters shall be sure to build rooms for the slaves that are spacious, dry, airy, strong, with separate parts for both sexes, and with a strong lock and key. . . . At eight o'clock, a roll call will be made, to insure that no slave is left outside, except those entrusted with keeping watch over the hacienda.
A light will be kept on all night in the slaves' quarters, and one or two keepers will insure that the slaves remain quiet in their beds, and report immediately anything out of the ordinary. . . .

Chapter IX

On the marriage of slaves. . . . The masters shall try to avoid any illicit contact between the two sexes, and try to promote marriage among the slaves . . . so that they may live together under the same roof. . . .

Chapter X

. . . a slave shall win his liberty if he reveals any conspiracy by persons of his class, or free persons, to disturb public order, kill a master, his wife, child, or parent. . . .

Chapter XII

Rewards for good service. . . . The slave who serves faithfully on a hacienda for thirty-five years shall earn the reward of no work during the first quarter of the day. *He* who continues for ten years more shall work only half a day, and he who reaches sixty-five years of age shall be given full freedom, but the master shall be responsible for helping and feeding him if he lacks the means of sustenance. . . .

[There is no record of a large slave insurrection in Puerto Rico. The presence of a Spanish military garrison was one deterrent, as was the fact that free men easily outnumbered slaves. In fact, many slave conspiracies were betrayed by slaves, who confessed to their masters, in exchange for their freedom. Small-scale revolts were attempted in 1527, 1821, 1822, 1825, 1843, and 1848. These caused scarcely a ripple. Of more concern was the turmoil in nearby islands, where slaves were in open revolt against governing white elites. This situation, in 1848, prompted an "Edict Against the African Race," by Governor Juan Prim, issued May 31, 1848, and published in the *Gaceta Oficial,* No. 67, June 3, 1848. The edict was designed to "prevent these calamities on our peaceful, loyal soil"].

INHABITANTS OF PUERTO RICO: Via the French ship Argus, which reached port today from Martinique, I have learned of the serious incidents in the French colonies of Martinique and Guadeloupe, due to the latest decrees of the French provisional government, emancipating the slaves in its colonies. The unfortunate immigrants aboard the Argus, who abandoned their families and interests, and came to this island in search of the security and protection they could not find in their own country, are the most evident testimony of the lamentable conditions in those colonies, and of the stupid ferocity of the African race, which—unable to appreciate the blessings conceded by their government—reacts with sentiments that are natural to them: arson, murder, and destruction. Happily, circumstances are quite different on this island. . . .

It is my duty to persuade you to ignore the fears that such news might instill in your spirits, and to assure you that your Captain General keeps constant vigil over the maintenance of order and tranquility. . . .

The critical circumstances of the times . . . oblige me to dictate measures that will prevent these calamities from occurring on our peaceful, loyal soil, and to establish quick punishment for all infractions:

Article 1—Infractions of any kind committed by individuals of the African race—be they free or slave—shall be judged by a Military Council of War. . . .

Article 2—Any African, free or slave, who takes up arms against whites, no matter how justified the aggression, shall—if slave—be executed by the firing squad, and—if free—have his right hand cut off; but, if he should have caused wounds, he, too, shall be brought before the firing squad. . . .

Article 3—If an individual of the African race insults, mistreats, or threatens with stick, stone, or in any way convinces his master that he plans to offend the person of a white, the aggressor shall be condemned to five years prison, if slave, and, if free, to punishment corresponding to the circumstances.

Article 4—Masters of slaves are authorized to correct and punish them for the slight infractions they commit, without need of consulting any military or civil official. . . .

Article 5—If . . . any slave rebels against his lord and master, the latter is empowered to kill him immediately, to set an example for the other slaves. . . .

[As racial tension eased in the French islands, Governor Prim's successor—Captain General Juan de la Pezuela—rescinded the harsh edict of June 3, and reestablished the regulations previously in force. Part of his proclamation of November 28, 1848 said:]

It is my duty, sons of the African race, to express my gratitude for your peaceful submission to your labors, and to warn you also to ignore the treacherous ideas which may perturb your spirits. . . . Via the law, you have the means to obtain your freedom. Your liberty is in your own hands, by purchasing it with savings from your own activity, and laborious work.[1] Resign yourselves, therefore, that man can only find happiness in this world by harnessing his desires, and by accepting his destiny.

---

1. Coll y Toste notes the "cruel sarcasm" of General de la Pezuela's remark, since the slaves were not paid wages for their daily labor.

MASTERS AND SLAVES

The institution of slavery began in Puerto Rico in the early 1500's, but slaves never formed as large a part of the island's population as they did on the British, French, and Dutch islands of the Caribbean. This, of course, was little consolation to the minority in bondage in Puerto Rico. Advertisements for runaways, so common in the United States, also appeared frequently in the island's *Gaceta Oficial*. The notice that follows appeared there in 1833.

On the night of Holy Week, the second of this month, a slave named Lorenzo fled from the Hacienda Los Cuatro Hermanos, Mayagüez District. He was wearing a tailcoat, straw hat, a new red wool shirt, and a

---

From George Coggeshall. *Thirty-six Voyages to Various Parts of the World, Made Between the Years 1791 and 1841* (New York: 1858). An excerpt is contained in Luis M. Díaz Soler, *Historia de la Esclavitud Negro en Puerto Rico* (San Juan: University of Puerto Rico, 1965), pp. 114-16.

three-pronged iron collar around his neck. He is crafty, short, not very black, good looking, and well built, from twenty-five to thirty years old. He previously belonged to the Hacienda San José, Bayamón, of the widow Vassallo. His owner, Dr. Felix García de Latorre, will pay the cost of his capture and return.

Except for the intensive scholarship of Puerto Rican professor Luis M. Díaz Soler and a few scattered research efforts, the history of slavery on the island has been largely neglected. A few contemporary accounts, however, have been discovered. One of these is a vivid description by a visitor to the island in 1831. He describes first the slave ship Sultana and its captain, then a disembarking of slaves on Puerto Rico's west coast, and finally a visit to Ponce, on the south coast, where he conversed with the captain and supercargo of the ship.

[T]he Captain] was a native of Paris, then about forty years old, rather above middle size, stout, strong and athletic, a good seaman, and of a bold and daring disposition. He spoke fluently four or five languages, and was altogether an original character. He seemed neither to fear God nor regard man, and appeared to be just fitted for the desperate business in which he was engaged. . . . And though so much is said in condemnation of these men who prosecute the slave-trade, still, they are merely instruments in the hands of capitalists, who in the end, reap the greatest portion of the gain.

Where do the capitalists reside? My answer is, I do not know; they may live sumptuously in England, France, the United States, elsewhere. One thing is certain, that very few of the planters in these islands have very much ready money to invest in this business, and but few merchants who reside in the West Indies can spare means to be employed in the slave-trade; still the business goes on from year to year, and no one knows who owns the ships engaged in the trade. For the information of those who have never seen a slave ship, I will just add that they were armed with great guns . . . they have a strong bulkhead to serve as a barricade, built athwart the after part of the vessel, through which are loopholes; and as all the muskets and pistols are kept in the cabin, the captain and the officers can fire from these holes and put down a revolt, should there be one among the slaves, without endangering their own lives. . . .

There have been imported, into the little bays of this part of Porto Rico within the last two months, three small cargoes of African slaves, say about 500 in number, men, women and children. I saw the remnant of these cargoes for sale in three enclosures. The best looking and most healthy of these miserable beings had been sold to the planters and removed to their estates; the remainder were extremely thin and sickly, and were selling at very reduced prices. There was a little stream of fresh water near where these slaves were kept, and in this little river they were made to bathe daily; if they showed any reluctance to go into the water, they were driven in like cattle. They had some rude instruments of music, such as banjoes and large gourd shells with strings, which made a rude, tinkling noise; on these instruments they were encouraged to play, singing and dancing at the same time to keep up their spirits. The venders of these negroes told me it was absolutely necessary to keep them in a good-natured mood, otherwise they would get the sulke, refuse all kind of food, and die with starvation.

Although the sight of these poor, unfortunate beings creates a melancholy feeling in the breast of a stranger, still there were circumstances connected with it that are so ludicrous, that they produce an involuntary smile even in the midst of this dark scene of degraded humanity. For example, at these depots, two large and healthy-looking negroes are selected, and made to stand erect outside the gate as a sign to indicate to the planters that slaves are sold here. The price of negroes at this time was about as follows: children of five or six years old, 100 dollars each; and what are here called prime slaves, that is, stout, healthy men or women, from eighteen to twenty-five years old, were worth 250 to 350 dollars each. They were generally retailed to the planters, and taken in small or large numbers as the case may be. At the time I visited this island, there were so many obstructions to the African slave-trade that the owners of large vessels dared not risk sending them, and were therefore in the habit of employing small, fast-sailing pilotboat schooners, to elude the vigilance of the men-of-war of different nations who were striving to prevent this inhuman traffic. These pilotboats carried from 150 to 200 of these poor creatures, and when chased by men-of-war, they crammed them all below deck to avoid detection; so also in bad weather they were all forced below to escape being washed overboard.

In hot climates like those between Africa and this island, to confine human beings under deck, where all must suffer, and many of them die with suffocation, is barbarous in the extreme. . . .

While I was here at Ponce, on the 18th. of February 1831, a large brig, under Spanish colors, arrived at a small port about a league to the eastward of this place, with 350 negro slaves from the coast of Africa. They were all landed under the direction of the government officers, and I was told their owners paid a duty to the government of 25 dollars per head. I went with my friend G. (Garrus) to see them landed; they were all taken to a neighboring plantation, and there exposed for sale. They were marched up from the vessel in parties of fifty; the men and women were all naked, except an apron which they wore about their loins; the children, both boys and girls, were in a perfect state of nudity, and, as far as I could judge, they all, both men and women, appeared utterly unconscious of any impropriety in their want of clothing. They were healthy, sleek, and in good condition, appeared pleased to get on shore and seemed to me an inoffensive, docile race of human beings. A large quantity of boiled plantains and salted herring was prepared for them. They all seemed to eat with a good appetite and enjoy their food. The planters from all this part of the island, soon came to this depot to purchase according to their wants or ability to pay; and here they were sold singly, in pairs, or in larger numbers, as was agreed upon by the parties.

During my stay at Ponce, I dined at a planter's house in company with the captain and supercargo of the slave brig; they were intelligent, sociable men, and when conversing on the slave trade, said it was a humane and most benevolent traffic; that in many parts of Africa the negroes were cannibals and extremely indolent; that the different tribes were constantly at war with each other, and if there were no purchases for their prisoners, they would be all put to death; that they were in the lowest state of degradation, and of no service to the world. On the contrary, when they were transported to the West Indies, they soon became civilized and useful to mankind. As a proof of what they had stated, they said that the boys and girls that were allowed to run about the vessel and mix with the seamen, soon learned English and Spanish, and acquired considerable intelligence in the course of a few months, and concluded by affirming that the African traders were benevolent and beneficial to mankind. The above was the substance of their conversation, and shows that a good deal may be said in favor of any system, however absurd it may appear to those who are opposed to it. After this conversation I remarked to these gentlemen that if the negroes were transported from Africa to these islands in large, comfortable ships, and sold to humane and benevolent masters, perhaps in many cases it would be better for the slaves themselves; but unfortunately, at present, this was not the case —on the contrary, they were crammed into small craft, and often perished with suffocation, while those who survived were liable to be sold to brutal masters, and receive inhuman treatment. Their reply was, that those who were engaged in the trade had been driven to adopt every expedient, in consequence of the persecutions they had received from short-sighted and ill-informed philanthropists. . . .

PART III

THE SPIRIT OF NATIONHOOD

Puerto Ricans . . . your brothers in exile have conspired—and they ought to conspire—because the colonial regime must some day be ended in our island; because Puerto Rico in the long run must be free, like the nations of the continent. . . .

—Proclamation signed by El Comité Revolucionario and circulated in July 1867; attributed to R. Emeterio Betances

After 300 years as a small, neglected Spanish colony, Puerto Rico "came of age" during the nineteenth century. The U.S. War of Independence, the French Revolution, the revolt of Haitian slaves in 1791, and the Latin American wars of independence in 1808-24—all had their impact upon the island.

Between 1800 and 1900, Puerto Rico's population exploded from 150,000 to nearly a million. Many of the new arrivals were Spanish royalists—soldiers, merchants, and landowners—fleeing from turmoil elsewhere. In addition to the large populations of Creole whites, Africans, mulattoes and resident Spaniards, there were also small French, English, North American, Danish, German, Dutch, and Italian colonies.

As early as 1809, Puerto Ricans were referring to the island as their *amada patria* (beloved homeland), although, politically, it was an overseas possession of Spain. That year, when Napoleon invaded Spain, the Spanish provinces rebelled and formed juntas under the Supreme Junta of Cádiz. The Junta declared Spain's colonies to be integral parts of the mother country. Puerto Rico's leaders rejoiced because this converted them from colonial subjects to citizens, with substantially increased civil rights. One of the delegates elected by the Puerto Rican ship to represent the island in Spain's Cortes was Ramón Power y Giralt. He took with him a list of demands: for free trade with foreign nations, for a university, for equal job opportunities for natives in government posts and the like. There was also the significant request that, if Spain was conquered, Puerto Rico should be granted the liberty "to choose its own destiny."

Some reforms were granted in 1812, when the Spanish constitution was extended to Puerto Rico and the island became an integral part of the monarchy. All free men were granted Spanish citizenship, and Puerto Rican deputies sat in the Spanish Cortes, with voting power. In fact, Power y Giralt rose to the vice presidency of the Cortes. Limited local power was also granted in the island's towns, where municipal assemblies were created, with nine government appointees and seven landowners.

But Puerto Rico's fortunes rose and fell in accord with changes in Europe, and civil rights were withdrawn as often as they were granted.

The first strong movement to secure a permanent working relationship with Spain and remove the stigma of colonialism began in 1887, in Ponce, when Román Baldorioty de Castro presided over the new Partido Autonomista Puertorriqueño.

The efforts of this movement bore fruit ten years later. In 1897, when Spain was fearful of losing its last grip in the Western Hemisphere, autonomy was granted to Cuba and Puerto Rico. It was too late in Cuba, where rebel patriots continued their battle for independence, but the royal decree of November 28, 1897, proclaiming autonomy for Puerto Rico, was well received. The cabinet of the new government was installed in February, 1898, and general elections for legislators were held in March. In July, however, American troops landed, drastically altering the course of Puerto Rican history.

The Autonomous Charter was not a grant of independence, but it promised more freedom than ever before. The crown named a Spanish Governor General, who was to be commander-in-chief of the armed forces and "supreme authority" on the island. The Insular Parliament consisted of an Administrative Council and a House of Representatives. The Council had fifteen members, eight elected by the people and seven appointed by the Governor General. All thirty-five members of the House were to be elected.

The Parliament was subject to the veto powers of Spain, but it could propose and approve its own laws, impose taxes, and enter into treaties with foreign nations. This was still colonialism, but with a very long leash—longer, in some respects, than the one that now binds Puerto Rico's commonwealth government to the United States.

SAILING TO SAN JUAN

As early as 1822, a visitor to Puerto Rico noted "some alarm" over "an intended insurrection of the slave population" and also learned of an expedition "that was about to sail from New York for the purpose of revolutionizing the island." Both of these attempts—to achieve freedom for the slaves and independence for Puerto Rico—failed. But they indicated considerable unrest simmering just beneath the otherwise placid surface of the Caribbean colony. The visitor was Joel Roberts Poinsett, a U.S. diplomat—long active and much resented in Latin America—who gained a certain immortality when he introduced into his country a Mexican flower, which was named the "Poinsettia" in his honor. At the time, Poinsett had been sent on a special mission to Mexico by President James Monroe, but en route he stopped briefly in Puerto Rico. His brief sketch also touches upon the island's social structure and housing conditions, as well as the piracy in Puerto Rico's coastal waters.

Beating to windward against wind and current—on the 20th, passed the Islands of Mona and Monica, and on the 21st, made the western extremity of Puerto Rico. We are now near enough to the land to distinguish the plantations of palms and bananas, and all the luxuriant vegetation of the tropics.

26th.—After passing one day in sight of the Moro Castle, we are at length anchored in the port of San Juan. The town is situated on the south side of the hills, and did not come in view until we had passed the Moro, and were within the harbour. Although closely built up, it does not appear capable of containing so many as twenty thousand inhabitants, the reported amount of the population.

We have just received the visit of the captain of the port, who informs us that some alarm has lately been excited by the discovery of an intended insurrection of the slave population. Although the slaves are not numerous, the vicinity of the republic of Hayti renders such a movement a probable event.

27th.—On landing this morning I was agreeably surprised to find the town very clean and tolerably well built. It is situated on the declivity of a steep hill, and at first I was inclined to attribute its cleanliness to the torrents of rain, so

From Joel Roberts Poinsett, *Notes on Mexico Made in the Autumn of 1822, Accompanied by an Historical Sketch of the Revolution and Translations of Official Reports on thePresent State of that Country. With a Map. By a Citizen of the United States* (Philadelphia: H. C. Carey and I. Lea, 1824). (Facsimile reprint—New York: Praeger Publishers, 1969), pp. 3-8.

frequent in this climate; but I find, on inquiry, that the police regulations are excellent, and are rigidly enforced. We strolled round the fortifications, which are well constructed and judiciously situated. They occupy a narrow island, about two miles long, on which the town stands, and which is connected with the main by a bridge strongly fortified with a tête de pont. This is united by a chain of small forts which the castle of San Christopher, a very strong fortress, situated so as to defend the eastern entrance of the town, and commanding all the works towards the north and east. . . .

For some time past our trade has been much harassed by privateers fitted out in the different ports of this island. The principal object of our touching here is to remonstrate with the governor against these depredations. Under the absurd pretext of blockading the whole coast of the Spanish main, a few small privateers cruise in the Mona and Sombrero passages, and capture all vessels bound to or from any port on that extensive coast. The prizes are carried into the small ports on the south and west of the island, where they are at the mercy of courts notoriously corrupt. The governor assured us that he had warned the commanders of privateers not to capture vessels sailing under the flag of the United States, and that he should in future exact a bond to a large amount from the Armateurs, in order to indemnify those who might sustain losses from illegal captures; that he had no authority to suppress privateering, as the commissions were issued by the government of Spain, but he promised to exert his influence to prevent their being fitted out. I look upon these professions as words of course, and am of opinion that these acts of piracy ought to be restrained by the strong hand of power, and the government of the island be made responsible for the illegal acts of its inhabitants. The dominion exercised by the mother country over these colonies is too remote and inconsiderable to enable her to control the lawless banditti that inhabit the coast of Puerto Rico and Cuba. The authorities of the islands can alone keep them within bounds, and they ought to be compelled to do so.

Desirous of obtaining an insight into the civil government and institutions of the island, of which I had received very contradictory accounts, I requested the commercial agent to introduce me to a *letrado;* we passed through several clean but narrow streets, the houses two and three stories high, with flat roofs, and latticed windows without glass, the shops neatly set off with French and English goods, and the lazy shop-keepers, with their coats off, sitting on chairs in the street, under the shade of the houses; and still lazier house-keepers swinging in hammocks suspended in the passage of their house, gazing listlessly at the passengers, and drawling away their existence. I found the man of the law wrapped in a loose morning gown, and swinging in a cotton hammock hung within a foot of the floor, with a client sitting by his side. He flung himself out of the hammock on perceiving us enter the room, and received us with great courtesy. He listened to my questions with exemplary patience, and answered them promptly and satisfactorily. Frequently, however, in his turn asking, "But why do you want to know that?" Nor could he comprehend that curiosity alone prompted my enquiries. . . .

By a census made about a year ago, the whole population of the island is stated to be two hundred and twenty-five thousand souls, of which twenty-five thousand, or thereabouts, are slaves. The greater part of the free inhabitants are coloured persons—the whites and free negroes bearing but a small proportion to the whole. Within a few years past the emigration from Europe has been very great, amounting it is said to between six and eight thousand persons. The inhabitants are divided into two classes—the nobles and the people. All the whites may be considered as forming part of the nobility; as custom extends to them an exemption from serving in the militia, and some other privileges that by law belong only to the *noblesse*. The laws know no difference between the white *roturier* and the coloured man; and this circumstance, as well as the Spaniard's being in the habit of mixing with the people of colour without those prejudices so common in the other West India colonies, prevents any jealousy or bad feeling towards him on their part, and forms a great security against the slave population and their neighbours of San Domingo. . . .

The authorities of the island have received information that an expedition was about to sail from New York for the purpose of revolutionizing the island, and are prepared to defeat the project, whatever it may be. It is much to be lamented that these expeditions could not always be arrested where they are fitted out. The object is so palpably plunder—for the pretended motive, the love of liberty, is too puerile to gain credit with the most credulous—and they involve so many innocent men in ruin and misery, and are so dishonourable to our country, that we ought to exercise a more vigilant police, and if possible prevent adventurers from disgracing us.

The rumour of an intended insurrection is confirmed. Sixty negroes, part free and part slaves, have been brought from the west side of the island, and are to be tried by a court martial. In the course of my walk this morning I saw several companies of the garrison on parade. They were of all colours, from the fairest European to the blackest son of Africa.

Dined with the American commercial agent, where I met the Marquis del Norte, a very intelligent and accomplished gentleman, from whom I have derived a great deal of information.

The young officers have this instant returned from a ball, delighted with the charming faces, delicate figures, and graceful movements of the Creole ladies. Those I saw in the streets had good persons, and delicate and well formed features, but very sallow complexions.

29th.—Set out this morning to make an excursion into the country. We crossed the bay in a small sail-boat, and on landing, found horses waiting for us. For saddles, they were furnished with straw pads, with baskets suspended on both sides, intended to support the legs. I found the seat not very commodious or secure, but the horse was quiet, and our feet and legs were elevated above being splashed. The road was a continued quagmire, and our horses frequently plunged up to the saddle girths.

The road, for about a mile from the shore, passes along a narrow valley, the hills on each side being steep and wooded to the summit. It then winds gradually up a chain of hills, passing near two large plantations with extensive buildings, dwelling houses, chapels, sugar mills and store houses. The summit of the ridge commands a view of a charming and highly cultivated plain, clothed with the richest verdure and with the most luxuriant vegetation. Lofty cocoa and date-palms, and plantations of coffee trees and bananas, cover the rising grounds, which skirt a plain cultivated in fields of Indian corn, sugar and cassava, and spotted with neat farm houses. A short ride from this enchanting spot, brought us to the habitation of a French gentleman, who received us with great urbanity and politeness. The house is large, and although it consists of only one floor, is commodious, and looked cool and clean. In front is a small garden, neatly laid out, exhibiting a great variety of flowers, and exhaling a profusion of sweets. We were introduced to a German Baron and to his lady, a fair Parisian; the latter, happy to meet with any one who had been in Paris, and who could understand her, overwhelmed me with her regrets and comparisons between the dull life of an Islander and the delightful life of Paris. . . .

After passing an hour very pleasantly, we set forth on our return. In the course of our ride, I had bought hogs, turkeys and ducks; for they were not to be found in market, and our conductor contrived to cram some into the baskets, and to sling the rest before his pack saddle: so that, on our march, we were accompanied by such a noise, that the folks ran out of their huts to look at us. If they were surprised at our appearance, I was equally so to see such crowds of men, women and children, issuing from habitations so small. The gable-end of every cottage projects about ten feet, with a rude portico, where they must sleep, for the interior cannot contain them all.

In the course of this ride, I met two whites only, but a great many people of different shades of colour. We reached the ship time enough for a late dinner, and all my hogs, turkeys and ducks arrived in safety, to the great consolation of the mess. The market is so badly provided, that we expected to be under the necessity of going to sea without fresh provisions. Limes, oranges, bananas, and other fruits are abundant and cheap, and we laid in a good store of them.

"ARRIBA, PUERTO RICANS!"

The spiritual leader of Puerto Rico's small pro-independence movement during the nineteenth century was Ramón Emeterio Betances, born in the coastal village of Cabo Rojo in 1827. A graduate in medicine from the University of Paris, he was well known in both the Caribbean region and Europe. Betances spent his lifetime trying to free Puerto Rico from Spanish colonialism. Also a militant opponent of slavery, he, at one time, purchased young slave children from their masters and gave them their freedom. Because of his controversial activities, Betances was forced to live part of his life in exile. In early 1864, the following proclamation was circulated on the island; it is believed to be the work of Betances. Its text, a call to arms against Spain, makes clear many of the islanders' grievances against their colonial condition.

Puerto Ricans, for more than three centuries, Spanish despotism has oppressed us. Until now, not a single son of this country has occupied a post of any distinction. On the contrary, any man who has dared to speak for the well-being of his countrymen has been persecuted, banished into exile, or ruined.

For more than three centuries, we have been paying immense taxes, and still we have no roads, railways, telegraph systems, or steamships.

The rabble of Spain—its soldiers and clerks—come to the island without a *peseta,* and, after they have squeezed us dry, return to their homeland with millions that belong to us, who have worked for it.

The *gíbaros* are poor and ignorant because of the Government, which prohibits schools, newspapers, and books, and not long ago refused to found a university, so that the poor, who cannot send their children abroad, shall never see them with the titles of doctor, lawyer, etc.

The Government insists that the *gíbaros* should remain nothing more than

Translated from Lidio Cruz Monclova, *Historia de Puerto Rico, Siglo XIX, Tomo I, 1808-1868* (San Juan: Editorial Universitaria, Universidad de Puerto Rico, 1958), pp. 477-78.

lowly day laborers with *libretas*.[1] And, lately, to exploit us even more, it tries to make us hate our brothers, the sons of Santo Domingo, forcing us to take arms and fight against them. . . .

Puerto Ricans, let us not be fools, let us not be deceived by the promises and falsehoods of the Government; we know from experience that Spain never fulfills its promises. Let us not sleep; the occasion is magnificent; there are no soldiers on the Island, and even if there were, the war in Santo Domingo must have convinced us that one *gíbaro* with his machete in hand is worth a hundred Spaniards.

Arriba Puerto Ricans! Let us show the rabble, who rob and insult us, that the *gíbaros* of Puerto Rico are neither cowards against their executioners, nor assassins against their brothers.

Let us join together, and rise en masse against the oppressors of our land, of our women and children. Our *grito* of Independence shall be heard, and supported, by all friends of Liberty; and there shall be no lack of arms and money to crush the despots of Cuba, Puerto Rico, and Santo Domingo into the dust.

---

1. Each worker had to carry a *libreta,* or notebook, which severely restricted his activities. This is explained by Juan Antonio Corretjer's article, later in this section.

"YOU SHALL BE FREE"

After the previous proclamation, General Felix María de Messina, the island's Spanish colonial governor, ordered Betances to appear before him in La Fortaleza, the governor's palace. As Betances told Messina of the need for independence, the governor interrupted and said, "If you continue this, I shall be obliged to hang you from one of the battlements of El Morro." Betances replied, "Well, keep in mind, General Messina, that the night of that day I shall sleep far more peacefully than Your Excellency." Betances was exiled, but he continued to support independence from abroad. The following proclamation, reproduced in leaflet form, was signed by Betances in November, 1867, and distributed on the island. He was still in exile, this time on nearby Saint Thomas. The proclamation sets forth "Ten Commandments," listing the conditions under which Puerto Rico would retain its association with Spain. It is virtually a declaration of independence.

Translated from photographic reproduction in *Lecturas Básicas Sobre Historia de Puerto Rico,* First Part, Curriculum Division, Social Studies Program (San Juan: Dept. of Public Education, Commonwealth of Puerto Rico, 1967), p. 174.

PUERTO RICANS!

The government of Queen Isabella is making a terrible accusation against us:

It says that we are bad Spaniards. The government is spreading falsehoods.

We do not want separation; we want peace and union with Spain; but it is only fair that we should also specify the conditions in the contract. They are very simple:

ABOLITION OF SLAVERY
THE RIGHT TO REJECT
ALL TAXES FREEDOM OF RELIGION
FREEDOM OF SPEECH
FREEDOM OF THE PRESS
FREEDOM OF COMMERCE
THE RIGHT TO ASSEMBLE
THE RIGHT TO BEAR ARMS
THE INVIOLABILITY OF THE CITIZEN THE RIGHT TO
    ELECT OUR AUTHORITIES

These are the
TEN COMMANDMENTS
of Free Men

If Spain feels capable of giving us these rights and freedoms, and does so, then it may send us a captain general or governor . . . made of straw, and we shall hang him, and have him burned during the days of *carnestolandas* [three carnival days before Ash Wednesday—ed.], to commemorate all the Judases who, until today, have sold us out.

THUS, we shall be Spaniards. If not, NO.

If not, Puerto Ricans, PATIENCE! You shall be free.

DR. BETANCES
St. Thomas, November 1867

THE DAY PUERTO RICO BECAME A NATION

"Spaniard became Spaniard and the Puerto Rican, Puerto Rican" on September 23, 1868, when a pro-independence insurrection broke out in Lares. The revolt lasted scarcely a day, but it was the first time that the island's sons had mustered an armed uprising of such dimensions, and it served notice to Spain that the days of colonialism were numbered. Lares was followed by Spanish efforts at reform, and—just five years later—by the abolition of slavery. As the author of the following essay notes, "The abolitionist movement had reached a point where its connection with the independence movement could only result in igniting a revolution." Juan Antonio Corretjer (1908-1985) was an accomplished poet and journalist, and a lifelong activist for Puerto Rican independence. A former member of the Nationalist party—he was a close associate of the late Pedro Albizu Campos—Corretjer was then president of the island's Socialist League. His essay was written to commemorate the one hundredth anniversary—in 1968—of the Grito de Lares, which is now celebrated as an occasion for the island's pro-independence groups to rally thousands of followers to that historic mountain town.

The centennial of the Grito de Lares tomorrow is a commemoration not so much of a short-lived insurrection against Spain as of the culmination of Puerto Rico's 19th Century revolutionary process. It is also the observance of an event which finally succeeded in forging a true Puerto Rican identity.

This does not mean that attempts to free Puerto Rico from Spanish colonial oppression had not occurred before or after. The red flag that waved under fire during the three attempts to take San Sebastián by assault the day after Lares was stormed, had appeared 30 years before in Carolina. The same bold spirit of Lares, with equal political intention, warmed the hearts of Fidel Velez and his followers in Yauco, March 24, 1897.

Just two years after Lares, in 1870, Captain General Laureano Sanz was forced to move to Ciales, where a serious insurrectionist organization had readied full development. Repression was severe—as was to be expected from the iron hand of General Sanz.

The Lares insurrection has been pointed out as the historical moment in which Puerto Rico's nationhood was defined. Our nationalist leaders and

---

Juan Antonio Corretjer, "The Day Puerto Rico Became a Nation," *San Juan Star Sunday Magazine,* September 22, 1968. Reprinted by permission.

theoreticians have maintained that that is the deep meaning of the Lares insurrection. National thought had developed enough to see independence as a necessary condition to solve Puerto Rico's social and economic problems, and national will sufficiently developed to carry this understanding to what some consider its logical conclusion of separation by force of arms.

History, Puerto Rican life itself, shows nothing was again the same in Puerto Rico after Lares. The Spaniard became Spaniard and the Puerto Rican, Puerto Rican. In the 1890's, commenting on a servile reference to the Lares Revolt made by Luis Muñoz Rivera, Ramón Betances who led the revolt, wrote to a friend: "Without Lares, *La Democracia* (Muñoz' newspaper) would not be published now in Ponce." Betances's clear words were a reflection of a well-guarded colonial opinion that all reform obtained from the Spanish crown after the Lares revolt originated from the Spanish fear of an independence insurrection in Puerto Rico at the time when the Spanish Army was fighting the Cuban war. That is to say, they feared a repetition of Lares.

In the 1930s, Tomás Blanco in "Prontuario Historico" wrote that the Lares insurrection was responsible for the abolition of slavery in Puerto Rico. He said just that. No more. But one must bear in mind the fact that the abolitionist movement had reached a point where its connection with the independence movement could only result in igniting a revolution.

The provisional government formed in Lares by the successful revolutionists immediately proclaimed that every slave that took arms in defense of a free and independent Puerto Rico would become a free man. Shortly after the military defeat of the revolution, the Spanish Government decreed the gradual abolition of slavery, making the decree effective on a date previous to the Lares uprising. Five years after, in 1873, slavery came to an end.

It was not only slavery that was solved at Lares. The so-called "free" laborer of the time was in reality a feudal serf. By decree of a General Pezuela, the "free" laborer, who lived as an "agregado" (something like a sharecropper) on a plantation could not leave the plantation limits without the owner's permission. Even his Sundays were spent as his master decided. He had to write his time of departure and return in a notebook that was always to be on his person and in this book he had to make note of every act of his life: work, expenses, morality. He was, in reality, a feudal serf.

And so the Liberation Army was joined not only by the Negro slaves but the laborers as well. And it was the laborers who piled up those notebooks and set them on fire in the center of Lares Plaza on Sept. 23, 1868. Shortly after, the Spanish government abolished the notebook system.

It is obvious that nations are not made with slaves and serfs. Nations themselves are part of the historical development of society. Slavery and serfdom come to a point, historically, when they chain the development of society. The slave owner's acquiescence to abolition had no altruistic motive. It was an economic, historical compulsion, idealistically phrased by their intellectuals in the resounding words of 19th Century liberalism. That is why we say that the Grito de Lares brought Puerto Rico to its definition as a nation.

The social contradictions steaming within the colonial society worked themselves to the point of what Marxism calls the highest form of struggle: insurrection. The property owner's protest against Spanish taxation and restrictions on trade; the general hunger for education; the call for freedom and a cultural consciousness on the part of the intellectuals—all this came to coincide with what many consider a logical revolt against imperialistic oppression. In Puerto Rico's history, its name is Lares.

The abolition of slavery and of the labor-notebook system put the colonial landed aristocracy on the road in a long march toward greater wealth. These beneficiaries of the crown's abolition of communal property now entered into a time of new prosperity. (In 1775 Charles III had abolished communal property on the recommendation of Alejandro O'Reilly, a Spanish general he had sent to the island to make a report of its progress. Up to then, all land was owned by the crown which could deed it to individuals but it reverted to the crown again after the second generation.) If the O'Reilly reform had permitted them to monopolize the land, the abolition of slaves and the labor-notebook system now gave them the benefit of a new working class, more willing to work and learn now that it was "free."

Results were seen immediately. Coffee production entered a time of unprecedented growth. Sugar and tobacco production multiplied. The Juntas de Agricultura, Industria y Comercio were formed and shortly after unified into a government bureau. The Junta Provincial de Estadísticas y Evaluación de la Riqueza came into being. Two agricultural experimental stations were founded, one of them in Río Piedras where the present station is located. The Asociación de Agricultores was organized and the Banco Territorial y Agrícola was founded. Agricultural "colonies" were established by law and a system of tax exemption was created to help their development. The Sociedad Anónima Para El Fomento de la Cría Caballar, the Liga Económica and the Negociado de Montes y Terrenes Baldíos; the Banco Crédito y Ahorro Ponceño, the Banco de San Germán and the Banco Popular, are all institutions born of this great surge of the economy as a consequence of the social forces freed by the abolition of slavery and the notebook system.

But there was also a shadowy side. After the revolutionary recession, colonialism as a way of life dug deep into the Puerto Rican upper and middle classes. Defeatism was politically systemized. It became, indeed, the very center of institutional life.

In 1870 the political parties were organized. With their coming into being duplicity came to reign in a colonial kingdom that has known no democratic overthrow. The reactionary elements barricaded themselves in religion, tradition, paper nobility and other forms of social simulation, and the Partido Conservador, Incondicionalmente Español. A large section of the independence forces hid within these parties, where consequently they were castrated. In time, their leaders became the masters of this game. Wrapped in the Spanish flag, kowtowing to María Cristina, they used independence and revolution as a source of prestige before the people and of blackmail against Spain. This forced them into partisan leadership and government positions. Thus the bombing of San Juan by American guns found them ready to kneel before a new god.

The leader of the nationalist movement was Ramón Emeterio Betances. . . .

Twice ordered to exile in Spain by the colonial authorities, he first fled to St. Thomas, then to New York, then to Santo Domingo. From exile, he organized the insurrection of 1868. He put into it all he had: his prestige, his fortune, his dreams of freedom and happiness for Puerto Rico. He was not, however, to be at Lares. His plans were discovered. The Dominican government seized the arms that were to be shipped to Puerto Rico. "El Telégrafo," the steamer he had bought to take him and his closest comrades to Puerto Rico, was confiscated.

What happened to Betances in Santo Domingo happened also to the conspiracy in Puerto Rico. The secret societies did their work well, but an indiscretion caused the arrest of Manuel María González, a distinguished member of the "Lanzador del Norte," the secret society in Arecibo. The Arecibo military found incriminating documents in González's Camuy residence which led to further arrests.

González's arrest precipitated the insurrection. The news was received by Manuel Rojas at his coffee hacienda in Lares. Rojas put the conspiratorial apparatus into immediate action. His call to the Mayagüez patriots brought 100 men to Roja's hacienda under the command of Juan Terreforte. At the suggestion of Mathias Brugman, Rojas was named commander of the Liberation army, over 400 men strong. The night of Sept. 23, at 9 o'clock, Rojas riding at the head of the cavalry, they set off for Lares. Without meeting any resistance, a little before midnight, he took the town.

A meeting was held at the Ayuntamiento (city hall) which was located where the plaza del mercado (market place) stands now. Spanish functionaries were arrested and the Spanish symbols replaced by those of the revolution. A provi-

sional government was formed. Francisco Ramírez Medina was elected president; Federico Valencia, minister of the treasury; Aurelio Méndez Martínez,
minister of government; Clemente Millán, minister of justice; Manuel Ramírez,
minister of state; and Bernabé Pol, secretary to the cabinet. Rojas was confirmed as military head.

Four decrees were immediately issued. One declared that all Puerto Ricans
were duty bound to fight for the revolution; another that every foreigner who
voluntarily took arms on the side of independence was to be considered a
patriot; that every slave who joined the revolution would automatically cease
to be a slave; and another abolished the labor-notebook system. Comments historian Lidio Cruz Monclova: "It is obvious that the revolution was affirming
with facts, from its very beginning, its decision to make a reality of the beautiful
trilogy of its supreme ideals of political, economic and social freedom."

Three flags flew at Lares. Two of them—a red flag, used 30 years before by
Vizcarrondo in Carolina and a white flag one ending in two points on which
Capt. Manuel Cebollero Aguilar, president of the revolutionary committee,
Junta Porvenir of San Sebastián, wrote with his cigar: Death or Liberty! Long
Live Puerto Rico Libre! Year of 1868—came under fire during the three attacks
on San Sebastián next day.

The other, a flag created by Betances and made by Mariana Bracetti, was
placed at the altar for a Te Deum celebrated by the Catholic Church and sung
in a small wooden hermitage near a corner of the plaza. It was the flag we know
as the flag of Lares. This was to be the official flag of the republic.

As the revolutionaries entered Lares, they say, cries were heard of "Down
with the taxes! Down with the Spaniards! Down with Spain. *Viva Puerto Rico
Libre."*

Tomorrow, Sept. 23, what we celebrate is, of course, not a defeat. It is the
military success of an action that took place 100 years ago. That military success enabled the leaders of the Lares insurrection to gather at the town hall,
proclaim Puerto Rico free of the Spanish crown, and organize a provisional
government based on the principles of democracy. This government, sovereign
in its moment, decreed the abolition of slavery and of the labor-notebook
system. In doing so, Lares forced the Spanish government to free the slaves
and put an end to the labor notebooks. . . .

Yet it is true that the Liberation Army was routed and disbanded at San
Sebastián the day after; that this defeat put Puerto Rico under a reformist
counter-revolutionary political preponderance that paved the way to both the
autonomous constitution of 1897 and the American invasion of 1898.

So Puerto Rico did not become a national state independent of Spain and
did become a colony of the United States. Lares failed, from this point of view.

Why?

Let us go back to Sept. 23, 1868.

Was the revolution not popular? Was Puerto Rico not ready for revolution?

Betances was not a daydreamer. The whole of his life, and the whole of his activities, the testimony of his contemporaries, show him as a well-balanced, extremely intelligent, widely read person whose scientific mind and apostolic zeal in no way carried him away from reality. He loved his people and knew them well. Yet Betances to the last day of his life repeated that in 1868 the country was ripe for revolution. His testimony is worthy of respect and consideration. It is well to remember, too, that he did not say the same of subsequent uprisings. . . .

Cruz Monclova believed all the factors so far mentioned were present and adds others: bad training of the military; no help from the outside world (due to the seizure in Santo Domingo of Betances's arms and ship): disorientation because of González's sudden, unexpected arrest; 30 years of consistent anti-independence propaganda.

It is well known that the insurrection was planned on a national scale and as Pérez Moris (the best informed and most anti-Lares historian of them all) suggests, it involved a section of the most influential people in the country. And, to a degree, it was politically convenient for the government to ignore that fact. It is equally known, that, because of the moving up of the date of the uprising caused by González's arrest, practically all the revolutionary committees never received Rojas's call to arms.

I give credit to Betances, on one side and to his most bitter enemy, Pérez Moris, on the other. Betances said that the country was ready and that it was the haste that caused the revolutionary abortion. Pérez Moris, a Spaniard, so near to the Spanish General Staff, said it was lack of armament, and implicitly, not a lack of popular support.

Now, why did Rojas concentrate on attacking San Sebastián? Why his apparently stubborn attacks on that city?

There were arms in the Spanish headquarters there. That fact is known. No student of history—military, revolutionary history—ignores what an effect a resounding victory has in fortifying a people's will to fight. Or, on the contrary, the depressive effect of a confrontation with defeat. Rojas was right to try to seize San Sebastián because the weapons were there that he needed to go on to Arecibo. He could not wait to be attacked at Lares. He was right in fighting with all he had to seize San Sebastián. If he had succeeded, the call to revolt he had issued to all the committees could have reached them on the wings of victory. Possibly, Puerto Rico's history could have been more similar to Venezuela's than to Saint Thomas's.

THE ABOLITION OF SLAVERY

The abolition movement in Puerto Rico was closely linked with the cause in Cuba. Both islands also linked the issue of slavery with that of political emancipation—of blacks and whites—from Spain. Eric Williams, Prime Minister of Trinidad and Tobago since 1956, is a distinguished historian and a specialist in West Indian politics. In this excerpt from a recent book, he puts the issue of Puerto Rican-Cuban abolition in a world perspective and shows how "the Puerto Rican situation was unique."

The slave system was abolished at different times during the nineteenth century throughout the Caribbean. The slave trade, abolished finally by Denmark in 1803, was abolished by Great Britain in 1807. Restored by Bonaparte in 1802, it was abolished by the French Government in 1817. In the same year the Spanish Government signed a treaty with Great Britain whereby it pledged itself to abolition in 1820. Holland proclaimed abolition in 1818, Sweden in 1824. Slavery was abolished in the British colonies in 1833. Sweden followed suit in 1846, France in 1848, Holland in 1863. Slavery was abolished in Puerto Rico in 1873 and in Cuba in 1880. . . .

Whereas the abolition of the slave system in the British, French, Dutch and Danish colonies in the Caribbean area was a metropolitan measure imposed on recalcitrant colonials, in the Spanish colonies, Cuba and Puerto Rico, it was the metropolitan government which insisted on the system in the face of powerful colonial opposition. The colonials rested their case chiefly on the economic ground that white, free labor was cheaper than the black slave. In Cuba it was estimated in 1862 that the sugar production from 490 acres and 74 free workers was equivalent to that from 635 acres worked by 142 slaves. . . .

The Puerto Rico situation was unique in the Caribbean, in that not only did the white population outnumber the people of color, but the slaves constituted an infinitesimal part of the total population and free labor predominated during the regime of slavery. The following table has no counterpart in Caribbean history:

Eric Williams, *From Columbus to Castro: The History of the Caribbean, U92-1969* (New York: Harper & Row, 1970), pp. 280, 290-95, 303. Copyright © by Eric Williams. Reprinted by permission of Harper & Row, Publishers, Inc.

Population	1827	1834	1860	1872
Total	323,838	357,086	583,181	618,150
Whites	162,311	188,869	300,430	328,806
Mulattoes	100,430	101,275		
Free Negroes	26,857	25,124	>241,015	>257,709
Slaves	32,240	41,818	41,736	31,635
Slaves as % of total	10	12	14	5
Slaves as % of coloured	21	33	16	11

These 31,635 slaves were divided among nearly two thousand owners. Few owners owned more than fifty slaves. Of the total there were only 21,000 between the ages of 15 and 50. Many were domestics; male laborers numbered 11,748. The explanation is that Puerto Rico's was a small farming and diversified economy, based on the cultivation of minor crops rather than plantation staples. In 1830 the total acreage under cultivation amounted to 120,721 cuerdas, divided as follows: starchy vegetables, 40,955; coffee, 17,247; maize, 16,674; rice, 15,290; sugar, 15,242; fruits, 8,301; cotton, 3,170; tobacco, 2,676; other crops, 1,166. . . .

Essentially a food-producing colony, with a birth rate of 56 per thousand in 1824, and a density of population of 180 per square mile in 1872, Puerto Rico did not need slavery, had an adequate supply of free labour, and could anticipate no shortage. The island sent delegates to Spain in 1866 to demand the abolition of slavery, not only as a moral necessity, but also as an economic necessity. "No really acceptable reason," they stated in their official memorandum, "can be given for its continuation in Puerto Rico. The general wealth of the island does not need it: its disappearance will not affect any productive element, and the self-interest of the owners must demand the overthrow of that institution."

Their arguments for the superiority of free labour over slave would have done credit to Adam Smith himself. They deserve to be quoted:

Let all the disadvantages of the one and all the advantages of the other be weighed; let the greater intelligence and interest with which free men work be appreciated, the fidelity and personal responsibility they display, the cheapness of their wages, the stimulus which is awakened in them, let all this be appreciated on the one hand, and then on the other consider the sickness, flights, captures, baptisms, marriages and burials of the slaves, all the expenses which fall on the owner; the thefts and the judicial proceedings to which they give rise; the absenteeism resulting from punishments, sickness and sometimes also indolence; finally, let the endless and continuous expenses of maintenance, medical care and so many others be added, and it will be seen that, in order to make slave labour cheaper than free, it is necessary for the master to dismiss from his mind every generous sentiment, every notion of justice, and to consider the Negro only and exclusively as a machine for production which, with a minimum of subsistence, can function fourteen hours a day, for four or five years at most.

If Puerto Rico, by the conventional standards of the final quarter of the nineteenth century, ranked as one of the most backward sectors of Caribbean economy, in intellectual perspective it was head and shoulders above its neighbours. . . .

From the standpoint of the Spanish colonials, the abolition of the slave system was an integral part of the struggle for independence in Cuba and autonomy in Puerto Rico. The first war of independence broke out in Cuba in 1868. Céspedes, who raised the standard of revolt, immediately freed the slaves. . . .

Like Lincoln before him, Céspedes understood that no nation could survive half slave and half free. Also like Lincoln, he used emancipation as a powerful political weapon in the struggle. According to the decree, the slaves were freed and drafted into the service of the country. Owners who supported the revolution would be eligible for compensation for their slaves if they so desired; those who opposed it would be ineligible. . . .

In Puerto Rico, also, the white population, openly bracketing together dictatorship, monopoly and slavery, placed the rights of the slaves before its own civil liberty. Rafael de Labra, one of the island's representatives in the *Cortes,* quoting Figaro's phrase that "liberty is not an overseas commodity," challenged the men of the 1868 (Spanish) revolution who had revolted for the imprescriptible rights of men to say that what was truth on one side of the Pyrenees was a lie on the other. "What example," asked another representative, Emilio Castelar, "can we give to Latin America, independent, republican, democratic, when it sees existing in Spanish territories white slavery and Negro slavery, the colonial regime and the slave regime, which the human conscience rejects in indignation?" Referring to the abolition of slavery by the Convention of France in 1794, Castelar, with a knowledge and appreciation of history rare in the protagonists of emancipation, asserted:

Even though the Convention had committed more crimes than it did, the tears of the pariah redeemed, of the eternal Spartacus emancipated, of the slave made man; those tears which condensed the gratitude of all the future generations and the blessings of all the past generations trampled under the vile heel of slavery, those tears sufficed to wipe out all the stains of blood.

It was widely suggested in Spain that the settlement of the slavery issue in Puerto Rico should await the outcome of events in Cuba, where the war of independence was in full swing. This was anathema to the Puerto Ricans. Sanromá replied to the *Cortes* in 1873:

> To subordinate the interests of Puerto Rico to those of Cuba . . . is a signal iniquity. I do not admit it; neither from the legal point of view, nor from the political, nor from the historical, nor from the economic can the interests of Puerto Rican be subordinated to those of Cuba. . . . When on earth will they leave us of Puerto Rico in peace with their eternal Cuba?

. . . .The establishment of the Spanish Anti-Slavery society in 1865 did not materially alter the situation. The government followed the beaten path of gradualism, though the Society itself stood committed to immediate emancipation. In the very years of Céspedes' emancipation proclamation, the Spanish republican government castigated slavery as an outrage to humanity and an affront to Spain; their humanitarianism was limited, however, to the modest proposal that all children born thereafter should be declared free. This so-called "law of the free stomach" was promulgated in 1870; in addition, freedom was decreed for slaves who had helped the Spanish troops in the civil war in Cuba, for slaves of the State, and for slaves who had reached the age of sixty. Eventually, emancipation was proclaimed [in Cuba] in 1880. But gradualism triumphed; a period of apprenticeship was instituted which lasted until October 7,1886.

Spanish paternalism was best illustrated by the case of Puerto Rico. The planters to a man demanded immediate emancipation with or without compensation. The metropolitan government decreed otherwise. On March 22, 1873, slavery was abolished. But the 31,635 slaves were required to enter into contracts with their owners for a period of not less than three years. If their owners refused to enter into such contracts, they were entered into contracts with other persons or with the government. Three funcionaries were appointed protectors of the freedmen. After five years the freedmen were to receive political rights. It was like using a sledge-hammer to kill a fly. . . .

"THE TROUBLES AT PORTO RICO"

The Lares revolt in 1868 was just a symptom of widespread distaste for Spain's absolutist rule. Despite strict press censorship, word of the growing schism between native Puerto Ricans and Spanish officials filtered abroad. In this article, a journalist, signing the pseudonym of "Quasimodo," described, in 1871, how the worried Spaniards had formed volunteer self-defense companies. The unpopularity of these loyalist volunteers is indicated by the fact that they were ordered "not to appear in the streets in uniform, so as to avoid complications." The article is also significant in that it contains an account of what is described as "the first time that the hitherto peaceful capital, San Juan de Puerto Rico, has witnessed a riot."

T he revolutionary spirit has been on the eve of breaking out for a long time past, and has only been kept within bounds by the leaders of the radical party, who were determined to wrest the island from Spain without fighting for it. . . . Some hot blooded spirits have long fretted over the apparent slowness of emancipation, and the outbreak of Lara [Lares?] was the first fruit of their untimely action. Flushed with their success at the recent elections, their numerical superiority over the Spaniards, and the tacit aid of many Spaniards themselves, these hot headed radicals have again preached and abetted open rebellion and instigated the colored population to begin the row, which the latter, many of whom are still held as slaves, are nothing loth to inaugurate. These extreme radicals also act under the impression that any disturbance in Porto Rico, no matter how small, will aid the revolutionary cause in Cuba, both morally and materially, and in this they are right; it is positively known that since

the outbreak of the revolution in Cuba more natives from Porto Rico have joined the Cuban rebels than from many a place in Cuba itself, but this is foreign to the subject, and only tends to illustrate the propensities of the Porto Ricans to become an independent Spanish American country.

The Spaniards in Porto Rico . . . began to form volunteer companies, and about one thousand volunteers are at the present time organized and armed in the island. The islanders saw this movement with disgust, and feared that a part of their countrymen might become tainted with *Españolism,* as so many hundreds of Cubans are; that they might even take up arms against their countrymen in case of an outbreak, and, as in Cuba, . . . organize those terrible counter-guerrillas, who, composed of natives of the island, commit such havoc among their revolutionary countrymen. But whatever the motive may have been, the ultra radicals refused to have any person dressed in volunteer uniform parade the streets, either singly or collectively. Wherever a volunteer appeared he was hooted by the populace, and threatened with violence in some cases. No demonstrations of hostility had been made against the regular troops until

---

"The Troubles at Porto Rico," *New York Times,* August 11, 1871.

the eve of the 25th, during the music on the Plaza de Armas in front of the Captain-General's palace, when several stones were flung from the neighboring jail, striking a couple of soldiers. The volunteers had received that same morning an order from the Captain-General not to appear on the streets in uniform so as to avoid complications. Another soldier who was walking along remarked: "This is getting unbearable. I advise nobody to fling stones at me else they'll suffer for it." He had hardly spoken these words when a stone struck him in the face. Seeing a dandified negro close by, he suspected him to be the author, and drawing his sword began the attack. Another negro, probably the one who flung the stone, saw the affair, and rushing up to the soldier stabbed him in the back. This enabled the first one to escape, the soldier cutting down the negro who had stabbed him. Negroes and soldiers flocked together, houses were barricaded, and a scene of indescribable confusion ensued, the cries of the combatants in the street, and the women and children inside of their houses, forming a strange contrast, this being the first time that the hitherto peaceable capital, San Juan de Puerto Rico, has witnessed a riot. The fighting continued in the streets wherever a negro met a soldier or a soldier a negro, until armed patrols appeared, and at 11 PM quiet was restored. The Captain-General immediately proclaimed martial law throughout the island and the capital itself in a state of siege. The result of the riot is stated to be three soldiers and one officer killed, nineteen men wounded, and five negroes killed and a very large number wounded. The police and armed patrols arrested a number of negroes during the night, and searched several houses for hidden arms. The Spanish party accuses the radicals of having hired the negroes to commit these excesses, and the natives say that the Spaniards purposely provoked the conflict. Either story is improbable, and the true explanation of the occurrence may be summed up in the fact that the natives, black and white, hate and execrate the Spaniards, and that the feeling is mutual. Until the morning of the 28th, the tranquility of the capital had remained unaltered, but reports were in circulation that outbreaks had occurred at Mayagüez and other points . . .

THE AUTONOMIST CONCEPT

Despite the widespread dislike for Spain, all of the armed might was in the hands of the military government, a substantial portion of the upper class was loyal to Madrid, and the illiterate peasants, who comprised the mass of the population, were too concerned with daily survival—and too isolated from each other—to join in an effective pro-independence conspiracy. Thus, most of the island's liberal leaders were discouraged by the prospects for armed insurrection, and sought a compromise. The spirit of their pessimistic views is captured in the following statements, by various leaders. In 1869, Román Baldorioty de Castro favored a Canadian-style autonomy as a means to resolve colonialism in Puerto Rico. He advocated free trade and the abolition of slavery, in accordance with the position taken by the Puerto Rican liberals who formed part of a commission in Madrid.

In the question of the public interest, as in an issue of private interests, compromises are frequently necessary. We seek solutions which are both practical and possible. However, we will never accept the colonial system, which places the province in humiliating conditions of inferiority, in contrast with the harmony of equality enjoyed by other provinces of the nation; nor will we accept a system based on slavery, whether overt or veiled, nor one which can permit, as has been the case up to now, the ruinous abuses of an irresponsible administration.

Such is and continues to be the colonial system which reigns in Puerto Rico; contrary to the true interests of the nation, this traditional regime represents blind opposition to the cultural, economic, and political progress of the island. We have protested against the colonial system, and we will continue to do so, accepting as an honor the calumny and vicious rumors perpetrated against our cause.

[In 1890, Baldorioty was leader of the Autonomist Liberal party. Here, he compares Puerto Rico with Cuba—then engaged in a bloody war for independence.]

The difference between Puerto Rico and Cuba is immense. Here, we have no man of stature, and they have many. Here, we would agree to a municipal life that is fairly reasonable, while they aspire or are driven on to the life of

Selections in this chapter:
1. Translated from Lidio Cruz Monclova, *Historia de Puerto Rico,* Vol. II (Río Piedras: University of Puerto Rico, 1958), pp. 34-35.
2. Translated from Pilar Barbosa de Rosario, ed., *La Obra de José Celso Barbosa* (San Juan: 1957), pp. 167-58.
3. Translated from *Barbosa,* pp. 167-88.
4. Translated from Luis Muñoz Rivera, *Campañas Politicas,* part of *Obras Completas,* Luis Muñoz Marín, ed. (Madrid: Editorial Puerto Rico, 1925), pp. 34-37.
5. Translated from Luis Muñoz Rivera, *Campañas Politicas.*
6. Translated from *Barbosa,* pp. 294-95.
7. From Edward J. Berbusse, *The United States in Puerto Rico, 1898-1900* (Chapel Hill: University of North Carolina, 1966), p. 50.
8. From a letter to Antonio V. Alvarado, February 16, 1892.

Canada or Australia. They desire a Cuban country within or without the national unity; we would agree to desire the life of a secondary province. . . . [Puerto Rico] will be reduced by misery or emigration; or it will, by entreaty, gain better conditions of government. Cuba will be an autonomic colony, or it will be lost through the war.

[In 1890, Julio Vizcarrondo, Puerto Rican deputy for Ponce in the Spanish Cortes, opposed the idea that Puerto Rico should join with Cuba in a revolt against Spain.]

I do not believe it fitting that Puerto Rico should follow the good or bad fate of Cuba . . . We have different inclinations . . . and other aspirations. . . . Let us live in friendly separation. I, who do not wish to see my island a colony of Spain, but rather a Spanish province, would never want to see it a colony of Cuba. The unhappiest slave is the slave of a freedman.

[Also pessimistic about independence was Luis Muñoz Rivera, the journalist who became the autonomy movement's *líder máximo.* Here, in 1890, he says:]

[Puerto Rico] is absolutely dependent upon the Castilian metropolis; and from it—or from annexation to a foreign country, which is a crime—we must hope for all. . . . [Compared with Cuba] we are lacking in the strength of the people, because of the ignorance of the country population. We are without a militant youth, because of the apathy and laissez-faire attitude of our youth. We are wanting in leaders, because they greatly fear creative statesmanship; and are motivated by an unpardonable selfishness. It is necessary to educate the first group, to stimulate the second, and to attract the third. . . .

[In 1891, Muñoz Rivera, writing in his newspaper *La Democracia,* urged a pact between his Puerto Rican Autonomist Party and the the Spanish Liberal Fusionist Party, led by Práxedes Mateo Sagasta. Six years later, when Sagasta gained control of the Spanish government, autonomy was granted to the island.]

We are not bent on fighting useless battles or pursuing the impossible. For those who cherish beautiful ideals, let us inquire whether the ideal is possible, and then make haste to follow its luminous path. If it cannot become a reality, let us limit our desire to the dictates of reason, rather than waste our energies in fruitless combat. We are men of our times, eminently practical in the noble and generous sense of that phrase. Today's world is not one of dreams and mirages. Platonism leads nowhere in our era.

[A year before the granting of autonomy to Puerto Rico, small revolutionary groups in exile were trying to join Puerto Rico with Cuba in the battle for independence. Here, Muñoz Rivera cites an interview in July, 1896 with Gerardo Forrest, of the Puerto Rican Revolutionary Junta of New York.]

My position is this, Mr. Forrest: I am a partisan of independence as an ideal. All have to be free. Nevertheless, I consider that the independence of my country is absolutely impossible. Our masses are even lacking in a complete civic education. They never fought, and will not fight, with the power of the Cuban masses. To attempt force is the equivalent of making a useless sacrifice. After twenty-five years of titanic struggle, Cuba has not been able to succeed. Puerto Rico would succumb without success and without glory . . .

[The exiled revolutionaries soon became frustrated over the inability of the island's leaders to aid the cause of independence. Claims were made that the Autonomists had become instruments of the Spanish colonial government. In a letter dated Jan. 23, 1896, Dr. José C. Barbosa wrote to Roberto Todd of the Revolutionary Junta in New York, replying that. "From New York all seems very easy, but it is necessary to be here in order to be able to judge the situation." Those favoring independence remained adamant. An example of this unyielding position is contained in a letter by Ramón Emeterio Betances in 1892, after he was asked to write an article honoring the memory of the late autonomist leader Román Baldorioty de Castro. In refusing, Betances explained:]

You know that in our country the separatists have been in disfavor for some time; and I do not feel capable of writing something which agrees with the thinking of the autonomists, neither those of today or yesterday. I know I have been defeated, but I harbor the hope that our people some day will say that if any party in Puerto Rico showed proof of its virility, it was the separatist party of Lares. The Spanish government has been able to calm down most of those who were with us by granting them the insignificant concessions which they now possess; but it is good to remember that all despotic governments throughout history have followed the same policy, whenever they have realized that the people are ready to claim their rights, with weapons in hand. Let us not forget that Lares means something in the Hispano-Puerto Rican struggle for obtaining freedom; and I, who have been, am, and shall die a separatist, believe that without a revolution, and without independence, we will never be anything but the eternal colony of Spain.

PART IV

MANIFEST DESTINY

I spent all of yesterday with the spyglass in my hands; from Desecheo to Ataud, from Punta Borinquen to Punta Ponce, I saw all of her, I looked and looked at her, I admired her, and blessed her, and grieved for her . . . I grieved for her, and with her, for her beauty and misfortune. I thought how noble it would have been to see her free by her own efforts, and how sad, and crushing, and shameful it was to see her change from one master to another, without ever being her own . . .

—*Eugenio Maria de Hostos, writing in his diary, September 13, 1898, while aboard the steamer* Philadelphia *as it left Puerto Rico*

As Carl Sandburg observes later in this section, the Spanish-American War was "a small war, edging towards immense consequences."

The war marked new eras for both the United States and Puerto Rico. It was America's first major step as an imperialist power; the first on a long road that led to the quagmire in Southeast Asia.

The United States had, for some years, contemplated expansion beyond its continental borders. The administration of President Franklin Pierce made overtures in Hawaii, Alaska, and Nicaragua. Perhaps the most brazen move was the Ostend Manifesto of 1853, which called for the annexation of Cuba (and probably Puerto Rico). If Spain did not accept a price for Cuba, said Pierce, "we shall be justified in wresting it from Spain."

In 1885, historian John Fiske wrote, in an article entitled "Manifest Destiny,"[1] that, "The work which the English race began when it colonized North America is destined to go on until every land on the earth's surface that is not already the seat of an old civilization shall become English in its language, in its religion, in its political habits and traditions . . ." He was not alone among influential Americans who believed in the inherent superiority of Anglo-Saxon culture.

---

1. *Harper's New Monthly Magazine,* LXX, pp. 578-90.

That same year, Congregationalist clergyman Josiah Strong mirrored the growing "Darwinian" surge in America when he wrote: "This powerful race will move down upon Mexico, down upon Central and South America, out upon the islands of the sea. . . . And can anyone doubt that the result of this competition of races shall be the 'survival of the fittest'?"[2]

Alfred Thayer Mahan, Captain in the U.S. Navy, and one of the nation's most influential "sea power" advocates, wrote in 1890, that "At present the positions of the Caribbean are occupied by foreign powers . . . a distinct advance will have been made when public opinion is convinced that we need them."[3]

In the same mood of expansion, U.S. Secretary of State James G. Blaine wrote to President Benjamin Harrison the next year: "I think there are only three places that are of value enough to be taken; one is Hawaii and the others are Cuba and Puerto Rico."

"From the Rio Grande to the Arctic Ocean, there should be one flag and one country," wrote U.S. Senator Henry Cabot Lodge, just three years before the Spanish-American War. England, he concluded, "has studded the West Indies with strong places which are a standing menace to our Atlantic seaboard. We should have among these islands at least one strong naval station . . ."[4]

In Boston's exclusive Middlesex Club, on April 27, 1898, Senator Albert J. Beveridge voiced the concern that "American factories are making more than the American people can use. . . . We will establish trading posts throughout the world as distributing points for American products." He went on to speak of "great colonies, governing themselves, flying our flag, and trading with us . . ."[5]

A few days later, the *New York Journal of Commerce* editorialized that it was necessary to have Puerto Rico or Cuba, and that, "Whatever territory of that nature falls into our hands must never be parted with."[6] At the same time, letters from American businessmen to the U.S. State Department urged the annexation of Puerto Rico as a "garden spot" that would boost American commerce.

There were, to be sure, some dissenters. Governor William O. Bradley of

1. *Harper's New Monthly Magazine,* LXX, pp. 578-90.
2. Josiah Strong, *Our Country: Its Possible Future and its Present Crisis,* Harvard University, Cambridge: Belknap Press, 1963, pp. 208-27 (facsimile of 1891 editorial).
3. "The United States Looking Outward," *Atlantic Monthly,* December, 1890.
4. "Our Blundering Foreign Policy," *Forum,* March, 1895.
5. Mr. Beveridge may have been clairvoyant, since Puerto Rico today is a "self-governing commonwealth" which flies the U.S. flag next to its own, and is America's fourth largest offshore trading partner.
6. *New York Journal of Commerce,* May 11, 1898.

Kentucky, for example, spoke out against "troublesome entanglements and complications" abroad, and the danger of converting Americans into "an aggressive and war-waging people."[7]

Recalling the withered empires of Rome and Spain, Bradley warned that "the acquisition of one piece of territory begets a desire for an other, and in the end an effort to take by force that which justly belongs to others will lead to the loss of all we have."

But he was in the minority. Even God, it seemed, was on the side of imperialism. On July 4, 1898, in the Central Presbyterian Church of Brooklyn, which was "ablaze with American, British and Cuban flags," The Rev. J. F. Carson read from the Holy Bible: "And Joshua took the whole land, and the land rested from war." He sermonized that "the high, the supreme business of this Republic is to end Spanish rule in America, and if to do that it is necessary to plant the Stars and Stripes on Cuba, Puerto Rico, the Philippines, or Spain itself, America will do it."[8]

Another clergyman foresaw a "widespread religious revival" because "the defeat of Spain will be the death knell of the Latin races. The Anglo-Saxons now hold the purest type of divinity."[9]

On the same night, in the Presbyterian Church of New York's Fifth Avenue, the Rev. Robert Mackenzie told parishioners that "God is calling a new power to the front. The race of which this nation is the crown . . . is now divinely thrust out to take its place as a world power."[10]

But terrestrial liberty and eternal salvation for the oppressed were only marginal reasons for America's entry into war with Spain. The so-called good old days of "the gay nineties" were neither so good, nor so gay. The period of 1893 through 1897, for example, was one of savage depression in America. Businesses failed, hungry tramps roamed the country, and Coxey's Army of the Jobless marched on Washington, demanding public works projects. In Chicago, federal troops battled against striking rail workers.

Unemployment, low wages, and strikes bred resentment toward the waves of alien workers from Europe, who worked for less, and were often trucked in under guard as strikebreakers.

The aliens were regarded as subhuman brutes, or as dangerous political radicals. In Chicago, an anarchist newspaper told its readers how to make dynamite. In Buffalo, in 1901, an anarchist would murder President McKinley.

---

7. *New York Times,* July 3, 1898, p. 3.
8. *New York Times,* July 4, 1898, p. 4.
9. Ibid.
10. Ibid.

Domestic turmoil engendered an upsurge of "nativism," and some states passed law? to exclude aliens from jobs. "Nativism" also bred "jingoism," a belligerent feeling towards not only aliens, but foreign lands.

It was not hard, then, for government leaders, aided by a sensationalist press that was engaged in its own little war to peddle papers, to divert the attention of the American people away from their domestic concerns, and towards Cuba, where a cruel, bloody war for independence was being waged.

Americans were urged to intervene in this war, to help free Cuba from the oppression of Spain. Fantastic stories of Spanish atrocities in Cuba abounded in the U.S. press. And, in early 1898, when the U.S. battleship *Maine* sank suddenly in Havana Harbor (although no one yet knows why), cries for war drowned out all appeals to reason.

Puerto Rico was a mere pawn in this power struggle. Spain, which had lost almost all of her Latin American colonies earlier in the century, was now embroiled in the Cuban conflict. In 1897, she granted a charter of autonomy to Puerto Rico. This charter gave Puerto Rico a substantial degree of home rule, and was the most liberal political status ever attained by the island until that time.

But the new autonomous government—which convened for the first time on February 11, 1898—never was able to flex its muscles. War was declared on April 25. Six days later. Admiral George Dewey crushed the Spanish fleet at Manila. On July 3, Santiago, in Cuba, was surrendered to American troops. On July 25, Americans landed on Puerto Rico's southern shore, and, on October 18, the island was formally surrendered by Spain.

On December 10, the Treaty of Paris released Cuba from Spain, surrendered the Philippines to the United States for $20 million, and ceded Guam and Puerto Rico to the United States "as compensation for the losses and expenses occasioned . . . by the war."

No Puerto Ricans took part in the Treaty of Paris negotiations. The fledgling autonomous government was stripped of its powers, and the island came under U.S. military rule.

PUERTO RICO AS A PERMANENT POSSESSION

From the United States, Puerto Rico was not viewed as the *patria* of nearly one million people with a distinct culture and nationality, but as a tract of tropical real estate: a fine naval station with a "commanding position between the two continents"; the "real gem of the Antilles," with "prolific" soil and an "exceptionally salubrious climate"; and a "charming winter resort." These enthusiastic remarks were made by an influential business writer on the editorial page of one of America's largest daily newspapers. If he did not speak with official government sanction, subsequent events proved him to be uncannily accurate. As he says, Puerto Rico "is an island well worth having." If his article rankles the sensibilities of those who abhor colonialism, it is at least refreshing for its candor, compared with the bland double-talk issued by today's power brokers. Some passages have been italicized here for emphasis.

There can be no question to perplex any reasonable mind about the wisdom of taking possession of the Island of Puerto Rico and keeping it for all time. There has been the same depressing misrule there as in Cuba, and the only reason why there has not been the same revolt against it is that the case was hopeless. The comparatively small and compact territory and the military weakness of the population have enabled Spain to crush out any attempt with merciless promptitude. At the same time she has taxed the little colony to help put down insurrection in Cuba as well as to enrich the Spanish officials. There can be no doubt that the people of the island, very few of whom are Spanish by birth, would rejoice to be relieved of the oppressive and exhausting rule of Spain, although they have been powerless to resist it, and have hardly dared to give vent to a desire to be rid of it.

There is the same reason for driving the corrupt despotism of Spain out of Puerto Rico as for driving it out of Cuba, save for the melancholy difference between a hopeless submission to wrong and a hopeless struggle against it.

The former condition is, indeed, the worse, for the cruelties practiced in trying to suppress chronic revolt excite sympathy and provoke interference from which rescue may come, while the deadening misery of hopeless submission may be allowed to go on forever. It is fortunate for Puerto Rico that Spanish outrages in Cuba have brought about an intervention which will rescue both islands at once. We are under a pledge to leave the fate of Cuba in the keeping of her own people when the Spanish sovereignty over them shall have been destroyed. They have created a claim to this by their own long and costly struggles for independence and by their own part in achieving it, and they have only to justify the claim by proving themselves capable of self-government and worthy of their heritage in order to become a free and prosperous nation. If they find

From Amos K. Fiske, *New York Times,* July 11, 1898, p. 6.

themselves unable to do this, they may yet call upon the United States to take charge of their future destiny, and *that may in the long run be better for them.*

But we shall free Puerto Rico from Spanish rule practically without any effort on the part of its own people, and at our own proper cost as an incident of the contest to expel it from Cuba. This result is necessary to make that expulsion complete and lasting, for to be rid of the Spanish disturbance to civilization in the Western World, Spain must be thrust from her last foothold on American soil. *We are not pledged to give Puerto Rico independence, and she will have done nothing to entitle her to it at our hands.* Besides, it would be much better for her to come at once under the beneficent sway of the United States than to engage in *doubtful experiments at self-government,* and there is reason to believe that her people would prefer it. It would be in accordance with the genius of our institutions to accord them self-government in local affairs as soon and as far as they showed themselves capable of it, and experience would soon teach them how much they had gained by their providential escape from the cruel stepmother country.

The circumstances of the conflict for the enfranchisement of Cuba and Puerto Rico fully entitle us to retain the latter as a permanent possession. Our need of a foothold in the West Indies for naval purposes has long been recognized, and it is now more obvious than ever before. We have made efforts to secure it on the island of San Domingo which were rendered futile by circumstances that we need not now recall. Once we secured it, so far as negotiation and agreement went, in the Danish Island of St. Thomas, and lost it again by the fatuous conduct of Congress in refusing to ratify the bargain, to the just resentment of Denmark and the humiliation of our Government in the eyes of its own people and of the world. *Now we have it within our grasp in a far better form, with Congress and the people in a mood for taking and keeping it, and with every just and proper consideration in favor of our doing so.*

As a naval station, the Harbor of San Juan de Puerto Rico is preferable in location to the Bay of Samaná, Mole St. Nicholas, or any other place on the island of San Domingo, and to Charlotte Amalia, the port of St. Thomas. Of the advantage of possessing all the land to which a naval station is appurtenant there can be no doubt. Puerto Rico occupies the central place on the eastern frontier of the great American archipelago, the outpost of the Greater Antilles, and the watch tower between the Bahamas and the Caribbees. The Mona Passage on the west and the Virgin Passage on the east are pathways to the South American coast. It is a commanding position between the two continents of the west, and upon the island rampart between the Atlantic Ocean and the Caribbean Sea. The most deliberate choice of a naval station in the West Indies could not have placed it better than the course of events, which has put the Island of Puerto Rico at our disposal. And it is an island well worth having—the real gem of the Antilles. . . . In spite of misrule, exhausting taxation, and a backward state of industry, it is a populous island, having more than 800,000 inhabitants, or about as many as Connecticut. This is because the soil is most prolific and the climate exceptionally salubrious; and twice as many people could live there in ease and comfort. . . .

Of the commercial value of Puerto Rico as a possession there is no possibility of doubt. Under a government that discouraged enterprise and prevented improvement, with an almost complete lack of roads and bridges in the interior to make communication and transportation economical, with primitive methods of cultivation and practically no manufactures, and with a stifling system of taxation and official corruption, it has supported a relatively large population and had a foreign trade of $35,000,000 a year. What is it not capable of under an enlightened policy and with a systematic application of enterprise and industry?

. . . . There is nothing in the tropical climate of Puerto Rico to prevent our people from going thither, but the labor force already there has never been half utilized. The real Spanish element is small even in the cities. The white population is mainly like the native element of Cuba—Creole descendants of European colonists alienated from the Spanish stock. There are many blacks, possibly a third of all the people, and much mixed blood, but the population is not ignorant or indolent or in any way degraded. It is not turbulent or intractable, and there is every reason to believe that under encouraging conditions it would become industrious, thrifty and prosperous. It is certain that a great advance could be made upon the present state of things, and the island could be rendered of no small commercial value to us and to its own people.

There is no reason why it should not become a veritable garden of the tropics and an especially charming winter resort for denizens of the North. Apart from the attractions of climate and scenery, there is a quaint picturesqueness in the old Spanish towns, and many interesting associations with the infancy of America. . . .

Whatever may be said or thought of keeping the Philippines or acquiring the Hawaiians, there can be no question of the wisdom of taking and holding Puerto Rico without any reference to a policy of expansion. We need it as a station in the great American archipelago misnamed the West Indies, and Providence has decreed that it shall be ours as a recompense for smiting the last withering clutch of Spain from the domain which Columbus brought to light and the fairest part of which has long been our own heritage.

"A DANGEROUS NEIGHBOR"

Mr. Fiske's views in the preceding article were not shared by Puerto Ricans. Members of the island's small elite were aware of growing U.S. influence in the Caribbean, and a few of them favored annexation by their North American neighbor. Others were steadfastly loyal to Spain, while others demanded outright independence. The party in power, however, supported a compromise position of autonomy, under loose Spanish rule. All, to some extent, were afraid that a change of sovereignty would bring a tidal wave of change that might overwhelm them. Even in 1892, six years before the outbreak of the Spanish-American War, journalist Mariano Abril could write:

To believe that the *yankees* will grant us all their freedoms and all their progress just for our pretty face is nonsense. Yes, they would grant us those liberties which they judged to be adequate, in exchange for guaranteed and ample exploitation.

Yes, we would have elevated trains crossing our streets; big, beautiful ports, with jetties and docks; bigger factories and commerce than ever before; but all of this in their hands; taken over and exploited by them; because all those things are not achieved without large amounts of capital, which would be *yankee* capital, because there is nothing here to support such enterprises. And, after a few years, industry, commerce, and even our agriculture, would be monopolized by the *yankees,* and the Antillean would be reduced to the condition of a miserable tenant farmer, without a homeland, without a home, and without fortune. . . .

And, as for liberties, we would have a *yankee* army, a *yankee* navy, a *yankee* police, and *yankee* courts, because they would need all of this to protect their interests. And this rich and beautiful Castilian would disappear from our lips, to be substituted for by the cold, barren English language. . . .

[In 1894, an editorial in the newspaper *La Democracia* said:]
The American nation is a dangerous neighbor, especially for Cuba, the Dominican Republic, and Puerto Rico. We must trust very little in her statements.

Selections in this chapter:
1. Translated from Lidio Cruz Monclova, *Historia de Puerto Rico* (Río Piedras: University of Puerto Rico, 1952), Vol. Ill, p. 386.
2. Translated from *La Democracia,* 1894, no. 1030.
3. Translated from *La Democracia.* May 4, 1898.

We must not fall asleep, and must keep watchful eyes on the Florida Channel. Anglo-American traditions are not the most reassuring.

There you have Mexico, invaded and dismembered, due to the greed of the Colossus. There you have Nicaragua, where they arrived one day, stirring troubles and difficulties. The North American Republic is too powerful to relax her pressure on the weak Latin American Republics.

On the alert, then. . . . the United States urgently needs to establish a position in the Antilles. In 1891, they talked and acted in this direction, without beating about the bush.

[As the war touched Cuba and the Philippines, and the invasion of Puerto Rico seemed imminent, an editorial expressed concern over the expected clash of cultural values.]

This war is the continuation of the terrible clash between two races, that started in the ancient times of the Roman decadence, and which sooner or later will shake the world. . . . We do admire the Yankee people for their gigantic activity, for their industrial power, for their extraordinary prosperity. But we prefer to be Spanish. We prefer death, rather than lose our nationality.

We do not wish to disown our blood, nor the sweet tongue with which our mothers lulled our sleep in the cradle.

"HAVE WE NOT SUFFERED LONG ENOUGH?"

While the American invasion force sailed to Puerto Rico, Eugenio María de Hostos, the eminent writer and educator, arrived in the United States. He sought an audience with President McKinley, to ask that Puerto Ricans be allowed to decide their political future by popular vote. A brief audience was later granted, but McKinley ignored the request. De Hostos was well known in several Latin American nations, where he had been awarded prizes for his literary works, and also founded institutions to help the Cuban revolutionary movement against Spain. He was held in particularly high esteem in the Dominican Republic, where he founded schools to train teachers, and in Chile, where he was commissioned by the government to direct the reform of that country's educational system. De Hostos also organized chapters of what he called The Puerto Rican League of Patriots, a pro-independence group. It was on behalf of the League of Patriots that he visited President McKinley.

"Señor E. M. Hostos Talks," *New York Times,* July 22, 1898, p. 2.

Referring to his mission to this country, Señor Hostos said: "It is my intention to ascertain as far as possible the plans of the United States Government relative to the disposition of Puerto Rico when that island becomes by right of capture its possession. It looks now as if my native land is destined to become American territory whether the inhabitants desire it or not, and to this I as well as many of my associates interpose serious objections. I wish, however, at the beginning to deny any reports to the effect that several Puerto Rican Juntas in foreign countries or in this country have advised their compatriots to offer any resistance to the United States troops in any manner. I fully realize that an expression of that character made on American soil would be treason, and I am quite sure that no sane person would ever utter it.

"Should I succeed in obtaining the desired interview with President McKinley I shall endeavor to impress upon him the fact that if Puerto Rico is to be annexed to the United States it should be with the consent of its population expressed through a regular plebiscite. If the majority of the people desire it we shall all bow to the majority and accept the inevitable.

"But neither I nor any other Puerto Rican patriot and republican would like to see the American people violate their mission as a great democratic nation by forcing our native island to become a dependency of the United States, instead of assisting it to shake off the yoke of its Spanish oppressors and then leave it to build up its own independent government and work out its own destiny.

"We should be only too glad to have the American people act in the capacity of our mentors, our teachers in the art of enjoying and making use of our liberty, which to the masses of the people who have lived for so many years under the ban of Spanish tyranny is a new feeling.

"As soon as I learn something of the readiness of the President and other high functionaries of the United States Government to receive me, I shall proceed to Washington and lay my mission before the President.

"To prepare the way for my coming and to ascertain the feeling in the White House with regard to my errand, Dr. [Julio] Henna, the President of the Puerto Rican Junta of this city, has sent Secretary [Roberto] Todd of our organization in Washington. I expect an answer in a few days, and in the meantime a meeting of all our people in this city will be held next Friday, and the situation will be thoroughly gone over.

Suggestions to Be Offered

"If I shall be allowed to offer any suggestions to the President, I shall make it my object to point out to him the cause which in my opinion is the only one worthy of the dignity and high aim of the American people. I am certainly entirely in sympathy with the course pursued in sending an expedition to Puerto Rico, as this is absolutely necessary to carry out the joint resolution of Congress on the merits of which the war was begun.

"Spain must be driven from the Western Hemisphere, and to do this requires men and arms; but there is another provision to this joint resolution which I think should not be left entirely out of sight. I refer to the declaration which says emphatically that this is not a war of conquest, but for the sake of humanity and the independence and liberty of a people entitled to both.

"If Cuba is to be free and its people their own masters, are not Puerto Ricans entitled to the same privilege? Have we not suffered long enough under the yoke of an oppressive government and should we not have an opportunity to show our capability of governing ourselves?"

Señor Hostos was asked to give his opinion of the strained relations said to exist between the Cubans and the Americans at Santiago. "It grieves me very much to learn of the unfortunate affair, but it should not, in my opinion, create surprise, after the conditions under which the Cubans have been living are looked into. Suffering for many, many years under a tyranny which drove them to extreme despair, is it at all to be wondered at that at the first opportunity that offers itself they should desire in some measure to avenge the wrongs they have endured? It but carries out the idea I have expressed, that all these peoples who have been buried in the thraldom of slavery do not appreciate the responsibilities of liberty, and for that reason must have mentors, teachers, to show them how to act and what to do for their own good. In this role I am sure the Americans, who have demonstrated so well their ability to govern themselves, will be accepted with gratitude and will receive the heartiest cooperation.

"Let them establish over all their conquered territory not a protectorate, that is too much on the order of sovereignty, but rather a mentorate, backed by a show of actual interest, and let them reward themselves in whichever manner they may see fit for their trouble, retaining if need be such control of the independent government as will insure their own interests and at the same time guarantee the rights of their proteges."

Señor Hostos is about fifty-five years old, short and slender, and bears a likeness to the portraits of Premier Sagasta. He knows the head of the present Spanish Ministry well, as they were both exiles in paris in 1867. Señor Hostos is a Puerto Rican by birth, but received his education in Madrid and took part in the September revolution of 1868.[1] After the revolution he came back to America, living for the most part in Venezuela and Chile. He is well known in South

---

1. The year of "The Grito de Lares."

America and among Republicans in Spain as the author of several works on political economy, with a decided leaning toward republicanism.

He speaks French excellently, in addition to Spanish, and while he understands English, it is difficult for him to speak the language. Since 1868 he has visited his native land but once, and that was shortly after the treaty of Zanjón, but after becoming convinced that the concessions supposed to have been granted the Puerto Ricans were such in name only, he decided to leave the island and devote himself to the cause of its emancipation, from a distance, where he would be free from prosecution.

"SEIZE SAN JUAN"

The invasion of Puerto Rico, at the south coast town of Guánica on July 25, 1898, came at a time when Spain was clearly beaten, and was pleading for peace. But America meant to have the island before the war's conclusion, in order to avoid disputes over its possession. In May, 1898, Assistant Secretary of the Navy Theodore Roosevelt, in a personal letter to Senator Henry Cabot Lodge, wrote: "give my best love to Nannie, and *do not make peace until we get Porto Rico.*"[1] Lodge replied: "Porto Rico is not forgotten and we mean to have it. Unless I am utterly . . . mistaken, the administration is now fully committed to the large policy that we both desire."[2]

On May 25, Washington correspondents observed great activity in the War and Navy Departments, and strong rumors indicated that President McKinley had decided to "seize San Juan de Puerto Rico and establish a permanent colonial government in the island." Influential congressmen explained that "the United States Government has awakened to the necessity of actually possessing Porto Rico before the end came. That island and the Philippines had come to be looked on as an essential recompense to the United States for its expensive intervention," while unless these territories were secured "before Cuba fell, embarrassing complications, leading possibly to grave international complications with European powers, might not be avoided."[3] These feelings were reinforced by millionaire industrialist Andrew Carnegie, who cabled from Europe, "Take Porto Rico first, for its effect on Europe."[4]

---

1. *Selections from the Correspondence of Theodore Roosevelt and H. C. Lodge, 1884-1918* (New York: Scribner's, 1925), Vol. I, p. 299.

2. Ibid.

3. Millis, Walter, *The Martial Spirit: A Study of Our War With Spain* (Boston: Houghton Mifflin), pp. 226-27. 1931.

4. Ibid. It should be noted that Mr. Carnegie later established a library in San Juan, as a "philanthropic gift."

In early July of 1898, a worried Dr. Ramón Emeterio Betances, exiled in Paris, wrote to Dr. Julio J. Henna, president of the Puerto Rican wing of the Cuban Revolutionary Party in New York:

"What are the Puerto Ricans doing? Why don't they take advantage of the blockade to rise en masse? It's extremely important that when the first troops of the United States reach shore, they should be received by Puerto Rican troops, waving the flag of independence, and greeting them.

"Let the North Americans cooperate in the achievement of our freedom; but not push the country to annexation. If Puerto Rico does not move quickly, it will be an American colony forever."

On July 21, a "practically official" statement by the U.S. Government was released to the press, saying that "Puerto Rico will be kept. . . . That is settled, and has been the plan from the first. Once taken it will never be released. It will pass forever into the hands of the United States. . . . Its possession will go towards making up the heavy expense of the war to the United States. Our flag, once run up there, will float over the island permanently."[5]

The United States expected little trouble in the occupation of Puerto Rico, where there had been no war (unlike Cuba), and no large, organized movement for independence.

As the time for the U.S. invasion of the island grew near, Antonio Mattei Lluveras, head of a Puerto Rican commission aboard the auxiliary U.S. cruiser St. Louis, wrote a letter to Washington. In it, he explained that some of his colleagues favored annexation to the United States, and others believed in independence, but "the main object . . . was to drive the Spaniards from the island."

---

5. "Diary of the War," *Harper's Weekly*, July 30, 1898, p. 754.

The Puerto Rican annexationists have formed a secret organization . . . and in nearly every city and village in the island they have established a branch. Every member of the society has been pledged to use his utmost endeavors to bring one or more friends or acquaintances into the society, which has annexation *or independence* [italics added] for its object. . . . A circular issued by the society, which has adopted for its name "Justicia" (Justice) explains to the ignorant native population of the island the injustice and tyranny of the Spanish government, and calls attention to the treatment which has been accorded a number of Puerto Ricans who have fallen into the hands of the Spaniards after openly favoring annexation. These prisoners were tried

---

Selections in this chapter:
1. From *New York Times,* July 30,1898, p. 1.
2. From *Harper's Weekly,* August 13,1898, p. 801.

by court-martial and shot without ceremony. At their trials they were tortured to make them reveal the names of their fellow-conspirators but the organization of "La Justicia" is so excellent that no one man knows another man by name, but only by signs.

All of the members of the society are not in favor of annexation to the United States. Their main object is to drive the Spaniards from the island. After that has been accomplished they are willing to take the best they can get from the United States Government, knowing that it will be *fair and equitable* [italics added].

Puerto Ricans opposed to Spanish misrule are firmly convinced that the United States, once the island has been rescued from Spanish control, will give them *independence to some extent* [italics added]. Even if the island is annexed, they believe that the United States will allow them the same home rule which is now accorded every State in the Union, and will not by military or moral force place Americans only at the head of affairs in the island.

Over 2,000 native Puerto Ricans, from different cities and villages in the interior, have assembled among the mountains on the southern coast to await the landing of the American army of invasion. They will immediately offer themselves, and thousands more will flock to the American standard. These people are a motley crew, armed with pistols, Remingtons, and old-fashioned guns, but they depend upon the American army to supply them with the necessary weapons. They are enthusiastic and will make excellent fighters.

[Sr. Mattei Lluveras's views in the previous article should be compared with those below, in a U.S. magazine. It notes that the Puerto Rican Junta in New York "has advocated independence," but those commissioners allowed to board the U.S. cruiser were annexationists. The glib final paragraph reveals how seriously the Puerto Rican views were received.]

On the opposite page is a picture[1] of the group of Puerto Rican commissioners who were selected, under direction of General Miles, by former Consul-General Warner P. Sutton and Captain Whitney of General Miles' staff, to land in Puerto Rico with our army and apprise the people of their several localities of the present status of the war between the United States and Spain, and of the intention of the United States to annex Puerto Rico.

They are to give their former neighbors a general idea of our institutions, and of the advantages to Puerto Rico which will follow annexation. They went to the island (from Newport News, Va.) on the cruiser *St. Louis.*

---

1. Photo showed Rafael Muñoz, Rafael Marxuach, José Budet, Mateo Fajardo, Emilio González, Domingo Collazo, P. J. Besoso, and General Antonio Mattei Lluveras, together with former U.S. Consul-General Sutton.

Their intention, as set forth by General Mattei and Mr. Fajardo, is to establish newspapers at once in Puerto Rico, through which, as well as by circulars, the announcements of General Miles may be circulated in the island. The Puerto Rican Junta in New York has advocated independence rather than annexation, but these commissioners have all along been annexationists, and were chosen for their present duty largely on that ground. Mr. Sutton has a large acquaintance in Puerto Rico, and understands the people there, and being on terms of warm friendship with the annexationist leaders is likely to be very useful in promoting good feeling between the people of the island and our forces.

The fact that the commissioners seem to have got their flag upside down indicates that they are not quite used to it yet; but the American flag is already much more familiar to the Puerto Ricans than it was when the picture was made.

OUR FLAG RAISED IN PUERTO RICO

Four Spaniards Fall in the First Fight of the Invasion

———

Americans Escape Unhurt

———

Guánica, on the Southern Coast, the Scene of the Landing

———

Enemy is Surprised

———

Excellent Military Road Leads to San Juan, 85 Miles Distant—
Good Work Done by the Gloucester

Copyright, 1898, by the Associated Press

Guanica, Island of Puerto Rico, July 25—Via St. Thomas, D.W.I., July 26—The United States Military expedition, under the command of Major Gen. Nelson A. Miles, which left Guantánamo Bay (Cuba) during the evening of Thursday last, was landed here successfully to-day, after a skirmish with a detachment of the Spanish troops and a crew of thirty belonging to the launch boat of the United States auxiliary gunboat Gloucester.

From *New York Times,* July 27, 1898, p. 1.

Four of the Spaniards were killed, but no Americans were hurt.

The American troops will be pushed forward promptly, in order to capture the railroad leading to Ponce, which is only about ten miles east of this place. From Ponce there is an excellent military road, running eighty-five miles north to San Juan de Puerto Rico, the capital of the island.

The ships left Guantánamo Bay Thursday evening, with the Massachusetts . . . leading. Capt. F. J. Higginson was in charge of the naval expedition, which consisted of the Columbia, Dixie, Gloucester, and Yale. Gen. Miles was on board the last-named vessel. The troops were on board the transports Nueves, Lampasas, Comanche, Rita, Unionist, Stillwater, City of Macon, and Specialist. This was the order in which the transports entered the harbor here. . . .

At noon yesterday Gen. Miles called for a consultation, announcing that he was determined not to go by San Juan Cape, but to go by the Mona Passage instead, land here, surprise the Spaniards, and deceive their military authorities. The course was then changed, and the Dixie was sent to warn Gen. Brooke at Cape San Juan.

Ponce . . . is a harder place to take. In addition, the water at Ponce is too shallow for the transports to be able to get close in shore. . . .

One advantage of this place is that it is situated close to the railroad connecting with Ponce, which means of transportation our troops will secure.

Early this morning the Gloucester, in charge of Lieut. Commander Wainright, formerly of the Maine, and one of the heroes of the naval battle off Santiago de Cuba, steamed into Guánica Harbor, in order to reconnoitre. . . .

The Spaniards were completely taken by surprise. Almost the first they knew of the approach of the army of invasion was in the announcement contained in the firing of a gun from the Gloucester, demanding that the Spaniards haul down the flag of Spain, which was floating from a flagstaff in front of a blockhouse standing to the east of the village. The first two three-pounders were fired into the hills right and left of the bay, in order to scare the enemy. The Gloucester purposely avoided firing into the town, lest the projectiles hurt women and children.

The Gloucester then hove to within about 600 yards of the shore and lowered a launch, having on board a Colt rapid-fire gun and thirty men, under command of Lieut. Huse. The launch was sent ashore without encountering opposition.

Quartermaster Beck thereupon told Yeoman Lace to haul down the Spanish flag, which was done, and they then raised on the flagstaff the first United States flag to float over Puerto Rican soil. Suddenly about thirty Spaniards opened fire with Mauser rifles on the American party. Lieut. Huse and his men responded, the Colt gun doing effective work. Norman, who received Admiral

Cervera's surrender, and Wood, a volunteer Lieutenant, shared the honors with Lieut. Huse.

Almost immediately after the Spaniards fired on the Americans the Gloucester opened fire on the enemy with all her three and six pounders which could be brought to bear, shelling the town and also dropping shells into the hills to the west of Guánica, where a number of Spanish cavalry were to be seen hastening toward the spot where the Americans had landed.

Lieut. Huse then threw up some intrenchments, which he named Fort Wainright. Barbed wire was laid in the street in front of it in order to repel the expected cavalry attack. The Lieutenant also mounted the Colt gun and signaled for reinforcements, which were sent from the Gloucester.

The Associated Press dispatch boat Cynthia II was the only boat in the harbor except the Gloucester. While the Mausers were peppering all around, Lieut. Commander Wainright called out to the Cynthia:

"They fired on us after their flag was down and ours was up, and after I had spared the town for the sake of the women and children. The next town I strike I will blow up."

Presently, a few of the Spanish cavalry joined those who were fighting in the streets of Guánica, but the Colt gun killed four of them.

By that time the Gloucester had the range of the town and of the blockhouse, and all her guns were spitting fire, the doctor and the Paymaster helping to serve the guns.

Soon afterward white-coated galloping cavalrymen were seen climbing the hills to the westward, and the foot soldiers were scurrying along the fences from the town. By 9:45, with the exception of a few guerrilla shots, the town was won and the enemy was driven out of its neighborhood.

The Red Cross nurses on the Lampasas and a detachment of regulars were the first to land from the transports. . . .

Gen. Miles . . . went ashore about noon . . . and said:

"Guánica and Cinga [?] are in the disinfected portion of the island. Matteo, the insurgent leader, lives at Yauco, a few miles inland. Had we landed at Cape San Juan, a line of rifle pits might have stopped our advance."

. . . Guánica is the most delightful spot yet occupied by our forces. It is a centre for the coffee and sugar industry and large herds of cattle are pasturing in the meadows, which are bordered by cocoanut palms. Many head of cattle and a large number of horses have been driven into the mountains by their owners. Some of them will be captured.

Ponce is the second city of the island, has a splendid harbor, and will make a good base of operations . . . [it] is sure to fall shortly before the combined attack of our army and navy. The main fighting until San Juan is reached will be along the line of a splendid military road leading from Ponce to San Juan. Street shields, of which a supply was brought with the expedition, will be used to protect the troops. . . .

At 9 o'clock to-night the commander of the Dixie said he had been almost around the Island of Puerto Rico and had not seen any men-of-war or transports, except the New Orleans, which was blockading the port of San Juan.

A heavy gale was blowing, causing the dispatch boat to consume nineteen hours in making the 125 miles to St. Thomas.

"TO THE INHABITANTS OF PORTO RICO"

On July 29, four days after the landing of American troops, Major General Nelson A. Miles, commander of the invasion force, issued a general proclamation from his military headquarters in Ponce. This was the first official public statement from the U.S. Government to explain its plans for Puerto Rico.

In the prosecution of the war against the Kingdom of Spain, the people of the United States in the cause of liberty, justice, and humanity, its military forces have come to occupy the Island of Porto Rico. They come bearing the banner of freedom, inspired by noble purpose to seek the enemies of our country and yours, and to destroy or capture those who are in armed resistance. They bring you the fostering arm of a nation of free people, whose greatest power is in justice and humanity to all those living within its fold. Hence, the first effect of this occupation will be the immediate release from your former political relations, and it is hoped, a cheerful acceptance of the Government of the United States. The chief object of the American military forces will be to overthrow the armed authority of Spain and to give to the people of your beautiful island the largest measure of liberties consistent with this military occupation. We have not come to make war against a people of a country that for centuries has been oppressed, but, on the contrary, to bring you protection, not only to yourselves but to your property, to promote your prosperity, and to bestow upon you the immunities and blessings of the liberal institutions of our government. It is not our purpose to interfere with any existing laws and

From Amos K. Fiske, *New York Times,* July 11, 1898, p. 6.

customs that are wholesome and beneficial to your people, as long as they conform to the rules of military administration, of order and justice. This is not a war of devastation, but one to give all within the control of its military and naval forces the advantages and blessings of enlightened civilization.

SOLDIER

Carl Sandburg, the famed poet and Lincoln biographer, was twenty years old when the Spanish-American War began. He enlisted and saw active service in Puerto Rico. This excerpt is from his autobiography.

We sailed out of Guantánamo Bay, three thousand troops on the transports. Rumors ran that we were going to Porto Rico. . . . Soon after daylight on July twenty-fifth we sighted a harbor and moved into it. Ahead we saw gunfire from a ship and landing boats filled with bluejackets moving toward shore. We were ordered to put on our cartridge belts and with rifles get into full marching outfits. We heard shooting, glanced toward shore once in a while and saw white puffs of smoke while we stood waiting our turns to climb down rope ladders into long boats called lighters. We were rowed to a shallow beach where we dropped into water above our hips. Holding rifles above our heads, we waded ashore. We were in Guánica, a one-street town with palm and coconut trees new to us. We expected to be ordered into action against Spanish troops somewhere in the town or near-by hills. So our talk ran. We were marched to a field near the town where we waited over noon and afternoon. We ate our supper of cold canned beans and hardtack and soon after were ordered to march.

When we came to a halt we waited in the dark and heard shots that seemed not far away. This was the one time on that island when most of us expected to go into battle, to shoot and be shot at. And it didn't happen. We waited and marched back to our fields near Guánica. A story arose that Sixth Illinois troops that night did some wild firing, some of their bullets hitting the transport on which General Miles was sleeping, others of their bullets hitting a ship carrying Red Cross nurses. . . . It could have been that the shots we heard sounding to

From Carl Sandburg, *Always the Young Strangers* (New York: Harcourt, Brace, 1953), pp. 403-24. Reprinted by permission.

us like enemy fire were from the Krag-Jorgensens of Sixth Illinois boys aiming at random at an unseen enemy. Some of us had been "shaking in our boots" and it would have been a relief to shoot at anything in any direction. We heard in the morning that bluejackets from the ship *Gloucester* and regulars with artillery had killed four Spanish soldiers, driven a troop of cavalry to the hills, and there was no enemy in sight or hearing. . . .

We marched to Yauco and on to Ponce, finding those towns surrendered. . . . On roads and streets as we marched were barefooted men and women smiling and calling to us *"Puerto Rico Americana."* For four hundred years this island had been run by a Spanish government at Madrid. Now it was to be American and it was plain that the island common people liked the idea and had more hope of it. More than once we saw on the roadside a barefoot man wearing only pants, shirt, and hat, eating away at an ear of parched corn. We saw kneehigh children wearing only a ragged shirt and their little swollen bellies told of something wrong with their food, not enough food and not the right kind. . . .

We camped at Ponce a few days and then began a march up mountain roads. The August tropic heat was on. We carried cartridge belt, rifle, bayonet, blanket roll, half a canvas pup tent, haversack with rations, a coat. We still wore the heavy blue-wool pants of the Army of the Potomac in '65 and thick canvas leggings laced from ankles to knees. On one halt after another there were men tearing their blankets in two so as to lessen weight to carry. I tore a third of mine away. Some let the whole blanket go. Men fell out, worn-out, and there were sunstroke cases. We passed more than one on the ground raving about the heat. It was an eight-mile march upgrade. . . .

We camped on a slope on the edge of Adjuntas, where we saw the American flag run up. Cook Metcalf over a long afternoon had boiled a tinned beef we named "Red Horse." For all the boiling it was stringy and tasteless, "like boiled shoestrings flavored with wallpaper." . . . About three o'clock in the morning a heavy downpour of rain kept coming. We were on a slope and the downhill water soaked our blankets. We got out of our tents, wrung our blankets as dry as we could and threw them with ponchos over our shoulders. Then a thousand men stood around waiting for daylight and hoping the rain would let down. . . . Midmorning the sun did come out and we dried and marched on to Utuado.

There at Utuado came news, "The protocol has been signed and peace is declared and we are ordered back to Ponce." Marching down the mountain roads we had climbed came easy along with rumors that we would take transports home from Ponce and replacements were on the way. Rains beat down and we were lighthearted and cried, "Hurrah for the Protocol!" It was a new funny word we liked. Instead of "Good morning," we said, "How's your old protocol?" We slept a night in a building used for drying coffee. Each man fitted nicely into a dry bin enclosure rich with a coffee smell.

At Ponce many of us weighed to see what we had sweated and groaned out. . . . My one hundred and fifty-two pounds in April had gone down to one hundred and thirty pounds in August. Many were gaunt and thin, with a slightly yellow tint on the skin of hands and faces. Uniforms were fading, here and there ragged and torn. Hats had holes in them. On some hats the fellows had written in purple with indelible pencils the names of the places we'd been. . . .

As for history, Theodore Roosevelt summed it up in a speech at the Stockyards Pavilion in Chicago which I (years later) covered for a newspaper. He happened to mention the Spanish-American War and added with a chuckle and a flash of his teeth, "It wasn't much of a war but it was all the war there was."

. . . . And the Mayor of Yauco, Francisco Mejía, whom we saw on a balcony, wasn't all wrong in his proclamation words: "Porto Ricans, we are, by the miraculous intervention of the God of the just, given back to the bosom of our mother America, in whose waters nature placed us as people of America."

The war, though a small one, was the first in which the United States sent troops on ocean transports to fight on foreign soil and acquire island possessions. At a banquet in Paris American citizens celebrated and offered toasts, the first one, "Here's to the United States, bounded on the north by Canada, on the south by Mexico, on the east by the Atlantic Ocean, on the west by the Pacific." The second speaker: "In view of what President McKinley has termed manifest destiny and in consideration of the vast new responsibilities that loom before our country, I offer the toast: To the United States, bounded on the north by the North Pole, on the south by the South Pole, on the east by the rising sun, on the west by the setting sun." The third speaker: "With all due humility in view of the staggering tasks our country faces across the future, I would offer the toast: To the United States, bounded on the north by the Aurora Borealis, on the south by the Precession of the Equinoxes, on the east by Primeval Chaos, on the west by the Day of Judgment." It was a small war edging toward immense consequences.

DIARY OF THE WAR

Angel Rivero, born in Trujillo Alto, Puerto Rico, in 1864, was captain in charge of a Spanish artillery garrison which defended Fort San Cristóbal in San Juan. His book about the Spanish-American War in Puerto Rico is probably the most complete account of the conflict ever written. Excerpts from the section called "Diary of the War" follow.

From the very day that I climbed the ramp of San Cristóbal castle to take command of its batteries, I began this diary. As my readers will see, they are spontaneous, disconnected, at times puerile. Upon looking over this document I've decided against adding or removing a single word; my desire is that it conserve its truthful *flavor* of the time. . . .

July 27—Today's *Gaceta* publishes an account of the enemy landing at the port of Guánica. . . .

July 29—Yauco captured. . . .

July 30—General alarm; it's advised that the enemy is landing at Boca de Cangrejos; the 3rd Provision marches there with all speed. They return a bit later . . . false alarm. . . . Since yesterday there have been two enemy ships in front of the [San Juan] port maintaining the blockade. . . .

July 31—Yesterday two coaches from the funeral parlor of Adrián López left for Caguas. This businessman, like the others, follows the scent of his clients.
. . .

. . . Last night I went down from the castle and stopped for some time at a refreshment kiosk owned by a fellow named Domingo in the Plaza de Colón. There, seated upon a bench, I found Luis Muñoz Rivera and José de Diego. We spoke . . . discussing for quite some time the alarm displayed by all of the residents who were passing before us en route to Santurce. As I left I said to them: "Perhaps we won't see each other again, because if the enemy squadron attacks . . . I could lose my life from one moment to the next, since my batteries are the most exposed of the fort and without protection. Since you are authorized by the Governor to live outside of the city, I advise you to leave as soon as possible and reunite with your families." Then, Luis Muñoz Rivera, getting to his feet and taking my hand, answered me: "It's true that they've given us permission, but we won't use it; as officials of the insular government, we have duties just as you do . . . and if our time comes, it, too, will find us at our posts . . . ; de Diego made a similiar declaration, the three of us embraced, I returned to my castle and they headed up Calle San Francisco towards the Plaza of Alfonso XII. . . .

August 2—News arrives that the Americans have captured Arroyo . . .

August 4—Last night a man from my battery, in a moment of madness, threw himself into the sea from the top of wall . . . we were able to recover him alive . . . ; two days before, another man from San Gerónimo tried to commit suicide also, hanging himself with a rope. The continuous nervous tension in which we live is the cause. . . .

Translated from Angel Rivero, *Crónica de la guerra hispánoamericana en* Puerto Rico (Madrid: Sucesores de Rivadeneyra Artes Gráficas, 1922).

August 6—Headquarters publishes a notice saying that in the combat sustained in Guayama against the invaders, the force led by Captain Acha had 17 dead and wounded, representing casualties of 20 percent. . . .

August 13—I think peace is very imminent, because censorship has been relaxed. Today's *La Prensa* publishes a few articles extolling the American flag, Old Glory. Signs of the times. . . .

. . . At one-thirty in the morning artillery Captain Aureliano Esteban, who has just reached the castle, said that he was in a meeting with the Captain of the Port, Eduardo Fernández, who claims to have seen a cable saying that the protocol of peace has been signed. General Ortega becomes furious and orders Esteban and me to go, immediately, to speak with Captain Fernández. We reach the Marina and, after waking him up, he tells us that the cable has been received, adding that among the conditions agreed so as to terminate the war, Spain renounces its sovereignty of Cuba and, furthermore, cedes Puerto Rico to the United States. . . .

. . . Such a sad night! I spend it, all of it, seated upon a cannon; as the sun comes out I affirm my resolution, taken before the war; as soon as the peace is signed I will leave the Spanish army and return to civilian life so as to share in whatever fortunes befall my country. . . .

August 14—I am sad. It seems as though someone very beloved to me has died; and yet many officers in the garrison do nothing to hide their joy. "At last the war has ended," they say. "And we'll be going home; Puerto Rico means nothing to us, and in the future we'll no longer dream of yellow fever and other tropical diseases. . . ." The conduct of these men contrasts with that of my artillerymen who looked extremely sad for not having had the chance to fight against the army advancing to occupy the fort. . . .

August 15—An American ship, one of the four in front of El Morro, has raised a white flag and after certain formalities some American officers disembarked by the arsenal docks. . . .

August 18—The *Gaceta* publishes an extra edition including the cable by the Minister of War, offering the news that the American government has lifted the blockade from Cuba, Puerto Rico and the Philippines, reestablishing commercial and postal communications.

August 22—Eugenio Deschamps in Ponce has commenced to edit the first newspaper written in English. It's called *The Porto Rico Mail.*

August 27—They tell me that signs have been placed upon many of the businesses in Mayagüez belonging to Spaniards. They say: *Don't enter you in here because it is a worst Spaniard.* The Spaniards may not be any good, but the English on the signs is much worse.

August 28—There is a great interest in learning English; men, women and children walk about the streets with a vocabulary that's just been put on sale and that's titled: *Idioma inglés en siete lecciones.*

August 29—A North American warship, the *New Orleans,* entered port today. Two officers disembarked, and one of them . . . was in the arsenal.

September 5—General Brooke, his escort and Chiefs of Staff arrived in Caguas today . . . ; at one in the afternoon he reached Río Piedras . . . ; at four the general and his staff came to San Juan . . . to greet General Macías, who awaited them in the Palacio accompanied by General Ortega . . . . the visit was very brief, purely a courtesy call, and then General Brooke and his companions went to the Hotel Inglaterra where they conferenced with Commodore Schley and General Gordon, returning soon afterwards to Río Piedras. . . .

September 11—General Wilson in Ponce made the following public declaration: "Puerto Rico will at first be governed by a military regime; then it will be declared an American territory, and later it will achieve the category of sovereign state within the Union. The duration of these periods will depend more or less upon the merits of the country."

September 12—In Río Piedras American and Spanish soldiers get along well together; they walk arm in arm down the streets, go to cafes and public places, as though nothing had ever happened. . . .

September 14—Today is the beginning of the evacuation of the Spanish forces. At eleven in the morning, the ships *Isabel II, Concha, Terror* and *Ponce de León* sailed for Spain. A great crowd followed the troops to the docks, offering them an affectionate farewell.

September 21—The surrender of the island has begun, town by town . . .

September 22—A seditious band of 40 men entered Fajardo last night, sacking three stores. . . .

September 23—Bands of arsonists are marauding through Garrochales. Factor and Hato Arriba, *barrios* of Arecibo, and also in Camuy. From Quebradillas one could see the flames last night. . . .

October 4—Today labor leader Santiago Iglesias has been freed after a long imprisonment resulting from political differences. . . .

October 9—Bands of robbers are spreading terror in the *barrios* of Adjuntas. . . .

October 11—A commission of American officers has visited the school established in Arroyo by professor Enrique Huyke, and they left highly satisfied over the English language examination given to the students. . . .

October 16—A daughter of Dr. Arrastia has flown the first American flag in Cataño; there was no objection on the part of the police . . . The Volunteer

Regiment of Kentucky is aboard the Mississippi, anchored in port. . . . The Red Cross still shows sign of life. D. Dolores Aybar de Acuña, president of the women's section, is tireless; she distributes clean clothes and many other articles to all the repatriated troops and administers medicine to all the sick and wounded. . . .

October 17—Some soldiers from the Kentucky regiment have left their ship without permission, and their presence causes some disorder. A patrol lands immediately and obliges them to get back aboard. . . . Press censorship has ceased as of today. . . .

October 18—Today is the day for the official surrender of San Juan. There's not a single Spanish flag in the town . . . since yesterday they'd been put away in a cedar chest expressly made for that purpose. . . . Pairs of soldiers with bayonets mounted have been stationed at the street corners . . . all businesses have closed their doors, fearful of what might happen.

. . . Today is a sad day, yet I take notes for my *Chronicle of the Spanish American War in Puerto Rico*. . . .

. . . This very afternoon the American forces took possession of Customs, allowing all employees to remain at their posts. *The Gaceta de Puerto Rico* has been published today, displaying on its front page the American eagle instead of the Spanish coat of arms.

. . . General Brooke has sent letters to all the secretaries of the insular government and the foreign consuls, inviting them to the official surrender of the city, which took place today at noon in the Palacio de Santa Catalina. . . .

. . . During the night there were serious disorders in the café La Mallorquina, incited by the American soldiers. . . .

October 21—Today an official commission arrived from Washington to study our laws, customs, commerce, agriculture and finance, with the purpose of proposing the best form of government for the country.

October 22—Boarding the ship *Montevideo* today were General Ortega, my battalion and some other forces; the only ones who have not yet been repatriated.

October 23—The *Montevideo* sailed this afternoon. Happy voyage!

PART V

"CITIZENS OF PORTO RICO"

Now, when I look into the depth of my soul, I can only perceive a portion of blue sea, and far away a white Latin sail, as a wing in flight. Where will it go? Where? Where?

—Translated from Eugenio Astol,
La Democracia, *February 19, 1907*

The United States had no clear plan for governing Puerto Rico, but one thing was clear: it would not relinquish the island. American newspapers clucked contentedly over the new prize—"a highly productive island . . . yielding coffee, sugar, fruits, nuts and tobacco"—and remarked that "the business of the country is in an unusually sound and healthy condition."[1] As for allowing Puerto Ricans some measure of self-rule, an editorial doubted the wisdom of "putting votes into the hands of men who can make no intelligent use of them. A few years of experimenting with the natives will instruct them in the duties of freemen and ourselves in regard to their capacities."[2]

Some Puerto Rican leaders welcomed the invasion, as did the pro-Republican newspaper *La Correspondencia,* which was not concerned "about the disappearance of the customs of this country . . . because if our people's customs are to continue being a matter of our peasants and workers walking with bare feet and legs, badly dressed and poorly nourished . . . it is better that such customs be substituted by others."[3] Two months later, the same paper applauded the material benefits expected under American rule, but warned: "Let us have the good sons of the North come and transform our minds, but let them not pretend to transform our hearts."[4] By 1912, the same paper would favor inde-

---

1. Editorial, *New York Times,* July 28,1898, p. 6.
2. Editorial, *New York Times,* July 27, 1898, p. 6.
3. Translated from *La Correpondencia,* August 22, 1898.
4. Translated from *La Correspondencia,* October 10, 1898.

pendence for Puerto Rico. There was criticism of the American takeover, but mostly from powerless sources. A small, liberal U.S. magazine editorialized that "Porto Rico is entitled to decide her own destiny by a fair vote of her people, and that she ought not to be forcibly annexed . . . without the consent of the inhabitants."[5]

As the months passed, it became evident that Puerto Ricans would not be allowed to vote upon their political destiny. The question then became: How would the United States govern the island? President McKinley assigned Dr. H. K. Carroll, a Protestant clergyman, to prepare a detailed report on conditions in Puerto Rico. Carroll concluded with a plea: "Let Porto Rico have local self-government . . . and she will gain by her blunders, just as cities and States in our own glorious Republic are constantly learning." He described Puerto Ricans as "industrious, law-abiding . . . and temperate."[6]

Robert E. Pattison, a former Governor of Pennsylvania, toured the island, and said that charges about ignorance prevailing in Puerto Rico were "not justified." He was favorably impressed by "merchants from San Juan and Ponce, tobacco planters from Cayey, doctors and businessmen from Coamo, the shop-keepers of Aibonito . . . the mayor and school-teachers from Barranquitas . . . the municipal emyloyees of Utuado," and described Federal Party leader Luis Muñoz Rivera as "one of the most capable and forceful men that I have ever met."[7]

And the powerful Senator J. B. Foraker of Ohio said that Puerto Ricans "have had no experience that would qualify them . . . for the great task of organizing a government, with all the important bureaus and departments needed by the people of Puerto Rico."[8]

The imperious attitude in Washington soon created resentment in San Juan. In February, 1899, Governor-General Henry abolished the Autonomous Council of the island government, on the grounds that its members were uncooperative. A few days later, an editorial in a Puerto Rican paper demanded more local participation in government and warned: "Let the generals from the North remember that they were greeted as friends; they should not labor in a way that tomorrow will cause the Germans or Russians to be so welcomed."[9]

There was little help from liberal circles in America. At its 1900 national

---

4. Translated from *La Correspondencia,* October 10, 1898.
5. Translated from *The Nation,* July 28, 1898, pp. 65-66.
6. *The Independent,* January 4, 1900. Vol. 52, pp. 57-77.7
7. *The New York Journal,* October 7, 1900.
8. U.S. Congress, Senate, *Congressional Record,* March 8, 1900.
9. Translated from *La Democracia,* February 20, 1899.

convention, the U.S. Democratic Party denounced Congress's treatment of Puerto Rico, saying, "In this, the first act of its imperialistic programme, the Republican party seeks to commit the United States to a colonial policy."[10]

But inaction by the Democrats in subsequent years suggests that they were merely using Puerto Rico as a political campaign issue. In fact, the Democratic Presidential candidate, William Jennings Bryan, who was running on a platform of "anti-imperialism," eventually voted to ratify the Treaty of Paris, which legitimized the U.S. takeover of Puerto Rico.

---

10. *Official Proceedings,* Democratic National Convention, Kansas City, Missouri, July 4-6, 1900, p. 114.

"THE PORTO RICAN INHUMANITY"

In 1899, as the United States prepared to remove its military governor from Puerto Rico, and establish a civilian government, a strong controversy emerged as the Republican administration in Washington proposed a temporary tax on Puerto Rican imports and exports. Supporters of the measure, such as Senator J. B. Foraker of Ohio, argued that the tax monies were needed to support the island's administration; in other words, Puerto Rico was expected to pay its own way from the start. Critics of the tax, such as the author of the following article, felt that it would cripple the already impoverished island.

The humane people of the United States cannot too soon be aroused to the fact that the Republicans in Congress are proposing to commit, in the name of this nation, an act of unparalleled and shameful cruelty. We refer to the bill taxing Porto Rican exports and imports to the extent of 25 per cent of the Dingley rates. There are strong reasons for thinking this bill unconstitutional. They are set forth in the minority report, and also in the individual report of Mr. McCall of Massachusetts, a Republican who has the courage of his convictions, and, what his Republican colleagues apparently have not, a sense of humanity. But we do not now insist upon the illegality of the measure. Chatham indignantly cried in Parliament: "I come not here armed at all points with law cases and acts of Parliament, with the statute-book doubled down in

---

From *The Nation,* LXX, No. 1807 (1899), p. 122.

dog-ears, to defend the cause of liberty." So we say to-day, be the constitutional right what it may; let the Supreme Court reverse itself if it choose; rule out all questions of fiscal need and policy—the fact remains that this proposed legislation is so cruel, so heartless, so charged with disaster and starvation for 900,000 human beings, that to adopt it would entitle Spain or Russia or even Turkey to send missionaries to us.

What are the facts? They are set forth in voluminous detail and with overwhelming force in the reports of our own officials. Governor-General Davis, Consul Hanna, Secretary Root, Commissioner Carroll, the President himself, have all shown how the immediate necessities of Porto Rico cry out for freedom of trade with this country. The inhabitants had practically a free market in Spain and Cuba. We destroyed that. Then we double-locked our own against them. The result is, as Secretary Root declared, that two crops of tobacco lie rotting in the warehouses of Porto Rico; that her coffee and her sugar are practically unsalable. This was true even before the hurricane of last August came to complete the ruin we had done our best to bring about by neglect. The hurricane was "an act of God." What can we call our deliberate attempt to prevent the Porto Ricans from living by honest labor but an act of the devil?

The tax on their exports is flagrant enough; but to make them pay one-quarter the Dingley rates on the necessaries of life would argue a perfectly fiendish ingenuity of malevolence. People do not generally understand this. The Dingley Schedule G, "Agricultural Products and Provisions," is a section full of "fake" duties, so far as we are concerned. These are the hoary old tariff taxes put in to fool the American fanner, and make him think that he, too, is "protected." But every one knows that the high duties dangled before his innocent eyes are not operative. They do not affect the cost of the prime necessaries in this country, for practically none are imported. In Porto Rico, however, these Dingley duties would take effect in crushing fashion. The island has long imported a vast amount of food products, paying for them with tobacco and coffee and sugar. Now the Republican plan is, on the one hand to refuse the Porto Ricans a market for what they raise, and on the other to tax them exorbitantly for the food they must have or starve.

Take a few sample figures. Commissioner Carroll returns the Porto Rican imports of rice in 1897 at 77,994,122 pounds. Here is a necessary of life, now free. We propose to clap on 25 per cent of the Dingley rate of 2 cents per pound. In other words, we propose to tax a ruined and starving people $389,000 on a single and necessary article of food! Did a Borgia or a Bajazet ever condemn his subjects to death with a more refined cruelty? The case will be very much the same with the other leading imports of Porto Rico—kerosene oil, pork, lard, flour, fish. Salt fish is taxed three-fourths of a cent a pound in the Dingley tariff; flour, 25 per cent ad valorem; lard, two cents a pound; pork, two cents a pound, and so on. In other words, all these sleeping Dingley duties on food, which are only a joke to us, are to be wakened by the bill before Congress, and set to clutching the throats of the unhappy Porto Ricans, whom we rescued from the tyranny of Spain in order to fling them into the jaws of our Moloch of protection.

This, we say, is an act of stark inhumanity, to which we do not believe the American people will ever consent. Certainly they will not if its monstrous nature is brought home to them. Why, we might as well turn our soldiers loose in the island to butcher the inhabitants as to decree their death by act of Congress. When Russia annexed the Crimea in the last century, she put 30,000 Tartars, men, women, and, children, to the sword. Is our proposed course a whit less unfeeling and bloody? Here are 900,000 fellow-men; if not fellow-citizens, they are at least our subjects, as even the Imperialists must admit. Their lives and fortunes are in our hands. We propose to rob them of both. And the leaders in the crime are the Senators from Connecticut—the State of schools and universities and churches! That State has no more inhabitants than Porto Rico; yet its representatives in Congress, some of them lights in the religious world, coolly urge a bill to extinguish the right of nearly a million men under our flag to life, liberty, and the pursuit of happiness.

The whole thing seems a ghastly joke—like Swift's proposal to kill and eat the babies in Ireland. But if this law is pushed in dead earnest, there will be need of Swift's *saeva indignatio* against its authors and abettors. Is this to be a final demonstration of the inhuman nature of protection? When the McKinley tariff worked distress in Vienna, its author exulted over the misery he had wrought. Will he now sit idly by and see a protective tariff made an instrument of torture for men and women and children under the American flag? We cannot believe it; nor can we believe that the religious and educated opinion of this country will tolerate the crime which the Republicans in Congress are intending to commit in the name of protection. The American people are not cruel. They do not want the blood of Porto Ricans or Cubans or Filipinos on their heads. But, if they would be guiltless, they must lose not a moment in letting their selfish and besotted representatives at Washington know what they think of this attempt to make the United States synonymous with greed and cruelty.

"WE ARE BECOMING AMERICANIZED"

The early years of the U.S. occupation were years of harsh adjustment. Change burrowed its way into every corner, even causing the island's name to be anglicized to "Porto Rico." New institutions sprang up to deal with health, education, and other central affairs. The island's traditional export markets were severed. U.S. investors came southward, buying up choice land for corporate farms that were gigantic by local standards.

The greatest strain was caused by the cultural impact, as a powerful English-speaking nation sought to mold a small Spanish-speaking colony into a more compatible entity. This was often a cruel, abrasive process.

The island's leaders had, for centuries, dealt with Spanish colonial administrators, sharing the same language and basic customs. Now—in their own homeland—they were forced to communicate in English with foreigners who held the reins of government.

Many despaired. In 1902, Luis Muñoz Rivera would write to a friend: "In the future there will be prosperity . . . but there will be no fatherland. And if there is, it will belong to Americans and their children and grandchildren. Within half a century, it will be a disgrace to bear a Spanish surname."

The brief U.S. military rule in Puerto Rico ended on April 12, 1900, when Congress passed a bill known as The Foraker Act. It provided for a governor, to be appointed by the President of the United States,[1] an Executive Council (with eleven Presidentially-appointed members, only five of whom had to be Puerto Ricans), and a Chamber of Delegates, with thirty-five members, all elected by the people. With this law, real power was in the hands of the American Governor and the six American members of the Executive Council. The power of the Chamber was restricted to minor local affairs. A Resident Commissioner in Washington, elected by the people, had a voice, but no vote, in Congress. Puerto Ricans were made "Citizens of Porto Rico." Congress reserved all powers to legislate on Puerto Rican affairs. A reaction to this situation appeared in an island newspaper editorial.

---

1. In theory, the President could have chosen a Puerto Rican, but appointed American governors held office for nearly half a century, until after World War II.

Selections in this chapter:
1. Translated from *La Democracia,* October 29, 1900.
2. From *U.S. Congressional Record,* 56th Congress, 1st session, Feb. 26, 1900, p. 2231.
3. From The Puerto Rican Papers of Victor S. Clark, Manuscript Division, Library of Congress, Washington, D.C.
4-6. Translated from La Democracia, Aug. 16, 1900.

Yes, we are becoming Americanized; . . . but not by the Constitution that is so wise, nor through freedom that is so great, nor through the law that is so magnificent; we are becoming Americanized through privilege, through monopoly, through injustice, through despotism. We are being Americanized the wrong way, and from this wrong Americanization the dealers who put on sale the honor of the country are to blame; not the American people, who have not yet come to know us, but the adventurers who fall upon the fields of Puerto Rico like swarms of ravenous locusts.

[Puerto Rican leaders also sent messages to Congress, such as this one:]

The United States has not been fair to those who gave their hand to their redeemer . . . who turned their backs upon the old conditions and accepted the new, only to discover themselves cut off from all the world—a people without a country, a flag, almost without a name, orphans without a father. . . . Who are we? What are we? . . . Are we citizens or are we subjects? Are we brothers and our property territory, or are we bondmen of a war and our islands a crown colony?

[One of the first acts of the United States was to establish a system of education, with the clear political goal of "Americanizing" the populace. This was attempted by organizing a highly centralized, islandwide school system, under an American Commissioner of Education. The first commissioner felt that:]

[Puerto Ricans do not have] the same devotion to their native tongue or to any national ideal that animates the Frenchmen, for instance, in Canada or the Rhine Provinces. . . . A majority of the people . . . do not speak pure Spanish. Their language is a patois almost unintelligible to the natives of Barcelona and Madrid. It possesses no literature and little value as an intellectual medium. There is a bare possibility that it will be nearly as easy to educate these people out of their patois into English as it will be to educate them into the elegant tongue of Castile. Only from the very small intellectual minority in Puerto Rico, trained in Europe and imbued with European ideals of education and government, have we to anticipate any active resistance to the introduction of the American school system and the English language.

[The following statement was attributed to U.S. Senator Teller of Colorado, and reported in the July 9, 1900 issue of *La Democracia*:]

I do not like the Puerto Ricans, they are not fighters as the Cubans, they remained subdued by Spanish tyranny for hundreds of years without showing themselves to be men in opposition. Such a race does not deserve citizenship.

[The next day, an angry editorial in *La Democracia* replied:]

Few, very few, are the Americans living in Puerto Rico who sympathize with the people of our country, believing themselves superior to us, when most of them do not attain the degree of culture and understanding of that large number of Puerto Ricans educated in Europe, and who constitute our intellectual circles. . . .

If that senator from Colorado, whose country [region] still is half savage, were not an ignoramus, he would know Puerto Rico never found itself in the same circumstances as Cuba did. . . .

[La *Democracia* continued its attacks, taking aim at racial prejudice in the United States.]

The extremely unfair treatment taking place in a country that calls itself free and democratic, cannot do less than dampen faith among those who believe that liberty and equality in the laws must govern the social world.

Since we don't want to see such a spectacle in our country, we defend our identity in every respect, since under its protection, Negros live here intermingled with Whites, enjoying the same rights and freedom, taking part in the administration of the country, something they have not attained in the United States, and exercising together with the Whites the right to vote.

Nevertheless, we observe with sadness that in Puerto Rico . . . the men of the colored race seem happy and satisfied with the absorption [by United States] menacing us all, without reflecting that they, more than anyone else, will suffer the consequences, the day when our island forfeits its personality.

"THEY ARE LOYAL"

Six years after the U.S. occupation, at a banquet in Washington for the local Yale alumni association, those gathered sang proudly of alumnus "Billy Hunt," who, as "Governor, he's steering Porto Rico's ship of State." The journalist who covered the banquet noted that "the people of Porto Rico are full of gratitude to the Americans" and earnestly desired Americanization." He observed that a new word had been coined: "spigotty"—later shortened to "spic"—which was a "new synonym for the Porto Rican native" who "delightedly" greeted American soldiers with the exclamation, "I speak de Inglish." The journalist acknowledged widespread poverty, but also remarked that "the native, while lying in his hammock, can pick a banana with one hand and at the same time dig a sweet potato with one foot."[1]

From *New York Times,* December 12, 1906, p. 7.

1. John Ball Osborne, *World's Work,* VIII (1904), pp. 4759-66.

In 1906, after President Theodore Roosevelt visited the island, he reported to Congress that the people of Porto Rico "are glad to be under our flag" and recommended the granting of U.S. citizenship.

To the Senate and House of Representatives:

On Nov. 21 I visited the Island of Porto Rico, landing at Ponce, crossing by the old Spanish road by Cayey to San Juan, and returning next morning over the new American road from Arecibo to Ponce. The scenery was wonderfully beautiful, especially among the mountains of the interior, which constitute a veritable tropic Switzerland. . . .

I doubt whether our people as a whole realize the beauty and fertility of Porto Rico and the progress that has been made under its admirable government. We have just cause for pride in the character of our representatives who have administered the tropic islands which came under our flag as a result of the war with Spain. . . .

I am very much struck by the excellent character both of the insular police and of the Porto Rican Regiment. . . . The insular police are under the local Porto Rican Government. The Porto Rican Regiment of troops must be appropriated for by Congress. I earnestly hope that this body will be kept permanent. There should certainly be troops in the island, and it is wise that these troops should be native Porto Ricans. It would be from every standpoint a mistake not to perpetuate this regiment.

In traversing the island even the most cursory survey leaves the beholder struck with the evident rapid growth in the culture of both sugar cane and tobacco. The fruit industry is also growing. . . .

Unfortunately, what used to be Porto Rico's prime crop—coffee—has not shared this prosperity. It has never recovered from the disaster of the hurricane, and, moreover, the benefit of throwing open our market to it has not compensated for the loss inflicted by the closing of the markets to it abroad. . . .

There is a matter to which I wish to call your special attention, and that is the desirability of conferring full American citizenship upon the people of Porto Rico. I most earnestly hope that this will be done. I cannot see how any harm can possibly result from it, and it seems to me a matter of right and justice to the People of Porto Rico. They are loyal, they are glad to be under our flag, they are making rapid progress along the path of orderly liberty. Surely, we should show our appreciation of them, our pride in what they have done, and our pleasure in extending recognition for what has thus been done, by granting them full American citizenship.

Under the wise administration of the present Governor and the Council, marked progress has been made in the difficult matter of granting to the people of the island the largest measure of self-government that can *with safety* be given at the present time. It would have been a very serious mistake to have gone any faster than we have already gone in this direction. . . .

In short, the Governor and the Council are co-operating with all of the most enlightened and most patriotic of the people of Porto Rico in educating the citizens of the island in the principles of orderly liberty. . . . It has not been easy to instill into the minds of people unaccustomed to the exercise of freedom the two basic principles of our American system—the principle that the majority must rule, and the principle that the minority has rights which must not be disregarded or trampled upon. Yet real progress has been made. . . .

THEODORE ROOSEVELT, The White House, December 11, 1906

"DISCIPLINE FOR PORTO RICO"

The first rebellion against American rule in Puerto Rico, albeit a peaceful one, occurred in 1909, when the insular House of Delegates refused to pass the appropriations bill for the next year's budget, on the grounds that appointed U.S, leaders wielded excessive power over island affairs. President William Howard Taft lost little time in rebuking the Puerto Ricans, in a message to Congress on May 10, 1909. "In the desire of certain of their leaders for political power, Porto Ricans have forgotten the generosity of the United States in its dealings with them," said Taft. He concluded that "the present development is only an indication that we have gone somewhat too fast in the extension of political power to them for their own good."[1]

Quite a different view of America's generosity was offered two years later by Tulio Larrinaga, Puerto Rico's elected Resident Commissioner in Washington.

That Porto Rico has been prospering for the last eight years—prospering from one viewpoint—is a fact which no one will deny. . . . Porto Rico has been exploited for eight years to develop her wealth-producing qualities, for the benefit of large money interests. Porto Rico has prospered, from

---

From The *Independent,* LXX (February 16, 1911) 356-59.

1. *The Independent,* LXVI (May 20, 1909) 1050-51.

that viewpoint. Under the protective tariff of the United States the sugar and tobacco interests have been greatly enlarged. From 69,000 tons of sugar exported in 1901 the production increased to 284,000 tons in 1910. It is a suggestive fact, however, that whereas there were then 345 sugar planters, the number is now reduced to less than 200, showing a concentration which is very undesirable in any country. And the increase in the production of sugar marked a corresponding decrease in the production of coffee, then the most important production of the island—still more important because the coffee farms, like the sugar farms at the start, were all comparatively small holdings owned and managed by the local planters, to their own profit and the benefit of Porto Rico. If it were not for the little money from sugar making which remains in the island today there would be great suffering among the poor. For with the advent of America and the tariff, there being no protective duty on coffee, the small farmers found it impossible to live, and their little farms were sold by the hundreds for taxes amounting to no more than ten or twenty dollars, and were bought up by the large interests. There was a law limiting the amount of land which could be bought by single interests, but there was no penalty affixed for disobedience, so no one cared.

No one denies the material prosperity, but the Porto Ricans are keenly alive to the fact that their political status, which should have kept pace with material progress, has been going down and that more and more they are losing their rights and losing their hold upon their island. In this connection one should not forget that Porto Rico has 1,100,000 inhabitants; that 100,000 children attend the public schools; that there are high schools, normal schools and a university in Porto Rico; that last year the exports of Porto Rico reached $30,000,000; that Porto Rico is more densely populated than any State of the Union; that we have a history and a Christian civilization centuries old.

During the past century, under the Spanish regime, the one aim of the Porto Ricans was to obtain political advancement toward their ultimate desire of self-government. Canada was their model. The English system in Canada was the goal of their aspirations. Toward this they made no mean progress. Several times during the past century they took real steps in advance—the promulgation of the Spanish Constitution, for example. In the first part of the nineteenth century they were granted representation in the Spanish Congress; a representation which made a brilliant record, in 1812, in the framing of the Spanish Constitution. In 1870 this representation was made permanent. Sixteen representatives and four senators were then allowed under the Spanish apportionment law. And with this as a fighting base they obtained several liberal reforms; such as an insular legislative body elected by a moderately restricted suffrage; in 1869 the abolition of slavery, and later the authority to make a loan to pay the slave owners; then the gradual suppression of the tariff was begun, which eventually was fully carried out, deducting every year one-tenth part of the duties on all goods exchanged between the colony and the mother country.

In 1887 the Autonomist party was formed and finally declared to be a legal party and admitted to an understanding with the Liberal party, then controlling in Spain. At last, in 1897, as a preparatory measure to the final establishment of self-government, the island was divided into two districts, and natives as well as Spaniards were appointed governors both of the North and of the South districts. In December, 1897, local self-government was at last granted, and besides there went with it the right to concur in treaty making with other nations thru special delegates chosen by the island for the purpose.

This was the status of Porto Rico at the time of the American occupation, and the arrangement was continued by General Brooke, the first military governor of the island, as established by his general order No. 1. But in December, 1898, General Brooke was succeeded by General Guy S. Henry, U. S. V., who began to introduce changes, and finally did away entirely with the autonomic organization. In April, 1900, an act of Congress established a civil government in Porto Rico, fashioned after the English system for their partially civilized colonies, such as the Fiji Islands. The act, commonly known as "The Foraker Act," granted a legislature composed of two houses. The lower house was to be elected by the people. The upper house, called the Executive Council, was formed mainly by the heads of the various departments appointed by the President.

This organization of an appointed, foreign body to make the laws of the country—a body whose members were at the same time the executive heads of departments—was naturally a great disappointment to the Porto Ricans. With the governor retaining the veto power and the Congress the right to amend or annul all acts of the local legislature, there could not have been any danger in leaving both houses in the hands of the people; nor could a better system have been furnished as a school for self-government training, if the advocates of the act were in good faith, in 1900, in their claim that we were not capable of self-government. Under the autonomic constitution which was taken away from us we had the right to name the major part of the upper house. They were simply to be citizens of Spain—and for thirty years previous we had been citizens of Spain; ever since the Spanish Constitution was extended to Porto Rico, when the colony was abolished and the island became a province of Spain. Now, after ten years of the Foraker Act, depriving us of the upper house appointments, why should we find ourselves given a legislature bereft of all power whatsoever, except that of amending criminal and civil laws already made? There was also added to the bill the provision that the legislature should not meet as often as it had. This was wise and, in the judgment of many, under such conditions it would have been still wiser to provide that the legislature should not meet at all.

Just a lower house, with practically no power at all, is a strange sop to hand to people who were enjoying almost complete home government, after they had been waiting ten years for the fulfillment of the early promises made upon American occupation. There are inconveniences, evils, injustices, wrongs inherent to a foreign executive council appointed by a foreign executive and responsible to no one in Porto Rico. Take the matter of granting franchises in the island, for example, The Porto Ricans have suffered several serious losses and great wrong in the granting of franchises to irresponsible people, for wildcat schemes known to be technically and economically impossible; to a bankrupt company, a company that was in the hands of a receiver. All these failures to protect the people of Porto Rico—the unjust and unwise franchises, the failure to keep the land from absorption by large foreign interests, and the rest—would never have occurred if the upper house had been elected by the people and responsible to the people. Members of the Executive Council now only await removal to go back to the United States, caring very little for what they leave behind. Some of them, indeed, have drawn salaries for long periods and have not been there half the time. There were members of the council in Washington for three or four months, their salaries being paid by the people of Porto Rico, while they carried on the campaign which resulted in Congress deciding to take away from the people of Porto Rico the right to concur in appropriation bills for the expenditure of their own taxes, for the benefit of their own island. Now we have no power whatsoever. The Executive Council may go on from year to year, appropriating the money of previous years, and they can dispose of this as they please. There is something which the Porto Rican cannot fully understand in this persistent tendency to reduce his rights instead of fulfilling any of the assurances given him in the past.

The chief open contention of those who claim that the people of Porto Rico cannot as yet be trusted with self-government is that they are not prepared for the duties and responsibilities of the status. But every one knows that, in the first place, they have already proven their capacity, when, in 1870, the Republican form of government was established in Spain as well as in Porto Rico, and when they organized their insular machinery by popular vote; also in the organization of their autonomic government in 1898. But suppose such experience was not conclusive of fitness for self-government; how are they ever to gain or prove that fitness without a limited opportunity? It is true that Porto Rico has prospered in a material sense in the past ten years. But it is also true that Porto Rico would have escaped several serious wrongs from which she has suffered, and who can say that her material prosperity would not have been still greater had she been allowed a voice in the conduct of her own affairs and the expenditures of her own resources. Would the new States which were admitted to the Union several years ago have made the rapid strides which have marked their progress if they had been kept down, under the arbitrary rule of a limited number of men sent there from outside, with the sole authority to make their laws and administer their material wealth and resources? Many of the territories did not have at the time of their admission to the Union anything like the favorable conditions which Porto Rico presents, in simply asking for the right of home jurisdiction.

Porto Rico has a civilization centuries old; has a larger population than eighteen States of the Union; has a greater commerce and wealth than several of them; has a larger trade with the continental United States than many of the nations with which they interchange commerce.

Those who demand colonial government for Porto Rico, and who realize that this first argument is absurdly weak, advance another which seems to be the only thing left upon which they can spread false accusations and incorrect impressions giving any apparent ground for depriving Porto Rico of the right of local jurisdiction. It is illiteracy. But even this cannot be taken seriously by one who knows anything at all about Porto Rico and is honestly trying to decide impartially in the matter. The proportion of illiteracy really existing is not really known. The only data upon which the argument is based are those quite inaccurately obtained and given out as the result of the first hurried census of ten or eleven years ago. But even supposing that the illiteracy of today is as high as 60 per cent, this, in the 1,100,000 inhabitants, will still represent a number of persons *not* illiterate, several times larger than there were inhabitants—with a degree of education or without it—in some of the territories admitted to the self-government of statehood in the United States several years ago.

Failing this, another, yet more absurd, argument is advanced. The large number of schools established and the many miles of good roads built in the last ten years—at the expense of Porto Rico—is used as an argument against any change in the present system of governing the colony. The Porto Rican feels that this progress is due mainly to his initiative and would direct attention to the fact that while the lower house retained the right of concurring in appropriations it readily agreed to every effort at progress. And if this co-operation and universal energy, under the present system, is to be used as an effective argument against improvement in their political status, then the Porto Ricans, with their industry and energy, are every day digging deeper into the grave of political oblivion. Why, upon this basis, they would be better fitted for home government if they deliberately combatted every effort at progress.

Now, if the partisans and advocates of the *status quo* are honest, and so sure of the incompetency of the people of Porto Rico to take care of themselves, let them accept this challenge and settle the controversy by putting it to the test. The governor of the island will always retain the veto power and the Congress of the United States will always have the right to amend or annul whatever vicious legislation may be enacted. There could be no possible danger either to the United States or to the island. Indeed, there could be no question raised unless with some sinister motive by money interests profitably exploiting Porto Rico. And this constant refusal to give them a chance in self-government has created a sentiment among the people that the partisans of the *status quo* really attach more importance to their control of the island and the benefit derived from it by outside interests than they do to the people of Porto Rico and their welfare.

Even the bill passed by the House of Representatives last year —which was meager enough in favorable provisions for Porto Rico—has already been shorn of its more liberal points by the Senate Committee and was so reported to the Senate, to be acted on, the other day, to the great chagrin and disappointment of the Porto Ricans, who are at this moment in grave excitement and distress, despairing of ever seeing fulfilled the promises made to them at the time of the occupation of the island, or of redress in harmony with the American claims of justice and democracy.

"INVERTED TERMS"

As the impact of American rule upon Puerto Rico spread, confusion—cultural and political—prompted different solutions to the dilemma.

Some wish to be Americans without ceasing to be Puerto Ricans; others want to be Puerto Ricans without ceasing to be Americans. It is a matter of inverted terms. Some of us want independence, but with the American protectorate, because it would be of great worth, because in that solution we glimpse the true bond of Union of feelings and interests between the small nation of the Caribbean and the big nation of the North. The others want annexation, where the State is free inside the Nation. They believe assured, in that way, the Independence of the country. But those countrymen . . . do not understand that, if it is true that we would achieve a personality in the Nation, we would lose it before the world. . . .

[Pleas for more home rule continued to receive little sympathy in the United States.]

The American residents in Puerto Rico have the same point of view that I have: it would not be the part of wisdom for us to surrender the government entirely into their hands, since they are of a different civilization, not looking upon matters of government in the same light as the Anglo-Saxons: They really have no conception of the true meaning of equality and liberty.

[Racial prejudice among some American leaders also helped to shape attitudes in Washington.]

. . . they have the Latin-American excitability, and I think America should go slow in granting them anything like autonomy. Their civilization is not at all like ours yet. . . . The mixture of black and white in Porto Rico threatens to create a race of mongrels of no use to anyone, a race of Spanish-American talkers. A governor from the South, or with knowledge of Southern remedies for that trouble, could, if a wise man, do much. . . .

[As English became the first language of the schools, and its usage quickly multiplied in commercial life, there were concerns about the survival of the mother tongue.]

The Castilian language cannot be banished from the country without the loss of the Puerto Rican personality. . . . Therefore, to relegate the Spanish language to a secondary position in our schools, not only because of the honor of the race that is so important, but because of the disaster that arbitrary action would bring, is a grave danger to the Puerto Rican people.

English must be taught in our schools, since it can be stated that it is the universal language. . . .

Selections in this chapter:
1. Translated from *La Democracia,* July 2, 1914.
2. From William D. Boyce, *United States Colonies and Dependencies* (Chicago: Rand McNally, 1914), pp. 414-15.
3. From letters of April 18 and July 21, 1913, to President Woodrow Wilson, from his friend, Judge Peter A. Hamilton.
4. Translated from an interview with poet Doña Trina Padilla de Sanz, known as "La Hija del Caribe," in *La Democracia,* February 20, 1915.
5. Translated from a column by poet-journalist Luis Llorens Torres, *La Democracia,* March 30, 1915.

Let us struggle, not just today, but always, so that our tongue be the Castilian . . . since a people who know how to preserve their language and their customs can never be crushed or swallowed up.

[Some Puerto Ricans resented the impact of American culture on the island, and others tried to ignore it. But others zealously adopted every new fad and wrinkle that reached Puerto Rico's shores. The new word *pitiyanqui*—which literally means "tiny yankee"—came into vogue, to describe in contemptuous terms the individual who casts aside his own culture, and becomes a 200 per cent American.]

. . . *pitiyanquis* are the Johns, the Peters, and the Williams, born in sweet potato fields, who sign themselves "Junior" and say that they are from Comerio or from Manati; they are the snobbish "boricuas" who smoke a pipe, who coil up their pants, who spit through their eyeteeth, and eat their avocadoes with a spoon. They are the native sons . . . who, aping truckdrivers, in the belief that they are imitating American "gentlemen," unhinge themselves dancing the native *danza,* to the style of the "turkey trot" and the "one step"!

And *pitiyanquis* are, finally, those hundreds of Puerto Rican insular government employees, who preach Americanization of the country, led by the sole self-interest of their greedy stomachs. . . .

PART VI

AMERICAN CITIZENSHIP

We request American citizenship with all the rights inherent to the great title of American citizens. This is citizenship with autonomy. And if one of these two, one independent of the other, which is absurd, is offered to us, we prefer self-government to American citizenship, rather than citizenship without self-government.

—Jose de Diego, July 1, 1907

It is no mere coincidence that, one year before the United States entered World War I, it purchased the Virgin Islands from Denmark for $25 million, and just one month before hostilities began, granted U.S. citizenship to Puerto Ricans.

It was a time when German ships prowled the Atlantic; when Herr Arthur Zimmermann, the German foreign secretary, sent the now famous telegram to his minister in Mexico, that Mexico and Germany should "make war together and together make peace," promising financial rewards, so that Mexico might "reconquer the lost territory in New Mexico, Texas and Arizona."

When a nation goes to war, it takes no chances. And America wished to take no chances in the Caribbean, a key strategic zone. Puerto Rico—unhappy with its colonial government and limbolike civil status—and the Virgin Islands were needed to shore up the U.S. presence in the West Indies.

This was not the first time that Americans or Puerto Ricans had discussed citizenship. The topic was born the moment that U.S. troops landed at Guánica in 1898.

But there was little sentiment in Congress to admit the Caribbean island as a full member of the Union. In Puerto Rico, some viewed citizenship as a means to achieve equal rights with Americans. The island's principal elected leaders, however, preferred self-government to Americanization.

José de Diego, for example, at a conference on the U.S. mainland in 1910, said:

The entry of our island in your brotherhood of states—let us be frank—is impossible; neither you nor we wish it, or believe in it. With that path closed, there remains only the explicit recognition of the Republic of Puerto Rico, under the protectorship of the United States.

At the same conference, Luis Muñoz Rivera said:

Our problem has three solutions: the proclamation of Statehood, which would blend us with you in national life; the concession of home rule, which would join us with you in a sentimental link of gratitude and would be a real bind for the exchange of commercial products; and the concession of Independence, by law of Congress, which would make us the sole masters of our destiny. Of these three solutions, we would prefer the first, we propose the second, and we reserve the third as the last refuge of our right and honor.

But Congress would grant no solution. It would merely impose citizenship upon Puerto Ricans, without allowing them to vote upon the question. Those who refused citizenship would become "citizens of Porto Rico," and be denied certain civil rights, including the right to hold public office in their own homeland.

"AN IDLE DREAM"

As the first decade of the twentieth century rolled by, the U.S. War Department continued to control Puerto Rican affairs, and Congress took no steps to resolve the colonial condition. By 1911, even the pro-statehood party had abandoned its ideal, and was courting the idea of independence. An American magazine, in describing the dilemma, said: "Our readers will remember Edward Everett Male's famous story, 'The Man Without a Country'; the Porto Ricans are all men without a country."[1] Pressure to allow more self-government for the island culminated in proposed legislation that came to be known as the Jones-Shafroth Bill of 1917. When Congress began to discuss the bill, Muñoz Rivera, the resident commissioner in Washington, supported it, because extra powers would be transferred to the island. But two clauses were

---

From Hearings before the Committee on Insular Affairs, House of Representatives, 63d Congress, 2d Session, on H.R. 138118, p. 61.

1. *The Outlook,* XCIX (November 18, 1911), pp. 643–44.

added to the bill; one granted American citizenship; the other gave absolute veto power to the Governor—an American—over all insular legislation. In 1914, Congressman John F. Shafroth of Colorado spoke with Muñoz Rivera at the Senate hearings in Washington.

CHAIRMAN (speaking to Muñoz Rivera): Your party's position is as follows, if I understand correctly: you want the part about citizenship to be left aside, because you believe that if you are declared citizens now, this will hurt your cause, and will preclude the chance in the future for obtaining complete independence, or independence as an American protectorate. Is that correct?

MUNOZ RIVERA: That is my position, exactly.

CHAIRMAN: Now, it seems to me, on the other hand, that the people of the United States desire that Puerto Rico remain as a permanent possession of the United States, but that it should be granted the most liberal form of government that it is capable of having. . . . The bill is already based on the idea that Puerto Rico should be a permanent possession of the United States. The idea is to resolve this question, and thus remove it from Puerto Rican politics. What do you say to that, Mr. Rivera?

MUNOZ RIVERA: That is a very difficult question for me, because as you know, the final aspiration of my party is nationalism, with or without an American protectorate, and according to the under standing of the Puerto Rican people, the concession of citizenship would interfere with their ambitions for independence.

CHAIRMAN: I don't think that changes the feeling of the United States, and I can say, speaking for myself, that this talk of independence is an idle dream of the Unionist Party, and it would be much better to resolve the affair right now, much better for the people of Puerto Rico themselves.

"THE FUTURE OF MY COUNTRY"

Soon afterward, Muñoz Rivera wrote to José de Diego, then president of the House of Delegates, to tell him of his "agonies and anguish" in Washington. "They are imposing citizenship upon us because they want to tie us to the Republic forever," he wrote, adding that, despite his tireless efforts:

No one helps us. No one supports us. Not one of the four Democrats who visited the island will speak out for our freedom. No senator, no representative, is with us. No newspaper is concerned about us, or responds to our propaganda, or will respond to our protest. The machine functions, and the machine is omnipotent.[1]

On May 5, 1916, Muñoz Rivera—realizing that his cause was lost—rose in the U.S. House of Representatives to discuss the Jones Act, and the issue of American citizenship. His statement reveals the complexity of the man, and the dilemma of a small island, seeking to retain its identity within the realm of a giant.

On the 18th day of October, 1898, when the flag of this great Republic was unfurled over the fortresses of San Juan, if anyone had said to my countrymen that the United States, the land of liberty, was going to deny their right to form a government of the people, by the people, and for the people of Puerto Rico, my countrymen would have refused to believe such a prophecy, considering it sheer madness. The Porto Ricans were living at that time under a regime of ample self-government, discussed and voted by the Spanish Cortes, on the basis of the parliamentary system in use among all the nations of Europe. Spain sent to the islands a governor, whose power, strictly limited by law, made him the equivalent of those constitutional sovereigns who reign but do not govern. The members of the cabinet, without whose signature no executive order was valid, were natives of the island; the representatives in the senate and in the house were natives of the island; and the administration in its entirety was in the hands of natives of the island. The Spanish Cortes, it is true, retained the power to make statutory laws for Porto Rico, but in the Cortes were 16 Porto Rican representatives and 3 Porto Rican senators having voice and vote. And all the insular laws were made by the insular parliament.

Two years later, in 1900, after a long period of military rule, the Congress of the United States approved the Foraker Act. Under this act all of the 11 members of the executive council were appointed by the President of the United States; 6 of them were the heads of departments; 5 exercised legislative functions only. And this executive council, or in practice, the bureaucratic majority of the council, was, and is in reality, with the governor, the supreme arbiter of

---

From *Congressional Record,* 64th Congress, 1st Session, 1916. LIII, pp. 7470-73.

1. Translated from *Revista del Institute de Cultura Puertorriqueña.* No. 4 (July-September, 1959), San Juan, pp. 35-36. Reprinted by permission.

the island and of its interests. It represents the most absolute contradiction of republican principles.

For 16 years we have endured this system of government, protesting and struggling against it, with energy and without result. We did not lose hope, because if one national party, the Republican, was forcibly enforcing this system upon us, the other national party, the Democratic, was encouraging us by its declarations in the platforms of Kansas City, St. Louis, and Denver. Porto Rico waited, election after election, for the Democratic Party to triumph at the polls and fulfill its promises. At last the Democratic Party did triumph. It is here. It has a controlling majority at this end of the Capitol and at the other end; it is in possession of the White House. On the Democratic Party rests the sole and undivided responsibility for the progress of events at this juncture. It can, by a legislative act, keep alive the hopes of the people of Porto Rico or it can deal these hopes their death blow.

The Republican Party decreed independence for Cuba and thereby covered itself with glory; the Democratic Party is bound by the priniciples written into its platforms and by the recorded speeches of its leaders to decree liberty for Porto Rico. The legislation you are about to enact will prove whether the platforms of the Democratic Party are more than useless paper, whether the words of its leaders are more than soap bubbles, dissolved by the breath of triumph. Here is the dilemma with its two unescapable horns: You must proceed in accordance with the fundamental principles of your party or you must be untrue to them. The monarchies of the Old World, envious of American success and the republics of the New World, anxious to see clearly the direction in which the American initiative is tending, are watching and studying the Democratic administration. Something more is at stake than the fate of Porto Rico—poor, isolated, and defenseless as she is—the prestige and the good name of the United States are at stake. England learned the hard lessons of Saratoga and Yorktown in the eighteenth century. And in the nineteenth century she established self-government, complete, sincere, and honorable, in Canada, Australia, and New Zealand. Then in the twentieth century, immediately after the Anglo-Boer War, she established self-government, complete, sincere, and honorable, for the Orange Free State and the Transvaal, her enemies of the day before. She turned over the reins of power to insurgents who were still wearing uniforms stained with British blood.

In Porto Rico no blood will be shed. Such a thing is impossible in an island of 3,600 square miles. Its narrow confines never permitted and never will permit armed resistance. For this very reason Porto Rico is a field of experiment unique on the globe. And if Spain, the reactionary monarchy, gave Porto Rico the home rule which she was enjoying in 1898, what should the United States, the progressive Republic, grant her? This is the mute question which Europe and America are writing today in the solitudes of the Atlantic and on the waters of the Panama Canal. The reply is the bill which is now under discussion. This bill can not meet the earnest aspirations of my country. It is not a measure of self-government ample enough to solve definitely our political problem or to match your national reputation, established by a successful championship for liberty and justice throughout the world since the very beginning of your national life. But, meager and conservative as the bill appears when we look at its provision from our own point of view, we sincerely recognize its noble purposes and willingly accept it as a step in the right direction and as a reform paving the way for others more acceptable and satisfactory which shall come a little later, provided that my countrymen will be able to demonstrate their capacity, the capacity they possess, to govern themselves. In regard to such capacity, it is my duty, no doubt, a pleasant duty, to assure Congress that the Porto Ricans will endeavor to prove their intelligence, their patriotism, and their full preparation to enjoy and to exercise a democratic regime. [Applause.]

Our behavior during the past is a sufficient guaranty for our behavior in the future. Never a revolution there, in spite of our Latin blood; never an attempt to commercialize our political influence; never an attack against the majesty of law. The ever-reigning peace was not at any time disturbed by the illiterate masses, which bear their suffering with such stoic fortitude and only seek comfort in their bitter servitude, confiding in the supreme protection of God. [Applause.]

There is no reason which justifies American statesmen in denying self-government to my country and erasing from their programs the principles of popular sovereignty. Is illiteracy the reason? Because if in Porto Rico 60 per cent of the electorate can not read, in the United States in the early days of the Republic 80 per cent of the population were unable to read; and even today there are 20 Republics and twenty monarchies which acknowledge a higher percentage of illiteracy than Porto Rico. It is not the coexistence of two races on the island, because here in North America more than 10 States show a higher proportion of Negro population than Porto Rico, and the District of Columbia has precisely the same proportion, 67 white to 33 per cent colored. It is not our small territorial extent, because two States have a smaller area than Porto Rico. It is not a question of population, for by the last census there were 18 States with a smaller population than Porto Rico. Nor is it a matter of real and personal property, for the taxable property in New Mexico is only one-third that of Porto Rico. There is a reason and only one reason—the same sad reason of war and conquest which let loose over the South after the fall of Richmond thousands and thousands of office seekers, hungry for power and authority, and determined to report to their superiors that the rebels of the South were unprepared for self-government. [Laughter.] We are the southerners of the twentieth century.

The House of Representatives has never been influenced by this class of motives. The House of Representatives has very high motives, and, if they are studied thoroughly, very grave reasons for redeeming my country from bureaucratic greed and confiding to it at once the responsibility for its own destinies and the power to fix and determine them. They are reasons of an international character which affect the policy of the United States in the rest of America. Porto Rico, the only one of the former colonies of Spain in this hemisphere which does not fly its own flag or figure in the family of nations, is being closely observed with assiduous vigilance by the Republics of the Caribbean Sea and the Gulf of Mexico. Cuba, Santo Domingo, Venezuela, Colombia, Costa Rica, Honduras, Nicaragua, Salvador, Guatemala maintain with us a constant interchange of ideas and never lose sight of the experiment in the colonial government which is being carried on in Porto Rico. If they see that the Porto Ricans are living happily, that they are not treated with disdain, that their aspirations are being fulfilled, that their character is being respected, that they are not being subjected to an imperialistic tutelage, and that the right to govern their own country is not being usurped, these nations will recognize the superiority of American methods and will feel the influence of the American Government. This will smooth the way to the moral hegemony which you are called by your greatness, by your wealth, by your traditions, and your institutions to exercise in the New World. [Applause.] On the other hand, if these communities, Latin like Porto Rico, speaking the same language as Porto Rico, branches of the same ancestral trunk that produced Porto Rico, bound to Porto Rico by so many roots striking deep in a common past, if these communities observe that your insular experiment is a failure and that you have not been able to keep the affections of a people who awaited from you their redemption and their happiness, they will be convinced that they must look, not to Washington but to London, Paris, or Berlin when they seek markets for their products, sympathy for their misfortunes, and guarantees for their liberty.

What do you gain along with the discontent of my countrymen? You as Members of Congress? Nothing. And the Nation loses a part of its prestige, difficulties are created in the path of its policies, its democratic ideals are violated, and it must abdicate its position as leader in every progressive movement on the planet. Therefore if you undertake a reform, do it sincerely. A policy of subterfuge and shadows might be expected in the Italy of the Medicis, in the France of the Valois, in the England of the Stuarts, or the Spain of the Bourbons, but it is hard to explain in the United States of Cleveland, McKinley, Roosevelt, and Wilson. [Applause.]

The bill I am commenting on provides for a full elective legislature. Well, that is a splendid concession you will make to your own principles and to our own rights. But now, after such a magnificent advance, do not permit, gentlemen, do not permit the local powers of the legislature to be diminished in matters so important for us as the education of the children. We are citizens jealous of this dignity; we are fathers anxious to foster our sons toward the future, teaching them how to struggle for life and how to reach the highest standard of honesty, intelligence, and energy. We accept one of your compatriots, a capable American, as head of the department of education, though we have in the island many men capable of filling this high office with distinction. We welcomed his appointment by the President of the United States. In this way the island will have the guaranty to find such a man as Dr. Brumbaugh, the first commissioner of education, who deserves all our confidence. But let the legislature regulate the courses of study, cooperating in that manner with the general development of educational work throughout our native country.

I come now to treat of a problem which is really not a problem for Porto Rico, as my constituents look at it, because it has been solved already in the Foraker Act. The Foraker Act recognizes the Porto Rican citizenship of the inhabitants of Porto Rico. We are satisfied with this citizenship and desire to prolong and maintain it—our natural citizenship, founded not on the conventionalism of law but on the fact that we were born on an island and love that island above all else, and would not exchange our country for any other country, though it were one as great and as free as the United States. If Porto Rico were to disappear in a geological catastrophe and there survived a thousand or ten thousand or a hundred thousand Porto Ricans, and they were given the choice of all the citizenships of the world, they would choose without a moment's hesitation that of the United States. But so long as Porto Rico exists on the surface of the ocean, poor and small as she is, and even if she were poorer and smaller, Porto Ricans will always choose Porto Rican citizenship. And the Congress of the United States will have performed an indefensible act if it tries to destroy so legitimate a sentiment and to annul through a law of its own making a law of the oldest and wisest legislators of all time—a law of nature.

It is true that my countrymen have asked many times, unanimously, for American citizenship. They asked for it when through the promise of Gen. Miles on his disembarkation in Ponce, and when through the promises of the Democratic Party when it adopted the Kansas City platform—they believed it not only possible but probable, not only probable but certain, that American citizenship was the door by which to enter, not after a period of 100 years nor of 10, but immediately into the fellowship of the American people as a State of the Union. Today they no longer believe it. From this floor the most eminent statesmen have made it clear to them that they must not believe it. And my countrymen, who, precisely the same as yours, have their dignity and self-respect to maintain, refuse to accept a citizenship of an inferior order, a citizenship of the second class, which does not permit them to dispose of their own resources nor to live their own lives nor to send to this Capitol their proportional representation. To obtain benefits of such magnitude they were disposed to sacrifice their sentiments of filial love for the motherland. These advantages have vanished, and the people of Porto Rico have decided to continue to be Porto Ricans; to be so each day with increasing enthusiasm, to retain their own name, claiming for it the same consideration, the same respect, which they accord to the names of other countries, above all to the name of the United States. Give us statehood and your glorious citizenship will be welcome to us and to our children. If you deny us statehood, we decline your citizenship, frankly, proudly, as befits a people who can be deprived of their civil liberties but who, although deprived of their civil liberties, will preserve their conception of honor, which none can take from them, because they bear it in their souls, a moral heritage from their forefathers.

This bill which I am speaking of grants American citizenship to all my compatriots on page 5. On page 6 it authorizes those who do not accept American citizenship to so declare before a court of justice, and thus retain their Porto Rican citizenship. On page 28 it provides that—

No person shall be allowed to register as a voter in Porto Rico, who is not a citizen of the United States.

My compatriots are generously permitted to be citizens of the only country they possess, but they are eliminated from the body politic; the exercise of political rights is forbidden them and by a single stroke of the pen they are converted into pariahs and there is established in America, on American soil, protected by the Monroe doctrine, a division into castes like the Brahmans and Sudras of India. The Democratic platform of Kansas City declared 14 years ago, "A nation can not long endure half empire and half republic," and "Imperialism abroad will lead rapidly and irreparably to despotism at home." These are not Porto Rican phrases reflecting our Latin impressionability; they are American phrases, reflecting the Anglo-Saxon spirit, calm in its attitude and jealous-very jealous—of its privileges.

We have a profound consideration for your national ideas; you must treat our local ideas with a similar consideration. As the representative of Porto Rico, I propose that you convoke the people of the island to express themselves in full plebiscite on the question of citizenship and that you permit the people of Porto Rico to decide by their votes whether they wish the citizenship of the United States or whether they prefer their own natural citizenship. It would be strange if, having refused it so long as the majority of people asked for it, you should decide to impose it by force now that the majority of the people decline it.

Someone recently stated that we desire the benefits but shirk the responsibilities and burdens of citizenship. I affirm in reply that we were never consulted as to our status, and that in the treaty of Paris the people of Porto Rico were disposed of as were the serfs of ancient times, fixtures of the land, who were transferred by force to the service of new masters and subject to new servitudes. The fault is not ours, though ours are the grief and humiliation; the fault lies with our bitter destiny which made us weak and left us an easy prey between the warring interests of mighty powers. If we had our choice, we would be a free and isolated people in the liberty and the solitude of the seas, without other advantages than those won by our exertions in industry and in peace, without other responsibilities and burdens than those of our own conduct and our duty toward one another and toward the civilization which surrounds us.

The bill under consideration, liberal and generous in some of its sections, as those creating an elective insular senate; a cabinet, a majority of whose members shall be confirmed by the senate; and a public-service commission, two members of which shall be elected by the people, is exceedingly conservative in other sections, most of all in that which restricts the popular vote, enjoining that the right of registering as electors be limited to those who are able to read and write or who pay taxes to the Porto Rican Treasury. By means of this restriction 165,000 citizens who vote at present and who have been voting since the Spanish days would be barred from the polls.

Here are the facts: There exist at present 250,000 registered electors. Seventy percent of the electoral population is illiterate. There will remain, then, 75,000 registered electors. Adding 10,000 illiterate taxpayers, there will be a total of 85,000 citizens within the electoral register and 165,000 outside of it. I can not figure out, hard as I have tried, how those 165,000 Porto Ricans are considered incapable of participating in the elections of their representatives in the legislature and municipalities, while on the other hand they are judged perfectly capable of possessing with dignity American citizenship. This is an inconsistency which I can not explain, unless the principle is upheld that he who incurs the

greatest misfortune—not by his own fault—of living in the shadow of ignorance is not worthy of the honor of being an American citizen. In the case of
this being the principle on which the clause is based, it would seem necessary
to uphold such principle, by depriving 3,000,000 Americans of their citizenship,
for this is the number of illiterates in the United States according to the census
of 1910. There is no reason that justifies this measure, anyway. Since civil government was established in Porto Rico, superseding military government—
that is, 16 years ago—eight general elections have been staged. Each time the
people, with a most ample suffrage law, have elected their legislative bodies,
their municipal councils, their municipal courts, and school boards. These various bodies have cooperated to the betterment and progress of the country,
which gives evidence that they were prudently chosen.

Perhaps one or a hundred or a thousand electors tried to commercialize their
votes, selling them to the highest bidders.

For the sake of argument I will accept that hypothesis, though it was never
proved. But even supposing that we had not to do with a presumption, but with
an accomplished fact, I ask, Were there not and are there not in the rest of this
Nation worthless persons who negotiate their constitutional rights? Did not the
courts of a great State—the State of Massachusetts—convict four or five thousand men of that offense? Was there not a case in which the majority of a legislature promised to elect and did elect a high Federal officer for a few dollars?
I do not think that these infractions of the law and breaches of honor reflect the
least discredit on the clean name of the American people. I do not think that
such isolated crimes can lead in any State to the restriction of the vote. They
are exceptional cases, which can not be helped. The courts of justice punish
the guilty ones and the social organization continues its march. In Porto Rico,
if such cases occur, they should have and do have the same consequences. But
it would be a sad and unjust condition of affairs if, through the fault of one,
1,000 men were to be deprived of their privileges; or, to speak in proportion,
if, through the fault of 160 electors, 160,000 were to be deprived of their
privileges.

The aforesaid motives are fundamental ones that require careful attention
from the House. But there are deeper motives yet, those that refer to the history
of the United States and of the American Congress. Never was there a single
law passed under the dome of the Capitol restrictive of the individual rights, of
the rights of humanity. Quite the contrary, Congress even going to the extreme
of amending the Constitution, restrained the initiative of the States for the
purpose of making them respect the exercise of those rights without marring it
with the least drawback. There is the fourteenth amendment. Congress could

not hinder States from making their electoral laws, but it could decree and did decree that in the event of any State decreasing its number of electors it would, ipso facto, decrease its number of Representatives in this House. The United States always gave to the world examples of a profound respect for the ideal of a sincere democracy.

I feel at ease when I think of the future of my country. I read a solemn declaration of the five American commissioners that signed, in 1898, the treaty of Paris. When the five Spanish delegates, no less distinguished than the Americans, asked for a guaranty as to the future of Porto Rico, your compatriots answered thus:

> The Congress of a country which never enacted laws to oppress or abridge the rights of residents within its domains, and whose laws permit the largest liberty consistent with the preservation of order and the protection of property, may safely be trusted not to depart from its well-settled practice in dealing with the inhabitants of these islands.

Congress needs not `be reminded of its sacred obligations, the obligations which those words impose upon it. Porto Rico had nothing to do with the declaration of war. The Cubans were assured of their national independence. The Porto Ricans were acquired for $20,000,000, and my country, innocent and blameless, paid with its territory the expenses of the campaign.

The treaty of Paris says:

> As compensation for the losses and expenses occasioned the United States by the war and for the claims of its citizens by reason of the injuries and damages they may have suffered in their persons and property during the last insurrection in Cuba, Her Catholic Majesty, in the name and representation of Spain, and thereunto constitutionally authorized by the Cortes of the Kingdom, cedes to the United States of America, and the latter accept for themselves, the island of Porto Rico and the other islands now under Spanish sovereignty in the West Indies, as also the island of Guam, in the Marianas or Ladrones Archipelago, which island was selected by the United States of America in virtue of the provisions of article 11 of the protocol signed in Washington on August 12 last.

You, citizens of a free fatherland, with its own laws, its own institutions, and its own flag, can appreciate the unhappiness of the small and solitary people that must await its laws from your authority, that lacks institutions created by their will, and who does not feel the pride of having the colors of a national emblem to cover the homes of its families and the tombs of its ancestors.

Give us now the field of experiment which we ask of you, that we may show that it is easy for us to constitute a stable republican government with all possible guarantees for all possible interests. And afterwards, when you acquire the certainty that you can found in Porto Rico a republic like that founded in Cuba and Panama, like the one you will found at some future day in the Philippines, give us our independence and you will stand before humanity as the greatest of the *great;* that which neither Greece nor Rome nor England ever were, a great creator of new nationalities and a great liberator of oppressed peoples. [Applause.]

"TREACHERY AND DISENCHANTMENT"

On May 23,1916, the House of Representatives passed the Jones Bill—with the provision for U.S. citizenship intact. In August, Muñoz Rivera—tired, disillusioned, yearning to go home—wrote from Washington to Mariano Abril, his old friend and fellow journalist in Puerto Rico: "Those mountains, that brook, those starry nights in Barranquitas always bring to my spirit a sweet, dreamy melancholy. . . . And politics? If you knew how tired I am, knowing that I keep to myself such treachery and disenchantment. We shall talk about it soon; not in San Juan, but up there, in the shadow of a tree, in the peace of a cool afternoon."[1]

On September 19, 1916, Muñoz Rivera sailed to San Juan, where he was greeted warmly by a large crowd of his followers. Two days later he fell ill, and, by the afternoon of November 15, he was dead. A few days before his death, he had dictated his "political testament" to Antonio R. Barceló, his young successor. Calling the Jones Bill "the first step in our evolution," Muñoz said, "The path is firmly outlined. . . . Although the final end to the problem is the independence of our homeland, we must have great confidence and absolute faith in the great people under whose influence and under whose protection our destiny must be determined." He called upon his people to "decide their destiny, according to the circumstances that the future may determine."[2]

On February 20, 1917, the U.S. Senate approved the Jones Bill, and, on March 2, President Woodrow Wilson signed it, making Puerto Ricans American citizens.

Before Wilson signed the bill, however, the Congressional Union for Women's Suffrage called a mass meeting at New York City's 48th Street Theatre, to protest against self-government for Puerto Rico "so long as it is denied

---

1. Translated from *Revista del Institute de Cultura Puertorriqueña,* No. 4 (July-September, 1959), San Juan, pp. 35-36.
2. Translated from *La Democratic,* January 5, 1917.

the women of the United States." A spokesman said: "The President has announced his desire for immediate action in the bill giving self-government to Porto Ricans *as a war measure. The imminence of war makes it wise, the President thinks, to insure the loyalty of the Porto Ricans.*"[3]

The passage of the citizenship bill created more confusion and dissent than before. Ostensibly designed to grant more self-government, it allowed the American Governor to retain final veto power. On its way through Congress, the bill was tinkered with by several legislators. A Senator from North Dakota, for example, added an amendment that imposed the prohibition of liquor, despite the fact that the island's impoverished economy derived great revenues from rum sales. This, too, was accepted by the powerless Puerto Ricans, who had no political "clout" in Washington. Above all, the Jones Act did nothing to resolve the long-range issue of political status. One of its most eloquent critics was José de Diego, who was then the leader of the insular House of Representatives.

N ever before in the realm of international law has such a thing been seen in the democratic nations of the world: 1,200,000 human beings, who by the law of the Congress of a Republic . . . are stripped of their natural citizenship, but under the menace and coercion of losing their right to vote or be eligible for public office, in the country where they are obliged to respect all the laws of the State, and pay military tribute to the dominant nation; in the country of their birth and life, where they aspire to be buried, Puerto Ricans who for some heretofore unknown crime—the love of their own citizenship—are reduced to the condition of being foreigners in their homeland; they are exiled from their land, and thus, out of fear, and due to the harshness of the punishment, only a tiny number of Puerto Ricans renounce the citizenship

---

3. *New York Times,* February 22, 1917, p. 20. Italics added by the editor.

Selections in this chapter:
1. Translated from *El plebiscito puertorriqueño* (San Juan: Tipografía Boletín Mercantil, 1917), pp. 75-76.
2–3. From *New York Times,* August 15, 1917, p. 4.
4. From *New York Times,* August 27, 1917, p. 8. © 1917 by the New York Times. Reprinted by permission.
5. From Woodrow Wilson, *The State: Elements of Historical and Practical Politics* (Boston: D. C. Heath, 1918), p. 357.
6. Translated from editorial in *El Mundo,* February 1, 1919.
7. From *New York Times,* March 2, 1919, p. 10. © 1919 by the New York Times. Reprinted by permission.

imposed upon them; almost all of them accept, and thus present—before the world—this unusual fact, the false demonstration that the Puerto Ricans did voluntarily and joyfully accept the citizenship of the United States, and with it abandoned the ideal of joining their country with the other free and sovereign nations of America.

[Six months after U.S. citizenship was granted, both houses of the Puerto Rican legislature sent resolutions to President Wilson, respectfully demanding complete self-government for the island. José De Diego sent the following telegram to Wilson and the Congress:]

. . . The House of Representatives has resolved unanimously to offer, through you, to the American people, a message of gratitude for the law which has caused a realization *in part of* the legitimate aspirations of the people of Porto Rico. The House also resolved to express to the people of the United States that the people of Porto Rico were ready to contribute with their blood, under the glorious flag of the United States, to the triumph of democracy throughout the world, and demand from the United States the completion of its work in Porto Rico by granting to our people the full right of self-government.

[Antonio R. Barceló, president of the insular Senate, also telegraphed the President:]

The first Porto Rican Senate greets President Wilson and relies on him and the American Congress for a greater development of the system establishing in Porto Rico a Government of and by the people to its fullest extent and purity.

[A few days later, a Puerto Rican in New York City wrote to the Editor of the *New York Times*:]

Reading your article under the heading "Texans Protest to President against Negro Soldiers in the South," I learn that the War Department contemplates the encampment of patriotic Porto Rican soldiers with the negroes in South Carolina. This plan is a great mistake and a revelation. It makes it clear that it will take long for us as a nation to understand the psychology of peoples of alien nationalities who come under our banner, and it teaches us Porto Ricans that our ultimate destiny is to possess one status in which we keep up the most cordial commercial and political relations, but as a distinct entity.

R. M. Delgado, New York, Aug. 24, 1917

[At about the same time, President Wilson saw little hope for statehood.]

With the acquisition of Porto Rico and the Philippines as a result of the war with Spain, the United States acquired noncontiguous lands, already inhabited by peoples differing from ourselves in language, customs and institutions.

Unlike the territory previously acquired—with the exception of Alaska and Hawaii—the insular possessions are not adapted for the progressive development from territories to states. They are dependencies, and will remain as such until they reach the stage when they may become independent or self-governing.

[It was not strange, then, that Puerto Ricans should be confused. One of the island's major newspapers wrote:]

We have come to the conclusion that the political program of the United States for Puerto Rico, in the final analysis, is *to have no program.* They send us diverse pieces to make a dress that does not correspond to a model or to a definite style. Congress decides that Puerto Rico is not even an incorporated territory. Evident it is that we enjoy rights, but they have not patterned a clearly defined status; they are beautiful frames for the structure, and with yearning, intelligence, and patriotism we will toil in order to select the best materials to organize them; not worrying about its outward appearance nor about the names under which the field of political architecture identifies it; but always looking toward Washington, whose Capitol is a lighthouse whose rays shine over the whole earth.

[The Puerto Rican legislature several times urged Washington to move in one direction or the other, to indicate a reasonable, sure road to end the political status dilemma. In early 1919, a headline in the *New York Times* said; "Porto Rican parties demand statehood. If that be denied, they want complete independence."]

SAN JUAN, Porto Rico, March 1—After a debate of more than two days in both houses of the Insular Legislature, the Unionists and Republicans today reached an agreement that now is the time to join forces on insisting that the American Congress make known what the future of Porto Rico is to be. It was agreed that if there can be no assurance that statehood is possible, the parties should work for independence.

The debate came after the receipt here of the full text of the speech made in the House of Representatives in Washington on Feb. 11 by the Resident Commissioner, Felix Córdova Davila, in which he urged Congress to state definitely whether statehood and complete self-government for Porto Rico were possible. If it was not possible, the commissioner told the House he would insist on complete independence. . . .

PART VII

THE GRIM YEARS

As we look back . . . we find that by 1936 we had hit a new low. . . . [We] were puzzled, distressed and angered by the sad and unacceptable plight of our society. We oscillated between frustration and revulsion. At times, incensed by our own helplessness, we felt the compulsion to close our eyes and charge. Some of the best among us did . . .

—*Jaime Benitez, President, University of Puerto Rico, in 1968*

The years between World Wars I and II were grim ones; thousands of Puerto Ricans were ravaged by starvation and disease. Absentee investors continued to acquire control of the economy, and some of them used their dollars to manipulate the elections. It was almost inevitable that, under such conditions, militant anti-American political forces should emerge.

In 1920, while Republican Presidential candidate Warren G. Harding was on the campaign trail, he spoke out against Puerto Rican independence; after his election, a number of anti-American cablegrams and letters from the island arrived in the White House. In March, 1921, Antonio Barceló, President of the Puerto Rican Senate, received a letter from Horace M. Towner, Chairman of the Committee on Insular Affairs of the U.S. House of Representatives, warning him that "friends of Porto Rico will find it difficult to help the island if this propaganda is continued. I assure you there is not now, and there is not likely to be, any considerable sentiment in this country for the independence of Porto Rico."[1]

Discord increased when President Harding paid off a political debt by appointing E. Montgomery Reilly, a Kansas City businessman, as Governor of Puerto Rico. In his inaugural address, Reilly rejected independence, adding "Neither, my friends, is there any room on this island for any flag other than

---

1. *New York Times,* March 10, 1921, p. 22.

the Stars and Stripes. So long as Old Glory waves over the United States, it
will continue to wave over Puerto Rico."

Then, in a letter to Barceló, Reilly said, "While discussing appointments,
I want you to fully understand that I shall never appoint any man to office who
is an advocate of independence. When you publicly renounce independence,
and break loose from your pernicious and un-American associates, then I will
be glad to have your recommendations."[2]

Early in 1922, Barceló's Unionist Party, trying to develop a *modus vivendi*
with Washington, removed independence from its platform, and proposed an
autonomous form of government that resembled the recently established Irish
Free State. The proposal asked that the island become an Associated Free State
(Estado Libre Asociado), the same type of status granted Puerto Rico in 1952.
But the proposal was ignored. Nor did Washington offer hopes of independence
or statehood. Puerto Rico, it seemed, was doomed to colonialism.

---

2. *New York Times,* August 18, 1927, p. 17.

IRELAND IN AMERICA?

Cayetano Coll y Cuchí was a member of the Puerto Rican House of Delegates
and of the Unionist Party. He was on record as favoring statehood for Puerto
Rico. Nevertheless, he was so irate at the unwillingness of the United States
to offer a status of political dignity to Puerto Rico that he once said: "Are we
going to be Americans? If so, all right, let us have it [statehood]. If not, let us
be independent. We would be as much an independent country in the Union
as out of it." In the following article, he traces the development of his views.

I entered public life in 1902, together with many other young men, all graduates of American universities. Almost immediately a phenomenon worthy
of note occurred. The men of my generation had been born at a time when
the radical parties in Porto Rico were engaged in their long and bitter struggle
against our Spanish rulers. We had grown up in an atmosphere of ardent longing

---

First appeared in Spanish in *Repertorio Americano,* a Costa Rican political weekly, on March
27 and April 3, 1922; later, in English translation, under the title "American Rule in Porto Rico,"
in *Living Age.* XXVII (1922), pp. 262-66.

to be free from Spain. We believed that every patriot should insist that Porto Rico become an independent republic, like her South American neighbors. All our political thinking and theories were based on these assumptions, at the time when we departed for the United States to study in the academic halls of the great Republic.

As students in American universities, we read and re-read the nation's great Declaration of Independence, and studied sedulously its Constitution and the principles upon which its government was formed, until we almost forgot the lessons of our earlier years. We spoke English better than our mother tongue. Our whole intellectual life was Anglo-Saxon. By the time we returned to Porto Rico, just as the United States was setting up a civil government in our homeland, we had thoroughly assimilated that nation's political ideals.

Naturally, we were ardent partisans of the Americanization of Porto Rico. But our old and battle-scarred leaders started an agitation against the new government Washington had imposed upon us, and when we had leisure to review our past, and to recall our glorious Castilian origin, we joined and speedily became the leaders of that movement. It fell to us, the graduates of American universities,

to voice Porto Rico's protest, to give her people a political programme, to show the logic and reason of her demands, and to become the champions of our traditions and our race.

I fancied, when I graduated, that I possessed an immense fund of political wisdom. I was filled with ardent enthusiasm for the great struggles for freedom of thought, for separation of church and state, and for the rights of man. My political standards had been formed in accordance with these doctrines. But I had forgotten my soul, which still retained the memories of my Spanish childhood. The moment that my artificial student personality came into conflict with my true native personality, with the traditions of my race, as soon as I discovered that what I had learned in the United States was repudiated by the spontaneous sentiments of my heart, I realized that it was impossible to change that part of us which God has shaped with his own hand. I still cherished profound respect for all that was great and noble and just in the North American people; but my Spanish soul asserted itself. My fellow students of Spanish ancestry passed through the same experience. It seemed to us abnegation of our rights as men, apostasy to our own higher impulses, to act otherwise than as we did. So we threw ourselves headlong into the battle to rescue our indestructible heritage— our traditions, our race, our language, our religion.

It was clearly an unequal battle. A million and a quarter people, inhabiting thirty-six hundred square miles of territory, defied one hundred and fifteen million people, possessing more than three million miles of territory. But even these figures do not measure adequately the immense power of the United States, which America's leaders so confidently expected would speedily Americanize Porto Rico and demonstrate the ease with which Anglo-Saxon civilization can establish its sway over a Spanish-American people. But we were undaunted. Political delegations from North America, the pressure of North American capital, the political philosophy of that country's thinkers, the efforts of her representatives to deprive us of our civil rights and to rob us of our Spanish civilization—all these things counted as nothing against our enthusiasm, which burned the brighter after every attempt to quench it.

So we accepted the challenge of battle, although we still welcomed, small country that we were, whatever the United States could give us that did not prevent the free development of our Spanish culture. This struggle culminated in 1909. That year an effort was made to abolish the teaching of Spanish in the public schools. Our schoolmasters were ordered to give their instruction exclusively in English.

We knew perfectly well that the soul of a people is incarnated in its language. We would have preferred being without a country, to losing our native tongue. Upon this issue, we joined battle, and spontaneously my friends and I threw ourselves into the thickest of the fight. That was quite natural. But it was the children—children of six, seven, and ten years of age—who really started the revolt. They were the first to rebel. The men at the head of the government were first apprised of the resistance to substituting English for Spanish by a pupils' strike. Children refused to attend their classes unless they might be instructed in the language of their fathers and their country.

A resort to brutal measures followed. Children were expelled from the schools. Those who did not attend English classes, or who refused to be taught in that language were turned into the streets. They could not continue their studies; their future was ruined. Then we got together and founded a Spanish school—the José de Diego Institute—where children expelled from the public schools were received and taught gratuitously.

We next appealed to the authorities at Washington. Immediately after President Wilson assumed office, we sent a commission to that city to describe the evils under which we were laboring. The President and the leaders of his party gave us a cordial welcome. A bill to confer upon us complete autonomy was submitted to Congress. Since that change could not be made immediately, Wilson sent a new Governor to the Island, to whom he gave most liberal instructions. All of the North American cabinet members were replaced by Porto Ricans.

At last we were given an autonomous regime. We elected our first independent legislature. My party, the party that championed a free Porto Rico, won in practically every precinct. The moment they had an opportunity to express their will, the Porto Rican people voted for liberty.

Then came the War. At the instance of the Administration, a bill was brought into Congress establishing compulsory military service, but expressly excluding Porto Ricans from this provision. Porto Rico protested at once, and insisted that her soldiers also should be sent to the battle fields of France, and should share both the sacrifices and glories of our national victory. Her protest was heard. Our Island, with 1,300,000 inhabitants, mobilized 140,000 soldiers, among whom there was not a single deserter. We witnessed the unusual spectacle of a people, not themselves entirely free, ready to die for the freedom of another nation, even though it were under the flag of a Government that refused them their full rights.

After the War was over, and Wilson left office, the new Administration at Washington adopted an absolutely reactionary policy toward Porto Rico. In place of the Governor appointed by President Wilson, we received a man who had previously been a commercial traveler, or something of the sort, in his own country. As soon as he arrived in Porto Rico, he began to denounce, in violent discourses, our national aspirations. Six hours after his inauguration, the Unionist party took up the challenge. The whole Island was aroused. The new Administration started out by dismissing Porto Rican officials, and replacing them with men from the United States.

So at present we are in a most unhappy situation, a situation likely to imperil seriously the good relations between our Island and the United States. The people of Porto Rico are more resolved than ever to resist such a reactionary policy, and are courageously confident that their protest will eventually be heard and their rights respected.

We cannot hold the noble people of North America responsible for the reprehensible deeds of an unjust and incompetent Governor, who has used the powers entrusted to him to serve men that are enriching themselves by oppressing a helpless community. The Porto Rican people rest their hope in a nation whose cemeteries in France are symbols of its love for liberty. We cannot conceive that the people of the United States, after liberating Poland and restoring Bohemia, will refuse freedom to Porto Rico, and thus create an Ireland in America.

What lesson does the recent history of Porto Rico, which we have here so briefly traced, teach to the Spanish-American nations? In the first place, that there are no grounds for fearing the results of the contact of Anglo-Saxon and

Spanish civilization. That is the fundamental lesson. Marvelous progress in industry, science, and commerce, and a successful pursuit of riches are not, exclusively, the patrimony of the Anglo-Saxons. But our culture of two thousand years belongs to us alone.

By studying Anglo-Saxon methods and accommodating Anglo-Saxon institutions to our own ideals and temperament, we can create Spanish-American communities where all men are equal, where there is no hereditary privilege, where justice is unbought, where every man's home is his castle. But our efforts and sacrifices will amount to naught unless the Spanish-American nations realize that they must work shoulder to shoulder. Such a union of effort, however, means something far more permanent and enduring than our present Latin-American rallies and banquets, and our exuberant floods of sentimental oratory.

We should bear in mind that we are one hundred and ten millions of people, that we dwell in the richest and most fertile territory upon the globe, and that nearly every great modern industry depends upon us for indispensable raw materials. Let us bear these facts steadily in mind as our gaze sweeps over the immense spaces of the American continent. Then we shall comprehend what Spanish-American union may come to mean; what the future of the Spanish race in the Western hemisphere may prove to be.

SWEATSHOPS ON THE SPANISH MAIN

A high birth rate, the collapse of family farms, and the seasonal nature of sugar cane employment created a huge surplus of workers—so desperately poor that they would toil for the lowest wages. This article describes the "sweatshop" type of business which emerged as a result.

Imagine yourself turning a corner in the city of Ponce, now four centuries old, and coming face to face with a modern concrete building, one tall story high, from which comes the familiar sound of the power-driven sewing machine, and reading over the door "A. Blaustein & Co., Blouse Manufacturers."

Nothing but the sound and the name is familiar. There are no overshadowing brick walls, no dark windows, no stuffy low-ceiled workrooms. Half-latticed

From G. L. Jones, *The Survey, LI* (November 15, 1923), pp. 209-10.

doors and windows admit the bright sunlight from all four sides; trade winds that blow twelve months in the year fan the workers; under the high ceiling a cushion of air as deep as a full story in an ordinary city building deflects the heat of the sun. Fancy if you can palm trees loaded with cocoanuts, bananas lusciously ripe on the stem, spreading guavas bent with their delicate fruit and a wealth of other tropical growth close to the rear of the building, and you will have a picture of surroundings such as palaces—out of the tropics—cannot boast.

The pleasing environment fades from the mind, however, when a local business man at your elbow remarks with unction on the progress manufacturing is making in Porto Rico. You remember the saying that the constitution follows the flag, but listening to the monotonous hum of the machines you are unable to keep back the cynical thought that, where profits invite, the sweatshop follows too.

With the constitution there came to Porto Rico medical science, education, prison reform, law enforcement and social order. But when, after these, there appeared the old, familiar face of the sweatshop, scarred and wrinkled, it seemed young and hopeful to Porto Rico, and now it goes by the name of industrial progress. In the United States, the sweatshop is recognized as a menace to workers and consumers; in Porto Rico it is thought of as the bearer of a kind of industrial salvation, and is welcomed by the government, business organizations and the unemployed. . . .

Hundreds and thousands are unemployed or find work irregularly, and are eager to work on any terms that will better their living conditions. To Porto Ricans of all classes, craving economic and social advancement, the need for new industries seems imperative, and their welcome to the needle trades is a hearty one. Porto Rican capital is ready to match American dollars, provided the Americans furnish the directing effort. The government backs the invitation strongly, and can point to an educational budget of $12,000,000, which emphasizes this year the addition of 300 new trade schools, as an earnest of its desire to supplement agriculture by new industries. New money in circulation seems to spell prosperity; every town is clamoring for its own row of sewing machines.

Such an invitation has very concrete appeal for the manufacturer who is facing the competition of the clothing-trade centers. Labor costs in Porto Rico may be judged from the fact that housemaids and cooks can be hired at from $4 to $15 a month, day laborers at from $.60 to $1.00 a day. The working day is as long as one chooses to make it. There are 1200 miles of paved roads, motor transportation is excellent, railroads girdle the island, tonnage rates facilitate carriage to and from the United States. It is said that the manufacturer can ship his raw materials to the island, make them up, re-ship the finished product to New York—and cut his manufacturing costs by a full third. There is of course no tariff wall to climb: Porto Rico is on a par with New Jersey or Illinois in that respect. Cheap water power, cheap and abundant labor—and no unions to deal with— give the booster a pretty good case.

Two noteworthy responses have followed these generous encouragements— the sweatshop and contract needlework in the home. In many respects, the general situation resembles that found in the old South immediately following the Civil War, when the cotton mills were introduced. Somewhat the same poverty, the same cheap power and cheap labor, found in the South by the New England mill owners, prevail in Porto Rico, accentuated by the same pressure of necessity created by the desire for higher standards of living. But the sweatshop finds advantages in Porto Rico that the cotton mill owner did not find in the South. The water power is developed and ready for him to throw in the switch, and a still greater advantage is found in the skilled hands of the Porto Rican women ready to be used in the sewing trades. The superior quality of this labor goes directly back to the time when lacemaking, drawn-work, embroidery and kindred arts flourished in the households of Spanish families, and were transmitted by them to their subjects and slaves. If this handwork seems widely separated from the field of the power-driven sewing machine and blouse making, the facts contradict it: the building of sweatshops, and the premium placed on Porto Rican garments by retailers in our American stores. For it is represented that these garments are better made than those manufactured in this country. Moreover, the adaptability of the skilled hand-workers in the sewing trades has become a part of the propaganda for more sweatshops in Porto Rico.

The hand crafts of lacemaking, drawn-work and embroidery are not for the present being sacrificed to the machine. This work is being stimulated by a system of contracts made by New York concerns that market the product. These firms have representatives all over the island who contract with native women in the villages and the hills, on a piecework basis, for fancy work, underwear, and also for dresses supposed to come from Paris. From all reports, these contracts have proved very profitable to the makers and have furnished employment to many hundreds of women, as well as material benefits to their families. The sweatshop and this home contract work have only scratched the surface of the available supply of labor. The one operates in a modern plant located in cities and towns; the other in the unsanitary shacks in which the masses of the people live. As they come into sharper competition for the choice of labor, the advantage would seem to lie with the sweatshop, for labor in Porto Rico, like any other, will sell to the highest bidder, and higher wages can be earned on the power machines than by artistic hand-work.

It took half a century to secure the existing safeguards for workers in the southern cotton mills, and the job is not finished yet. How long it will take to accomplish the same for sweatshop workers in Porto Rico it is hard to say. The proper protection of contract workers in their homes, and of the consumers of their products, is even more difficult. Where labor so greatly exceeds the demand, the workers themselves can accomplish little to improve their condition. And Porto Rico lacks experience, even if it had the desire to establish the rights of the workers. Certainly legislation now proposed in the interest of the workers, or tending to eliminate the Porto Rico manufacturer's advantage over his American competitor, would be interpreted as discouraging new industries. For that reason, if for no other, the proposal must wait upon a popular movement growing out of a more equalized supply and demand of workers . . .

"THE GENTLEMAN'S TIME HAS EXPIRED"

In 1926, Felix Córdova Dávila, Puerto Rico's Resident Commissioner in Washington, rose in the House of Representatives to ask that Congress allow the island to elect its own governor. This right would not be granted until twenty-two years later. *The Congressional Record* incorrectly calls him "Mr. Dávila," using his second—maternal—surname.

THE CHAIRMAN. . . . The gentleman from Porto Rico is recognized for 10 minutes.

MR. DAVILA. . . . We are not asking for independence. We have not lost our faith in the United States of America; and it is our honest opinion that the association of Porto Rico with this country would not only secure freedom to our people but also that happiness which is the main objective of human activities. . . . Our paramount purpose is to make our people happy, and any solution which will mean the realization of this idea will be favored by us.

But it is only fair that the Representative of Porto Rico should state once more on the floor of this House that my country will not be happy and satisfied with anything suggesting inferiority in the solution of our permanent status. We come to you on the basis of equality, always ready to share the national responsibilities and to do our duty in the supreme hour of sacrifice, but claiming

---

From *Congressional Record,* House of Representatives, March 24, 1926, pp. 6203-4.

the same privileges, rights, and liberties that are enjoyed by American citizens in the continental United States. . . .

Of course, if the granting of statehood is an impossibility, as has been held by prominent American statesmen, and if the right to complete home rule with the election of the executive [island governor] is denied to the island of Porto Rico, then we would be justified in asking for the absolute independence of our country. But it is our belief and hope that the island of Porto Rico can secure her happiness under the guidance of American institutions. We have entire confidence in the American people, and your sense of justice and our faith in the Almighty God incline us to believe that Congress will not unduly delay the recognition of our right to enjoy complete home rule with the executive elected by the people. What we need is a sincere and frank understanding, mutual confidence, and mutual respect. Most of our evils and frictions in life are due to misunderstanding. Have faith in the Porto Ricans, believe them, trust them. They are good and lovable people. They are true to this country. It was proved beyond any doubt during the crisis of the World War. But if you want to apply once more the acid test to the loyalty of the people of Porto Rico, wait till the arrival of a national crisis—God grant it will never come— and pronounce your request of us in only one word: Sacrifice. [Applause.]

MR. GARRETT of Tennessee. Mr. Chairman, will the gentleman yield?

MR. DAVILA. Yes.

MR. GARRETT of Tennessee. The gentleman desires that the people of Porto Rico be given the right to select the governor?

MR. DAVILA. Yes. We want complete home rule with the election of the governor.

THE CHAIRMAN. The time of the gentleman from Porto Rico has expired.

MR. DAVILA. May I have two minutes more?

THE CHAIRMAN. The gentleman from Porto Rico is recognized for two minutes more.

MR. DAVILA. I have introduced a bill in the House providing for the election of the executive in the year 1932. It is the same bill that unanimously passed the Senate last year and which was favorably reported by the Committee on Insular Affairs. There is no reason in the world to delay the passage of this bill, and I hope that the Committee on Insular Affairs will understand the advisability of enacting this legislation at this time. [Applause.]

THE CHAIRMAN. The time of the gentleman from Porto Rico has again expired.

LINDBERGH'S VISIT

Even nature seemed to be against the luckless colony. In 1928, Hurricane San Felipe swept through, followed four years later by Hurricane San Ciprián—the final toll, 567 dead, hundreds of thousands homeless, and more than $125 million in property damage.

Also in 1928, the island welcomed an eminent visitor, Charles Lindbergh, who was on a goodwill tour a year after his famous nonstop solo flight from New York to Paris. It was February 3, and thousands of children and adults honored the young aviator on the parade grounds of El Morro Castle. Later, at a special session of the legislature, a medal was pinned on Lindbergh's coat by Senator Antonio Barceló. Then, the Speaker of the House, José Tous Soto, read a joint resolution of the legislature, asking Lindbergh to take the following message "to your country and your people":

> You will convey a message of Porto Rico not far different from the cry of Patrick Henry—'Liberty or Death!' It is the same in substance with but a difference imposed by the change of time and conditions. The message is . . . grant us the freedom that you enjoy, for which you struggled and which you worship; which we deserve and you have promised us.[1]

Barceló and Tous Soto then sent a cablegram to President Calvin Coolidge, stating that:

> Puerto Rico feels humiliated because of the inferior condition she is subjected to in spite of the hopes that the Treaty of Paris awoke in us; in spite of the unfulfilled promises made to our people, and in spite of the repeated legitimate demands in favor of a regime that may enable our island to exercise her own sovereignty over her own internal affairs and to freely solve the grave economic situation she is undergoing.[2]

President Coolidge's reaction was an angry letter to Governor Towner on February 28, which was made public on March 15.

From *New York Times,* March 16, 1928, pp. 1, 12.

1. *New York Times,* February 4, 1928, p. 1.

2. *U.S. Congressional Record,* 70th Congress, 1st Session, March, 1928, p. 6,584.

The request is made that Porto Rico be constituted as a "free State" and not "a mere subjected colony." Certainly giving Porto Rico greater liberty than it has ever enjoyed and powers of government for the exercise of which its people are barely prepared cannot, with propriety, be said to be establishing therein "a mere subjected colony."
. . .

We found the people of Porto Rico poor and distressed, without hope for the future, ignorant, poverty-stricken and diseased, not knowing what constituted a free and democratic government and without the experience of having participated in any government. We have progressed in the relief of poverty and distress, in the eradication of disease, and have attempted with some success to inculcate in the inhabitants the basic ideas of a free, democratic government. We have now in Porto Rico a government in which the participation by Americans from the United States is indeed small. We have given to the Porto Rican practically every right and privilege which we permitted ourselves to exercise. . . .

It is not desired to leave the impression that all progress in Porto Rico was due to continental Americans. Without the cooperation and assistance of Porto Ricans progress would indeed have been negligible, but the cooperation is largely due to the encouragement of American assistance, American methods and an increase in the reward of efforts made. . . .

Perhaps no Territory in the world has received such considerate treatment in the past thirty years as has Porto Rico, and perhaps nowhere else has progress been so marked and so apparent. . . . We are certainly entitled to a large part of the credit for this situation. . . .

There is no disposition in America, and certainly not on my part, to discourage any reasonable aspiration of the people of Porto Rico . . . but it certainly is not unreasonable to ask that those who speak for Porto Rico limit their petition to those things which may be granted without a denial of such hope. Nor is it unreasonable to suggest that the people of Porto Rico, who are a part of the people of the United States, will progress with the people of the United States rather than isolated from the source from which they have received practically their only hope of progress.[1]

---

1. In Washington, Resident Commissioner Córdova Dávila replied, "There is not so much as a word in the President's letter to suggest . . . that, in holding Porto Rico, the United States derives benefits of a political and economic character." Complaining of "a point of view of American charity," Córdova Dávila declared "emphatically" that "we are not asking for charity, but for rights."—New *York Times,* April 13, 1928, p. 14.

"THE SAD CASE OF PORTO RICO"

Luis Muñoz Marín, the son of the late Resident Commissioner Muñoz Rivera, was thirty-one years old when this article was published. Born in San Juan in 1898, the young Muñoz was raised in the United States, and now began to take an active role in island affairs. At the time Muñoz wrote this, he was Economic Commissioner of the Legislature of Porto Rico in the United States. Two decades later, he would become the island's first elected governor.

Two major problems perplex the old Spanish province of Porto Rico, arising out of its enforced relationship to the United States. One deals with the consequences of American economic development, the other with cultural Americanization. Both go to the root of the drama now being acted on that gorgeous stage; both are portentous in their potentialities.

The importance of the economic problem is obvious to all, whatever their views or interests. Americanization is more insidious. The tendency works while you sleep. It changes the expression of your eyes, the form of your paunch, the tone of your voice, your hopes of Heaven, what your neighbors and your women expect of you—all without giving you a chance to fight back, without even presenting to you the dilemma of fighting back or not. Certainly no two things are more important than to have what you want and to live as spontaneously as you can manage. These two hopes are now in process of being shot to hell in my country.

The American flag found Porto Rico penniless and content. It now flies over a prosperous factory worked by slaves who have lost their land and may soon lose their guitars and their songs. In the old days most Porto Rican peasants owned a few pigs and chickens, maybe a horse or a cow, some goats, and in some way had the use of a patch of soil. Today this modest security has been replaced by a vision of opulence. There are more things that they can't get. The margin between what they have and what they can imagine has widened monstrously. While there are many more schools for their hungry children and many more roads for their bare feet, their destiny is decidedly narrower now than it was when they were part and parcel of one of the most interesting and incompetent nationalities in the world.

From Luis Muñoz Marín, *The American Mercury,* XVI, No. 62 (February, 1929). Reprinted with permission.

In 1898 Porto Rico was a semi-feudal country, typical of the old Spanish provinces in America, willing and capable of assuming with a natural grace and a natural awkwardness its position in the Spanish commonwealth of provinces, or to venture into a simple, old-fashioned Latin-American national form. Its economics were those developed by Spain in the tropical New World: fiscally rotten, socially humble and sound. Culturally, it was a slow, calm place. Racially, it shared with Costa Rica one peculiarity: a predominantly unmixed European peasantry—if Spain be Europe.

Schools were few, roads were fewer; chickens laid eggs under thatched cottages, goats cavorted outside and were corraled for a milking and sometimes killed for a stuffing, the squall of pigs and not of factory whistles woke up the countryside. Pale, wiry, moustached, sleepy-eyed men tumbled out of hammocks pulling up their trousers for the day, and barefooted women in terribly starched dresses of many colors began preparing strong coffee in iron kettles and serving it steaming in polished cocoanut shells. Although Porto Rico was not then one of the great sugar producing centres of the world, there was usually sugar at the bottom of the cocoanut and the sleepy-eyed man stirred it lazily with a wooden spoon, tasting it with his eyes and his nose. Inside the hut the brats wailed; one of them soothed itself by finding five eggs, certified by cackles, under the floor, another by plucking from the wall the image of the Virgin, printed in screaming blue and red. The men left for the field to cut cane, to lead the oxen on their sugar grinding merry-go-round, to prune or pick the coffee bushes in the sloping shade of the tall guavas, to pick and seed the cotton or sift the tobacco leaves or spade in their master's truck field. As they wound their way along the coastal plain or twisted along the precipitous mountain paths a very few pennies jingled in their pockets.

At noon the jíbaro comforted himself, for two cents, with a tumbler of rum bought at the store under the ceiba tree, and went home to a meal of codfish with sweet potatoes and rice mixed with beans. The rice and beans were plentiful; he ate of them until he had enough, and then he slept. After the day's work he loafed in the starlight, sang fantastic songs, usually depicting a topsy-turvy grandeur of some sort, made love to one or two girls, and then went home and made love to his wife.

Of a Sunday, he might with a number of his friends eat a barbecued pig, get drunk in the shade and go to cockfight. If there was sickness in the family, the master of the plantation would send his doctor, and the master's wife might send some quinine or rhubarb or cadillo leaves. I don't believe he ever went to bed hungry or muddled through a spell of sickness without attention.

As he could not read, it was unlikely that he would discover that Porto Rico's total production for the year came to something less than $9,000,000, and that 950,000 human beings were living, sleeping, eating, drinking, feasting, gambling, singing, and loving on that money.

His master, the feudal lord, rose out of an enormous mahogany bed, washed his hands and face in cold water out of an enamelled bowl with a design of roses, and breakfasted on a cup of coffee, rolls, butter, and cheese. Then he shouted for his horse and rode over his land, seeing that everyone was at work, inquiring after those who were sick or lazy, listening to gossip, giving advice on marriages. It was not until later in the morning that, coming upon a secluded bend of the stream where the pomarrosales bent over the water, he took off his clothes and bathed.

He owned his house; his hills and ravines were lightly mortgaged or not at all; he chose out of several horses for his tours of his domain; he bred, bought or swapped roosters to uphold the honor of his judgment; he fathered his men gruffly or kindly, intelligently or stupidly. Perhaps he wanted a house in the nearest town, or, perhaps not in the nearest town but in the capital of the district.

Maybe some day he would even move to San Juan. Someone had a horse or a rooster he coveted. They said that Madrid was a lively place, but it would probably bore him, so far from home, where no one would know him or greet him with deference or seek his advice. His son might be sent across to study, and might receive a visit from his parents during his last year at the university. It was a long trip though.

In San Juan, a city of many colors crowded within thick brown walls, occasional carriages clattered over the cobblestones; high ceilings made cool dark interiors; a rare cocoanut shell mounted in silver gave evidence in certain old houses of the time when glassware was an infrequent importation; the cafés were clubs where politics and women were discussed over ice cream, chocolate, or rum; and a bowlegged mulatto was famous as a procurer. Regional autonomy had been granted by Spain, and a native Cabinet with a native Premier ruled the green fields and polychromatic towns.

If you didn't own a house, you might own one. If you didn't have a carriage, you might have one. If you did have these goods and a little money in the bank for a trip to Madrid or Paris now and then, you were at the top, and peace, romance, or prestige were your remaining goals. Porto Rico was a land of opportunity. Opportunity in a serene Spanish sense. Opportunity within classes. All that a man of a given class could imagine himself as attaining, he could attain. His economic imagination wasn't stimulated by the brash parade of contraptions which were later to become badges of honor and tokens of social superiority. You didn't have much, and you could only want a little more. There was only one millionaire on the island, but there were many lords and masters of the soil.

II

Presto, the flag! The one and only. The magic carpet on which Rotary, benevolence, and interference fly over the crumbling liberties and inefficiencies of the earth. It found a dignified little world, bearing with an easy penury, playing the tiple, and dreaming of a moon which was attainable. Its servitors set to work to transform that little world into a hasty one, pushing great iron wheels, slipping innumerable bills of lading across Grand Rapids desks, and dreaming of automobiles, which are mostly unattainable. "Mother," the troubadours used to sing.

> I bought a toy
> In the market-place of love. How pretty it was, oh, how pretty it was.
> But what price I had to pay!

But soon they were singing:

> The automobile, oh, mother, is something
> That surprises all people, oh, mother,
> And is prodigious.

Spain had recently granted Porto Rico an autonomous form of government. The island was run by Porto Ricans under a responsible Cabinet system, and the Governor-General, barring his military command, was as purely ceremonial as his colleague of Canada. Porto Rico had control of her customs, a measure of treaty-making power, sixteen representatives in the Madrid Cortes. She was empowered to develop her economic life as best suited her tastes and interests. Her statesmen and politicians had the future in their hands. Theirs was the responsibility for molding this quiet lovely place into an image of unassuming prosperity and justice. Porto Rico is small, not very complex, and the task was—and is— an easy one, if only it be undertaken in a spirit of objective statesmanship, with no axes to grind.

But there seems to be a feeling in the United States against permitting others to be responsible for their own welfare. Under American rule the native Cabinet, tolerated at first, soon found its existence made unendurable by the encroachments of the Military Governors. It resigned. A mongrel system of government, under the Foraker Act, took the place of the ample autonomy established by Spain. The Lower House was elected by popular suffrage. The Cabinet was the Upper House, blithely combining legislative and executive functions. This Cabinet-Senate was composed of six Porto Ricans and five Americans, all appointed by the American authorities.

It was not difficult to find six adequate Porto Ricans. They were found. But, although a community can be ruled by a few men willing to rule it in a nice way, some kind of supporting majority is demanded by the democratic yen. So a majority was found. To be a member of this majority all you had to do was to proclaim yourself an ardent American in bad English, or in no English at all. If you were a member of the majority, you could become a street-cleaner or a health inspector, or you could recommend some poor henchman for either job.

Then the tariff wall was thrown around the island. Sugar became the chief beneficiary and cane spread over the valleys and up the hillsides like wildfire. The Spanish economy had been somewhat haphazardly predicated on small land-holding. The American economy, introduced by the Guánica, the Aguirre, the Fajardo and other great *centrales* was based on the million-dollar mill and the tight control of the surrounding countryside. By now the development of large absentee-owned sugar estates, the rapid curtailment in the planting of coffee—the natural crop of the independent farmer—, and the concentration of cigar manufacture into the hands of the American trust, have combined to make Porto Rico a land of beggars and millionaires, of flattering statistics and distressing realities. More and more it becomes a factory worked by peons, fought over by lawyers, bossed by absent industrialists, and clerked by politicians. It is now Uncle Sam's second largest sweat-shop.

It is a sweat-shop that has a company store—the United States. American dollars paid to the peons are so many tokens, redeemable in the American market exclusively, at tariff-inflated prices. The same tariff that protects the prices of sugar and tobacco, controlled by the few, skyrockets the prices of commodities that must be consumed by all. Porto Rico obtains tariff prices and pays tariff prices. The appearance of justice is maintained, but the reality is a pawnbroker's reality.

The favorable trade-balances, so naively emphasized by the official reports, are therefore a choice bit of irony. During the last twenty-eight years of American rule the island has enjoyed an unfavorable trade-balance only twice. In each of the other twenty-six years the exports have exceeded the imports in the same manner that the exports of a burglarized house exceed its imports. In brief, the renowned favorable balance is nothing but the profit of the absentee landlords and industrialists.

Here, as Al Smith would say, is the lowdown. From 1901 to 1927

$228,000,000 was extracted from Porto Rico and reported as a favorable trade-balance. But if the island had been privileged to forego that flattering balance, a reasonable proportion of those millions would have gone into the development of its industrial resources. As the whole island is now valued at about $300,000,000, the effect of such reinvestment on the living standards of its overcrowded population would have been very important. To the American people, on the other hand, that money spread over that number of years, means nothing. Its ingress, even in one single year would have no more appreciable effect on their prosperity than a bucket of water on the tides of the Great Lakes. Yet these life-giving pennies have been filched from the pocket of a pauper by the fingers of an opulent kleptomaniac.

Of course, no such gorgeous dividends could have been declared had not the influence of American enterprise and the actual investment of American capital increased Porto Rico's output of dollars so fabulously. Certainly, the imperialists could argue if they felt compelled to, those millions represent but a small percentage of the increase of wealth brought about by the American regime. In dollars, they represent a profit of 16%. In value they represent incalculably more. The operation of the tariff against the consumer and the expanding land monopoly explain the discrepancy. So far as the bulk of the population is concerned, only an eighty-cent wage paid during six months of the year to the head of each family, and redeemable only in the world's highest market, separates them from the angels.

III

It is close contact with the United States rather than the influence of the small group of resident Americans that has given a decided, if superficial, direction to the institutional life of the island. The Y.M.C.A. has its swimming pool, its basket ball court, its inspirational talks, but I doubt that such implied notions as Christ's disapproval of cigarettes get much serious attention from the local young men. Rotary slaps backs, sings, and hears speeches in a bored and genial way, but when I gave it a somewhat fantastic talk on the culture of light ladies as an index of civilization, the members really had a good time. The Elks and Odd Fellows play with their rituals, charity becomes slightly organized, evangelical preachers thunder in the villages. Holy Rollers roll in the back alleys, three or four prominent citizens become Protestants and are considered funny, women are beginning to be feared as the rolling-pin follows the flag, virginity still abounds and often attains to old age, but is perceptibly on the wane.

It is probably through the women that the largest doses of Americanism are being administered. The Latin-American attitude in this respect is confusing to a narrowly egalitarian world. Certainly we are wont to make a sharp nonsensical distinction between good and bad women—there is hardly any middle ground between chastity and prostitution. But this has not heretofore meant that the mere goodness of good women gave them any appreciable influence on the social point of view. Good women have been powerless and tame among us, and have grown smug in the consciousness of their hard luck. Generally speaking, there were only four things Latin women could be: old maids, wives, mistresses, or prostitutes. Now they can be girls. They can be girls for a long time.

They can also be stenographers, bookkeepers, telephone operators, shop assistants, and feminists. They may speak in public and harass legislators.

Porto Rican politicians may now be publicly accused of keeping mistresses. The charge doesn't come near defeating them, but evidently there is some suggestion in the atmosphere that makes it seem relevant. Twenty years ago it would have seemed preposterous to advance such an argument as in any way affecting a man's fitness for office.

The indications are that we may soon find ourselves adopting a subtly feminized point of view as unsatisfactory to both men and women as the one now prevailing in the United States. The change, in spite of the stupid simplicity of our traditional mores, would seem to be for the worse. We were groping toward adjustment; now we are drifting toward equality.

There are two kinds of Americanized Porto Ricans: the young men freely and spontaneously shaped into the image of whatever happens to be the Young Generation up here, just as young Germans, Italians, and Swedes are shaped in New York or Pittsburgh; and the older fellows who Americanize themselves out of a sense of their inadequacy as Porto Ricans. The former may be as charming and as innocuous as the youths who play tennis in the Saturday Evening Post. The latter are a sight for the gods. Their manner is as unctuous as that of Y.M.C.A. secretaries and quite as unreal. They approve and disapprove of many things. They have Ethics and go in for Service. They emphasize the importance of their smallest actions to the working of the sacred social machinery. They need the crutch of a principle to support their conduct as it hobbles along the straight and narrow path where the primroses grow—and, of course, they always find one.

Whether as a result of American tailoring or of psycho-biological imitation, their paunches no longer grow in the reticent Spanish fashion, but rather in the aggressive, imperialistic, genial American fashion. They are gregarious and dull and oversimian, and try pathetically to find innocent amusements. They immolate the paramount heritage of Spain—individuality—in the altar of regular-fellowship. The girls don't like them, and I maliciously suggest this fact as an issue to the Porto Rican nationalists.

The tone of life in the cities has been speeded up. A certain efficiency is observable. Clerks take shorter siestas after lunch. Telephone connections are quickly achieved, although private messages may still be conveyed through the operators if they like your voice. Transportation is rapid and cheap. Good liquor is delivered within a few minutes—Scotch, $5 a quart; champagne, $7; Holland gin, $8. Soda fountains suffuse the narrow streets with their sweet odor. Cafés are arranged to look more and more like glittering American beaneries, but conversation and not food is still the major inducement for tarrying in them.

The population is about as susceptible to nationalist emotions as to American manners. While the latter grow like a monstrous parasite on the island's Latinity, it remains a fact that whenever a politician of intelligence and prestige has taken up the issue of national independence, he has swayed the island. It is the students at the university, however, who give expression to the most conscious and complex form of nationalism, not only as a sovereign control of the jobs, but as a cultural continuity.

They don't want the local temperament violated by the bayonets of education or by the contagion imminent in close commercial relationships. They want Porto Rico to be Porto Rico, not a lame replica of Ohio or Arizona. They want its spirit to be part of the great Spanish spirit, now in process of saving itself from its political and economic ruin.

IV

The university authorities, under the leadership of Dr. Thomas Benner, who is far from sharing the political viewpoint of the students, follow a policy that is friendly to this end. The university can boast of the most brilliant Spanish department on American territory. It is in fact among the soundest of any to be found in Spanish-speaking countries, having enjoyed at one time or another the services of such men as Vasconcelos, ex-Minister of Education of Mexico; De Onís, head of the Spanish department at Columbia; Amado Alonso, of the Centre de Estudios Históricos of Madrid; Américo Castro of Oxford, and many other first-rate men.

What effect this may have on the destiny of the island is of course doubtful. However, saving a culture, even an inferior one, from becoming the monkey of another, even a superior one, is a good in itself. And in the present case it is by no means certain that the heritage shared by Porto Rico is to be unfavourably compared with the heritage to which the blind forces of production and exchange now seek to hook it up.

The haphazard manner in which the character of the island spars for survival may influence its political future. Whether the island is to be semi-independent, like Cuba, or autonomous under some special dispensation of Congress, is a question to be determined by the interplay of politic and economic interest. But it is certain that it will never be incorporated into the Union as a State save through the operation of cultural forces: that is, not unless, and until, our manner of life and thought has been respectably Americanized.

Will this ever come about? Will the island retain its historical personality? An unqualified answer to either of these questions would necessarily fall short of the possibilities. Perhaps a more absurd fate is in store for us. Perhaps we are destined to be neither Porto Ricans nor Americans, but merely puppets of a mongrel state of mind, susceptible to American thinking and proud of Latin thought, subservient to American living and worshipful of the ancestral way of life. Perhaps we are to discuss Cervantes and eat pork and beans in the Child's restaurant that must be opened sooner or later. Perhaps we will try not to let mother catch us reading the picaresque verses of Quevedo. Perhaps we are going to a singularly fantastic and painless hell in our own sweet way. Perhaps all this is nothing but a foretaste of Pan-Americanism.

"JOKER IN THE DECK"

[In scrutinizing Puerto Rico's apparently favorable economic trade balance, two American authors reveal the "joker in the deck"—the fact that most of the benefits accrue to absentee investors. This book excerpt shows in considerable detail how U.S. corporations quickly monopolized the economy of Puerto Rico. The authors discuss the impact upon the island worker who is "forced to work for a wage far below his needs," and ask the question, "Can we (the United States) govern the island for its own best interests?"]

After thirty-two years of American occupation . . . anyone who wishes to face the truth of the situation must recognize that the progress made in certain lines has been astounding. No country ever started nearer the bottom than Porto Rico did and few, if any have ever set about climbing in any more determined manner. . . .

From Bailey W. Diffie and Justin Whitfield Diffie, *The Broken Pledge* (New York: The Vanguard Press, 1931), pp. 199-220. Reprinted by permission.

Among the most prominent changes . . . are those in the realm of economics. . . . Fruit growing sprang from nothing in 1898 to occupy the third place in value of the agricultural exports in recent years. . . . This crop is more nearly dominated by local men . . . but still the percentage of absentee ownership is large, and will probably increase. . . .

About one per cent of the cultivated area was in tobacco in 1898 and today the percentage is more than five. . . . Today it is the second industry in importance, being surpassed only by sugar.

The sugar industry . . . furnishes more than half of the exports and at least half, if not more, of the wealth is due to this one business alone. Occupying but 15 per cent of the cultivated area at the time of the American occupation, it today claims more than 44 per cent of all the land in cultivation. . . .

The needlework industry, famous for its quality but not for its quantity in 1898, reversed this and by 1929 showed an export trade of . . . $15,000,000. The total export trade, made up in the main of the four industries just named, grew from less than $5,000,000 gold in [1897] . . . to more than $100,000,000 in 1928. The apparent trade balance has been in favor of Porto Rican products almost continuously in the last 32 years, becoming adverse only when some unusual upset like the hurricane of 1928 struck the Island.

But this favorable trade balance has long been proclaimed the "joker in the deck" by the Islanders. . . . In 1928 the apparent excess in favor of the Island was more than $14,000,000. . . . That this was a false balance may be seen . . . in casting up the items resulting in a net outgo from Porto Rico. Freight payments to steamship companies and marine insurance, commissions collected by outside houses, remittances to Porto Ricans abroad, tourist expenses, other types of insurance, motion picture royalties, lottery tickets bought in the lotteries of Spain, Santo Domingo and other nations, interest, dividends, rents and miscellaneous items amounted to more than 125,000,000, leaving a net deficiency for all trade and service operations of something over $10,000,000. . . .

In other words, each year shows a net deficit of several million dollars which has been met so far by handing over Porto Rico, bit by bit, to the absentee. . . .

Let us turn now to what social improvements have been made with this vast new wealth and revenue. . . . Few countries can match the road building achievements of the Porto Ricans in the last generation. Unaided they have built more than 1,500 kilometres of hard-surfaced roads in regions which would defy a mountain goat. . . . Public health, too, has engaged the interest of Porto Rican statesmen . . . As a result, the death rate was lowered from an average of 30 per thousand for the period from 1888 to 1892 to about 23 per thousand for the ten year period ending with 1930. But it is in the field of education that we find the most decided progress . . . expenditures increased to where they claim more than 38 per cent of the Insular budget. . . . Illiteracy has decreased from around 80 per cent to something less than 50. The number of schools increased from 560 to 2,238. The total registration of pupils was less than 30,000 in 1898 and by 1928 had increased to 230,000. . . .

But what is the American share in Porto Rican progress? There are some who point to every forward step as the work of the United States. . . .

Hundreds of American teachers have gone to Porto Rico to teach English, but they were paid with Porto Rican dollars. None of this came out of the public purse of the United States. Their salaries, along with other expense attached to English instruction, have been a crushing burden on the slender resources of the Island. Why spend millions of dollars to teach English to people who were 80 per cent illiterate, in preference to teaching them their own language? Why teach them English when the majority live and die within twenty miles of the ocean and never see it? Why teach them English when they are ragged, hungry, unskilled and might better have learned a trade or been taught something of scientific agriculture? The last thing that the Porto Rican masses needed was English. . . . And to the teaching of English the American Government has never contributed one penny. Only to the College of Agriculture have we given financial assistance. . . . But in spite of the burden placed on the Insular and Municipal Governments for education there are almost 300,000 children for whom there are no school facilities. . . .

In the field of public health we have been equally as liberal. Outside of a meager amount of work carried on by the Army there has never been any serious effort to stamp out the atrocious health conditions . . . [which] today can be depicted in just about the same language as in 1898. Diphtheria has been increasing constantly since 1915, while in the United States it has decreased 95 per cent since 1900. Typhoid tells the same story. . . . The death rate from tuberculosis is likewise growing. . . . The dreaded hook-worm disease has still the preferred place among the causes of sickness, and though thousands are cured each year the poor cannot afford the necessary shoes to protect them from reinfection.

When we come to our participation in road building, we find a record wholly devoid of anything to which the continental American can point with his accustomed pride. . . . Up to the hurricane of 1928, the United States Government had never contributed one cent for road building in Porto Rico. All of the more than 1,200 miles of hard-surface roads have been built by Porto Rican initiative and with Porto Rican money. . . .

But where the American Government has been neglectful, American capital has not. In every branch of Porto Rican business, American corporations have steadily absorbed the interest once belonging to Spaniards, or natives. The sugar industry, tobacco manufacturing, fruit growing, banks, railroads, public utilities, steamship lines and many lesser businesses are partially or completely dominated by outside capital. . . .

Approximately 60 per cent of the [sugar] crop is ground by American and other absentee companies. Sugar cane growing has absorbed about all of the fertile valley land, and the absentee companies dominate the four chief sugar cane sections. More than 100,000 acres of the most fertile soil are the property of men who seldom or never see the Island and who have no interest in it except to make it pay dividends.

The assets of the four principal companies, all American companies owned by men who for the most part dwell outside Porto Rico, were more than $63,000,000 in 1928. These properties have paid dividends over long periods sufficient to replace their original investment many times over. From 10 to 30 per cent per annum is the rule and dividends exceeding 100 per cent a year have been known.

An examination of the taxes paid on their holdings show them to be at most half and sometimes not even one-fourth of the true value. . . . In 1928, the Aguirre Sugar Company was assessed at less than $4,500,000 and its net income capitalized at 10 percent was more than $27,000,000! . . . High profits and low assessments have not inspired these companies to be liberal with Porto Rico or the Porto Ricans. The *colono,* the farmer who grows the cane, is receiving his substance from the little end of the funnel. He gets less than 65 per cent of the sugar from his cane, but has to pay 80 to 89 per cent of the cost of production. The cost of financing his crop, the low return he receives, the disadvantage in which he finds himself compared with the owners of the sugar manufacturing Centrals is tending to drive him out of his farm and make of him a day laborer. The result is that his land is passing into the hands of a few large corporations, in opposition to the Organic Law of Porto Rico, which forbids corporate ownership of land in excess of 500 acres. The Congress of the United States which passed this provision and placed it in the Organic Law of Porto Rico has never bothered to make it effective. The men who own the sugar companies control both the Bureau of Insular Affairs and the Legislature of Porto Rico. . . .

The effect of this land concentration has been disastrous to the agricultural economy. While sugar acreage was increasing almost four times, crops devoted to food were declining to about two-thirds their former acreage. . . . Porto Rico has only one acre of food crops today for every 15 people, whereas only 30 years ago she had an acre for every six people. . . . After 30 years of sugar economy, during which time millions have been made from Porto Rican soil, Porto Rico is facing the fact that sugar has not paid. . . . Tobacco may have paid the grower a little better return, but it is the absentee capitalist who has made the real profit. . . . The case of fruit is somewhat different. This crop is owned more largely by residents who live on the land and market their own product. Sugar and tobacco have paid the manufacturer; fruit has paid the owner; but none of them has paid the laborer!

. . . this monopolization . . . is carried into every branch of business. Practically every mile of public carrier railroad in the Island belongs to two companies—the Ponce and Guayama and the American Railroad Company, which are largely absentee owned. . . . The public utility service is likewise the property of those who for the main part live outside Porto Rico. Every trolley ride taken by a Porto Rican pays tribute to a foreign owner, and about half the towns depend on absentee companies for their lights and power, and more than half the telephone calls go over wires owned by outsiders. . . .

. . . . the island consumer . . . is buying in the dearest market in the world, or he pays such a high tariff that the resulting price is many times what it would otherwise be. The price of rice, his chief food, is more than doubled. Beans, potatoes, bread—in fact everything he eats—cost him twice what they would in the cheapest market. And this same tariff, while apparently protecting him, is rendering him every day more subservient to the absentee interests.

The native is forced to work for a wage far below his needs. The unemployment situation, like that of many other countries, is a temporary problem that has become permanent. Starting in 1899 with only 17 per cent unemployed, Porto Rico has made such startling progress in this line that she had 36 per cent unemployment in 1929. . . . This good business for the owner has driven the wage down to where the day laborer is compelled to work 33 days to supply himself with rice today, as against 25 in 1898. He spends more than 20 days for flour now, whereas only 10 were formerly necessary, and for his dry vegetables the number of days work rose from three and a half to more than 13. Altogether he must today spend 104 days working to buy imported foods that once cost him only 70 days to work!

. . . the Porto Rican . . . uses more of his income for food than the Oriental laborer does, about 94 per cent being so spent, as compared with only 90 per cent in the Far East. . . . What seems more incredible, he pays in actual money more for the same foods than the New York City laborer! By actual test, 17 articles comprising 65 per cent of the food used by the Porto Rican *jíbaro* cost from eight to 14 per cent more than the same articles in New York City. . . .

The average Continental American will immediately say that Porto Rico's troubles are vestiges of the evil and incompetent Spanish regime. The patriotic

Porto Rican nationalist believes just as firmly that the breeze which unfurled
the stars and stripes was an evil breath which has since that time cursed the
Island. Neither of these opinions can be entirely correct. . . . Porto Rico was a
sadly neglected little Island during most of its existence. . . . It was in such condition when it fell into the willing lap of Uncle Sam. Why it is still in about the
same condition is a question that should be of interest to every American and
a true answer might do something to rectify our present policy of "muddling
along" with our possessions. . . .

The injunction of President McKinley to the first governor to "prepare them
for statehood as rapidly as possible" was in the mind of the United States the
only solution needed. Once they had statehood they would automatically
become a 49th section of paradise! . . .

Officially, the United States has been doctoring its patient for thirty-two
years without counting the pulse or taking the temperature. The first reason we
can assign, then, for American failure to remedy bad conditions, is the failure
to diagnose the trouble and to meet the issue squarely once the trouble was
known.

The second is a peculiar mixture of "laissez-faire" and mercantilism of the
twentieth century type. We are great worshippers of "give business a free rein"
and of "rugged individualism." We seem to believe honestly that all a man
needs is a chance, to become a president or a Henry Ford, regardless of the fact
that we have only one president at a time and only one Henry Ford. . . .

. . . the bitterest complaint against us today is not on political grounds; nor
are the main problems political. It is the economic and social condition which
draws the shafts of critics, and these are the ones most in need of solving. . . .

The problem of the United States in Porto Rico . . . resolves itself into one
question: can we govern the island for its own best interests? As long as the
United States Government has the ultimate word in policies, the island will be
governed for the good of those interests considered "American." Porto Rico is
at once the perfect example of what economic imperialism does for a country
and of the attitude of the imperialist towards that country. Ragged, hungry, diseased and dispossessed, Porto Rico has just been examined by the President of
the United States and has been given his official approval. Its land owned by
absentee capital; its political rights resting in the hands of the United States
Government; its people in the depths of deprivation, it has been told to help itself. That is the "remedy" which the President prescribes—imperialism's answer to problems of its own creation! . . . Porto Rico can hope for no relief
under the existing system. This is well proved in the fact that the President of
the United States visited Porto Rico and "saw that it was good."

THE RISE OF ALBIZU CAMPOS

The Great Depression in the United States hit Puerto Rico with extra force, tumbling wages from their already miserable level. In 1933, a study on the offshore municipality of Vieques Island showed that its 11,000 inhabitants were surviving on a *total* income of $500 a week—less than seven cents per person, daily.

In the political arena, many of Washington's appointed American officials were inept, and at least one governor misused public funds. The U.S. sugar corporations had strong lobbying power in Congress, and in the colonial legislature.

Relief and public works projects, founded after Franklin D. Roosevelt's "New Deal" government took power in 1933, staved off starvation for many, but these programs were—at best—a cosmetic cure for a host of deeply rooted ills.

Four years earlier, Theodore Roosevelt, Jr. was named Governor of Puerto Rico by President Herbert Hoover (he served in the post from April 7, 1929 to January 18, 1932).

Like his father, Roosevelt was an energetic man, who traveled through the island's poverty-stricken countryside and saw "farm after farm where lean, underfed women and sickly men repeated again and again the same story—little food and no opportunity to get more."

"I have seen mothers," he wrote, "carrying babies who were little skeletons, I have watched in a class-room thin, pallid, little boys and girls trying to spur their brains to action when their little bodies were underfed. I have seen them trying to study on only one scanty meal a day, a meal of a few beans and some rice. I have looked into the kitchens of houses where a handful of beans and a few plantains were the fare for the entire family."[1]

The Nationalist Party, headed by Pedro Albizu Campos, became a focal point for radical protest, and—though few Puerto Ricans would admit it—a loudspeaker for the pent-up anger and frustration of the long-silent, long-abused masses.

Pedro Albizu Campos was a graduate of Harvard Law School and served as a second lieutenant in the U.S. Army during World War I.

He entered politics in the 1920's, and, by 1930, was president of the Puerto Rican Nationalist Party. During the 1932 elections, the party received 5,300 votes; from then on, Albizu preached abstention from "the colonial elections."

"Puerto Rico must create a grave crisis for the colonial administration in

---

Translated from *Claridad,* Puerto Rico, November 1, 1970.

1. *Review of Reviews,* January, 1930, which was a condensation of a December 8, 1929, article in the *New York Herald Tribune Magazine.*

order that its demands be heard. . . . A nation like the United States, with enormous national and international problems, has no time to pay attention to submissive, servile men. What is needed is a rebel organization . . . to make a clean break with the colonial regime, and to request recognition of our independence from the free nations of the world," he wrote.

"Nationalism," he wrote later, "is the only salvation, because it causes to be reborn in each of us the conscience of a free man, for whom human dignity is priceless, and who cannot conceive why he should not have the right to direct the destinies of his children or his homeland."[2]

Although always in the minority during the next two decades, the Nationalists had moments of genuine popular support. Albizu was a fiery, compelling speaker, and a man who did not shrink from his self-appointed role as martyr for the cause of independence. Here are excerpts from one of his speeches, made in 1930 "to mark the first 30 years of *yanqui* intervention." It was a prelude to a long, turbulent career, marked by violence and imprisonment in Federal jails. Albizu died in 1965, after a long illness that left him partially paralyzed. Puerto Rico's pro-independence militants regard Pedro Albizu as the "apostle" of their cause, and they have adopted as their slogan his statement: "*La patria es valor y sacrificio*" (The homeland is courage and sacrifice).

Although the sinister purpose of the United States was always to take possession of the Antilles, convert the Caribbean into a *yanqui* lake, and thus exercise strategic influence over Mexico, and Central and South America, the true purpose of the conquest could not be revealed to the North American people. They were told of a war for humanitarian reasons. The case of Cuba and Puerto Rico under Spanish sovereignty was presented as something so intolerable to civilization that it forced a nation, anxious not to disturb the peace, to interfere, so that our right to freedom would be respected.
. . .

The *yanqui* invasion in 1898 . . . meant the coming of a regime of liberty, equality, fraternity, and material prosperity, to judge by *yanqui* propaganda. And all that happiness would be generally heaped upon us by North American philanthropy and humanity. The invaders imposed the Treaty of Paris upon Spain. We were never consulted in the preparation or approval of the treaty. They forced Spain to cede Puerto Rico, as war indemnity.

All this revealed the true face of *yanqui* humanitarianism, but their propa-

---

2. Translated from *El Mundo,* November 16, 1933.

ganda did away with Boricuan [Puerto Rican] concern, and with international suspicion.

Puerto Ricans—without distinction of political party—offered to cooperate in this supposed coming of liberty.

No one believed that the invader had decided to profane mankind's most sacred words.

They imposed a regime with absolute powers, to control all taxes and privileges, and to determine the displacement of all native wealth into the hands of the invaders. Thus, agriculture, industry, commerce, and the communications media all practically became theirs.

Today, barely twenty per cent of these [sectors of the economy] are under native control.

Voices of alarm, shouts of patriotism, and imprecations against the invader were heard.

But *yanqui* propaganda again benumbed the Boricuan conscience. With our fears becalmed, we were presented to ourselves and nations abroad as a country enjoying extraordinary prosperity, owing exclusively to the presence of the magical North American flag.

Workers came to believe that their good salaries depended upon the *yanqui* government; many intellectuals pinned their greatest hopes on occupying a high position in the North American Government, especially in the diplomatic and consular service; farm owners were warned against the possible demagoguery of the working class; commerce was attracted by the supposed advantages of tariff-free transportation between Puerto Rico and the United States; businessmen became convinced that they ought to deposit their money in the banks of the invaders, because *yanqui* propaganda subtly accused everyone of lack of honesty; teachers were convinced that they should teach everything in English; in sum, the nation assented to its moral and material dismemberment, anesthetized by so-called good intentions.

The patriotism of some natives was not enough.

The worker could not believe that the *yanqui* government was actually encouraging *latifundismo* and absentee-ownership, and the destruction of all native industries, so that unemployment would grow on a large scale, and so that cheap labor would be available, in order for *yanqui* corporations to accumulate enormous profits.

Commerce lost all sense of accounting. It did not expect its own inevitable bankruptcy, as a result of the tariff-free structure that requires us to sell to the *yanqui* at the price he wishes to pay, and to buy from him at the price he wishes to stipulate.

The naive businessman, attracted by foreign propaganda, believed that the branches of foreign banks were backed by many millions of dollars, and deposited his cash in them, so that the invader could finance his own enterprise; with this money retired from the market, interest rates were raised, making it impossible for native business to survive.

The land owner became a slave of exploitative enterprises, and sooner or later had to hand over his farm to the creditors who hounded him.

The government assessed his farm at the highest price possible. But foreign interests were—and are—permitted to hide all types of wealth; low prices are fixed for their declared wealth, and their nonpayment of taxes is tolerated.

Meanwhile, year after year, native farms are systematically auctioned off, in many cases for less than two dollars.

Still, with the excuse of teaching English, a public education system is maintained that uses the language of the invader as the only vehicle for instruction, at a cost of $4 million a year. In reality, English is not taught, and the only result is to brutalize our young, forcing them to study science, and Latin, in English, and languages in the tongue of the invader.

The invader reached the point where he no longer needed to justify himself. There were paid natives to do it for him. Thus, we have outstanding "pedagogues" in the Department of Education sanctioning the barbarities that we have pointed out.

Lawyers to defend foreign interests are in abundance.

There is a group of pseudointellectuals who have dared to preach the creation of a hybrid type, a monster that is half *yanqui,* half Boricua.

North American propaganda had triumphed. Despite these facts, it insisted that our prosperity was real, and that ours was a most advanced civilization.

Abroad, we were advertised as a prosperous, happy people, enjoying such a good standard of life that we deserved to be emulated.

Then, a nationalist movement arose, that refused to be trapped in colonialism. It sought international cooperation. It pointed out the lie of North American kindness in Puerto Rico. It is painful to confess, but even abroad there were Puerto Ricans who accepted the assignment of the government to continue maintaining its falsehoods.

With public opinion focused upon the nations of our race, the colonial legislature sent a cablegram to the Sixth American Conference, being held in Havana.

Everyone knows how that message produced such anger in the despot [President] Coolidge.

In his reply, although he continues to claim that Puerto Rico's progress is owing exclusively to North American leadership, he outlined the new propaganda of misery. When Puerto Rico was supposed to be prosperous and happy under the American flag, there was no reason to lower it. Now that the island is composed of suffering hungry people, there is no reason to lower the flag, either, because it is needed to help our people.

With the propaganda of prosperity worn out, the propaganda of misery is begun.

Then came the San Felipe hurricane, and colonial Governor Roosevelt, to justify our poverty.

This man, with the sense of a vulgar *barrio* politician, tries to pass as our friend; he goes up into the mountains, and takes photographs of our nudity and our hunger. Propaganda in the United States asks for public and private North American charity, alleging that we have no resources to attend to our needs.

The gullible fall quickly. The servile, as always, grow emotional over the voice of the master. Others fear to fight him. All applaud.

The Nationalist Party raises its voice of protest against this perverse propaganda, which demeans our prestige as a people.

The party says this, in the very legislature of the colony. It points out that there is neither public nor private charity in the United States for Puerto Rico. It affirms, with dignity, that if there were, we do not want it. We only demand justice for our nationhood.

The colonial governor asks for special powers from the legislature to solve the supposed crisis. He walks right into the Capitol building to give orders. No one dares protest against his presence.

He wants all municipal administration to be submitted to his complete authority—which is the only thing that is partially in Puerto Rican hands. There are suspicions. The legislature refuses.

But, he obtains from the legislature the creation of various bureaus that will function under his direct command. They are too important to be located in any department of the cabinet. . . .

He speaks of industrializing the country. Everyone is confounded by such a pleasing hope.

He introduces the party leaders in the legislature to the David-son Brothers, as our saviors. These newcomers are going to build, Roosevelt says, a great refrigeration plant for native fruits; they have many millions of dollars, and they can distribute many millions.

But the Legislature must give them 6,000 square meters of land on San Juan's waterfront, to build the great docks that will permit the entry of large ships. The solvency of Davidson Brothers is investigated. They are incorporated in Florida with a capital of $25,000.

We have just been informed that these gentlemen are mere agents for the *yanqui* octopus, the United Fruit Company, and now we understand the presence in San Juan of a representative of United Fruit.

We say that we shall not permit our misery to be used as an excuse to rob us. The industrialization gets off to a bad start.

Now, Roosevelt tries to make us believe that the salvation of Puerto Rico depends upon a donation of $3,000,000 from the United States Congress, which has always begrudged the expenditure of a cent. . . .

Three million! What good are three million for solving a national crisis? Let us stop this farce. . . .

And now we have the report of the Brookings Institute. Its publication coincides with the presence of Roosevelt in the United States.

This surprises no one who understands something of the *yanqui* propaganda system.

The "experts" paint a gloomy picture. They recommend drastic measures to solve the crisis. Let us see a few: Eliminate the colonial senate!

In practice, this body has never existed. It has always submitted to the will of the colonial governor. . . .

Since the colonial legislature is a comedy, accepted until now, according to the Institute, it would not be surprising if it accepted bare-faced despotism.

It is dangerous to maintain a comedy, if you give serious actors the opportunity to convert it into a tragedy.

Restrict municipal power, increase the direct central power emanating from Washington, etc., etc., are measures necessary for our salvation, according to these "experts."

The important thing is to legalize *latifundismo* [they say]. The law restricting land ownership to 500 acres should *be* eliminated, because it no longer exists. The colonial legislature never enforced it.

Let Puerto Rico be a factory. Peons, foremen, and cheap policemen are needed. A factory needs neither a legislature nor political power.

We must economize. Get rid of superfluous jobs. When all of Puerto Rico's wealth passes to the invaders, they, for the first time, will have to carry the entire weight of the budget. There will no longer be natives to cover up their expenses.

Public power will openly be a department of the administration of the factory.

Puerto Rico will be another Hawaii. Puerto Ricans will be peons, foremen, and policemen, to guarantee the invaders the enjoyment of our riches, and to oppose any complaints that might arise.

And, still, some people dare plead for tolerance of the invader. The time has come to apply sanctions against those who cooperate with the invader.

There is misery, but not for lack of resources.

The monopolizing of these resources must be discouraged. We must distribute them among our people. The legion of landowners that we had in 1898 must rise again.

The Nationalist Party is not surprised by the declarations of the Brookings Institute. We know the maquinations [sic] of *yanqui* propaganda. . . .

The politicians not in our party must be warned that the Puerto Rican nation demands the immediate suppression of this regime, and it will not permit itself to be disoriented in its effort to definitely end this situation.

We shall not tolerate feigned acts of rebelliousness. If there is sincerity—as is to be expected—before this great collective tragedy, why not call together immediately the general assemblies of each party, and resolve to demand recognition of our right to constitute a free, independent nation? The Puerto Rican nation demands definite action from those who pretend to be her representatives.

REBELLION IN PUERTO RICO

[n 1933, an eminent U.S. historian described the situation in "our one Latin American colony (which) would without question vote to leave us tomorrow if given a chance." His article is a strong indictment of the patronage system employed in appointing overseas representatives of the U.S. Government.

Two of the smaller Atlantic islands—Manhattan and Puerto Rico—now have a common bond. President Roosevelt gave both to Postmaster Parley. Parley picked Joseph McKee to rule Manhattan and Robert Gore to rule Puerto Rico. Both islands rebelled; Manhattan has achieved a rousing success, and Puerto Rico will probably soon rid itself of Gore.

In the long story of American ineptitude in Puerto Rico the last chapter must be written down as the most melancholy. For thirty-five years we have extended what General Miles termed in 1898 "the fostering arm of a nation of free people." The governors bestowed by this fostering arm have usually been gen-

From Hubert Herring, "Rebellion in Puerto Rico," *The Nation,* CXXXVII (Nov. 29,1933), pp. 618-19.

tlemen of good intentions; they have perhaps been deserving of political favors; they have rarely been distinguished for their ability. The worst was Mont Reilly, Harding's gift; the best, Theodore Roosevelt, Hoover's appointee; the dullest and most pathetic, Robert Gore, lifted from oblivion by Parley and about to be retired to oblivion by the grace of God, supported by the rage of the Puerto Rican people.

The case of Robert Gore might be forgotten were there not danger that the President may absent-mindedly allow his postmaster to repeat the performance. That cannot be, and the record must contain the entry showing the price which we exact from our subject people in Puerto Rico in the name of political expediency. Mr. Gore had made money in Florida and spent large sums on the Roosevelt cause. He was given Puerto Rico. True, he had other qualifications —genuine human sympathy and vestigial traces of a liberalism acquired in the days of Eugene Debs. He went to Puerto Rico in the sincere hope of translating the ethical ideals of the New Deal into practical terms for the island. He saw the struggle between the possessors and the dispossessed. He wanted to do something about it. That from the beginning he was unable to obtain results commensurate with his sympathies was because of defects of the head, not the heart.

It is reported that when he was appointed, Mr. Gore was not quite sure where Puerto Rico was. After a talk with him, it is clear to me that he is still confused on that point. Someone in Washington, someone near the Great White Throne, told Mr. Gore that the Puerto Ricans were children, and that the wise governor would treat them as children. The unnamed misinformant should be warned not to make that mistake again. Whatever may be said of the Puerto Ricans, they are not children. For 400 years they served Spain. Other colonies revolted and escaped, but Puerto Rico was peaceful and small. The Puerto Ricans had recourse to politics, and they became expert. They outplayed Spanish governors and cabinets systematically and malevolently. Mr. Gore arrived with his trunkload of colored beads; the politicians took his beads away from him, they took everything from him, and he is returning to the United States, unhappy and sick, with no glimmer of an idea what happened in this island, seemingly so innocent and peaceful. He is, however, obsessed by the conviction that the island is seething with a dreadful thing which he calls "anti-Americanism." Those who oppose him are perforce "anti-Americans."

From the beginning Mr. Gore talked and played politics. His predecessor, Theodore Roosevelt, had escaped that pitfall; he had talked about the suffering children, about the exploited needle-workers, about the plight of the sugar workers. But Gore put his head into the political trap, and it clamped down with a dull crunching of gubernatorial bones. The complicated political picture includes three major parties: first, the Union Republicans, composed of the respectable people who own things or work for people who own things, the lawyers, doctors, and business men; second, the Socialists, of a breed which has forgotten Karl Marx and thinks William Green a labor leader. They are a pathetically ineffective but honest group, sincerely working for the improvement of the lot of the workers. Their greatest spiritual handicap is too long and too close association with the American Federation of Labor. Third, there are the Liberals, a new hopper into which has been gathered a miscellaneous collection of old conservatives and young liberals. For the most part they are the habitual followers of Antonio Barceló, the most picturesque politician of the island, honest, magnetic, an opportunistic patriot. The chief plank in the Liberal platform is insular independence, and it is upheld honestly and tenaciously by the rank and file of the younger leaders in the group. The first two of these parties are at present united against Barceló's Liberals. This coalition received 210,000 votes in the last election, against the Liberals' 175,000, thereby winning control of the Congress. Gore, innocently thinking that things are as they seem, decided to be realistic and to play ball with the coalition. He forgot its complete artificiality and seemed not to realize that while Barceló and his party were for the moment submerged they have an obstinate capacity for rising again. Gore played the coalition game and showed decided animosity toward the Liberals. This animosity was natural to a man of Gore's type. The Liberals were "anti-American." They wished to have Spanish taught as the language of the island, and they proposed at the earliest possible moment to pull down the Stars and Stripes. His distaste was promptly reciprocated. Unfortunately for Gore, the Liberals have several men who know how to express distaste in stirring fashion. One of them is Luis Muñoz Marin. The columns of *La Democracia* have kept Mr. Gore awake nights. Nothing has been left unsaid, and Mr. Gore gave a clever editor plenty of things to say.

The first too astute political move of the new governor was a requirement that all new appointments should be filed with undated resignations. The inevitable storm aroused by this affront to the dignity of appointees was met by a blanket denial of the order from Gore. Whereupon Barceló's *La Democracia* came out with a streaming headline in English. "Governor Gore, you are a damn liar!" Muñoz Marín in his editorial suggested that the Governor bring a libel suit. The Governor didn't.

The patronage question came next. Gore had reason to know that to the victors belong the spoils. He had profited under that accepted principle. The Democratic Party is represented in Puerto Rico by a select group of 175 hopeful

Democrats. President Roosevelt owed much to this group. Their six votes in the convention that nominated him were his from the first day. Parley saw to that. The local leaders of this valiant band were quick to press their claims. One Mrs. Whittemore was open-minded on the subject of being appointed governor. Failing in that, she revealed her willingness to serve as commissioner of education. This post was held by José Padín, whom Theodore Roosevelt had persuaded to give up a more lucrative business post in order to take it. Padín had made a conspicuous success, and he was acclaimed wherever educators foregathered. From the beginning Gore showed marked dislike for Padín. Padín, it seemed, spoke Spanish, approved of teaching Spanish, had no interest in politics, refused to allow the politicians to meddle with his schools—obviously he was "anti-American." A cable from Washington requested Padín's resignation. Things looked bright for the Mrs. Whittemore who had helped to elect Roosevelt. Then the storm broke. Almost everyone in Puerto Rico who knew or cared about schools wrote or wired to Washington. American educators entered the lists and told the President in unmistakable words exactly what they thought of paying party debts with the schools of Puerto Rican children. Padín is still commissioner, and Parley had to find other jobs for his staunch Puerto Rican henchmen. Mrs. Whittemore was given the post of collector of internal revenue, Mr. Horton of attorney-general, Mrs. Dooley of chief of immigration—all well-paying jobs which should have gone to more competent Puerto Ricans.

The most spectacular scene—and probably the last in which Gore will play a part—was staged on the campus of the University of Puerto Rico in Río Piedras. The university has been the football of island politics ever since it was founded, but under the able direction of Carlos Chardón, a brilliant scientist and able executive, it has made steady progress. It is the proud center of island culture and is dear to Puerto Rican hearts. It symbolizes the spiritual independence of the people in the face of alien domination. Faculty, students, alumni, and islanders generally have repeatedly demanded that the politicians keep their hands off. The Governor soon gave evidence of suspecting the university. It too was put on the anti-American list. A place on the board of trustees became vacant, and it was the Governor's duty to make an appointment. He has wide latitude under the law, the only requirement being that the nominee must have made a name in the arts, in science, or in letters. Gore appointed Alonso Torres, an active politician, a congressman, a labor leader, a Socialist, an honest and zealous protagonist for the workers of the island. The appointment was inspired by two motives, one political and one emotional. Torres was a leader in the dominant coalition, chairman of the finance committee of the house. Furthermore, he was a recognized leader of labor, and Gore thought that he was striking a blow for the dispossessed by making the appointment. If it had been a clear case of appointing a labor man to a place on the university board, Gore might well have been applauded, but the case was not clear. The appointment was definitely political. The coalition was determined to control the university and to "Americanize" it. Further, Torres did not qualify as competent in the field of arts, science, or letters. He had on numerous occasions expressed his dislike of the university. His literary efforts were brought out to confound him, especially the report of an economic commission of which he had been chairman. Included among the proposals for the betterment of economic conditions in the island was one which suggested the possibility of raising nightingales, these to be trained to sing the Star Spangled Banner and to be sold in the United States for fifty dollars each. The appointment of Torres evoked a cry of rage from students and alumni, parents and friends. It was the *cause célébre* which solidified the island against the Governor. A delegation of students sought an appointment with the Governor, but was refused. The students paraded with a coffin labeled *Cultura,* and in the shadow of the Governor's home shed tears over the bier. They sent three girls with a copy of a book of etiquette for Mr. Gore. They called an assembly and voted a student strike. The Governor broke into a cold sweat. Here was anarchy, insubordination, ingratitude, and—anti-Americanism. He decided to call out the militia, but was dissuaded by men of calmer mind. He decided to close the university altogether, but someone reminded him of Machado. In the meantime the students laughed and marched and sang. They campaigned throughout the island. Alumni and parents joined forces with them. Chancellor Chardón kept his head. Commissioner Riggs of the insular police talked with the boys and suggested that all retain their sense of humor, and the university voted a recess of two weeks. The Governor ordered extra guards for his house, and the two weeks went by. Torres, under orders, or out of his own wisdom, resigned. The students went back to work. They had captured the respect of practically all sections of the population, for they had expressed the stored-up resentment against a man who presumed to ride rough-shod over the dignity and self-respect of the island. They won the strike, and more. They made it certain that Governor Gore must retire.

The most heartening experience one can have in Puerto Rico is a talk with the leaders of the student directory. I have just talked for three hours with five of them. They are young men of poise and idealism. They stand out in welcome contrast to Puerto Rican old-guard politicians. They are thinking in fundamental economic and social terms of the island's future. Their minds are not closed. Many of them believe that Puerto Rico should be allowed to work out its destiny as a separate nation. They have not been "Americanized," and I hope they will not be. The word has a bad connotation in Puerto Rico.

I regret the necessity of writing these words about Robert Gore, but he represents a political habit which must be rooted out. He has gone far toward undoing the excellent work of Theodore Roosevelt in building up relations of mutual respect between the island and the mainland. Yet the fault is not primarily Gore's. The real culprit is Postmaster-General Parley together with the spoils system of which he is belated administrator.

On the eve of the Seventh Pan-American Conference in Montevideo it is fitting that the Administration take swift measures to make honorable amend to the Puerto Ricans. The Latin American peoples question our good intentions. Puerto Rico is a test of the reality of those intentions. We have failed miserably there during the greater part of thirty-five years. Our one Latin American colony would without question vote to leave us tomorrow if given a chance. It is a sorry commentary on our handling of the island's affairs.

VIOLENCE AND NATIONALISM

On Sunday, February 23, 1936, Puerto Rico's insular police chief, E. Francis Riggs—an American— was shot to death by two young Nationalists while he walked to church in San Juan. The youths, Elías Beauchamp and Hiram Rosado, were taken to the police station and shot to death but not before one of them posed solemnly for a news photographer outside and preferred a stiff military salute. It was a clearcut political assassination, causing severe repercussions on the island and in Washington.

Soon afterward, legislation was proposed in Congress to grant independence to Puerto Rico. This caused a furor on the island, because the terms of separation were considered punitive, even by many independence advocates. For example, after four decades of colonialism, the island would have to bear the full brunt of U.S. tariffs in four years.

A prominent U.S. magazine called Washington's "offer to free Puerto Rico . . . little more than window trimming for the coming Pan American conference."[1]

"The best-informed authorities in this country," the article went on to say,

---

Arthur Garfield Hays, "Defending Justice in Puerto Rico," *The* Nation. CXLIV (June 5, 1937), p. 647.

1. *Business Week,* May 2, 1936, pp. 41, 43. The reference was to a conference in Buenos Aires, "to prove to the Latin American countries . . . that the United States has no intention of forcing its sovereignty over any territory when the people in those lands no longer wish it."

"feel confident that Puerto Rico cannot afford to sever its connections with the country under the terms of this proposal."

The article adds that "Our naval base on the island would be all that would remain of American control." That, apparently, was not negotiable.

"Puerto Rico is almost entirely dependent on the United States as a market outlet . . . due to a policy carefully cultivated over the past years. . . . The new bill . . . will . . . give the United States a fresh slate to deal firmly with a terroristic minority without being accused of being an imperialistic oppressor by the rest of Latin America," the article concludes.

Tension continued in Puerto Rico, as the Nationalists pressed their demands for independence, and the island government reacted by taking repressive measures. Perhaps the most infamous moment of this period is the so-called Ponce Massacre, which occurred on Palm Sunday of 1937, when more than twenty persons were killed and 150 wounded on Ponce's Marina Street as the Nationalists began a parade. Many different versions of the carnage were offered, and an official of the American Civil Liberties Union was asked to head a commission that would investigate. Here, he summarizes the results of the inquiry.

In the fall of 1935 five members of the Nationalist Party of Puerto Rico sought to make their way to a meeting which students at the Puerto Rico University were to hold to protest against certain remarks made by Pedro Albizu Campos, the Nationalist leader. The story is that the Nationalists were stopped by the police, that they shot at the police, and that, as a result of the fracas, four of the five Nationalists in the automobile were killed. It was said that they carried bombs and guns.

In February, 1936, Colonel Riggs, head of the insular police, was assassinated by two Nationalists. The assassins were seized and, while in the hands of the police, were shot. Although Colonel Riggs was popular with the Puerto Ricans and was himself a believer in independence, the cold-blooded murder of the two Puerto Rican "martyrs" aroused not only the Nationalists but great numbers of Puerto Ricans who opposed Nationalist methods. Americans thought of the murder of Colonel Riggs; Puerto Ricans thought of the murder of the two assassins.

Albizu Campos and other Nationalist leaders were charged with conspiracy to overthrow the government of the United States and later, in July, 1936, were convicted and sentenced to six years in jail. Governor Blanton Winship apparently felt it was necessary to deal with the Nationalists with a heavy hand and acted to suppress not only those who were militantly demanding Puerto Rican freedom but also a united front of groups opposed to the conviction of Albizu

Campos. Parades and meetings of Nationalists and other protesting groups were prohibited. The Puerto Ricans take seriously their Organic Act guaranteeing the rights of free speech and assemblage, and resentment grew apace.

On March 21, 1937, the Nationalists announced that they would hold a parade and meeting in the town of Ponce. A permit was first given by the mayor of the town. At the last moment it was canceled. The insular police commanded by Colonel Orbeta, who was acting under orders of the Governor, prohibited the parade as it was about to start. The national hymn of Puerto Rico was played, the crowd cheered, the parade advanced. Suddenly there was shooting, and when it was all over, it appeared that the casualties were 20 killed—including those who died later, among whom were two police officers—and from 150 to 200 wounded, among among whom were 6 police officers.

Governor Winship reported to Washington that several "divisions" of the so-called "Army of Liberation" had arranged a concentration in the town of Ponce; that a parade was forbidden; that nevertheless the Nationalists insisted upon proceeding; that when the command "Forward march!" was given, a Nationalist fired a shot killing a policeman on the left of the chief of police and another Nationalist fired a shot killing a policeman on the right of the chief of police; that shooting then broke out from all sides as well as from roofs and balconies where Nationalists were stationed; and that casualties resulted. He ended his report by commending the patience and consideration of the police.

The leading citizens of Ponce formed a committee of prominent citizens of San Juan and asked that they make an investigation. The proposed commission consisted of Emilio Belaval, president of the Athenaeum, who acted as secretary; Mariano Acosta Velarde, president of the Puerto Rican Bar Association; Lorenzo Pineiro, president of the Teachers' Association; Dr. Manuel Díaz Garcia, president of the Puerto Rican Medical Association; Antonio Ayuso, editor of the *Imparciale;* Francisco M. Zeno, editor of the *Correspondencia;* and Davila-Ricci, assistant editor of the *Mondo.* None of the commission were Nationalists. Request was made to the American Civil Liberties Union to appoint the chairman of the commission, and the writer was so appointed. The commission undertook to investigate not only the events in Ponce on March 21 but the general subject of civil rights and liberties in Puerto Rico.

Hearings were held at Ponce beginning Friday, May 14, and were thereafter adjourned to San Juan. Evidence as to what happened on March 21 was adduced not only from disinterested eyewitnesses but from a series of photographs which tell the story in incontestable fashion. Photographs show that the "divisions" of the "Army of Liberation" consisted of about eighty young men wearing black blouses and white trousers, about twelve girls dressed in white as nurses, and a brass band of about six pieces. The Nationalists, known as "cadets," carried no arms; the girls did not even have Red Cross kits.

A photograph shows the scene just before the shooting. About eighteen policemen armed with revolvers, shotguns, and tear-gas bombs, stood in front of the line of these eighty boys and twelve girls; about twenty policemen armed with Thompson submachine-guns were in the rear; a number of armed police were on the street along the side; a crowd of men, women, and children stood across the way watching the parade. The Nationalists had brought their wives, mothers, and children along to see the parade. The evidence showed that there was no shooting whatever from any roofs or balconies, and this was confirmed by the district attorney of Ponce, Pérez Marchand, who made the first investigation and who later retired as district attorney because, according to him, he was not given a free hand in his inquiries. One of the photographs shows a policeman actually firing at the crowd and other policemen drawing their guns, all in menacing posture. The police who were wounded or killed seem to have been caught in a cross fire.

The commission unanimously reported that the people of Puerto Rico have properly described the occurrence as the "massacre of Ponce."

I shall never forget the photograph of those cadets whom newspapers have described as "ruffians" and "gangsters," standing quietly with their hands at their sides waiting to be shot—defenseless but not one of them running away.

PART VIII

"¡JALDA ARRIBA!"

He [Muñoz Marín] is, more and more, a Puritan in Babylon. He likes to dream of American capitalism as a non-sacred cow to be rationally utilized by rational Puerto Ricans. He fails to see that, in grim reality, it is a raucous tiger not easily tamed.

—*Gordon Lewis,* San Juan Review, *October 1964, p. 47*

Puerto Rico took a giant leap forward during the two decades that followed World War II. A poor, rural island transformed itself into a "semi-developed" society; factories replaced farms as the chief means to earn a living; schools and medical care were made available to virtually all citizens, a large middle class emerged, cars clogged new cement highways, and thousands of tourists streamed in each year, to bask in the Caribbean sun.

There were still awful slums, and long lines of unemployed, but Puerto Rico had thrust itself into the modern world.

Why all this happened precisely when it did is a complex story. After World War II, the U.S. economy enjoyed an unheralded boom, and spillover profits were used by mainland investors to build factories abroad; many of them chose Puerto Rico, which offered liberal tax benefits—under the "Operation Bootstrap" industrialization program—and a plentiful supply of jobless people, willing to work for low wages.

The once dormant economy was also spurred upward by Puerto Rican GIs returning from the war, who received federal loans for housing, and grants for education. It was stimulated, too, by the availability of FHA mortgages for homes, and easy credit plans for consumer purchases. Puerto Rico was guided through this period of rapid change by the left-of-center Popular Democratic Party, which took power in the elections of 1940, and ran the government for the next twenty-eight years. Senator (later Governor) Luis Muñoz Marín and his colleagues, many of whom favored independence, undertook bold programs designed to provide decent jobs, housing, and education for the island's impoverished majority. Between 1940 and 1970, personal income per year spiraled from $118 to $1,200; this was a dramatic improvement, even when one takes into account the rise in living costs, and the fact that income was not distributed on a wholly equitable basis.

It is most interesting to note that Puerto Rico progressed in the same proportion as its powers of home rule increased.

Not until 1941 did the United States appoint a governor—Rexford Guy Tugwell—who was competent, imaginative, and sympathetic to the aims of the elected Puerto Rican leaders in the island government. Not until 1948 was Puerto Rico allowed to elect its own native governor. And it was not until 1952 that Puerto Rico was granted more self-rule, under the Commonwealth form of government.

Puerto Rico made its greatest economic progress in the 1950's and 1960's, at a time when Puerto Ricans—not Americans—directed the island's local affairs.[1]

There are numerous books and shorter studies that chronicle the Muñoz era. Here, we shall look at a few selections that describe highlights of the time when *¡jalda arriba!*—up the hill!—was coined as a battle cry against poverty and social injustice.

---

1. A number of Americans lent their expertise as consultants and aides, but all key cabinet and legislative posts were held by Puerto Ricans.

"A TIME OF NATIONAL CRISIS"

In 1939, President Franklin D. Roosevelt chose a military man—Admiral William D. Leahy—to govern Puerto Rico; America was readying itself for war with Germany and Japan. Almost immediately, Congress appropriated $30 million to build large air and naval bases on the island, in order to shield the Panama Canal.

The threat of global war dwarfed Puerto Rico's internal problems, which were never of great concern to Washington. Even a liberal U.S. magazine said at the time: "If, in the interest of national defense, Puerto Rico must be turned over to military rule, we can think of no better choice [than Admiral Leahy]. Naturally, we would prefer a world in which such a disposition of Puerto Rico was unnecessary."[1]

Puerto Rico was well on its way to becoming an island fortress, much as it was during Spain's heyday, by the time Admiral Leahy was reassigned. Soon afterwards, President Roosevelt appointed Rexford Guy Tugwell, a member of his "Brain Trust," to govern the island. At the same time, the zealous, reform-minded "young Turks" of the Popular Democratic Party had taken power in the insular elections. Their leader was Senator Luis Muñoz Marín. Tugwell, who governed from 1941 through 1946, worked closely with Muñoz in laying the groundwork for an ambitious socio-economic reform plan. Tugwell's writings offer perhaps one of the most intimate accounts of relations between Puerto Rico and the federal government. Here, he explains his—and President Roosevelt's—views on the island's strategic importance during wartime, and on its future political development. Italics are added for emphasis.

B ecause no Colonial Office existed to assume the complex administrative responsibilities involved in the relationship [with Puerto Rico], the President was quite unable to see to it that Puerto Rican interests were effectively protected. The power to interfere was willfully retained by the Congress and protected by refusal to establish an adequate office in the executive establishment. Actually a Bureau of Insular Affairs was set up in the War Department to look after both Puerto Rico and the Philippines when they were occupied, and military Governors were appointed. That Bureau in the War Department continued, right down to 1934, when President Roosevelt moved it to Interior—to be all there was of colonial administration in the executive branch of the federal government. . . .

From Rexford Guy Tugwell, *The Art of Politics* (New York: Doubleday, 1958), pp. 36, 147-51. Reprinted with permission.

1. *New Republic,* XCIX (May 24, 1939), p. 58.

Before 1934 a certain change had taken place in the formal relationship— the Jones Act of 1917 had modified the Foraker Act of 1900. As to this, it *should not escape notice that 1917 was again a time of national crisis, when certain grudging concessions could be got from an unwilling Congress on the plea of national security. There would not be another change until World War II, when the same arguments would again apply —that the principles we professed to be fighting for were very poorly observed in our own dependencies, and that the loyalty of Puerto Ricans was important. . . .*

I was inclined at first to consider immediate independence, or at least an announcement of eventual independence, as necessary. About this I had several talks with the President [Roosevelt]. He was against it. It was not that he thought the Puerto Rican affiliation of any advantage to the United States, except in a *strategic sense,* but that he felt we had a serious obligation we had not discharged. The most I could get from him was a willingness to give way to advance. It seemed to me that unless Puerto Ricans were to accept independence—which I felt certain Congress would grant for the asking—they must move toward a more agreeable status than now existed.

The attitude of President Roosevelt toward Puerto Rico was partly, then, shaped by misinformation. But partly, also, it came from the same general impulse that led him to prefer retired admirals and generals as Governors for all non-self-governing areas. I had had to join [Harold] Ickes in a fervent plea in 1934 to prevent the President from returning the Virgin Islands to the Navy administration; and the smaller Pacific possessions never had a civilian government during his time. The imperialist ideas in his mind were still warring with more recent ones. When he had been Assistant Secretary of the Navy he had visited Haiti and Santo Domingo on a historic occasion and had taken credit in his 1920 campaign for the vice-presidency—unjustifiably—for bringing order to these republics by way of the Marines and new constitutions. There was an admiral concealed somewhere in Roosevelt and had been, I suppose, ever since his ambition for a naval career had been thwarted by his father. . . .

. . . . Actually Muñoz's ambitions for Puerto Rico had their climax in Truman's acquiescence—and, perhaps it should be said, his ignorance. It would not be fair to say that Muñoz took advantage of the President's lack of experience; nevertheless, Truman was willing to have the United States, at that time, assume the generous posture involved in the Commonwealth status without many safeguards. *This did not, and could not, have happened with Roosevelt's consent.*

Looking at Puerto Rico as a problem for the United States, it is well to recall that Muñoz happened to be rising to power when a change of attitude was in process. Until the end of the war in 1945, the dominant consideration had been a *strategic one*. The military dispositions of the decade preceding had naturally been determined by the weapons available, and the source, the objective, and the direction of the possible attack. The source was Germany, the objective was the Panama Canal, and the direction was through the Caribbean island arc from Florida to Trinidad. In this arc *Puerto Rico was central. Bases there were, in the strict sense, strategic and essential. Puerto Rico therefore had to be maintained as a controlled and, if possible, friendly base. As wartime Governor, this was my first responsibility.*

But when the African invasion was established, there was a complete change, somewhat tardily acknowledged by the military bureaucracy, but apparent at'once to one with such a responsibility as mine. There was no longer any possibility of actual invasion, although the submarine blockade was still a serious problem; and the development of new weapons, together with the acceleration in airplane range and speed, made it unlikely that Puerto Rico would ever again be strategically important even if there should be another threat to the United States from the east. The significance of this was that policy could be revised. And it was then that I laid before President Roosevelt my analysis of the change and my proposals for new relationships.

In general I urged that local government should be freed from outside controls. I told the President he was quite wrong to think of the Puerto Ricans as politically immature or incapable of administering their own affairs. They were, in fact, more advanced than many of the states of our Union. We ought to begin successive changes as rapidly as the Congress could be got to grant them. Specifically we ought to begin at once with the elective governorship, proceeding to a status somewhat short of full statehood—it could not be full because for a long time more economic, assistance would be needed than the federal government gives to the states. We need not worry about local protection for military bases; they were no longer necessary to our defense. . . .

While I was arguing thus with President Roosevelt, Muñoz was consolidating his political power. . . . He was extremely cautious about encouraging hopes. He had so little faith that anything would happen that he isolated the question of status and for years refused to discuss it. He even had the reluctance I have mentioned to serve on the committee I persuaded the President to set up for making the first recommendations to Congress. He balked badly at my proposals and my timetable. Not only that, he made up his mind that Roosevelt would be defeated in 1944, as he had similarly made up his mind in 1940, and this confused his planning. He succeeded in alienating both Secretary Ickes and President Roosevelt, and neither of them made any energetic effort to implement the committee's recommendations about the governorship.

But President Roosevelt was re-elected. Then, within a few months, he was succeeded by the former Senator from Missouri. . . . [In 1946] Truman showed an active interest. He saw half the problem—the need for autonomy; but he missed the other half—the continuing interest of the nation—thus reversing Roosevelt, who saw the half Truman did not see but missed the rest . . .

"PUERTO RICO IS THE CENTER"

President Roosevelt, in 1943, supported an unsuccessful bill to amend the law that defined U.S.-Puerto Rican relations, in order to allow the people to elect their own governor. In his message to a Congressional committee, Roosevelt reaffirmed the importance of Puerto Rico as the "center" of an "island shield" to protect the Panama Canal. "There is no reason why their Governor and other officials should continue to be appointed from without," he said. But he was quick to add that "the ultimate power of Congress" would not be altered. Italics are added for emphasis.

D uring the 45 years which have passed since the occupation of the island by the United States the economic situation of the Puerto Rican people, although materially improved in some respects, has not changed in essential character. Instead of development toward economic self-reliance, there has been a steady tendency to become more dependent upon outside markets for disposal of the single great crop— sugar—and upon outside sources for food, clothing, building materials, and most of the other necessities. Partly because of economic and geographical factors and partly because of tariff preferences and shipping laws, these relationships, are, by now, almost wholly with the continental United States. . . .

During the 45 years of our sovereignty, the elements of world military and naval strategy have changed also. When the island was brought under our flag, the Panama Canal had not yet been dug, and the airplane had not yet been

Selections in this chapter:
1. From U.S. Congress, House, Committee on Insular Affairs. To amend the act to provide a civil government for Puerto Rico. S. 1407. August 26, 944, pp. 14-15.
2. From U.S. Congress, Senate, Subcommittee of the Committee on Territories and Insular Affairs, Hearings on § 1407, A Bill to Amend the Organic Act of Puerto Rico. 78th Congress, 1st Session, 1943, p. 364.

invented. The Caribbean was something of a backwater in the broad current of world affairs. When the present war became imminent, however, it was obvious that the chain of islands running in a great arc from Florida to the shoulder of South America, enclosing the Caribbean Sea, formed a vast natural shield for the Panama Canal, suited in distance and conformation to the uses of the military plane. *And of this island shield, Puerto Rico is the center. Its possession or control by any foreign power—or even the remote threat of such possession—would be repugnant to the most elementary principles of national defense.*

It has long been the policy of the Government of the United States progressively to reinforce the machinery of self-government in its territories and island possessions. The principles for which we are now fighting require that we should recognize the right of all our citizens—whether continental or overseas—to the greatest possible degree of home rule and also of participation in the benefits and responsibilities of our Federal system.

Puerto Ricans of all political parties, however divergent their views as to the political future of the island, are united in asking for the right to elect their own Governor. I believe that they are entitled to it. . . . The fiscal relationship of the insular government to the Federal Government would not be altered, nor would the *ultimate power of Congress to legislate for the Territory.* The people of the island would, however, be given assurance of the intention of Congress to obtain the concurrence of the people of the island before imposing upon them any further changes in the Organic Act. . . .

[The question of granting real autonomy to Puerto Rico was never seriously entertained. When the elective governor amendment was discussed in 1943, Federal officials suggested that a U.S. High Commissioner might be appointed to serve as liaison with the Puerto Rican governor. When island officials objected to this, Abe Fortas, Undersecretary of the Interior, and later a U.S. Supreme Court Justice, impatiently shot back:]

The U.S. Government will continue to be supreme in Puerto Rico, and that is that. There just is not any question about it. We might just as well quit if we are not going to proceed on that basis, and you might as well all have that very clearly in mind that the United States, under this scheme, will continue to be supreme in Puerto Rico.

"WE HAD BETTER WAIT"

In 1943, a bill providing for Puerto Rican independence was also submitted to Congress. Testimony was heard from many persons, for and against. Vicente Geigel-Polanco, Floor Leader of the Popular Democratic Party in the Puerto Rican Senate, called the bill a "just, adequate, democratic, and historically feasible solution to our problem of sovereignty." The island's legislature, by unanimous vote, asked that "the colonial system of government be ended," and encouraged "free, democratic elections" so that the status problem could be solved "by the free will of the people of Puerto Rico themselves." Congress, however, was heeding other voices, such as that of John J. McCloy, U.S. Assistant Secretary of War.

W **• • •** e do not consider it to be within our purview to comment on the political wisdom of the independence of Puerto Rico at this time. We do have rather strong feelings from a purely military point of view.

The bill . . . provides for . . . a transition of sovereignty during the period of the war. For military reasons, we believe that to be unwise. . . . I think perhaps the political disturbance that might occur in connection with these various steps [of transition] would be unwise during the war period.

I do not need to dwell upon the military significance of Puerto Rico. . . . It is an outpost in our Caribbean defense; it is one of the islands which is farthest removed from the Panama Canal, and constitutes a bulwark in the defense of that area.

There are likewise some features of the bill that we think should require elaboration. . . . We think some of the reservations that are in there providing for the establishment of military installations should be broadened in a substantial degree. . . .

Senator HAYDEN. Mr. Chairman, I think there is considerable force in what the secretary says, because you will remember that although we took great care and trouble with respect to the bill providing for the independence of the Philippines, it was afterwards discovered that there were certain military installations in the islands that were transferred to the Government of the [Philippine] Com-

From U.S. Congress, Senate, Committee on Territories and Insular Affairs. Puerto Rico. *Hearings before the Committee on territories and insular affairs, United States Senate, 78th Cong., 1st session, on S.952, a bill to provide for the withdrawal of the sovereignty of the United States over the island of Puerto Rico and for the recognition of its independence, and so forth.* Washington, U.S. Government printing office, 1943, pp. 9-21.

monwealth that might better have been retained by the United States.

Mr. McCLOY. That is quite true, and the same situation came up in Panama, which embarrassed us very much in this war.

The CHAIRMAN. We do not want to make that mistake the third time, so we are going to look to the War Department to clarify the defense features of this bill in every possible way.

Mr. McCLOY. But I also want to make it clear that even with that improvement in the bill, we think it unwise, from a military point of view, to pass the bill during wartime. . . .

The CHAIRMAN. In other words, your concern is to keep the status quo there during the period of hostilities?

Mr. McCLOY. That is right. I would like to make this suggestion also, that you do not limit it precisely to the date of the armistice. . . . We ought to have a "look-see" in regard to what the Caribbean area is at the end of the war, who occupies the adjacent islands, who is controlling the Atlantic, and so forth.

Senator VANDENBERG. . . . How do you think our interests would be adversely affected by starting the processes [for independence] during the war? They still have elections there anyhow. They have heated political contests.

Mr. McCLOY. Well, a heated political contest in an area as limited as that is not too advisable in the course of a war, since the entire island is largely a garrison, and a contest on such a substantial issue as this might be most disturbing. . . .

Senator CHAVEZ. People get excited when they talk about independence, and it is liable to interfere with the general [defense] program.

Senator VANDENBERG. They get excited down there, anyway. . . .

The CHAIRMAN. I do not want to bring out military secrets, but I think we could generalize by saying there is a considerable amount of our Army and Air Force there from time to time. Is that true?

Mr. McCLOY. That is true. There is also a very substantial Puerto Rican Army. It is part of the American Army.

The CHAIRMAN. You are familiar, too, with the fact that the conditions in Puerto Rico for the last 10, 15, or 20 years, even going back to 25 years ago, have been—well, more or less in a turmoil?

Mr. McCLOY. Yes; so I understand.

The CHAIRMAN. There is more activity there politically, economically, and otherwise than you find in most places, but the amount of lawlessness, from a governmental standpoint, has been very, very, very small; is not that true?

Mr. McCLOY. That is my impression. . . .

The CHAIRMAN. You would not be opposed to it [independence]from the standpoint of the War Department after the war period, is that correct?

Mr. McCLOY. With suitable protections, that is right.

Senator BONE. You would have no objection to this Government doing for Puerto Rico what was done for Cuba after the Spanish War?

Mr. McCLOY. With improvements, perhaps, on our military reservations— reservations in a general sense rather than the territory. . . .

Senator TAFT. Mr. Secretary, I do not understand your position exactly, because if it is unwise to have Puerto Rico independent during this war why isn't it unwise to have Puerto Rico independent at any time, as long as war is not insured against in some way? Will not Puerto Rico always occupy the same strategic position that it occupies in this war?

Mr. McCLOY. Well, it will . . . I suppose, speaking in a purely military vein, it would be always easier if we had sovereignty over any area, to make our military dispositions over that area. But those considerations are minor, or can be minor in the face of the general desire or of political considerations.

Senator TAFT. Puerto Rico occupies, does it not, today, a strategic position, a very key position in the defense of the Caribbean?

Mr. McCLOY. Yes.

Senator TAFT. Is there any reason why it will not always occupy that position?

Mr. McCLOY. It will always be a key position in the Caribbean,

Senator TAFT. Puerto Rico is about 35 miles wide by 100 miles long. In order to have an effective military and naval base, will not you require practically that much land to use for that base? For instance, you have the Borinquen Field at one end of the Island . . . you have the base at San Juan. How can you possibly have a military base at San Juan Harbor and still have San Juan the capital that is governed and ruled by an independent nation?

Mr. McCLOY. Well, perhaps I put too much faith in the reservations we write into the bill to give us free access between the two ends of the island. It is, as you say, not too large an area for our military dispositions in the event of war. . . .

Senator TAFT. You have enough troops there to make a large-size city. . . . Borinquen Field [now Ramey Air Force Base] is on the west end of the Island, a large new naval base at the east end of the Island [now Roosevelt Roads], and San Juan in between. . . What I cannot see is how you can effectively permit an independent nation to be operated in a base so important in which you are using so many parts of the island. . . . I can understand a certain amount of autonomy, but I cannot understand how you can reconcile complete independence of the Island with the effective and necessary use of Puerto Rico for military control of the Caribbean.

Mr. McCLOY. Well, it depends on what you mean by complete independence. I do not think any area as small as that is completely independent if it has any soldiers of any foreign government on it, or if it has military installations of any size on it. . . .

Senator TAFT. . . . There are 25,000 trained Puerto Rico soldiers who are now in the American Army but who would immediately become a Puerto Rican army upon Puerto Rico obtaining independence . . . surrounding and operating between the different Army and Navy posts of the United States. . . .

The CHAIRMAN (to Mr. McCloy). Of course, what you are saying is even if the people of Puerto Rico want independence and even though they give you all the bases that you want, there might still arise a question where you would want a watershed or a valley.

Mr. McCLOY. Yes; or a right of access. . . .

The CHAIRMAN. So that, in the end you would rather have no independence at all. That is a logical conclusion, isn't it?

Mr. McCLOY. Yes; from a purely military point of view. The soldier wants to have a chance, without consulting anybody, to issue his orders. . . .

Mr. TAFT. I think the (War) Department might consider also the question of some kind of autonomous government under which we would retain control of foreign relations and military control of the island. I think the department, in making their general study of this question, might consider whether that condition was not more consistent with the military needs than complete independence when you make your final report.

The CHAIRMAN. I think that is a very good suggestion. . . . I do not mean to say we can get everything we want without hurting the Puerto Ricans somewhat or that they can get everything they want without minimizing our rights somewhat, but I think there is a fair field where the War Department can get substantially what it needs now, and that it thinks it must need in the future, without any impairment of the sovereignty of the Puerto Ricans if they do vote for independence. . . .

Senator BONE. So, if you want to give Puerto Rico independence with certain prescriptions in the bill as to military and naval installations and means of egress and ingress, a reservation of certain rights for the acquisition of watersheds, and the like, control over foreign affairs, and all other things incident to protecting ourselves against the disturbed conditions in the world today, those can be made by prescriptions in the legislative formula that you adopt; there is no doubt about that, is there?

Mr. McCLOY. I think there is no doubt about that.

Senator VANDENBERG. I disagree with that completely. I want to make that perfectly plain. I think our experience in Panama proves it. There is something inherent in independence; there is something inherent in sovereignty which constantly arises. Any peacetime reservations you make are an infringement on that sovereignty and independence, and slowly but surely you will find, in spite of all the formulae you can write, that your reservations are gradually being eaten away.

Mr. McCLOY. The Senator used the word "status." I said "yes" to status. If he used the word "sovereignty," I think I would have had made a reservation. What the implication of the status that he sets up may be is another question.

Senator BONE. . . . I am not prepared to admit that the lawyers of Congress, together with the assistance they are able to get from the legal departments, are unable to work out a formula. . . . Here you are starting from scratch with a piece of white paper upon which you may write. Whether it is good or bad, I am not trying to say. I do not assume the Congress is capable of writing a prescription, in the event we decide Puerto Rico should have independence, in which I think you can preserve all the rights that the Puerto Rican Government wants. We know what we are likely to meet in the future in the way of air power and sea power, both on the surface and under the surface. I am not prepared to admit we cannot take a fresh sheet of white paper and write on it exactly what Congress wants to write. I think we can write that. I believe Congress would have the power to do it, but if it did, then it would not be independence.

The CHAIRMAN. Well, if they accepted it, then there would be a meeting of the minds. That is what we are after.

Senator VANDENBERG. For the time being.

The CHAIRMAN. I am not one of those . . . who believes you can write an independence bill and that forever after there never will be a dispute arise over the bill, but that, to me, is a minor point. The major objective is to protect America in that area and to give these people the God-given right to govern themselves if they want it.

Senator TAFT. Mr. Secretary, I want to suggest that the problem we meet here may be repeated hundredfold all over the world after the war, in the postwar settlement, and whether it is not better to hold up the determination of it until that time. Many islands throughout the world will have a semi-autonomous status. This is only one phase of the problem, it occurs to me. We had better wait and see what develops out of the treatment of colonies, territories, and islands after the war before we determine exactly what we ought to do with Puerto Rico. . . .

THE BARD OF POLITICS

Between 1940 and 1968, while the United States was led by a Roosevelt, a Truman, an Eisenhower, a Kennedy, and a Johnson, in Puerto Rico, there was only Luis Muñoz Marín.[1]

Because Muñoz had been a poet and journalist in his early years, he was popularly referred to as *El Vate* [The Bard]. His literary talent notwithstanding, Muñoz's forte was politics, which he practiced with the flair and discipline of a fine poet. Muñoz had an uncanny rapport with the people, whether it be from the speaker's platform in the dusty plazas of the island's small towns, or in their rustic homes, where he sipped their home-grown coffee and listened sympathetically to their concerns. As a consummate politician, Muñoz gathered together a host of talented colleagues with differing ideologies and sensitive egos, and united them under a single party banner for three decades.

Born in 1898 (the same year of the U.S. invasion), Muñoz spent much of his youth on the American mainland; he was perfectly bilingual. He rose to power as head of the insular Senate in 1940, became Puerto Rico's first elected governor in 1948, and was the guiding spirit behind the establishment of the Commonwealth status in 1952. During his long, eventful career, Muñoz won international fame for his role in Puerto Rico's dramatic transformation.

Muñoz began as an advocate of independence and socialism, but as the years passed these goals were diluted by multiple pressures.

In the early 1940's, Puerto Rico launched "Operation Bootstrap," an ambitious program to create industrial jobs. In the first phase, the island government opened a small nucleus of factories that produced basic products such as cement (for homes and highways), glass (for rum bottles) and boxboard paper (for shipping export products). The government also bought the electric companies and vast tracts of land, set up a central planning agency and a development bank, and adopted a socialist-style approach to numerous other socio-economic problems.

But the obstacles to such a plan were many. It was soon realized that a few factories, even under optimum conditions, would not generate enough profits to build more factories and make a noticeable dent in unemployment. There was a shortage, too, of trained technicians, who are so essential to a large-scale manufacturing network.

Perhaps even more important, leaders in Congress and in the U.S. business world viewed Puerto Rico's "socialist experiment" as inimical to the free enterprise system.

San Juan Star, July 25, 1962, p. 18.

1. In the latter four years, 1964 to 1968, Roberto Sánchez Vilella governed the island. But he was hand-picked by Muñoz, who served in the Senate, led the Popular Democratic Party, and played a major role in the 1967 status plebiscite campaign.

An influential American business writer reflected this concern when he described Puerto Rico's cement plant as "an ugly sign of growing bureaucracy and state socialism . . . frightening away investment capital."[2] In his hostile report, he called Puerto Rico's development plan "a Utopian-Marxist-Soviet dream," and sounded the alarm that "public money is being used to launch a new beef cattle product, and make Porto Rico independent of U.S. meat packers."

Considerable pressure, public and private, was put upon the island, and Puerto Rico soon sold away its factories to private interests. Instead, an aggressive promotion campaign was launched to attract U.S. factories, offering tax exemption and other inducements. (Since then, about 2,000 factories have opened, creating more than 100,000 direct jobs, and earning an average of 20 per cent profit yearly for their investors.)

Thus, Puerto Rico under Muñoz evolved into a hybrid of government welfare statism and laissez-faire capitalism; many essential services remained under public control, but private enterprise (largely absentee-owned) dominated manufacturing and commerce.

In politics, the same pragmatic course was followed. The federal government discouraged independence, and Muñoz felt that Puerto Rico had neither the military nor the economic strength to force the issue. Statehood had little support in Washington or San Juan. Faced by the *status quo* of colonialism, Muñoz, in the late 1940's, began to explore a midway course, a third alternative, that would hopefully achieve a dignified form of self-government for the island.

Muñoz has explained his rationale many times, perhaps best in the following speech, which was given on July 17,1951, in the mountain town of Barranquitas, the birthplace and resting place of his father, Luis Muñoz Rivera.[3]

One year and one week later, on July 25, 1952, the Commonwealth status was formally inaugurated, and Puerto Rico became known as an *Estado Libre Asociado*: a "state" that was "free" and yet "associated" with the United States.

Advocates of independence and statehood called the new political formula a "perfumed" type of colonialism. The *independentistas* argued that Puerto Rico's "permanent union" to the United States under Commonwealth would never permit true sovereignty. The statehooders called Commonwealth an insidious trick, a way of allowing independence to sneak in "through the kitchen door."

Muñoz, near the end of his speech, emphasizes that "what we have done is to initiate a process of political creation," which "needs to grow."

How it will grow, and in what direction, is unclear. Muñoz and other spokesmen for Commonwealth believe that the present system can, and should, be perfected, allowing for more autonomy. The final answer, as Muñoz himself has said, rests with future generations.

---

2. Emmett Crozier, *New York Herald Tribune.* Dec. 4, 1946.
3. July 17 is a holiday in Puerto Rico, marking Muñoz Rivera's birth in 1829.

L anguage was given to man to enable him to make himself understood by his fellow man. But one of the frailties of language is that there are some words which for a time prevent understanding. In Puerto Rico *patria*—the homeland—has been such a word. At first blush this may see strange, as there is no people of the earth who love their native land more profoundly than do the people of Puerto Rico.

To the Puerto Rican, *patria* is the colors of the landscape, the change of seasons, the smell of the earth wet with fresh rain, the voice of the streams, the crash of the ocean against the shore, the fruits, the songs, the habits of work and of leisure, the typical dishes for special occasions and the meager ones for everyday, the flowers, the valleys, and the pathways. But even more than these things, *patria* is the people: their way of life, spirit, folkways, customs, their way of getting along with each other. Without these latter things *patria* is only a name, an abstraction, a bit of scenery. But with them it is an integral whole: "the homeland *and* the people." Those who profess to love their country while taking an irresponsible attitude towards the destiny of its people suffer from spiritual confusion. The implication of their attitude is that we must save the country even though we destroy the people!

Love of country must mean love of all of the country—both the *patria* and the people. But some of us confused love of the homeland with the narrow and bitter concept of the national state. We felt that love of Puerto Rico has as a necessary corollary the desire for separate independence. We had not yet comprehended that no law, divine or human, commands that countries must be suspicious, vain, and hostile, that they must live separate from other countries whose peoples are a part of the broad equality which the Lord created on the earth. Because of the rigidity of our thinking, we could not disentangle the concept of love for our country from the fixed idea of separate independence. Anything other than independence seemed to clash with our love for Puerto Rico.

The Dawning Light

The difficult process of clarifying these ideas began when the Tydings bill was introduced in Congress in 1936. On the one hand this bill offered the separate independence for which many of us had asked because of our feeling for the abstract idea of the *patria*. On the other hand, it condemned the people of our homeland to extreme poverty from which they could never hope to escape. Suddenly what had seemed to be an integral idea—the homeland and separate independence—turned out to be two conflicting ideas: one, acceptable as an abstract idea; the other, a mortal enemy of the people. The Tydings bill would have made Puerto Rico independent; but it would have shackled the people with economic misery.

It was not easy to change our views on this subject. Our minds could grasp the point that if we could have separate independence only under the economic conditions of the Tydings bill it would be not independence but a living death of hopeless poverty for Puerto Rico. Yet our emotions led us to search for other economic conditions under which independence would be possible. At the time, our emotions were stronger than our powers of reasoning. Rationalization works where understanding is the servant, instead of the master, of emotion. Instead of using reasoning objectively to seek the truth, we used it to justify our emotions. Just as one might confuse the glittering uniform of a doorkeeper with that of a king, our powers of reasoning were led astray by rationalization induced by our emotions. We were the victims of wishful thinking in believing that separate independence would be feasible if the economic conditions in the Tydings bill came into effect over a period of ten years instead of immediately. This was also inadequate; but it served for a time to protect, in the minds of many of us, the preconceived idea of separation.

The Untaught Wisdom

We were gripped with this emotional confusion wanting independence but not wanting economic upheaval—when the campaign to found the Popular Democratic party was running its course between 1938 and 1940. At this point, well aware of the great economic needs of our people, and knowing our simple people well, I set out to talk with them. I learned many things from these talks.

I learned that there is a wisdom among the people in the towns and in the countryside which education may lead, but cannot improve, in its magnificent human essence. I taught many of them something, but they taught me more. I learned that the people are wise—wiser than we think. I learned that to them freedom is something deep in the heart, in the conscience, in everyday life, in personal dignity, in the furrow, the plow, and the tools. I learned that among the simple people the nationalistic concept does not exist, because in its place there is a deep understanding of freedom. I learned that in their wisdom they prefer—if they have to choose—one who governs respectfully from a distance to one who governs despotically from nearby. And that understanding is the unequaled basis and root of every great federalist concept, of great unions between countries and between men which cut across climates, races, and languages. The nationalistic concept prefers the despotic government of the nearby to the democratic government of the remote. Naturally, democratic federalism requires respect and liberty in the local as well as in the federal levels of government.

I learned many things, probably many more than I think I learned; for we learn by planting things in the mind which later bear fruit in understanding. And I learned better something I already knew: that it is unworthy of the conscience, that it is the denial of all ideals, to risk, for abstract concepts, the hope for a better life, the deep belief in the integral freedom of the good and simple people who populate the long paths, which sometimes cross the streets and squares, which are Puerto Rico. I learned all this, and I also learned that the great majority of the people of Puerto Rico prefer close association with their fellow citizens of the American Union and with all men on earth, to the bitter narrowness of separation.

I realized that with a program calling for separate independence we would never obtain the support of the people for economic development—equitable distribution and production—which the people needed so much. The profound intuition of the people was quick to point out the contradiction in a program which on the one hand talked about the struggle to reduce their extreme poverty and on the other hand talked about separate independence which would destroy any hope of ever conquering that extreme poverty—which in fact would rapidly aggravate the seriousness of that poverty.

From the instinct of the people which I observed in my journeys among them, from the doubts in my own mind and the minds of others, and from the compulsion to deal with the great economic and social problems of so many good people in Puerto Rico, there emerged the formula which made possible everything that was to come, the formula that "the political status is not in issue." The votes in favor of the Popular Democratic Party would not be counted either for separate independence or for federated statehood; they would be votes in favor of an economic and social program. Our political status would be decided by the people on another occasion, wholly apart from the regular elections—presumably in a plebiscite.

This new concept of separating the economic from the political problem of Puerto Rico liberated the Popular Democratic party from a platform which was its own worst enemy—a platform in which the political plank could destroy the economic planks with the devastating fury of a tropical hurricane. This liberated those of us who had suffered from an intolerable perplexity of spirit. It enabled us to tackle the economic problems of Puerto Rico in a way that introduced a new, large movement of reform, creation, and hope. We are still engaged in that great task; in spite of the great deal which we have accomplished, there is much more to be done.

The Either/Or Concept Persists

However, we were free of this perplexity of the spirit for only a short period. We continued to be preoccupied as a collective group with the notion of a plebiscite in which we would be required to choose between separate independence and federated statehood—despite the fact that under either alternative the economic life of our people would be gravely threatened. It must be understood that it was not the people who were insisting on this course. This came from the political assemblies, who in this respect were not so representative of the people as they were in economic questions.

Those of us who participated in these assemblies were not insincere. With more learning and less wisdom, we continued to believe, although assailed by anguished doubts, that the choice must be between separate independence and federated statehood under economic conditions different from those in the Tydings bill and from those which existed for the states of the Union. We persisted in this view without examining closely the question of whether it would be possible to obtain these necessary economic conditions without any deviation from the two rigid alternatives. We were impaled on the horns of the dilemma which seemed to force an inexorable choice between separate independence and federated statehood. Actually, the instinct of the people used the idea of a plebiscite between these two classical forms of government to provide time for a better and autochthonous solution of the problem to appear. We can see this now. It was not easy to see it at that time.

In the 1944 campaign the promise to the people that the political status was not in issue was repeated. However, it was still imperative that we find a solution for that problem. The wisdom of the people, which I have mentioned, does not consist in a belief that the question of political status is of no importance whatsoever. Rather, recognizing that man does not live by bread alone and is in part a political being, the people have wisely refused to be bound by the intellectual straitjacket of rigid and preconceived formulas which stifle the creative will and energy of men. It was this instinct of the people, which at times their leaders must channel into action, which engendered the happy thought that the solution might well lie in some form other than the two inflexible formulas upon which the political assemblies had long focused their attention.

A Third Possibility Recognized

We were thus one step farther along the road to reality: in a request to Congress for a plebiscite we used language which permitted consideration of solutions other than the two rigid classical alternatives. True, we committed the error, at the insistence of some of the members of the political assembly, of inserting a deadline; we asked for a solution of the problem when World War II ended. But we had freed ourselves from the tyranny of the labels, separate independence and federated statehood. We were making progress.

In 1945 I went to Washington for discussions on the question of the political status of Puerto Rico. As a result of this visit, a bill was introduced in the Senate by Senator Tydings and in the House of Representatives by Resident Commissioner Piñero. That bill presented *three* alternatives: separate independence, federated statehood, and dominion status; the economic conditions were completely different from those of the original Tydings bill and from other Tydings bills. Under either of these alternatives, free trade between the United States and Puerto Rico would continue, the internal revenue taxes which now revert to the Treasury of Puerto Rico would continue to be covered into our Treasury, and federal aid for roads, hospitals, school lunchrooms, and many other public works and services would be extended for a long period of time.

During these consultations in Washington I became aware that such a bill could not pass. However, it did serve to present graphically to Congress and to the people of Puerto Rico the minimum economic conditions we needed in order to survive, irrespective of our political status.

The Object Lesson of the Philippines

In April 1946 I went again to Washington as a member of the Status Commission which was created by the Legislature of Puerto Rico and on which all the political parties with members in the Legislature were represented. Once more we tried to find a solution to the problem of status as we saw it. During that time hearings were being held before congressional committees on a bill to establish the economic relations which would exist between the United States and the Philippines when the latter became a republic. I read carefully the record of those hearings because of their obvious bearing on the question we were raising. It convinced me that Puerto Rico would never obtain the right to choose separate independence in a plebiscite except under economic conditions which would destroy any hope of continuing to improve their standard of living. The most important factor which led me to this conviction was the most-favored-nation clause found in trade treaties between the United States and many other countries.

The plan at the time was to give the Philippines economic treatment which would preserve for them the advantages of union with the United States for only eight years; this preference would be gradually reduced until the Philippines had no preference whatsoever in their economic relations with the United States. The principal reason for this treatment of the Philippines was the most-favored-nation clause in trade treaties to which the United States is a party. Under this clause the United States is required to give each nation with which it has a trade treaty containing the clause the most favorable economic treatment provided in a treaty with any other nation.

Obviously, the United States could not maintain its present good economic treatment of Puerto Rico, which is vital to our continued development, if we acquired a status which had all the legal paraphernalia of separate independence. It became clear that only under some form of status in association with the United States in which we retained our American citizenship could we preserve the good economic conditions which are necessary for our survival as a people. It could not be gainsaid that any status for Puerto Rico which connoted loss of American citizenship and disassociation from the American Union meant the discontinuance of our present favorable economic conditions, except perhaps for a few years on a diminishing graduated scale. The hard fact was that the present free trade between Puerto Rico and the United States could not be continued if Puerto Rico were a separate, independent nation. To provide for such free trade would require the same treatment for all the most-favored-treaty nations. And this, of course, was out of the question. Moreover, added to our economic situation was the affection and mutual respect which had developed between the peoples of Puerto Rico and the United States within our common citizenship.

We concluded that we must stop wasting time groping for a solution to the problem of political status which we knew beforehand was impossible for Puerto Rico to attain—impossible not for the American Union but for us. The Philippines with their greater territory and natural resources in relation to population, could manage under such stringent economic conditions. Our destiny lay in a different direction. It was incumbent upon us to devise creatively a realistically free form of political status which would not be at war with the solution of the economic problems of Puerto Rico and yet would protect the dignity of our people within our association with the American Union.

The Path of Progress

Once we forthrightly faced this task in the middle of 1946, things began to happen. The political status lost its role of enemy of the solution of our economic problems; instead we considered it in the light of and in harmony with the effort to solve the great economic difficulties of our people. We moved at an unprece-dentedly accelerated pace which proved beyond peradventure that the log jam on status had finally been broken.

There had been no progress in self-government for Puerto Rico since 1917. Less than two months after this new approach to the problem of status had been adopted, the President of the United States appointed Jesús Piñero, who had been elected by the people of Puerto Rico as their Resident Commissioner in Washington, to the post of Governor of Puerto Rico. And it took only four years for Congress by Public Law 600 to offer to create a relationship between Puerto Rico and the United States based on a compact approved by the people of Puerto Rico and on a constitution written by the people of Puerto Rico themselves.

The wisdom of halting the divisive and futile debate on status, which para-lyzed our progress towards self-government from 1917 until 1946, has been dramatically demonstrated by the swiftness of the events which occurred be-tween 1946 and 1952. With this hindrance removed, the long-repressed political energy of our people soon created a new form of status, a new form of political relationship in the American Union and in all America, a new form of political harmony with the economic freedom of our people, in place of the rigid and sterile formulas which threatened the full development of Puerto Rico, which had immobilized for generations the great creative political powers of its people.

It should be made clear that what we have done has been to initiate a process of political creation in Puerto Rico, and not merely to invent just another formula. Precisely because it needs to grow in so many phases in its life as a people, Puerto Rico cannot become engaged in formulas. It must use its energy in development and continuous growth. Nothing could enslave us more than handicapping our great drive towards a happy future with a rigid, obsolescent, unprogressive, or inapplicable formula.

Interpretation of the Constitution

Every constitution is subject to different interpretations which are made in good faith. But our thesis is that by their votes in the referenda in which Public Law 600 and the constitution were approved, the people adopted the interpretations of these documents advanced by those who campaigned for their approval. We submit then that when the time comes for judicial review of the compact and the constitution, they should be interpreted in accordance with the understand-ing of the people as to their meaning and scope when they approved them. We are confident that such interpretations will prevail, and that they will yield the results which will be most favorable and liberal to Puerto Rico and which will promote fraternal understanding between Puerto Rico and the American Union.

Blanca Canales (1906–1996) and the Jayuya Revolt

The document excerpted here is part of a longer autobiographical account, written by Blanca Canales between 1967 and 1969. Canales was sentenced to life in prison for her role in the attack against Jayuya, a small town in the central highlands of Puerto Rico which took part in the Nationalist uprising that shook the island on October 30, 1950. This excerpt corresponds to pages 19-49 of the Spanish version, published in San Juan, Puerto Rico (1997), under the title La Constitución es la Revolución. The publication was sponsored by the Comité de Estudios of the Congreso Hostosiano. Authorization to translate the entire Canales account and publish it in English was granted to me by the past Director of the Instituto de Estudios Hostosianos, Professor Vivian Quiles-Calderín.

In 1898 Puerto Rico became a colony of the United States, following its involvement in the Spanish-Cuban-American War. Puerto Rico was ceded by Spain in the Paris Peace Treaty, despite the fact that it had granted the island autonomy the previous year. The fact that members of the Puerto Rican government were not consulted during the peace negotiations became a bone of contention for those who wished to see Puerto Rico independent.

During the first half of the twentieth century, two groups consistently advocated for Puerto Rico's independence. One of them, the Puerto Rico Nationalist Party, founded in 1922, at first favored independence via the ballot but gradually revised its strategy in favor of armed struggle. The man responsible for this change was Pedro Albizu Campos, a Harvard-educated lawyer, who joined the party in 1922 and became its president in 1930. There are numerous speculations but no hard evidence as to Albizu's motives. There is evidence, however, that he was kept under constant surveillance and was increasingly harassed, eventually arrested, and sent to prison in 1936. Convicted of advocating the overthrow of the U.S. colonial government in Puerto Rico, he was sentenced to a prison term of ten years, six of which had to be served in a federal penitentiary in Atlanta, Georgia. Shipped to Georgia in 1937, he remained absent from Puerto Rico until December 15, 1947. His return was greeted by thousands of well wishers.

Translated and edited by Olga Jiménez de Wagenheim.

The warm welcome of so many and the fiery speeches of a more radicalized Albizu led the local legislature to enact a gag rule, Law #53, in June 1948, as a deterring measure. Law #53 turned out to be essentially a Spanish version of the Smith Act enacted in the United States. Also known locally as Ley de la Mordaza, the new law made it a crime to print, publish, sell, or exhibit any material that advocated independence. Once in effect, Law #53 sought to restrict the right of citizens to demonstrate, organize, and publicly assemble for any activity that could be construed as an "attempt to overthrow the existing government." Violators were threatened with arrest, fines of $10,000, and prison terms of up to ten years. None of these threats deterred Pedro Albizu Campos or his followers. In fact, between the summer of 1948 and October 1950, they planned an armed uprising that erupted in October 1950, as Canales' account makes evident.

As one of the rebel leaders involved in the planning of the revolt and the attack against Jayuya, Canales explains that she was "destined" to play a role in the liberation of her homeland. Due to space limitations, I offer here only an edited portion of the chronology of events that led her and her comrades to obey the orders of Pedro Albizu Campos to attack the police headquarters and federal agencies in the town of Jayuya on October 30, 1950.

She explains: "On October 27, 1950, I was driving to Jayuya and stopped at a friend's home in Manatí where I learned that [some of the] men . . . escorting Don Pedro had been arrested the previous evening. . . . That evening, October 26, Don Pedro had gone to Fajardo to honor the birth date of General Antonio Valero [Bernabé] . . . and near dawn the men were detained as they were returning [to San Juan]. I had not known [this] because I had not been listening to the radio (pp. 19-20).

"After I heard [the news] . . . my friends begged me to stay in Manatí, but I drove on to Jayuya, my home and base of operations, in case there had to be a confrontation with the puppet government (p. 20).

"I reached Jayuya by nightfall, and as I headed home to Coabey I found cousin Elio [Torresola] in a local store and relayed the information. The news required that we be prepared, as I will explain later, primarily because we feared that they (the authorities) would try to arrest Don Pedro . . . a feat that would cost them dearly because this time it would not be like the last time when Don Pedro had insisted that we remain calm when he was arrested (p. 20).

. . .

"Since the decade of [the] thirties the imperial power had been trying to do away with Don Pedro. It is known that there were attempts on his life, but they all had failed because of Albizu's personal valor and because a Nationalist guard protected him at his home, at meetings, and during his travels throughout the island. [The need to protect Albizu] led us to acquire arms . . . and to [enlist] our youth, which included Elio and Griselio Torresola, Carlos Irizarry, and his cousins Fidel and Mario Irizarry. [They all took turns] guarding Albizu during the three months he remained at my house in 1948 (pp. 21-22).

"[And while training] the youth to handle firearms was difficult, they carried on, sometimes forced to train by the river's edge, under the pretext of hunting for birds. Practice shooting in the valley of Coabey was particularly difficult because it is surrounded by mountains, and the shots echoed throughout the area and alerted the neighbors. [Nonetheless] I practiced with a caliber 38 revolver that Don Pedro had given me (pp. 21-22).

. . . .

"[The order] to activate the Nationalist military camps was not given by Don Pedro until after Law #53 was enacted in [June] 1948. [At the time], the Nationalists in each municipality were organized into two sub-groups: a civil junta and a military camp that was in charge of military operations. [In Jayuya] the president of the civil junta was the cabinet maker Ramón Robles, [later] known as 'a hero of the uprising of 1950,' while the one in charge of military affairs was Elio Torresola. His brother, Griselio, 'later known as hero and martyr,' had gone to New York on a special mission, [part of which] included purchasing arms (pp. 23-24).

. . . .

"I remember one day that Don Pedro was pacing back and forth in the living room of my house in Coabey, as a form of exercise. I was sitting in the dining room and noticed that he paced with his head down, as if in meditation. Suddenly, he stopped, and said to me: 'I am thinking that it is necessary to prepare for the revolution because the government will try to arrest me at any moment. I am also getting old, and that is what they are waiting for: my old age and my death. So, that means that we have to speed up the preparations' (p. 24).

". . . When Public Law 600 was approved by the U.S. Congress (a major step towards the creation of the Commonwealth of Puerto Rico), [and] given the onerous requirement of military conscription for the [U.S.] Korean War . . . he could not wait [any longer and] . . . issued his call to revolt: 'La constitución es la revolución,' during his visit to Lares on September 23, 1950 (p. 24).

. . . .

"On Saturday, October 28, a group of inmates revolted in the State Penitentiary [in San Juan]. While that event may not have been part of the [revolutionary] plot, it seems to have precipitated matters and to lead the government to order home searches and the arrests of Nationalists, as Don Pedro confirmed a few days later. [Fear of arrest] led Don Pedro to give the order to begin the attack . . . the following Monday, three days after his guards were detained . . . (p. 24).

. . . .

"I have already recounted how I reached Coabey, Jayuya, the night of [October] 27 and told my cousin Elio what I had heard . . . and how we needed to get ready.

"The next day, Saturday, [October] 28, I went down to the town of Jayuya to run some errands and buy the newspaper. As I drove into town, I saw Mr. Juan Jaca, a well-known Nationalist from Arecibo, on the street near the bridge that leads to Coabey. I stopped the car. As he got in he told me that he had a message for Elio and me. In questions of military matters we (Jayuyans) answered to the commander of the northern area whose headquarters were located in the District of Arecibo (p. 25).

"Once in my house in Coabey we sent for my cousin Elio and when he arrived, Jaca explained the situation and conveyed the order that the revolution was to begin on Monday. We were to start by attacking the police station at 12:30. The [lunch] hour was deemed [appropriate] for a surprise attack. Jaca did not stay for lunch because he had urgent business in Arecibo. He accepted only an orange juice from the oranges from my farm.

"As I drove Jaca back to town we talked about the importance of the step we were about to take, and I remember telling him: 'I have been waiting for this moment for many years. I am very pleased that we have finally decided [to act] now because we have been planning this for a year-and-a-half and I am tired of waiting. And while I understand that we don't have enough firearms, we have to act without delay' (p. 26).

"The truth is that a revolutionary or conspirator who struggles to free his homeland lives [on two planes]: the secret one in which he plots and prepares; and the public one in which he deals with the problems of daily life. [In my own case] I was dealing with the matter of how to make my farm productive, possibly by starting a gardening business . . . in addition to my job as a social worker. At the time, I was on an extended, unpaid medical leave because of health issues (p. 26).

"Jaca's trip to Jayuya had to be kept confidential. In order not to arouse suspicion I left him on the bridge that connects Coabey to the town, but since he seemed unsure as to which 'público car' to board . . . we agreed that he would walk to the plaza . . . and I would follow at some distance until I saw that he found his way out of town. I then went to the gas station, filled up the [tank], and returned home to Coabey (pp. 26-27).

"Elio, the person in charge of military affairs, had to recruit the men and find the firearms [needed for the assault.] Although my farm was the place where men conspired and the firearms were hidden, I did not know how many there were in either case. Elio was taking care of everything, in a hurry. On Sunday afternoon he convinced Carlos Irizarry 'our now known martyr' to stay home and fight rather than go back to the University of Puerto Rico, where he was a senior. Carlos had served in the U.S. Army, in Germany, during World War II, and we needed him (pp. 27-28).

"Since I had not been feeling well (since the oral surgery) I stayed home making some remedies and burning 'papers and documents' I did not want to fall into enemy hands.

"On Sunday evening [October 29] I approached Elio and Carlos, who were meeting in a corner of my porch, to ask them what they had done. They explained that they had few firearms. It was decided they would make a few Molotov cocktails with the gas from my car. The firearms had already been stored under the house, and the Molotov cocktails would be stored in an empty pigeon coop to the northeast of the house. I asked whether they planned to cut the communication lines and blow up the bridges. 'Unfortunately,' they replied, 'the dynamite we had was sent to Mayagüez and other places, and is no longer available to blow up the bridges and telephone facilities.' The weekend was not a good time to go looking for dynamite without calling attention and blowing the cover of the surprise attack. [We recalled that] Don Pedro had stopped coming to Jayuya lately, to deflect attention from us, so we could take the town by surprise and proclaim the republic (pp. 28-29).

". . . We agreed that once we had seized the police station we would take the microphones and bullhorn at City Hall, to issue a manifesto to the townspeople. We also agreed that since Carlos Irizarry had military experience he would be the one to take charge of the military operation and lead the charge against the police station (p. 29).

"I lived practically alone in the summer house in Coabey, except for . . . Uncle Raúl . . . who had [recently] moved in . . . and helped with chores at the farm. [On weekends] nieces, cousins, and sometimes friends were likely to visit. . . . The one who came most often was my cousin Gladys Torresola, but she was of no concern because she shared our ideals . . . (p. 29). [This weekend] I was alone with Raúl . . . [since] not even the women who used to take turns cooking and cleaning for me [had come] . . . ; they had told me three weeks ago that their whole family would be moving to Ponce. This [move] seemed so sudden . . . that I began to suspect whether they had become informants for the police. . . . I became almost certain that one of them might have seen a bayonet my cousin Griselio had carelessly left in one of the bedrooms when he last visited (p. 30).

"We hoped the evening of October 29, 1950, ended quietly, without any undue incident. [To that end] Elio decided to postpone calling on the men for the attack . . . until Monday morning. Only Reinaldo Morales was there, guarding the firearms, in the lower level of my house. But he was a very brave lad . . . who had been a member of Don Pedro's guard during the time he lived at my house. . . . [The time he] shot himself accidentally in the thigh, I had secretly taken him to . . . Dr. Pelegrina, a great doctor, friend of the family . . . [who] treated him twice but never reported the incident to the police. We had kept him (Morales) at the house for about three weeks while he convalesced. I served as his nurse and the lad remembered and appeared to be grateful . . . (pp. 30-31).

". . . Over the [weekend] I had time to meditate on the step we were about to take but remained calm and determined. At my age (three months short of my forty-fourth birthday and six years short of twenty years of service as a social worker), after nineteen years in the Nationalist Party, I understood that the step we were about to take was one of life or death, or at the very least would land us in jail [when we were] defeated by the great forces of the Yankee empire, which included the National Guard and the Insular Police, which on the advice of the FBI, persecuted even those who sought independence through peaceful means. I understood [also] that this was our chance to rise and let the world know that we were a people who wanted to be free. The bigger the uprising and the longer it lasted, the better it would be (p. 31).

. . . .

"As I thought about all of this . . . I became reaffirmed in my decision that we needed to take the town of Jayuya.

" . . . On Sunday afternoon, I went into each of the rooms in the house; I sat on a rocking chair in the living room and looked for a long time at the Puerto Rican flag on the foyer wall. Conscious that I may never again set foot in the house of my childhood . . . the family's favorite house . . . I went into the room Don Pedro had occupied when he visited, and looked at the trees outside the window . . . and the mountains beyond, and thought of Lares (pp. 32-33).

. . . .

"Convinced that I was about to take . . . a transcendent . . . necessary step in the history of our beloved Puerto Rico, I slept soundly for a few hours and rose at six the next morning.

"Contrary to what has been said, Elio Torresola did not round up his men the night before, but began to do so on Monday morning, when he asked each of them to come to my house. The first he sent for was a driver we used to hire whenever Don Pedro needed to go somewhere, or be picked up in San Juan. His name was Carmelo [Maldonado], known as 'El Cano.' I was up in my room, listening to the radio, to see how the country fared, while Elio and Carlitos [Irizarry] were instructing the men who were gathering in the front yard and below the house. The news [at first] revolved around the breakout at the Insular Penitentiary . . . (p. 34).

"[Without help in the kitchen] and with so much to worry about that Monday morning, there was no time to think about preparing meals. We hurriedly drank coffee and ate some crackers, standing up, as soldiers do when they are in a hurry. Around 9:00 in the morning I asked my Uncle Raúl to serve coffee and crackers to the men gathered on the patio (p. 35).

. . . .

"At 10 or 10:30 in the morning a news bulletin came over the radio, saying that there had been a shoot-out in Peñuelas. [The previous night] several Ponce Nationalists, afraid their homes would be searched, moved the firearms [they had] to Peñuelas, to the farm of the engineer, and 'now martyr,' Guillermo González-Ubides. During one of their trips, sometime around dawn . . . one of them let out a shot, and that brought a confrontation with the police (p. 36).

"The plan to take the various police headquarters [by surprise] at 12:30 on Monday, October 30, was aborted in Peñuelas. News of the shoot-out in Peñuelas spread quickly and we heard it at 10:30 [Monday] morning. I reported it to Elio through the open window, and can't recall what he replied (p. 36).

". . . Around 11:00 in the morning we heard that the Arecibo Nationalists had attacked the police headquarters. I called Elio up to my room and we agreed that the uprising had started. . . . Arecibo [we reasoned] had struck earlier [than planned] because of the incident in Peñuelas, and we, too, needed to hurry. Elio asked me to talk to the men gathered in the basement, because 'in circumstances such as this, a woman's words infuse men with valor' (p. 36).

"Elio left because he still had much to do, while I tried to think what I would tell the men. Recalling something Don Pedro had said one day . . . I removed the flag from the wall . . . and went with it downstairs, [for this] was a flag with a history; it had been flown at the San Juan gate by a group of independence supporters the day Don Pedro returned home, on December 15, 1947. . . . That flag had [also] been to Lares and to Manatí, on June 11, 1948 (pp. 36-37).

"I went down to the patio . . . and Carlos summoned most of the men to the basement. . . . I entered . . . and told those comrades the news about the arrest of Don Pedro's guard three days earlier . . . and that this was the moment to act. I don't recall what else I said, but I ended by telling them that we would go and seize the town, and while displaying the flag I asked them 'to swear to defend the flag, Don Pedro, and the liberty of Puerto Rico with their lives.' Then I cried out, 'Swear, on your knees!' Carlos knelt, signaling to the men [to do the same]. And in a booming voice, Carlos cried, 'I swear,' which the others repeated, in unison. Then they rose and we left the basement (p. 37).

"[Outside] I ran into Elio who told me that he had only 15 men and needed more . . . and had to obtain more firearms. . . . Carlitos [Irizarry] and I agreed that we better hurry and get to [Jayuya] . . . before we were met with heavy resistance. . . . [Also] with 15 men milling around the patio we were likely to be noticed if we lingered. . . . Pistol in hand, Carlitos and another man commandeered a van that was headed to town. . . . The driver was uncooperative but when threatened handed over the van and let out the passengers on the patio (p. 38).

"I noticed that a woman was crying and screaming, so I took her up to the porch and [reassured] her that there was nothing to fear. 'This,' I said, 'is a revolution, which we are doing for you, for the good of the people. You see that I am well off economically, but I risk all this for you, for the liberty of my homeland' (p. 38).

"I left her [still] on the porch and . . . I left last . . . in Cano's car. Mine . . . had been taken by the men assigned to attack the police station. Elio and Carlos had assigned me to 'silence the phone' in town . . . and then go and display the Puerto Rican flag and proclaim the republic from the hotel in the center of town (p. 39).

"I went to the telephone center but found I was unable to cut the wires with the tool I had. Just then the bag where I carried my revolver flew open and the operator (a woman) became frightened and promised to lock up and hide. I went to the center of town looking for one of our men to keep an eye on the telephone operator, but I could not find anyone (p. 39).

"When I reached the hotel, which was [located] above Guillermo Hernández' pharmacy, a boy came to tell me that the owners had left that morning for Ponce. . . . But since I knew they sympathized with [our cause], I went up to the balcony, where I had a view of the entire town. I saw smoke coming out of the police station but could not see the men attacking it. . . . I proceeded to wave the flag, holding it by the blue triangle and letting the rest fall downward. I waved it many times while I cried out, 'Long Live Free Puerto Rico!' I asked the people gathering below to join the revolution (pp. 39-40).

"The place where I stood was on the corner of Main Street and the street heading to Coabey . . . a heavily trafficked area. In addition to the persons who stopped to smile and cheer there were others who walked by hurriedly. Some did not seem to understand what was happening. Several (women) teachers walked by, two of them screaming hysterically. But in general the townsmen and the students understood what was happening and gave their tacit assent to the cry 'Long Live Free Puerto Rico!' (p. 40).

. . . .

"I waited on the balcony for Elio and Carlos to come [so we could] issue a formal proclamation. Around 1:00 in the afternoon Elio came by with a platoon but told me that they were going after a few policemen who were said to be hiding. . . . A few minutes later a young man came to tell me that Carlos had been wounded and had been denied treatment at the local hospital. I went down to find my car. . . . [While a] student helped me with the search . . . another messenger came to tell me that Mario Irizarry, Carlos's cousin, wanted to take him to Utuado (p. 41).

. . . .

"I drove up the hill and found Carlos lying on a patch of grass, in front of the Jayuya hospital, where he had been refused treatment (p. 41).

. . . .

"[When] I approached [I saw that though] Carlos had a bullet wound in his chest he was not visibly bleeding nor had lost consciousness. [And he] with the gallantry of a patriot said to me: 'Do not take me to Utuado. Leave me here and continue the struggle.' His words put me momentarily in a quandary: 'Should I obey his plea and return to town? Or should I give succor to our heroic commander?' I decided to do whatever I could to save his life. 'Comrade,' I replied, 'the town has been captured and other men have joined the struggle, so we want to take you to Dr. Pelegrina's clinic in Utuado. . . . Then we will return here' (pp. 41-42).

"Mario helped him up and laid him in the back seat, holding his head on his lap. . . . I drove to Guillermo Hernández' pharmacy and had him give [Carlos] a shot to contain the bleeding . . .

"Since we were on a Red Cross mission, and thinking that in war those who offer succor to the wounded are respected, I left my revolver with one of the rebels. I also left the flag, so that it could be flown at City Hall when the republic was proclaimed (p. 42).

"When we left, the police station was on fire, forcing us to change our route. Although the trip took [only] 40 to 45 minutes . . . Carlos was already fading. At the entrance of Utuado he began asking for water so we stopped at a nearby house and Mario got the water . . . and held him up while he drank. When he was finished, he cried out, 'Viva Puerto Rico Libre!' Those would prove to be his last words. Perhaps he knew that he was dying and as a revolutionary, a hero, he wanted to leave [this earth] with a proclamation of liberty [on his lips] (p. 42).

. . . .

"As I write these lines, 19 years later . . . my heart leaps and my eyes are teary. I am proud to have belonged to the Jayuya group, which, inspired by Don Pedro Albizu Campos, proclaimed Puerto Rico's right to be a free, sovereign republic (pp. 42-43).

. . . .

". . . When we reached the town [Utuado] looking for Dr. Pelegrina's clinic . . . we [found] the streets had been blocked . . . because the police and the Nationalists were engaged in a shoot-out (p. 43).

. . . .

". . . Told about another clinic on the other side of town, I drove in that direction. . . . Carlos had become weaker. . . . He had to be supported by Mario when he went into the . . . clinic, which turned out to be Veterans Hospital. . . . Since Carlos was a veteran of the Second World War, he was admitted . . . after Mario gave [the information needed] (p. 44).

. . . .

"[On the way back to Jayuya] as we approached the small bridge at Jayuya Abajo, a man driving a van yelled something I did not understand. . . . Mario thought he said, 'We could not get through.' We smiled, thinking that the revolutionaries [had taken over] (p. 45). A little later we saw an abandoned car, but did not know why. [But] as we rounded the curve by the now defunct sugar mill Santa Barbara, we came face to face with a 'police patrol.' [I] didn't have time to . . . speed up, even if they had shot at us.

"They asked us to stop, and naively thinking that they could not arrest us because we were not carrying firearms, or anything that could incriminate us, I stopped the car. Two policemen, pointing guns, approached us and ordered us out of the car. The one on the right aimed at Mario, and the one on the left aimed at me. He searched me roughly [and] took away my purse, where I carried money and other valuables that were never returned to me. He put me into the patrol car alongside Mario (p. 45).

"He then picked up a microphone from the front seat and asked to be connected to San Juan, and told them, screaming, 'We have arrested the Nationalist leader Blanca Canales and her companion Mario Irizarry.' That was [the moment] I realized that they did not need evidence. They already knew that we were the persons who had attacked the town of Jayuya . . . even if he [mistakenly] said Mayagüez. . . . I, who always thought of myself as a modest rank and file soldier, was being proclaimed the leader of the uprising by the enemy (pp. 45-46).

"It was a hot day . . . around 2:30 in the afternoon . . . and the police van was all enclosed, except for the wire mesh that separated the back from the front seat. I suffer from a thyroid condition and was not feeling well. Being locked up made me dizzy. The lack of air was nauseating. . . . I begged God to help keep me from making a spectacle in front of my enemies, as they would [very likely] interpret it as lack of courage. I sat up closer to the wire mesh (p. 46).

"I began thinking about . . . [the policemen] who . . . in exchange for a government salary . . . persecute, jail, and even kill those who struggle to free the homeland so that they no longer have to be slaves. Then the policemen entered the van . . . saying, 'Let's hurry into town and put them in front so they can catch their comrades' bullets.' Mario and I merely looked at each other. We did not talk, so as not to provoke those furious beasts (p. 46).

"But the cowards did not dare enter the town [Jayuya] even after they called for reinforcements. About 4:00 in the afternoon they took us out of the police van . . . and transferred us to the back seat of my car, [which was being guarded] by a policeman holding a rifle with a bayonet attached. The policeman [now] guarding us . . . appeared to be both angry and afraid . . . he kept peering at the cane fields around the sugar mill. At one point he stopped pacing around the car and pointing his rifle at me yelled, 'I feel like killing this old hag.' I remained inscrutable, yet I confess that I was more upset by his reminder of my age than by the thought that he might kill me (pp. 46-47).

"The way the car was parked . . . allowed us to see smoke still coming out of City Hall. We heard a man say that the City Hall had been torched. We were pleased because that meant that Elio had continued the fight despite having lost Carlos and Mario. The patrolmen were not moving . . . as a man had come to tell them that 'there were many revolutionaries about, that around 200 men were in control of the town' (p. 47).

. . . .

"At nightfall a Police Lieutenant . . . took the wheel of my car while another policeman sat in back seat. We were led away. We had no idea where they were taking us. But as we began to climb the Pica road I realized that we were being taken to Ponce. We remained quiet, but I began asking myself why they weren't taking us to Arecibo, since in judicial matters Jayuya falls under the jurisdiction of the District of Arecibo (p. 48).

"The rest of the story, what became of me, the trials, my long jail sentence, etc., I have sketched elsewhere (p. 48).

"Let us turn to what happened in . . . [Jayuya] after I left it. I will base the little I know from the confidences comrades shared with me during the trials, and from a few exchanges I have had with others after they were released . . .

"The municipality [Jayuya] remained under rebel control for three days. The [Puerto Rican] flag was raised on the very spot where I had issued the cry of liberty while the men were attacking the police station. The town was bombed from the air by the National Guard, and then the military forces entered and recaptured the town on October 31. The revolutionaries retreated to Coabey but did not surrender until November 2 (pp. 48-49).

"The Nationalists, under the command of Elio Torresola, set fire to the office of the U.S. Selective Service and destroyed its records. They torched the U.S. Post Office, the Court, the Tax Office, and City Hall. They also set fire to the homes of policemen and other sworn enemies of independence, such as the Inspector of Schools and other informants who had spied on us" (p. 49).

"I LOVE MY COUNTRY"

Despite the fact that the island's economy was on the move, and living standards were rising, not all Puerto Ricans were willing to peacefully accept the Commonwealth status as a solution to colonialism.

On July 4, 1950, President Harry S. Truman signed Law 600, which allowed Puerto Ricans to draft their own constitution under a Commonwealth form of government. On October 30, that same year, five armed Nationalists attacked La Fortaleza, the Governor's mansion in San Juan; there were bloody uprisings in other island towns, causing twenty-seven deaths and ninety gunshot injuries. On November 1, two Puerto Ricans—Griselio Torresola and Oscar Collazo—made an amateurish, but headline-catching, attempt to kill President Truman in Washington. Despite this unrest, and despite the fact that many voters abstained in protest, the Commonwealth constitution was approved by a vote of 374,000 to 82,000 on March 3, 1952. But the Nationalists did not give up. On March 2, 1954—exactly thirty-seven years after Woodrow Wilson signed a law that made all Puerto Ricans citizens of the United States—headlines on the front pages of newspapers throughout the world screamed out that a band of Nationalists had opened fire in the halls of Congress of the most powerful nation on earth.

From Edward F. Ryan, *The Washington Post,* March 2, 1954, pp. 1, 12-13. © The Washington Post. Reprinted by permission.

A squad of Puerto Rican terrorists, led by a woman, fired a wild fusillade of pistol shots from a visitors' gallery into the crowded United States House of Representatives yesterday, and wounded five Congressmen, one so severely he was given only a 50-50 chance to live.

Critically wounded was Rep. Alvin M. Bentley (R.-Mich.), a freshman member. A bullet plowed into his chest, down through his abdomen, and out his side. . . .

The four other Congressmen, one with a flesh wound in the back, three with wounds in the legs, were all reported in good condition last night. . . .

The "suicide squad," a woman and three men, were identified by police as belonging to the Puerto Rican Nationalist Party. Two other party members had tried to assassinate President Truman in November, 1950, at Blair House in Washington. Police said the four yesterday bought one-way tickets from New York, expecting never to return alive. . . .

All residents of New York, the four terrorists *are:* Mrs. Lolita Lebrón, 34, divorcee, of 315 W. 94th St., New York City; Rafael Cancel Miranda, 25, 120 S. First St., Brooklyn; Andrés Figueroa Cordero, 29, and Irving Flores Rodríguez, both of 108 E. 103rd St., New York City.

The woman boasted the shooting was planned on George Washington's birthday, was staged for Puerto Rican independence, and was timed to coincide with the opening of the Tenth Inter-American Conference in Caracas, Venezuela. . . .

In the wake of the attack, both Houses speedily adjourned while police threw heavy guards around the Capitol, and leaders ordered immediate extra security measures for future sessions.

In addition, extra guards were assigned to protect Vice President Richard M. Nixon and his family, as well as Interior Secretary Douglas McKay and Agriculture Secretary Ezra Taft Benson, both of whom canceled a scheduled joint visit to Puerto Rico.

The attack was without precedent in American history. One veteran legislator called it "an attack on representative Government."

The woman stood up without warning, waved a flag, and fired the first shot, according to her story to police. Her shot was the signal for the others to fire. There were a score or more of shots, fired staccato within a few seconds. The woman screamed, witnesses said, in Spanish. It sounded like "Vive La Mexico" to some and "Vive Puerto Rico" to others.

Their fantastic fusillade shattered the routine of the House of Representatives at 2:20 P.M.

The House was halfway through a vote on a resolution to permit debate on a bill that would authorize continuation of a program for admitting Mexican farm laborers for temporary employment in this country.

Speaker Joseph W. Martin, Jr. (R-Mass.) said "I had just finished counting the "ayes"—168—and was about to call the "noes" when I heard the first two or three cracks. I looked up to see what was going on and I moved back against the wall.

"The gunfire was coming from the back row of the gallery at the southwest corner. A women there was waving a flag and shouting. She was shooting too, and so were some men."

Members thought at first it was a demonstration with blanks. Then they started feeling bits of plaster hit them. . . . There was a sudden rush for the doors, while some members ducked behind chairs. Others hit the floor. . . .

Two bullets slapped into the majority leader's desk. . . . Other bullets hit the rear walls of the House, the ceiling, and punctured the chairs where members sit. . . .

A score or more of bullets had been fired in a few agonizing seconds. Then there was silence. A visitor in the gallery, Frank Wise, of Tacoma Park, Md., said he was five seats away from the Puerto Ricans. When the shooting stopped, he jumped at one of the gunmen, and "pinioned his arms."

Wise said he rushed the man out of the Gallery and pushed him into the hands of people there. Then he turned just as a second man came through the door. "I grabbed him around the arms and said 'here, this man's got a gun, too.'"

Both men were disarmed in a wild melee.

Mrs. Lebrón and two men, Miranda and Cordero, were seized at the Capitol, while Rodríguez was picked up later at the Greyhound Bus Terminal, police said. Police also seized three other Puerto Ricans from Florida at the bus station, but concluded after questioning the Florida trio that they had nothing to do with the shooting.

According to Murray [Police Chief Robert V.—ed.] Mrs. Lebrón said the quartet got together in New York on George Washington's Birthday and agreed to come to Washington to stage a demonstration for the freedom of Puerto Rico.

Murray said documents found in her pocket indicated she was a member of the Nationalist Party of Puerto Rico.

According to Tom Kennamar, House Doorkeeper, the woman's purse contained a note which said:

"Before God and the world, my blood claims for the independence of Puerto Rico. My life I give for the freedom of my country. This is a cry for victory in our struggle for independence which for more than half a century has tried to conquer the land that belongs to Puerto Rico.

"I state forever that the United States of America is betraying the sacred principles of mankind in their continuous subjugation of my country, violating their rights to be a free nation and a free people, in their barbarous torture of our apostle of independence, Don Pedro Albizu Campos."

On the back of the paper . . . was written:

"I take responsible for all."

. . . . Secret Service and FBI agents also questioned the four. Police had some trouble at the outset because all the group spoke broken English. Interpreters were called in to help question them in Spanish. . . .

Mrs. Lebrón and Miranda told newsmen in an interview last night that they shot the Congressmen to bring to the attention of the American people and the world that Puerto Rico is not free.

Mrs. Lebrón said as long as Puerto Rico is not free such a shooting "may happen again."

. . . . She said she was treated well by police. "Somebody has to be punished and I want the law to punish me," she continued. . . .

She said she came to the United States six years ago and was employed in a sewing machine factory in New York. She said she had an eighth grade education and was a Catholic.

Miranda, who said he was not sorry they shot the Congressmen, told newsmen he was jailed for two years in Puerto Rico as a draft dodger.

He said he left Puerto Rico about a year ago and now operates a punch press in a shoe factory in New York. . . .

Boyd Crawford . . . staff administrator of the House Foreign Relations Committee, was in the committee room when he heard the shooting. . . .

"I recognized it as gunfire and I tore out of the committee room to see what it was all about. I saw a small slender woman there and heard her scream something in Spanish and heard her say in English 'I love freedom, I love my country.'"

WORKER IN THE CANE

While the industrialization program pushed ahead in the 1950's, Puerto Rico remained largely rural, and most of the country's working men still earned their "rice and beans" by toiling in the sugar cane fields. Anthropologist Sidney Mintz, who spent several years observing the lives of Puerto Rico's plantation workers, here provides a close-up view.

From the air the narrow coastal plain of southern Puerto Rico looks like an irregular green ribbon. It contrasts sharply with the blues and azures of the sea to the south, and with the sere vegetation of the uplands to the north. The plain itself is covered with sugar cane. A road cuts through the cane, paralleling the sea, and linking towns along the coast. Most of the people live in rural areas rather than in the towns: in shacks that hug the shoulders of the road or stretch around the bays and inlets; in barracks and houses around the plazas of the old-time sugar haciendas; or in company towns built up near the monster cane-grinding mills. The mills are the most conspicuous landmarks from the air: their chimneys cast long shadows over the shacks and across the cane. From the air, the workers' shacks look regular and neat. There is a picturesqueness about the thatched roofs, the waving palms, and the nearness of the sea. But walking through a village destroys such impressions. The ground is pounded hard and dusty, littered with tin cans, paper, coconut husks, and cane trash. The houses are patched with old Coca Cola signs, boards torn from packing cases, and cardboard. Only a few are painted. The seeming order dissolves into disorder and crowding. Large families are packed into tight living places. The houses are variously divided into two, three, or more sections "by partitions which never reach the ceiling. The cooking is done in ramshackle lean-tos behind the living quarters. And all around the houses grows the cane.

Such a village is Jauca. The barrio called Jauca contains clusters of houses, some on the edge of the sea, some along the east-west highway, and others bunched around the centers of the *colonias* —the great farms of the corporations which control over 95 per cent of all the cultivated land in the municipality. In Barrio Jauca the largest aggregation of houses is along the highway; this village is called Poblado Jauca. The nearest large groupings are at the beach to the south and to the northwest near the plaza of the largest colonia in the barrio, Colonia Destino. There is a company store at Colonia Destino; 36 little two-room shacks provided rent free by the corporation to resident workers; a two-story house for the *mayordomo,* or overseer; two barracks left from slavery times and still occupied; and the ruined shell of the hacienda warehouse, now used to store machinery and fertilizer. The only trees in view are some palms growing near a point on the beach, the twin rows of tamarinds which line the approach to Colonia Destino, and a few scattered fruit trees among the houses of Poblado Jauca.

Poblado Jauca consists of a string of shacks lining the highway, and a sub-

From Sidney M. Mintz, *Worker in the Cane* (New Haven: Yale University Press, 1960), pp. 12-22. Copyright © 1960 by Yale University Press. Reprinted by permission.

stantial cluster of additional houses—on an acre plot of land called Palmas Oril-
lanas—which extend from the road southward toward the sea. There are fewer
than a dozen small stores and bars, two school buildings, and, at one end of the
village, the crumbling mill and chimney of an old sugar hacienda. The village
has standpipes along the road to supply its water, many of the houses are elec-
trified, and the road which connects the village to the towns of Santa Isabel to
the west and Salinas to the east is well surfaced. In its outward appearance,
Poblado Jauca does not differ significantly from hundreds of other such "line"
villages in the sugar areas of Puerto Rico.

At five o'clock in the morning Poblado Jauca is still and deserted-looking.
An occasional touring car goes by on the coast road carrying passengers from
Ponce to San Juan. The roosters crow and the dogs bark and the surf sounds
softly. Every shack is shut tightly—the wooden shutters of the windows closed
against the "night air," the doors barred. The cookhouses behind the shacks are
cold; the sun is still low. An easterly breeze stirs the cane, rattles the Coca Cola
signs, shakes loose a ripe nut in the palm grove near the water.

But by six o'clock the village comes to life. The first signs are the swinging
back of the shutters that give on the back yard and the tendrils of smoke curling
out of the stoves. The first need of the morning is food: the food, coffee. In the
early morning the air has a deceptive chilly freshness. Everything is coolly
damp and stimulating. In less than an hour the entire quality of the morning is
transformed. By the time the men have drunk their coffee, tied their cuffs to
their ankles with cords, and picked up machetes or hoes and the food for the
midmorning breakfast, the sun is high and glittering; it weighs on the skin like
something tangible, burns away the dampness from every surface, almost crack-
les as it grows hotter. The men leave the houses, carrying their breakfast and
tools and dressed in rough work clothes, wide-brimmed straw hats, and old
shoes. They go to "defend themselves" *(se defienden)* in the cane, which is their
phrase for the struggle of making a living. These men have lived with the cane,
most of them, from the time they were born. It grows up to the edges of the
house plots. When it is in full glory it stands fifteen feet high, and the villages
are choked in it. It litters the roads; during harvest the smell of it fills the air,
the "hair" of its surface works into the skin like peach fuzz. Men who work in
the cane speak of "doing battle" *(bregando)* with it.

From the thatch shacks along the beach, from the wooden ones along the
highway, the men move toward the plazas of the old haciendas to get their work
orders for the day. Some will form the cutting lines; others will lay rails for the
wagons that are loaded in the fields or will do the loading. There are cultivators
and seeders, seed cutters and winch operators, ditchers and gang bosses. Most

of the jobs can be done by nearly everyone, but individual workers have pref-
erences and some have special skills. Old Don Tomás, like many of the oldest
Negro people in the barrio, is a *palero*—a ditcher—the most skilled, the high-
est-paid, and the most prestigeful "dirt" job in the fields. The cutters come
mainly from the shacks at the beach; they are white men, most of them named
De Jesús, whose families migrated to the coast from nearby highlands. The De
Jesús are set somewhat apart by other Jauqueños. Some of them take their
Catholicism seriously and go to church; they try to grow little vegetable gardens
at the beach, and they fence their houses; they "marry cousin with cousin"; and
unlike the old coastal working families, they prefer cane cutting on a piecework
basis to most other jobs. Aníbal and Fredo are truck drivers; they were in the
Army, and learned some skills there most Jauqueños, and especially the older
ones, could never acquire. Truck driving pays relatively well and it is easy work
compared to cutting or loading. Don Daniel likes to plant seed. It is a curious
choice, for Don Daniel is very tall and seeding requires that one bend over continuously, setting and tapping the seed—which is not seed at all, but cuttings
of cane stalk—into place.

By seven o'clock those who have work are out of the village. The children
eat and start for school, or begin their jobs at home—toting pails of water, mop-
ping the floors, tending the baby, ironing—or play in the yards with toys made
of old tin cans and bits of wood. As the sun climbs, each woman begins to prepare the hot lunch which must be carried out to her man in the fields, no matter
how far away he may be working. No Puerto Rican cane worker will settle for
a cold midday meal. At nine o'clock he has his thermos of black coffee and a
piece of bread smeared with margarine or topped with a slice of cheese or
sausage—he feels it gives him the strength he needs to work till noon— but at
noon someone must bring him a hot luncheon. Nests of pots hung on wire
frames are the lunchboxes of the Puerto Rican countryside. Sometimes the pots
hold noodle soup, or a quantity of starches such as boiled green bananas, taro,
yams, and Irish potatoes; fish broths, cornmeal cakes, and salads mixed with
bits of boiled salt cod are common. But no matter what else, one tin container
is always full of rice, another of red or white beans in a mild sauce. Rice and
beans are the staple of the lower-class Puerto Rican.

After lunch the cane workers pick up their machetes once more. Back home
the wives are busy with the laundry. They scrub the clothes on washboards,
remove stubborn dirt with scrapers fashioned from coconut shell, and hang the
clean clothes on fences or stretch them over pieces of corrugated iron to dry.
Then water is boiled for the afternoon coffee, and the youngest children must
be bathed and dressed to await their fathers' return. By three or four o'clock

the men have all returned, and the heat of the day has begun to abate slightly. The men bathe, crouching over the washtubs in the cookhouses or in showers fed from hand-filled tanks if they have them. It is in the late afternoon that the social life of the day begins. Men shave after their afternoon baths; young girls and boys put on their good clothes; the radios loudly announce the baseball scores, carry political discussions or Puerto Rican and other Latin American music.

Dinner is not eaten by the whole family seated at a table, but by each family member independently, down to the littlest, during a two-hour period. The father sits at the table and is served by his wife, who hovers about him, often with her youngest child in her arms. Again rice and beans and black coffee are the core of the meal but there may also be cornmeal slabs in fish broth; or stewed goat or beef; or boiled salt cod. Children eat standing in the kitchen, or sitting in the yard and feeding the chickens from their spoons. The dog and the chickens scour the floors and yards and follow the housewife about with friendly but cautious importunacy.

After dinner the street becomes the setting for conversation and flirting. Loafing groups gather in front of the small stores or in the yards of older men, where they squat and gossip; marriageable boys and girls promenade along the highway. Small groups form and dissolve in the bars. The women remain home; married couples rarely walk together, usually only on their way to revivalist prayer meetings. The more worldly young men—who have probably served in the Army and have a little money—may hail passing public cars and go to the movies in the nearby towns, or to see girls in neighboring villages. If it is a Tuesday or a Saturday night, illegal numbers-games sellers will be making their rounds, collecting bets placed on credit at an earlier time. The winning numbers (which are based on the winning numbers in the national *legal* lottery) will be announced the next morning over the radio, and nearly everyone in the village, knowing the favorite numbers of their fellows, will know who has won.

By nine o'clock—unless it is a Saturday—Jauca has grown quiet. Activity continues within the houses, the stores, and the Pentecostal chapel. Youths may prepare to hunt octopus and lobster on the cays, while their younger brothers are catching crabs in the cane fields, along the irrigation ditches. Couples in love say their good nights in the shadows. By ten even the stores are closed; one bar or two may still be open. The Pentecostals come home from their services. Only if there is a wake, a local political meeting, or a fight will activity continue outside the houses. The surf, scarcely noticeable during the noise of the day, can be heard again after ten o'clock, and the dogs and roosters vie with the gentle little croaking frogs—the *coquí*—in breaking the night's stillness.

During the course of the week the character of a day's activity varies. Saturdays are paydays, and Saturday nights are special. The nickelodeons play late into the night, and many people of all ages dance. Old Tomás Famanía, who has all his teeth and walks straight, though he carries a cane of *frescura* with a brass tip, and glories in his more than sixty years, comes up from his thatched shack at the beach to dance. He usually picks rumbas, and his partners will be Ceferino Hernández' daughters and granddaughters, none of them more than eight years old. The bachelors stand at the bar drinking their rum neat—each drink downed in a swallow from a tiny paper cup. The more affluent buy half pints of rum (called "Shirleys" after Shirley Temple) and finish them sitting at the tables. The teen-age males play pool on the much-ripped table in Cheo's bar and watch the girls walk by. Sometimes the barbecue pit at Cheo's will be going. A youth will crouch by the bed of hot charcoal, casually turning the long pole on which a whole pig is impaled.

On Saturday evenings during harvest the front doors of the houses are open. One can peer in to see the dimly lighted "parlor," which is separated from the "dining room" by a low wooden partition. There is the mother with one child nursing, another sleeping in her lap, a third perhaps drowsing at her feet or pulling at her skirt. The grandmother may be visiting, rocking in a chair, sometimes smoking a cigar. Conversation is animated and humorous: Don Fonso had to chase his mare two miles tonight down the main road; Barbino has nearly worn out the record called *Vuelve* (Return) at the bar, because his girl friend Wilma is leaving for "El Norte"; Don Fico hit on the *bolita* (numbers game) for $2,300 last Sunday; there is an elopement expected, or a revival meeting; how long will the *zafra* (harvest) last? The father returns from his visit to a *compadre* (godparent of one of his children) and greets his mother-in-law with respect and care. A man must maintain very good (but circumspect) relations with his mother-in-law. The children, those still awake, cling to him. He may put them to sleep by rocking and fondling them as the hours pass. When the front door is closed and the shutters are swung to, it is time for the parents to go to bed. One teen-age son may still be abroad; he will creep in after the house is dark, feast on the cold rice-and-bean leftovers from dinner, and crawl into bed, often alongside two or three brothers. And the bed may be a folding cot.

Sundays are quieter than weekdays, as Saturdays are noisier. The Pentecostal church has its day and its night services. Older people dress up on Sunday, though very few ever go to church. In the summer townspeople come to swim at the Jauca beach, to sit under the palms and drink soda or coconut water. Passing cars may stop in Jauca—a merchant or salesman seeks to purchase a dozen succulent land crabs to take home to San Juan. Jauqueños wander down to the beach to watch the townsmen swim. These are a different sort of people. They are not explicit about how they regard each other, but town and country are not quite the same, and the townsmen who come to swim or to buy crabs are not merely cane cutters who may live in town but storekeepers, civil servants, and teachers. And, parenthetically, it is not their color that sets them apart but their class.

Just as Saturday and Sunday differ from weekdays, so the harvest time differs from *el tiempo muerto*—dead time. From Christmas until early summer the cane is cut, and much cane is planted. The fields are alive with activity. Long lines of men stand before the cane like soldiers before an enemy. The machetes sweep down and across the stalks, cutting them close to the ground. The leaves are lopped off, the stalk cut in halves or thirds and dropped behind. It is a beautiful thing to watch from a hundred yards' distance. The men seem tiny but implacable, moving steadily against a green forest which recedes before them. When the cane has been piled and then scooped up, either by men who load it on carts brought into the fields on movable tracks, or by the new *arañas* (spiders), machines that load it on rubber-wheeled carts, the oxen may graze among the trash. And soon the field may be cleared for planting a new crop, which will be sprouting within weeks of the harvest.

From a distance, the scene is toylike and wholesome. Up close it is neither. The men sweat freely; the cane chokes off the breeze, and the pace of cutting is awesome. The men's shirts hang loose and drip sweat continuously. The hair of the cane pierces the skin and works its way down the neck. The ground is furrowed and makes footing difficult, and the soil gives off heat like an oven. The mayordomo sits astride a roan mare and supervises the field operations. He wears khakis and cordovan riding accessories. To see him ride past a line of men bent over and dripping sweat, to hear the sounds of the oxen in the fields behind, the human and animal grunting, and to feel the waves of heat billowing out of the ground and cane evoke images of other times. The men of Jauca grow drawn in the first two weeks of the harvest. This is the time to make the money to pay debts from the past dead time and to prepare for the next. It is a way of life that can make menial jobs in the continental United States seem like sinecures.

When the cane is entirely cut the intense activity ceases. The last trainload of cane, from the westernmost plantations serviced by the Machete and Aguirre mills, is pulled through Jauca by the little engine to the accompaniment of an unceasing whistling. The train is crying; the next day the whistles of Machete and Aguirre will cry. And then, people joke sourly, the people will cry. The nickelodeons play less. The drinkers of bottled rum turn back to *cañita*—"

the little cane," the illegal white rum. Don Tomás has no more dancing partners, because there are fewer nickels. The little account books each Puerto Rican family has for its food purchases begin to carry more unpaid entries. *Fia'o*—credit—gets extended two weeks instead of one, or four instead of two. Back before World War II, when Puerto Rico was much poorer, dead time was marked by a sharp increase in infant mortality, supposedly from a disease diagnosed as gastroenteritis; the correlation with the cessation of income does not seem to have been a coincidence.

In dead time one hears more reminiscence, there is more fishing, the ways to turn an extra penny are given more thought. Around the houses one notices little treasures that were overlooked before because they mean much less during the harvest: the bedraggled chickens, a melancholy goat, perhaps even a duck. There is a lime tree behind Don Cosine's house, and it will yield large quantities of lime drink. And if coffee is really short, one can brew *hedionda,* which grows all over. Headache powders may be better, but some headaches do pass if you crush a leaf of *naranja,* dip it in oil, and press it to the brow. Cheo has a hive of bees; and if one has a compadre who is a fisherman, he may make a present of the *carey* (turtle meat) that he could not sell or use this morning. A little corn-meal will make the land crabs fatter, and one's sons keep the crab traps going throughout the rainy season. The land is crowded with the growing cane and the yards are dry and sterile, but there is a tree here and a bush there, one hen still is laying, and octopuses live in the rocks of the cay. Everything belongs to Corporation Aguirre, it seems; but there is a little left that belongs to the people. The feast day of the patron saint of Santa Isabel—who is not Saint Elizabeth, despite the town's name, but Santiago Apóstol—comes in the summer, at a time when money is scarce. (Some wags have suggested that the town fathers should pick a new saint, preferably one whose birth may be commemorated during the harvest.) In October and November there is some work in the fields, for this is the planting period for the *gran cultura* (big growth) cane, which is allowed to stand fifteen or even eighteen months before it is cut. Some Novembers there are elections. The baseball season gets into swing. And when Christmas comes, the harvest is near once more. The year begins and ends with the swish of the machetes.

DON ABELARDO

Not all Puerto Ricans worked on large sugar cane plantations, which are mainly located along the flat coastal plains of the island. Many others lived in the mountainous interior, where tobacco, coffee, fruits, vegetables, and live-stock were important. Grinding poverty persisted in much of the countryside, and unsung heroes struggled to survive. Here, John Hawes—a long-time res-ident of the island—recounts an incident about a remarkable *barrio* leader, and the plight of strong men, with families, and without work.

D on Abelardo Reyes Rivera is a fiery little fighting cock of a man. In his middle sixties, with a shock of white hair that stands straight up on his head, large observant black eyes, three remaining front teeth which have turned yellow with age, like old ivory, he has been President of the Barrio for twenty years. For twenty years he has acted as the intermediary between his neighbors, in the valley that makes up Barrio Flores, and the municipal au-thorities. He has judged minor offenses that never reached the police; found work, whenever possible, for those who needed it, and settled disputes. His only authority derives from the neighbors who chose him, and like the judges of medieval Castille, he judges by no set code of laws, but *por sus sesos* (by his own wits and experience). His wits are sharp, and his experience encom-passes most of life in Barrio Flores.

Abelardo was born in the Barrio, and he has spent all of his sixty odd years there. He has seen the days of the tobacco boom, when everyone had money in their pockets, and life was good and the times, after a hurricane passed, when people collected palm nuts and wild beans from the scattered weeds, roasted them, and made a substitute for coffee. He survived the terrible time when the great Northern Tobacco Companies went into bankruptcy, and men went about the hills at night, burning the barns that had tobacco in them, to maintain their strike for a chance to live.

As long as he may live, he will never forget the night when he heard muffled voices outside his house at midnight and roused himself to see who the intruders were. At the first flicker of the match that he started to light the lamp with, a familiar voice called to him:

"Don't light the lamp Abelardo, and don't open the door. We will kill the

John Hawes, *The Island Times,* San Juan, Puerto Rico, March 25, 1960, p. 24. Copyright © 1960 John Hawes. Reprinted by permission.

cow, because people are hungry, and we will leave a share for you, but we don't want to be forced to hurt anyone."

He would never forget it, just as he would never forget that they left the head and a filete for him, propped up on sticks, where the dogs couldn't reach them.

"Fair enough," he said. Needless to say, he never said anything about recognizing the voice of his midnight visitor. In times of really desperate need, anyone might do such a thing. When his midnight visitor died, 15 years later, Abelardo was President of the Barrio. He went to the wake early in the evening. At three o'clock in the morning, when a group of people were about to leave, they offered to accompany him to his house.

"No," he said, "we have something in common, the dead man and I. I'll see him through." He stayed through the night, and in the first clear light of dawn, he helped to carry the coffin over the tortuous mountain trails, up and down, but mostly down, leading to the town, and he was present when the grave was filled in.

These are things that people remember, and they are still mentioned in the neighborhood. Apart from these inevitable disorders, provoked by crises, in the world in which he lives, don Abelardo is familiar with ordinary weakness. He knows why the men who work all day, five or six days a week, on the steep slopes of the tobacco talas, or weeding and cutting the hill cane, get drunk at the end of the week. He knows why they fight with their wives, and quarrel with their children and neighbors. He knows how people get killed on such occasions, how sudden anger leads to death. He understands and sympathizes with the remorse of the murderer, at the same time that he sympathizes with the bereaved, but he is sentimental about neither. Violence is a mistake, but once started, it has to run its course like a canefire or a sickness. A man is killed—the killer must be punished. And the whole Barrio suffers in both instances. This might not be just, but it is the law. Abelardo shrugs and repeats the bitter proverb:

"For the poor, there is no justice."

Abelardo's moral judgment is firmly based on the teachings of the church, but with certain individual amendments, founded on his own experience and knowledge of his neighbors, that would shock a parish priest.

Underneath all of his patience and understanding, even his seeming resignation in adversity, Abelardo is a fighter. He has fought hard and well for the people of his Barrio. Flores is one of the poorest barrios in the municipality, and one of the most thinly populated. Lacking any rich and important residents who might raise their voices in the municipal councils, or a large number of votes that would compel the attention of politicians, the barrio might well be

almost forgotten, were it not for Abelardo. Armed with nothing but his bound-
less energy, ready wit and love of reasoning, Abelardo sees to it that nobody
forgets Flores.

People say that the Mayor winces whenever he sees Abelardo coming, but
Abelardo's demands are never unreasonable, and he takes most of the unpopular decisions upon himself. In times of drought and hardship there is a fierce
competition for the jobs that the municipality offers, repairing the roads, trimming the undergrowth and clearing the drains. It was Abelardo who established
the principle that the roads in Barrio Flores should be tended by residents of
the Barrio. This was clearly a popular decision among his neighbors, but he
went further. No man who is not the father of a family, he decreed, may work
on the roads. And more, in hard times, no man may work more than one day a
week on the roads.

Not unnaturally, this decision was resented by some, but its essential justice
made it acceptable to the Barrio. It was questioned, one night, in don Abelardo's
little store. Feeling ran high,—and several of the participants were a little tight.
Don Abelardo came out from behind the counter. He liked to fight in the open.

"Miren señores," he said, "is there anyone here who wants to go to New
York?" He waited for a minute and a half. Someone in the back started to
answer, was kicked by his neighbor, and kept quiet.

"We all want to stay here with our families, and there's only one way to do
it." The little white-haired man stood in the glaring light of the electric bulb
over the doorway. His big gnarled hands made an encircling movement. "We
all want to live here. So we all have to sacrifice. I could pick you, and you, and
you," his root-like finger indicated three men in the semi-circle that faced him,
"and say that you are the best workers, and so," he shrugged, "you should have
the jobs." He paused, and then his spatulate index finger pointed to the first
man that he had picked out, "would you, *could* you, provide for your sister and
all her children? No sir. You couldn't. It is better to have one day's work for
the head of every family, so that everyone has something, even if it's only a little, than to have seven or eight prosperous families in this hunger-bitten barrio,
and the rest starving to death. Am I right, gentlemen or am I wrong?"

For a long moment, the old man stood in the harsh light of the bare bulb,
facing the half circle of neighbors, gathered around the counter. Then someone
said:

"Don Abel, we're dry. Isn't there any beer here?"

Slowly, muscle by muscle, don Abelardo relaxed. *"Joven,* I have more than
you could drink in a year." Two minutes later, Abelardo was behind the counter,
providing drinks for the men and doling out eight cents worth of dried codfish

to a small boy who had been sent on an errand by his overworked mother.

Many times Abelardo has threatened to resign as president of the Barrio. But Flores without Abelardo would be like rice without beans—like an asopao without olives, like bread without salt,— unthinkable.

THE STATUS DILEMMA

The dilemma of Puerto Rico's political status, which has plagued the island since it was a colony under Spain, was not resolved by the granting of citizenship in 1917, nor by the founding of the Commonwealth government in 1952. There still remained a growing minority that urged statehood, and an equally determined movement that condemned colonialism, and demanded independence.

In 1959, Muñoz Marín tried to rewrite the Commonwealth, adding greater powers of home rule, but he was ignored by Congress. In 1963, when John F. Kennedy occupied the White House, he tried again. Here, a former aide of Governor Muñoz tells what happened when the groundwork was being laid for a plebiscite.

We have to go back once more to 1963. . . . Efforts were directed towards Congress to try and get a commitment that commonwealth could be permanent, to enable it to confront in a plebiscite the traditionally "permanent" solutions of statehood and independence. Promises of help were extracted from then-President John F. Kennedy. A bill was introduced in Congress that would have made commonwealth "permanent and irrevocable." Hearings were held in the House of Representatives on May 16-17, 1963. In the early afternoon of May 16, Governor Muñoz visited President Kennedy at the White House. The word spread among the faithful that the agreement to make commonwealth permanent if the people voted for it had been sealed. It was a very, very happy occasion.

Selections in this chapter:
1. From Juan M. García Passalacqua, San *Juan Star,* February 3, 1970. Reprinted with permission.
2. From U.S. House of Representatives, Subcommittee on Territorial and Insular Affairs, Committee on Interior and Insular Affairs, Hearing on H.R. 5945 and other bills to establish a procedure for the prompt settlement in a democratic manner of the political status of Puerto Rico, May 17, 1963, p. 50.
3. Ibid., pp. 128-30.

On the afternoon of May 17 came a betrayal. Harold Seidman, acting assistant director for the Bureau of the Budget—the "acting" and "assistant" reinforce the importance that the administration gave to our issue—came before the committee. He was categorically clear: "We strongly favor the perfection of existing arrangements with the understanding, however, that actions taken now cannot and should *not* be considered to be binding for all time in the future. . . . We believe the words 'permanent union' as used in section 2 of the bill, may give rise to misunderstandings."

People who knew of the Kennedy commitment couldn't believe their ears. Even some members of the congressional committee thought for a moment that this could be a fourth-echelon bureaucrat let loose, and felt compelled to ask: "Do you know if there is a position from the Administration that you would like to state?" Without blinking an eye, and for posterity, the man answered: "I am here, I should make clear, representing the views of the Administration." That is historical fact. This writer was there. That was then, and (for all we know) is now, the *official* position of the United States of America. . . .

[During the 1963 hearings on political status, the Commonwealth status came under attack from various circles, including members of the U.S. Congress. This sharp exchange between Governor Muñoz and Representative John Saylor of Pennsylvania was one of the most dramatic.]

GOVERNOR MUÑOZ. I would say that the basic thing is to clarify the non-colonial nature of a commonwealth status. . . . The basic importance is to clarify a feeling, a relationship of dignity, of political dignity between Puerto Rico and the United States beyond any shadow of a doubt. . . .

MR. SAYLOR. Governor, I was looking this morning at the statement of Mr. Crawford who, you will recall, was the eminent chairman of this committee when the basic legislation was passed. I have found it. What he said on the floor of the House on June 30, 1950, and what you are saying are as opposite as it is humanly possible to get. On page 9592 of the *Congressional Record*, Mr. Crawford, in addressing the House, said:

We are not offering the people of Puerto Rico anything except the right to vote on a constitution to be submitted to the President of the United States who in turn is to submit it to the Congress of the United States for approval—and all of this commonwealth that you keep talking about, and the clarification, I am satisfied are things which have been built up under your administration in Puerto Rico and have not been the intention of Congress then, and I hope not now.

GOVERNOR MUÑOZ. Congressman, I have had a great friendship for Mr. Crawford, and I have a great respect for his memory, but I would not agree with him on that. If he was right, then Puerto Rico is still a colony of the United States. If it is still a colony of the United States it should stop being a colony as soon as possible, for the honor of the United States and for the sense of self-respect of the people of Puerto Rico. (*Applause and jeers.*)

[At the same hearings, congressmen heard the testimony of Juan Mari Bras, leader of the Pro-Independence Movement. The text incorrectly uses his second surname, calling him "Mr. Bras."]

MR. BRAS. . . . The forces of independence will not accept anything short of a full, unconditional transfer of all sovereign powers to the people of Puerto Rico. We do not deny the right of both Puerto Rico and the United States to enter into some type of association in the future. But, such association will not be valid if it springs from our present colonial status. Only free and independent nations can validly associate themselves.

And regarding the pretension of this bill to establish the permanency and irrevocability of the present colonial setup of the Puerto Rico-United States relationship; I warn you, in the name of thousands of patriots struggling for independence in my country, that the attempt to secure, on a permanent basis, the chains of our colonial subjugation, will only produce such friction and struggle that the situation in Puerto Rico could very well degenerate into an American Algeria. . . .

. . . . We have never exercised sovereignty in the past. The constitutional convention that we held in 1952 was not in the exercise of sovereignty but in the exercise of the delegate powers of Congress that asked the people of Puerto Rico to elect a convention and to submit through that convention a proposal for a constitution that would again be approved by Congress.

MR. O'BRIEN. Then your first step would be independence. If Puerto Rico as an independent nation decided to water down or even turn its back on complete independence, then you would feel that would be the decision of a sovereign independent people, and you feel that the steps that have been taken so far . . . have not been taken by a sovereign independent people.

MR. BRAS. That is right. . . . You cannot consent to a contract if you don't have the freedom to do that. . . .

The same happened in the international law on politics. A colonial people is like a minor. He is incapable of consenting to anything. You should have to emancipate it in order to have some sort of compact or treaty or agreement with that people. That is what the United Nations have asked. It is very simple. Just relinquish sovereignty, put it in the hands of the people . . . of Puerto Rico. . . .

MR. GILL. I understand your position. However . . . you are predetermining the result. In other words, you would already be out of the United States and then we will talk about your future status. Did you not mention the unemancipated child who needs to be set free? Take it another way. This unemancipated child is now in our house. I don't feel free to kick him out in the cold weather and say "Get out" if he doesn't want to go.

MR. BRAS. The thing is, we are not in your house. You are in ours . . .

A YANKEE FROM MASSACHUSETTS

Before a plebiscite was held in 1967 to allow voters to choose between Commonwealth, statehood, and independence, a detailed study was made of all aspects of Puerto Rico. Public hearings were conducted. On July 28, 1965, the U.S.-Puerto Rico Commission on the Status of Puerto Rico heard Elmer Ellsworth, who had spent most of his life as a local farmer. In the 1940's, as a founding member of the Popular Democratic Party, Mr. Ellsworth also served in the insular House of Representatives. Here, he describes how times have changed in Puerto Rico—not always for the better—and he protests against the drafting of Puerto Ricans into the U.S. Armed Forces. "How many boys from this peace-loving island," he asks, "must now die in Vietnam?"

MR. ELLSWORTH. Honorable members of the committee, to introduce myself I must say that I am a Yankee from Massachusetts who has made my home in Puerto Rico for some 46 years. So I have come to put in my two cents' worth before this committee.

As many here know, I was associated with my old friend Luis Muñoz Marín in "la lucha" to set up the Popular Democratic Party and to win the elections in 1940, under the theme "Pan, Tierra y Libertad." Years later in the mind of Don Luis there emerged a brilliant solution to the status of Puerto Rico, the associated free state or Estado Libre Asociado. I never was sold; I couldn't buy it because basically it had an obvious fault which I never could stomach. Under this status Puerto Ricans will continue to be drafted into the Armed Forces of the United States. Coming from an old State that has a fame for its democratic tradition, it never appeared right to me that a people with second-class political rights should be forced to serve the mother country.

From U.S. Senate, 89th Congress, 2d Session, Document No. 108, Vol. II, "Status of Puerto Rico, Hearings Before the United States-Puerto Rico Commission on the Status of Puerto Rico, Social-Cultural Facts in Relation to the Status of Puerto Rico," Washington: U.S. Government Printing Office, 1966, pp. 109-11.

Don Luis is an intelligent man. I waited through the years to see him give some sign of appreciating that obvious defect in the status; but there was no word, there was not even a whisper. Not even when the awful tragedy of Korea in which Puerto Ricans, not rugged people, not rugged marines, but people generally of small physical stature from a tropical colonial country, were sent into the subarctic region of North Korea and were thrown into some of the most bloody sections of that terrible war. I don't know if any of you have ever had a chance to visit the Juliá Clinic: I have. And there I found scores of Puerto Ricans whose lives have been ruined by their battle experience in Korea. Scores of them, today, and how many years has it been since Korea? How many?

Now, that does not seem to be enough. Now, there is a new field for Puerto Ricans to be thrown into a slaughter—Vietnam. How many boys from this peace-loving island must now die in Vietnam? . . .

I am a farmer and have stayed close to the "jíbaro" of the mountain interior. . . . I know that they are not happy over this prospect of having their sons drafted and sent to Vietnam. But can they protest? What would happen? As everyone knows they would immediately be accused of being Communist. . . . Anyone with a deep feeling and understanding of democracy has to be outraged by this drafting of Puerto Ricans, without a voice, nor a chance to vote in approval or disapproval of the President of the United States who is making these dreadful decisions. Is this true democracy or simply an ugly hangover of the worst of colonialism?

Now I must tell you frankly, gentlemen, that I don't believe much in committees. I have seen a lot of them in my 46 years. How many committees have come to Puerto Rico about the status? And still no solutions. Don Luis himself tried to sell the people that this Estado Libre Asociado was at last the final permanent status of Puerto Rico. That illusion lasted him for a few years and then even he had to realize its temporary nature and how it had to evolve further.

Now, if anything is to come out of the committee, gentlemen, for God's sake, try to get an amendment through Congress to eliminate the drafting of Puerto Ricans until the final status of this island is decided or they have true representation in Washington. That's all.

The CHAIRMAN. Perhaps some of the members of the Commission would like to ask you questions, sir. . . .

By MR. FERRÉ:

Q. Just one question. Excuse me. Mr. Ellsworth, you have been in touch with the people of Puerto Rico at the grassroots for a long while. Do you feel that they are eager and anxious for Puerto Rico to become a State of the Union?

A. No. The people of Puerto Rico have been told for a number of years:

"It is not status, status is not the problem; it is social justice." They have been sold on that for a long time and the Popular Party keeps saying the same thing. The people of Puerto Rico aren't very happy with anything going on in Puerto Rico today. I don't know how some of you leaders get around to talk to the people. But Puerto Rico today is not the Puerto Rico of 10, 15, or 20 years ago. I lived in a house in Manatí when I first came to Puerto Rico. I was a pineapple grower, I was the manager of a pineapple plantation. We lived in one old two-story big house under the mango trees, and we never shut the doors of that house in the 8 years I lived in it. In fact, when a new manager came and I went to live in Cidra—into the wilderness of Cidra—his wife was a little scared. She was afraid of the peons with their "machetes" in their hands; so she tried to shut the door at night but the doors were so warped out of shape they wouldn't shut.

Now, this status thing has been kicked around so long that there are other problems that are more pressing. Agriculture is dying in Puerto Rico, and a country without any basic agriculture isn't a happy one. The other day I went up by my old farm, which I had to sell because the town grew and crept up close to me. . . .

I ran into a man, a "trabajador" who had worked for me for many, many years. He stopped me. He said: "Mister, las cosas están malas. Es tamos ganando más chavos, pero ayer yo tuve que pagar más de un peso por un racimo de guineos verdes."[1]

Nothing has grown. The new laws which protect the "agregado" were passed with good intentions, but they were not practical. As a "patrón," which I was once, I insisted and urged my men to keep planting their crops. But now the "patróns" are fearful that there would be a problem when they wanted one of their agregados to leave. So now in general there are no more agregados and nobody plants food crops. So, today, two things mainly are being planted in Puerto Rico—cement houses and pangola.[2] True, human beings can eat the steers that the pangola produces and it produces good steers; but the only two phases of agriculture that are up in Puerto Rico are dairy and cattle raising. All the other phases of farming are down. This year we had a bad drought and "plá-tanos" were sold in Caguas for 12 cents a "plátano," and a miserable little fruit at that.

So, we are getting houses, automobiles, and all the gadgets of the great

---

1. "Mister, things are bad. We're earning more money, but yesterday I had to pay more than one dollar for a bunch of green bananas."
2. Pangola grass is planted, with government cash incentives, for cattle grazing.

United States of America, but we are not growing much of any of our food. Yes, there are more and more automobiles, television sets, and every kind of gadget. There are also other things but there is not much food produced and there are not very many books.

So I say that this is not a happy country, because the happy man was the worker who had his wage and also had his bananas and "plátanos" and "yautía" and "malanga" and chickens and a pig or two. He never starved. There are urbanizations in Puerto Rico, as you may know, that they call Campbell, Urbanización Campbell, because the people live mostly on Campbell's soup.

"THE CONSCIENCE OF HIS PEOPLE"

The decade of the 1960's was a turning point in Puerto Rico's history. In 1964, Governor Muñoz stepped down and nominated a younger man—his long-time aide, Roberto Sánchez Vilella—to run for the post. In the 1967 plebiscite, the Commonwealth status was favored by 60 per cent of the voters, while 39 per cent chose statehood, and a fraction voted for independence. In 1968, a pro-statehood candidate, Luis A. Ferré, won an upset victory for the governorship, and Muñoz Marín went into virtual retirement.

It was also a time when the foremost modern figure in Puerto Rico's independence movement passed into legend. Pedro Albizu Campos, the militant Nationalist, died in San Juan on April 21, 1965. He had spent eighteen of his seventy-three years in prison. In April, 1936, Albizu was sentenced to ten years in Atlanta Federal Penitentiary after Nationalists killed insular police chief Francis Riggs. When he was pardoned, six years later, thousands of persons met his ship as it docked in San Juan. In 1951, Albizu was jailed after a Nationalist uprising broke out in several island towns, and an attempt was made on the life of President Truman in Washington. He was pardoned in 1953, but this was revoked the next year, after Nationalists wounded five Congressmen. Albizu suffered a stroke in 1956, which left him partially paralyzed. He was sent to Presbyterian Hospital in San Juan, where he remained until he was pardoned by Governor Muñoz in November, 1964. Journalist César Andreu Iglesias wrote this stirring epitaph shortly after Albizu's death.

Translated from César Andreu Iglesias, *El Impartial,* San Juan, April 24, 1965, p. 30. Reprinted by permission of the author.

D on Pedro Albizu Campos entered into history before he died. Now the legend begins. . . .
It would be illusion to believe that Albizu's life has ended. It is just now beginning. His death marks the end of an epoch. He was, without doubt, the last vestige of our patriots of the previous century. Without that link, who knows if we might have lost our roots!

To define Albizu, a single word suffices. Albizu was the conscience of Puerto Rico. He was for those who followed him, and even more so for those who rejected him.

In deep crises, a single conscience can save a people. Puerto Ricans were lucky to have Albizu. What would have become of us without him?

Albizu accepted his role as his inexorable destiny. Nothing is more terrible than to be the conscience of a people. He spoke when it was necessary to speak. He denounced when denunciations were needed. He accused when it was necessary to accuse. And he was always ready to accept the consequences.

He knew no compromise or surrender. He acted as he was: an unyielding, absolute conscience. That is where the incomprehension began.

If Albizu had only spoken with less anger. If Albizu had only denounced with less fire. If Albizu had only accused with less passion. Ah! Then he would not have been our conscience.

Some have tried to minimize Albizu, saying that his people rejected his words, and repudiated his acts. But that is juvenile logic. It is quite unimportant whether he was repudiated or rejected at one time or another. What gives the measure of Albizu is the impact of his words and of his acts upon the conscience of all Puerto Ricans, to some degree. . . . That will last!

And that, precisely, is the difference between an apostle and a politician.

The politician is with everyone, or pretends to be. The apostle is alone, with his conscience. He is not with others; they are with him . . . to whatever extent and number that may be! . . .

The most important decision is that which each individual makes when he is alone with his conscience. Above the formal vote is the silent vote of the people. And as every critical moment has shown, at the eleventh hour, people and conscience reach an understanding.

Even the hardest-skinned Puerto Rican feels this, although he may not understand it. It is felt by those who adapt to circumstances, for their own good. It is felt by the politician who has not lost all his dignity. It is felt by the teacher, the lawyer, the laborer, the government clerk. . . . They feel it and know it—by intuition if not by conviction—rich and poor, men and women, young and old. And the proof is that no man inspired greater admiration from his people than Albizu.

It had to be thus, because Albizu is the conscience of all Puerto Ricans. And a conscience is seen and heard, even when we look the other way, and pretend to be deaf.

The person who represents the conscience of a people can hardly hope to triumph. His mission is not to save himself, but to save us. In that self-sacrifice is his victory: the final triumph of the cause to which Albizu devoted his entire life.

PART IX

EXODUS

We have to share everything. We share poverty with the Negroes, religion with the Irish and Italians. We don't even have our slums for us alone.

—Jack Agüeros, a Puerto Rican in New York City government,
New York Times, *April 23, 1968*

I have great hope for their education and great fear of the streets.

—Enrique Paoli, father of ten children,
Cleveland Plain-Dealer, *April 26, 1971*

L ike the waves of immigrants before them, Puerto Ricans came to the United States in search of work. This is borne out by hard statistics over the years: each time there is a recession or a slowdown in the U.S. economy, the number of migrants from Puerto Rico decreases; when the mainland economy "heats up," and jobs are plentiful, the northward flow of manpower resumes.

Since the end of World War II, economic conditions in Puerto Rico have improved immensely, but not nearly enough to employ all who needed work to support their families. What was once a trickle of migration turned into a torrent when inexpensive air travel became available between San Juan and America's industrial centers on the East Coast.

By the late 1950's, several American cities had large Spanish-speaking *barrios.* Most of the newcomers were ill-prepared for their new way of life, but they tenaciously held on to the hardest, poorest-paying jobs, lived in over-priced substandard housing, and struggled to establish themselves. Some fell by the wayside, into public welfare dependence, or—far worse—into drugs and crime. Soon, U.S. newspapers began referring to "our Puerto Rican problem," in much the same way that newspapers at the turn of the century complained of the "filthy Hebrews," or "the dangerous Italians."

Inch by inch, the Puerto Ricans have gained a toehold in America, but many of them have paid a terrible price. The following selections describe the exodus from Puerto Rico, and some facets of those first hard years.

THE EARLY DAYS

Back in 1910, there were a mere 1,513 Puerto Ricans scattered through 39 states of the Union, according to the national census. A decade later, compared with the mass of newcomers from Europe, the Puerto Rican community on the mainland was still small: 11,811 islanders were reported to be living in 45 states. Among these pioneers was Jesús Colón, born in the tobacco region of Cayey. He worked his way north during World War I as a bus-boy aboard a freighter—that soon afterwards was torpedoed to the bottom of the Atlantic by a German submarine. These excerpts are from his book, which—in his words—offers "a modest attempt . . . through the medium of personal experience to throw a little light on how Puerto Ricans in this city *really* feel, think, work and live."

t must have been around 1918. . . .

My brother's job was to keep the long, cold desolate platforms of a subway station nicely clean, to wash the toilets and see that the drunks didn't spoil his artistic brooming. Among his other multiple little tasks he had to collect all the newspapers and press them into bales that were stacked at the end of the station. For this he got about sixteen dollars a week for working from seven to four in the morning.

While he worked nights I worked days. So we hardly talked to each other during the week.

But one thing we did every evening as I came in was for me to hand him my working pants. He put them on, the pants still warm with the heat of my body. Then he said "Hasta mañana" and left. When he came at 4:30 or 5 in the morning I was fast asleep. At seven in the morning I took back my working pants, put them on, without disturbing his sleep and off to work I went until the evening. When I came in at about six he took my—our—pants back.

The question might be asked: "And what did you do when both of you would

From Jesús Colón, *A Puerto Rican in New York & Other Sketches* (New York: Mainstream Publishers, 1961), pp. 25-28, 115-17. Reprinted by permission.

go out say—on Sunday?" To that I would answer that we had our Sunday suits. I could not call them Sunday best, because "best" implies that there were other suits in our wardrobe . . . we had no other suits. Just two. His and mine. And a pair of working pants for the both of us. Then again we could not call our suits "Sunday best," because our two Sunday suits had seen their best days already many, many, years ago. They were two blue serge suits whose seat-shine seemed to have permanently permeated the other parts of the cloth. . . .

But the fact remained that we only had one pair of working pants between the two of us. And that was a fact for months, until the day when we were not too tired after one of us came from work, to go out and buy one pair of pants. By that I really mean, until we could spare the few dollars—the cost of a pair of good working pants—without disturbing the very delicate balance between what we earned and what we had to spend on room, food, and other incidentals. . . .

Early in 1919, we were both out of work, my brother and I. He got up earlier to look for a job. When I woke up, he was already gone. So I dressed, went out and bought a copy of the *New York World* and turned its pages until I got to the "Help Wanted Unskilled" section of the paper. After much reading and re-reading the same columns, my attention was held by a small advertisement. It read: "Easy job. Good wages. No experience necessary." This was followed by a number and street on the west side of lower Manhattan. It sounded like the job I was looking for. Easy job. Good wages. . . .

The place consisted of a small front office and a large loft on the floor of which I noticed a series of large galvanized tubs half filled with water out of which I noticed protruding the necks of many bottles of various sizes and shapes. Around these tubs there were a number of workers, male and female, sitting on small wooden benches. All had their hands in the water of the tub, the left hand holding a bottle and with the thumb nail of the right hand scratching the labels.

The foreman found a vacant stool for me around one of the tubs of water. I asked why a penknife or a small safety razor could not be used instead of the thumb nail to take off the old labels from the bottles. I was expertly informed that knives or razors would scratch the glass thus depreciating the value of the bottles when they were to be sold.

I sat down and started to use my thumb nail on one bottle. The water had somewhat softened the transparent mucilage used to attach the label to the bottle. But the softening did not work out uniformly somehow. There were always pieces of label that for some obscure reason remained affixed to the bottles. It was on those pieces of labels tenaciously fastened to the bottles that my right hand thumb nail had to work overtime. As the minutes passed I noticed that the coldness of the water started to pass from my hand to my body giving me intermittent body shivers that I tried to conceal with the greatest of effort from those sitting beside me. My hands became deadly clean and tiny little wrinkles started to show especially at the tip of my fingers. Sometimes I stopped a few seconds from scratching the bottles, to open and close my fists in rapid movements in order to bring blood to my hands. But almost as soon as I placed them in the water they became deathly pale again.

But these were minor details compared with what was happening to the thumb of my right hand. From a delicate, boyish thumb, it was growing by the minute into a full blown tomato colored finger. It was the only part of my right hand remaining blood red. I started to look at the workers' thumbs. I noticed that these particular fingers on their right hands were unusually developed with a thick layer of corn-like surface at the top of their right thumb. The nails on their thumbs looked coarser and smaller than on the other fingers—thumb and nail having become one and the same thing—a primitive unnatural human in-strument especially developed to detach hard pieces of labels from wet bottles immersed in galvanized tubs.

After a couple of hours I had a feeling that my thumb nail was going to leave my finger and jump into the cold water in the tub. A numb pain imperceptibly began to be felt coming from my right thumb. Then I began to feel such pain as if coming from a finger bigger than all of my body.

After three hours of this I decided to quit fast. I told the foreman so, showing him my swollen finger. He figured I had earned 69 cents at 23 cents an hour.

Early in the evening I met my brother in our furnished room. We started to exchange experiences of our job hunting for the day. "You know what?" my brother started, "early in the morning I went to work where they take labels off old bottles—with your right hand thumb nail . . . Somewhere on the West Side of Lower Manhattan. I only stayed a couple of hours. 'Easy job . . . Good wages' . . . they said. The person who wrote that ad must have had a great sense of humor." And we both had a hearty laugh that evening when I told my brother that I also went to work at that same place later in the day. . . .

It was very late at night on the eve of Memorial Day. She came into the sub-way at the 34th Street Pennsylvania Station. I am still trying to remember how she managed to push herself in with a baby on her right arm, a valise in her left hand and two children, a boy and girl about three and five years old, trailing after her. She was a nice looking white lady in her early twenties.

At Nevins Street, Brooklyn, we saw her preparing to get off at the next sta-tion—Atlantic Avenue—which happened to be the place where I too had to get off. Just as it was a problem for her to get on, it was going to be a problem for her to get off the subway. . . .

And there I was, also preparing to get off at Atlantic Avenue, with no bundles to take care of—not even the customary book under my arm without which I feel that I am not completely dressed.

As the train was entering the Atlantic Avenue station, some white man stood up from his seat and helped her out, placing the children on the long, deserted platform. There were only two adult persons on the long platform some time after midnight on the eve of last Memorial Day.

I could perceive the steep, long concrete stairs going down to the Long Island Railroad or into the street. Should I offer my help as the American white man did at the subway door placing the two children outside the subway car? Should I take care of the girl and the boy, take them by their hands until they reached the end of the steep long concrete stairs of the Atlantic Avenue station.

Courtesy is a characteristic of the Puerto Rican. And here I was—a Puerto Rican—hours past midnight, a valise, two white children and a white lady with a baby on her arm palpably needing somebody to help her at least until she descended the long concrete stairs.

But how could I, a Negro and a Puerto Rican, approach this white lady who very likely might have preconceived prejudices against Negroes and everybody with foreign accents, in a deserted subway station very late at night?

What would she say? What would be the first reaction of this white American woman, perhaps coming from a small town. . . . Would she say: Yes, of course, you may help me. Or would she think that I was just trying to get too familiar? Or would she think worse than that perhaps? What would I do if she let out a scream as I went toward her to offer my help?

Was I misjudging her? So many slanders are written every day in the daily press against the Negroes and Puerto Ricans. I hesitated for a long, long minute. The ancestral manners that the most illiterate Puerto Rican passes on from father to son were struggling inside me. Here was I, way past midnight, face to face with a situation that could very well explode into an outburst of prejudices and chauvinistic conditioning of the "divide and rule" policy of present day society.

It was a long minute. I passed on by her as if I saw nothing. As if I was insensitive to her need. Like a rude animal walking on two legs, I just moved on half running by the long subway platform leaving the children and the valise and her with the baby on her arm. I took the steps of the long concrete stairs in twos until I reached the street above and the cold air slapped my warm face. . . .

"WHAT IS PREJUDICE?"

Bitter experience taught the early migrants that in the United States there was racial prejudice of an intensity unknown in Puerto Rico. In the 1950's, as thousands of migrants flew north to seek jobs, the island government made sincere, but feeble, attempts to prepare them for the "culture shock" that awaited them. Part of this effort was a series of pamphlets that was distributed in rural areas of the island. Excerpts from one of these pamphlets deal with the question of racial prejudice. The message is written in simple terms, for people with little formal education.

W hat is prejudice? Prejudice is the judgment or opinion that one forms without having enough information about something . . . without taking the truth into account. Let us take an example:

If we don't know the Jews, but we insist that all Jews are traitors, we are judging something without knowing it. We are committing an injustice. We are being prejudiced. Why are we prejudiced?

Well, perhaps we recall the Bible, where we read that Judas betrayed Jesus. And Judas was a Jew. Then, without thinking or reasoning, we say that Jews are traitors. Should all the Jews pay for what Judas did? That wouldn't be just. Jesus himself was a Jew. Would anyone dare to say that Jesus, being Jewish, was a traitor? . . .

Let's suppose that in the United States a black American commits a crime. There are many white Americans who are prejudiced against the blacks. What happens? The act of a single black is paid for by the others. Because people with prejudice say: "Look, that's what the blacks do." And it isn't true. Because when a white American kills someone, it doesn't occur to anyone to say that all white Americans are killers. In the same way, the other blacks are not guilty of what a single black did. . . .

The same thing can happen to the Puerto Ricans in the United States, as it does with the blacks or the Jews. . . .

If one Puerto Rican steals, Americans who are prejudiced say that all Puerto Ricans are thieves. If one Puerto Rican doesn't work, prejudiced Americans say all of us are lazy. If one Puerto Rican throws his garbage into the street instead of into the trash can, prejudiced Americans say that all Puerto Ricans

---

Translated from *Emigración*, Libros Para El Pueblo-Número Ocho (San Juan: Department of Education, 1966), 2nd Edition, pp. 49-51.

have filthy habits. So, each mistake by a Puerto Rican in the United States is paid for by all. How?

We pay, because a bad opinion of us is formed. And the result may be that they discredit us, they won't give us work, or they deny us our rights.

Of course, not all Americans are prejudiced. There, as in Puerto Rico, there are all kinds; good people and bad people, stupid people and intelligent people, honorable people and thieves. . . .

How can we defend ourselves against prejudice? Not with violence or insults. We cannot attack the prejudice of others with our own. One means of defense and attack against prejudice is to set a good example. Another is to have the knowledge of all our rights and duties as citizens.

But we must keep something else in mind. We must be alert, so as not to contaminate ourselves with the prejudices of some Americans.

Some Puerto Ricans have grown cowardly, in the face of prejudice in the United States. Their solution to the problem has been to believe in the prejudice of some Americans. There is nothing more terrible to see than a Puerto Rican in the United States who is contaminated by the prejudice there. He begins by attacking the American blacks, and winds up attacking his own Puerto Rican brothers. He betrays his own, and even winds up denying that he is Puerto Rican. That type of wrongly "Americanized" Puerto Rican is one of our worst enemies . . .

LONG NIGHT'S JOURNEY

The exodus of Puerto Ricans that began in the 1950's was so massive that the route between San Juan and New York soon came to be known as an "air bridge." Day after day, planeloads of migrants were lofted from their *patria*, and a few hours later descended the stairway to a new world, 1,600 miles to the north. During the flight, they were crammed together in planes that jounced about in the air like ships in a storm-tossed sea. It was a frightening, often nauseating, baptism. Dan Wakefield, the well known American journalist and novelist, who lived for more than a year in New York's Spanish Harlem, also made the trip.

From Dan Wakefield, *Island in the City: The World of Spanish Harlem* (Boston: Houghton Mifflin, 1959), pp. 23-43. Reprinted with permission.

Ricardo Sánchez came from where the sugar cane is higher than a man to the plaza in old San Juan where the buses marked *Aeropuerto* stop. He came with his wife and two daughters and three suitcases and a paper bag and the promise from a brother in Harlem, New York, that there was work to be found in *fábrica*. The work in the sugar cane was over for the season and Ricardo had found nothing else. The government would pay him $7 every two weeks for thirteen weeks before the season began again, and then with the season he would get $3.60 a day for eight hours in the sun. He had done it before, as his fathers had done it, but this time he told himself he wanted something more. "It is," he said, "no good to be poor." His lean brown face was twisted in a grimace of disgust as he said the words, and remained that way, in the memory of poverty, slowly relaxing as he fingered the three fountain pens neatly clipped to the pocket of his new brown suit, and turned to face the dark from where the buses come.

Christopher Columbus, migrant by trade, stood by frozen in the stone of a statue, the accidental patron saint of the plaza that serves as a boarding place for those who go away. Even more practically, Columbus' weathered figure serves those who stay, for around it sit the old men who sit around the statues of the plazas of the world; these by the chance of Columbus' mistaken discoveries (and Ponce de León's mistaken hopes) speaking the language of his creditor the Queen. But the Queen is four centuries dead, and the island's highest ruler is a president from Kansas—a place whose name and language are totally foreign to the old men who sit by the statue.

Their fathers before them were Indians here, called Borinqueños, and Spanish followers of Ponce de León, seeker after gold and youth and captor of neither. His body is buried up the street. Their fathers were Negro slaves from Africa, brought here to fill the vacuum left when the Indians painfully vanished, by death and escape, from the Spaniards' rule. . . .

The city is quiet, and the old men who sit in the plaza seem unconcerned. Their fathers are gone and their sons are free to go.

For more than a century the sons have left the plazas and the dust-and-green towns of the interior to come to New York. Ricardo Sánchez is young, but his journey is old. The first Puerto Ricans came to New York in the early 1800's, along with other men of good hope from the underfed islands of the Caribbean who decided that "it is no good to be poor." From Cuba and Santo Domingo they came, from San Juan and Haiti and Jamaica. Some survived and others were lost, and in 1838 the men from Puerto Rico who had managed to make themselves merchants of New York City formed a Spanish Benevolent Society for those of their brothers who had failed and were hungry.

Others went west, and by 1910 there were Puerto Ricans living in thirty-nine states of the Union. Twenty years later the people of the island were in every state, though the great majority were still in New York City. The journey north from the Caribbean became a regular route for those seeking something better (and having the money to make the search), and for most of the first half of the twentieth century an average of 4000 came from Puerto Rico to the mainland every year.

No one seemed to notice. It was not until near the end of the Second World War that the quiet, steady migration became the great migration—the promise of the mainland suddenly expanding with more new jobs than ever before and the word passing on from relative to relative, friend to friend, employment recruiter to unemployed. During the war there was little transportation available for Puerto Ricans who wanted to leave the island, but toward the end of it the U.S. War Manpower Commission brought workers up in army transports to help fill the booming job market. In the first year after the war 39,900 Puerto Ricans came to the mainland, and the annual stream reached an average of roughly 50,000 in the postwar decade. As it has throughout its history, the Puerto Rican migration curve followed the business curve on the mainland, and the start of the greatest postwar recession in 1957 was reflected by a 28 per cent decrease in migration from the year before. Downturns in the volume of business on the continent have always meant downturns in migration from the island, and during the worst depression years of the thirties the flow of migrants actually reversed itself, with more returning annually to the island than came from it. But barring an extreme and prolonged depression, the total of 600,000 first- or second-generation Puerto Ricans in New York City in 1958 was expected to rise to a million by the early 1970's. And, for the first time, the great migration had begun to spread more heavily in cities and towns throughout the country. In 1950, 85 per cent of the entering migrants settled in New York City, but by 1956 and 1957 the average was down to 65 per cent, with others going to expanding Puerto Rican settlements in cities such as Philadelphia (New York's largest Spanish-language newspaper now carries a special column of Puerto Rican news from Philadelphia), Chicago, Cleveland, Ashtabula, Bridgeport, Milwaukee, and others farther west.

The journey from the island had become not only more promising because of the market for jobs after World War II but also much easier to make because of the airplanes that rose from San Juan and landed at Idlewild, New York City, 1600 miles up the ocean, in only eight hours and for only $75 on regular airlines instead of the former price of $180. Besides the approved commercial lines that opened up regular service after the war there were secondhand planes making unscheduled flights for $35—they could charge that price because they were paid off later by men from the states who came to Puerto Rico and charged "employment agent" fees that often consumed life savings sweated from sugar cane as payment for nonexistent jobs in New York City. Some of the victims never found out because they first became the victims of ill-equipped planes that crashed in the ocean. After several such tragedies the government outlawed the small, unscheduled airlines from making the San Juan-New York run.

But the regular, legal air travel flourished—not only giving a boost to the old migration to the mainland cities but also opening up a new migration. Cheap and fast plane travel made it possible to transport idle agricultural workers from Puerto Rico during the heavy harvesting season on the mainland in the spring, and back again to the island when the sugar-cane season began in the fall. A new seasonal migration began on that basis after the war and has grown to an annual flow of about 30,000 workers (not counted in the regular migration figures of those who come and plan to stay). Contrary to popular belief, the great majority of Puerto Ricans who come to New York, and other U.S. cities, are not laborers but city people who have held city jobs on the island.

Ricardo Sánchez, who waited in the dark for the bus marked *Aereopuerto,* was one of the small but slowly growing number of Puerto Ricans who have left the sugar-cane fields for the city. The desire to escape from the backbreaking work of the cane cutting is still not easily fulfilled, but the dream has become much more widespread since many young men saw the world in service with the U.S. Army in Korea, and returned home with higher aspirations. Frank Ruiz, the secretary-treasurer of the *Sindicato Azucarero* (Sugar Workers Union) in Puerto Rico says that it is harder now to get the young men to work in the cane fields because "the army has refined them."

Ricardo Sánchez was able to make at least a partial transition in his work before the drastic change from the island fields to the New York fabric shops. During the idle season a year before, he had found a job doing piecework in a garment shop in the small town of Vega Baja. But the work didn't last, and after another season in the fields he decided to try his luck—and his brother's help— in the *fábrica* shops of New York City.

Ricardo held for himself and his family tickets on the $52.50 night coach Thrift Flight to Idlewild airport. It leaves six nights a week from San Juan at eleven o'clock and arrives the next morning at Idlewild at seven. The adjective "thrift" is the only term of distinction between this flight and the other night coach flight, which costs $64, leaves a half hour later, and arrives in New York City two hours earlier. The Thrift Flight is not recommended—or even suggested at the ticket counters—to non-Puerto Rican travelers. English-speaking people who ask about it are told that it is better to spend the extra money and go on the eleven-thirty flight.

There were only Puerto Ricans on the *Aereopuerto* bus that Ricardo Sánchez boarded in the plaza of Christopher Columbus. They stayed together when they reached the San Juan airport, checking in baggage and then joining friends and relatives and watchers in the crowd on the observation deck. When the flight was called, it was as if a troop plane were leaving for a war, or a group of refugees being shipped of necessity out of their native country. It is that way every night around eleven o'clock at the San Juan airport—the women crying and the men embracing them; the old people staring out of wrinkled, unperceiving faces and the young engrossed with the wonder, rather than the pain of it, pressing up against the iron rail of the observation deck and squinting through the dark to watch the line of human travelers move as if drawn by a spell through the gate below and into the still, silver plane that swallows them, closing silver on silver to complete itself, and then slowly moves toward the dark and disappears.

Inside the airplane Ricardo Sánchez had seated his wife and one of his daughters on the left-hand, two-seat aisle, and taken his other daughter and himself across to the right in the three-seat row with a stranger. The flight was full, as these flights are nearly always full. . . .

The plane was hot—hotter than the 75° weather outside—and many of the men, already sweating, had taken off their coats. A young, dark-skinned woman in an aqua silk dress was crying softly and fanning herself with the plastic *Ocupado* sign from the pocket of the seat in front of her. The stewardess appeared at the head of the aisle when the door was closed and gave a demonstration while the steward explained on the loudspeaker, first in Spanish and then in English, the instructions for putting on life jackets in case of an emergency.

The engines began, swelled, and the plane crept forward. The woman in the aqua dress pressed her face against the porthole-style window, crying much louder now. The balcony of watchers grew smaller and darker; became a few white handkerchiefs waved in the night, and then was gone. Babies began to cry as the plane rose, moving above the red, white, and green pinpoints strung geometrically and sparkling in the pattern of the city and suburbs of San Juan. In several minutes the dark had covered it. The no-smoking and safety-belt signs in the plane blinked off, the overhead lights went out, and only the small, individual reading lights above the seats were on. The babies stopped crying, and the temperature of the plane began to cool. Seats were pushed back, and soon the thin beams of light from the few remaining reading lights were thickened with cigarette smoke. The stewardess came by and asked Ricardo Sánchez if he wanted her to hang up his suit coat. The stewardess did not speak Spanish and Ricardo, looking at her quizzically and smiling politely, clutched his coat when she reached for it and held it folded on his lap. He leaned his head back against the seat, folding his hands on his lap, and stared straight ahead, the view slightly tilted with the angle of the seat; his mouth in a tight, tentative smile. After a while he closed his eyes.

The dull, steady roar of the engine was the single sound, growing louder and fuller as other sounds stopped, until, in its constant drone and throb, the sound of the engine became no sound at all, but a part of the plane's suspended life. It became a sound again several hours later when the screams woke Ricardo Sánchez from his tilted sleep:

"Ay, ay, *ayyyy!*"

The women screamed as the plane fell forward through the dark. The sound of the two engines heightened and throbbed. The plane leveled off from the drop, leaving the stomachs of the passengers with the sickening, overturned sensation that comes on a roller coaster during the sudden, steep descent. The steward hurried down the aisle with smelling salts.

Ricardo Sánchez leaned forward to look across the aisle at his wife. Her head was leaning across on her daughter, who sat in silence, her eyes widening to watch the steward stop by the seat and wave the smelling salts. Ricardo's mouth opened and his white teeth were clenched together as if he were being struck. He started up, but the safety belt was fastened on his waist. He looked at it a moment, then leaned back into his seat. The plane dipped again.

The steward stopped and explained to the only non-Puerto Rican passenger that the plane had hit a storm.

"We felt it quite a bit," he said. "The planes for this flight aren't pressurized. If you take the eleven-thirty flight—the $64 one—you fly above all this."

There was no announcement in Spanish about the storm. Ricardo Sánchez's wife, revived, pulled the white bag for vomiting out of the pocket of the seat and leaned into it. Lightning flashed as the plane pitched again in the dark— the tiny green light on the end of the wing was the only thing visible. Ricardo Sánchez tightened the safety belt of his daughter who sat next to him. She clutched at the arm of the seat, in silence, and pressed against the back of it, her thin legs sticking out with the shiny black patent leather shoes not touching the floor. Her father stroked her hair, then leaned back himself and touched the palms of his hands together, pointing upward, in his lap. Through the crack of the seat in front, the brown, large-veined hands of a woman twisted and knotted and pulled on a rainbow-colored silk handkerchief.

The dips became slighter and the screams lower, several becoming soft, con- tinual moans that rose with the fall of the plane. A man walked back to the stewardess who sat reading a copy of the *Saturday Evening Post* and asked her in English if the worst of the storm was over. She looked up annoyed and said, *"I'm* not the pilot," touched her forefinger to her tongue, and flipped the page of the magazine.

A little after five o'clock in the morning the silver wings of the plane became visible, and then a layer of clouds below the plane. A pink strip grew at the end of the layer of clouds in the east, and an orange streak grew from the pink. The billowed layers of clouds below became blue-gray, then lighter blue. Ricardo Sánchez tapped his daughter's shoulder and told her to look. She leaned across on his lap and he explained, "It is dawn. Look—it is beautiful."

About six o'clock the stewardess came by with a tray of steaming paper cups and asked each passenger, in English, "Would you like some coffee?" Some didn't seem to understand so the stewardess repeated the question in more distinct tones, "Would you like some coffee?" There were those who still did not understand and the stewardess, seemingly annoyed, passed on. Some people nodded, or held out their hands, and were given coffee.

The woman in the aqua silk dress stood up in the aisle and pulled up her stockings. She sat back down, pulled a small bottle from her purse, turned it on her finger, and dabbed at her neck. The strong, sweet smell of perfume spread across the aisle. The plane had broken through the clouds and there was water below. Soon there was land—another island; this one, too, striped and set with rows of white lights and green lights, fewer lights in the growing gray dawn than were seen in the night above San Juan. The island that the plane approached seemed not so much larger than the island it had left. Lower, the land turned brown and barren, with a swamplike series of protrusions in the water, and the plane moved closer till the brown high grass on the land and the wind-ruffled waves of the water were clearly visible. The plane seemed about to touch the water and suddenly touched on land—the end of the Idlewild airstrip. The babies again were crying.

The plane stopped, and the passengers looked out the window at the quiet runways, the long, low buildings, and the high, silver lampposts that arched in a long and graceful curve like the neck of some thin and watchful animal, repeated row on row. The women stepped out of the silver door, clutching at their flimsy, bright-colored dresses, into the morning chill of New York and the gray, surrealistic landscape of Idlewild.

Friends and relatives waited at the gate with scarves and coats and kisses and handclasps and took the passengers out of the airport and into cars and buses to the Bronx and the lower East Side and the upper West Side of Manhattan and also to New York's first large Puerto Rican neighborhood, known as Spanish Harlem.

"I'M FREEZING TO DEATH"

The migrant soon learns that getting used to cold weather is just the first of several harsh adjustments. Next come finding a place to live, a job, a means to communicate, and a way to make your children respect you in a city where you yourself are insecure. Via the tape recorder, and exhaustive research, the late anthropologist Oscar Lewis spent a lifetime trying to "give a voice to the people who are rarely heard." Here, he listens to Puerto Ricans in New York City as they describe the dreams, and nightmares, of migration.

U pon arriving, many informants experienced an initial feeling of dejection and a strong desire to return to Puerto Rico. They expressed disappointment and even disgust at the ugliness and dirtiness of the city.
. . .

"The truth is that I was disillusioned when I saw New York because I thought that it would be a cleaner and prettier place and that the houses would be newer. I was disappointed to see so many slums. I thought, 'Puerto Rico is much prettier than this!'"

The cold weather bothered most people and they disliked the fact that New Yorkers lived "all shut in" even in the summer, in contrast to the open porches, doors and windows of the houses in Puerto Rico. . . .

"When I arrived I wanted to turn around and go right back to Puerto Rico because it was so cold. I came in January of 1961 and there had been a tremendous snow-storm. There were about seven inches of snow on the ground and it was below zero. I said to myself, 'Mmmm, I'm not liking this country very much.' But then I told myself, 'Go on, get off the plane. Let's see what it's like.'

"I came with nothing but a sweater and a suit, one of those wash and wear suits. I had written to my brother asking him to bring a coat to the airport because I didn't have one.

"As I was getting off the plane a girl said to me, 'Excuse me, can you help me carry this baby? I have two of them.' But I said to her, 'I'm very sorry, *señora,* but I'm freezing to death and I don't have a coat.'

From Oscar Lewis, *A Study of Slum Culture: Backgrounds for "La Vida"* (New York: Random House, 1966), pp. 126-28, 144-45, 160-61, 182-84, 201. Reprinted with permission.

"I got off the plane and ran to the terminal. My brother was waiting with a coat so I put on the coat over my sweater. I put on gloves, I put on everything!

"It was three o'clock in the morning and I kept looking and looking to see what kind of a country this was. Somehow we got to a subway, and that was a crazy thing. I thought they were the same as the buses in Puerto Rico and that when you wanted to get off you stood up and pulled the cord. But my brother told me, 'No, it's not like that here. This isn't a bus, it's a train, and it stops where it likes.'

"There were a lot of people on the subway, but I wasn't paying any attention to them. I kept looking out the window to see what the country was like. But what could I see? Nothing. The train was going underground! All I could see was the wall. I'll never forget that in all my life."

Complaints about the impersonality and anonymity of living in New York and its effects upon morality and behavior patterns are well illustrated by the following excerpt: . . .

"Here you may move into the apartment next to mine and it will be ten years before I find out you are there. When I go out to work in the morning I don't see my neighbors who live in the same building. I once saw an American girl in the building where I lived and I asked someone if he knew her. 'Why that girl lives right here,' I was told. Yet, as long as I had lived in that building, I had never seen her before.

"In Puerto Rico, it's different. Suppose you live somewhere in Río Piedras—everybody in the whole barrio knows you. If you move, there isn't one neighbor who can't tell me, 'She moved to Cantera, in Santurce.' . . . Even if someone wants to cheat you by moving away they can't, no matter how far they move. But here one can move two blocks away and even his nearest relatives can't find him. . . ."

There was a general feeling among our informants of being exploited and discriminated against—mainly, they believed, because of their language handicap.

"Hispanos are the only ones in New York who have to work for practically nothing. The colored people are a bit better off than the Hispanos because at least they know English. Negroes are the laziest people you'll find here. They're born lazy. A colored man gets a job in a factory and the boss explains clearly to him what he is supposed to do. But suppose he's working at something and the boss says, 'Look, hand me that piece of paper.' He'll tell the boss, 'Pick it up yourself,' and go on with what he is doing. With an Hispano it's different. Like if the boss says, 'The only thing you have to do here is to dust that little chair,' you can be sure that before he's through they've made him scrub the floor, clean the toilet, wash down the walls. And if there's a heavy package to be carried, it's the Hispano who has to carry it. . . .

"What else can he do? He doesn't know the language and if he quits the job he will have a hard time finding another one. All because he doesn't know English. That's what keeps us down. In a factory we have to do all the odd jobs because we don't have the advantage of speaking English, and the Hispanos who do know English get the best of the others and hold them back instead of helping them out. When a boss tells an Hispano who knows English to order another man to do something and the other says, 'Tell the boss that if I am to do that he should pay me more, 'the first will come back at him, 'If you don't like the pay, you can quit.' A man of one's own race!"

. . . Many parents questioned the right of law enforcement officials to prevent them from beating their children. They believed that beatings were a necessary part of child discipline and they attributed much of the delinquency to over-protection of the young. . . .

"Here the children become very independent at an early age. If you give a kid a good wallop and his bruises show, the police can get after you. It's not like that in Puerto Rico. Here in New York one day I was giving my little boy a good strapping and a policeman came and warned me to stop beating him. . . . That happened because my boy took $20 from my purse and went to the dime store in the neighborhood and bought everything he could lay his hands on. When I found out about it, I took him back to the store and had him return the things and get the money back. And for each thing I gave him a good spanking. That's when the cops stopped me. But if I had let my son get away with that, God only knows what he would be like today.

"So anyway, when the policeman butted in, I said, 'You can warn me about hitting my child now, but when he's eighteen and you see him on the rooftops robbing apartments and acting shamelessly, don't say anything to me. Bring him down with a bullet and leave me in peace.' The cop never said another thing to me about spanking my child." . . .

Our informants were very critical of the manner in which Puerto Ricans behave toward each other. Although some insisted that there is no friction among Puerto Rican migrants, many others lamented their lack of unity and the presence of discrimination and exploitation within the group.

"The Hispanos also have a little—let's say a little—discrimination among themselves. Not actually because of color, you understand, but because some Hispanos are in better positions, they live in better sections of the city and earn more money than the rest of us. This class may own a business and wants to segregate itself from the other Hispanos. Sometimes they even disown us. They say that they're not Hispanos but South Americans or something like that. . . .

"If we had any kind of unity, all those things that happen to us here wouldn't occur. Instead of offering a hand, the ones that come first try to keep the others down. If a veteran Hispano is working as a salesman, he goes from door to door to exploit his compatriots rather than going to the houses of Americans who have money. . . .

"The trouble with the Puerto Ricans in New York is that each lives for himself and they're all scared to death. They don't dare to protest against anything. They won't picket a police station for fear of getting shot. Most Puerto Ricans here don't even dare speak up when the factory bosses make them work overtime and then don't pay for it. They belong to unions but the unions don't do a thing for them. They are afraid to complain to the Department of Labor for fear the boss will find out and fire them. They think they would starve if they did. They hold back and won't talk.

"I don't know what's the matter with our leaders! The leaders were all born and bred in the States. They have no feeling for Puerto Rico, nor for us Puerto Ricans who come here. They have gone to school here from the first, they live well, so what do they care about the rest of us? They think, 'Let the rest of them sink or swim. Why should I bother as long as I have what I want, earn a good salary, and live well? If the rest don't know how to get as far as I have, let them stay where they are.'

"If you go to them with your complaints, they are the first to rob you. You go to one of those lawyers because he speaks Spanish the same as you do, and the first thing he'll tell you is, 'Bring $50 or $60 and I'll see what can be done about your case.' Suppose you want to bring suit against the company where you work. As soon as your back is turned, your man will seek out the company lawyer and you are out on the street, fired from your job. . . ."

So many of the families harbored hopes of returning to Puerto Rico that it suggests that Puerto Ricans were, psychologically speaking, not really immigrants at all, but migrant workers. . . .

"As soon as I can, I want to leave New York with all its 'modernization.' This 'modernization' doesn't go back with me. It's for those who have ability, money, education, and who are on their way up. Perhaps it's for my children in the future, but not for me. . . .

"When I leave here I'm going to take $800 or $1,000 with me to Puerto Rico. But I'm not going to live like a rich man in the center of San Juan. I'll work in San Juan but I'm going to take my family to live in the countryside, where I can have a little house of my own, even if it's made of planks and has a tin roof. At least I won't have to pay rent. I'll buy a few acres of land and I'll come home and raise my animals and cultivate something. I'll educate my children and perhaps the whole family can live peacefully. Of course it's always possible that it won't work out. And what I think now is that if luck is not with me, and I fail, I'll throw myself under a car."

AMERICAN-BORN "FOREIGNERS"

The Puerto Rican migrant has much in common with the people of other ethnic groups who poured into America's "melting pot" during the past century: He is new, he must cope with a strange culture, and he is poor. Yet, in certain very important respects, he is unique: He is born an American citizen, he is often wrongly lumped together with the American blacks (with no consideration or understanding of his own heritage), and he rarely intends to settle permanently on the mainland. These important differences are explored by a former priest, who for many years was involved with Puerto Rican communities in New York and on the island. Since 1968, the author has directed the Center for Intercultural Documentation, CIDOC, in Cuernavaca, Mexico.

After the introduction of the quota system in 1924, it seemed as if the melting process in New York City were finally about to catch up with the number of people tossed into the pot. Then, in the late forties, the city was presented with a novel challenge, an invasion of American-born "foreigners," the Puerto Ricans. . . .

These Puerto Ricans are not foreigners, and yet they are more foreign than most of the immigrants who preceded them. About this seeming paradox the well-meaning should be well-informed, since to be received kindly because you are a foreigner is not much different from being received kindly because, "after all, all men are alike." In both cases, chances are that the man who receives you is determined never to come to know you. . . .

This fallacy is at the bottom of the attitude of many well-meaning people toward the Puerto Rican immigrants: Let them do what the Irish or Italians did, or let them attempt what the Jews attempted; let them grow gradually through their own national parishes, territorial ghettoes and political machines to full "Americanization"; let them vociferously assert that they are as good Americans as the man next door. These attitudes are very common in New York, where the arrival of successive migratory waves is taken for granted. It is too often gratuitously assumed that the future novel about the Puerto Rican journey will be fashioned after either The Last Hurrah or Marjorie Morningstar, or will be a combination of both.

The welfare investigator who says to José Rivera, "My parents went through

From Ivan Illich, "Puerto Ricans in New York," *The Commonweal,* June 22, 1956, pp. 294-96.
Reprinted with permission.

the same experience," neither lies nor expresses xenophobia—he just oversimplifies, like the politician who tries again to use methods which worked when Italian was spoken in Harlem.

When the Irish and the Germans came here a century ago, New York City was faced with a challenge of a kind never experienced before and of a size never to be duplicated. In 1855, one-third of the city's population (500,000) consisted of immigrants who had arrived in the previous decade; against this proportion the one-fifteenth of the city's population which in 1955 consisted of recently arrived Puerto Ricans (again 500,000) seems insignificant.

In the days of the heavy influx to America, wave after wave of immigrants arrived, settled down and became accustomed to new patterns. The newcomers spoke different languages, worshipped in different churches, came from different climates, wooed in different fashions, ate different dishes and sang different songs. But under these apparent differences they had much in common. They came from the Old Continent and arrived as refugees or settlers to become Americans and to stay for good. They brought their own clergy, rabbi, priest or minister, and the symbols of past millennia which were their own, St. Patrick, the Maffia or Loretto, no less than the Turnverein. They settled in special sections of the city and kept to themselves for years before they ventured to take part in that experience new to all of them, life in a pluralistic society. They fell into a common pattern, and it is no wonder that those who had been here long enough to consider themselves part of a settled stratum fell into the habit of assuming *a priori* that each new incoming group would be analogous to theirs. This assumption, in fact, proved to be true until after the second world war, with the exception of two groups, the Orientals and the Southern Negroes.

Then, suddenly, the Puerto Ricans arrived en masse. New York had never before known such an invasion, an invasion of Americans who came from an older part of the New World into New York, which had been part of the diocese of San Juan long before Henry Hudson had discovered Manhattan. And New York had never had to deal with born American citizens who in their schools had learned English as a foreign language, yet who went to the polls to vote.

These strange Americans were sons of a Catholic country where for centuries slaves had found refuge, where the population of a little over two million is overwhelmingly white but where a difference in the shade of the skin is no impediment, either to success or to marriage. Yet theirs was the first sizable group coming from overseas into New York to be tagged by many as "colored," much less because of the racial heredity of some than for the vaguely sensed great difference between them and former new arrivals.

This was a new type of immigrant: not a European who had left home for good and strove to become an American, but an American citizen, who could come here for one harvest and return home for vacation with a week's salary spent on a coach ticket. This was not the fugitive from racial or religious persecution in his own country, but the child of "natives" in a Spanish colony or perhaps the descendant of a Spanish official in the colonial service; not a man accustomed to be led by men of his own stock—priest, politician, rebel or professor—but for four hundred years a subject in a territory administered by foreigners, first Spanish, then American, only recently come into its own.

The new arrival from Puerto Rico was not the Christian in his own right who received the Faith from the sons of his own neighbors, but the fruit of missionary labor typical of the Spanish empire. He was a Catholic, born of parents who were also Catholics, yet he received the Sacraments from a foreigner because the Government was afraid that to train native priests might be to train political rebels.

Even the physical configuration of the world from which he came was different. He was a man from an island where nature is provident and a friend, where field labor means much more harvesting than planting. When nature rebels every few decades, he is powerless; in the hurricanes he cannot but see the finger of God.

Until recently, nobody in Puerto Rico built a house with the idea that it should survive the elements with its strength or withstand the climate with its air-conditioning. What a difference from the Pole and the Sicilian, both of whom built to withstand nature, climate and time, both of whom built to separate their lives from that of nature. One might have come from the Russian steppe or the ghetto and the other from an olive-grove on the coast, but both knew what winter meant; they knew that a house was there to protect them from the cold, a place within which to make a home. It was easy for the Pole and the Sicilian to settle in tenements and to live confined there. But the new immigrant from the tropics knew no winter, and the home he left was a hut in which you slept, but around which you lived with your family. The hut was the center of his day's activities, not their limit. To come to a tenement, to need heat, to need glass in your windows, to be frowned on for tending to live beyond your doors—this was all contrary to the Puerto Rican's traditional habits, and as surprising to him as it is for the New Yorker to realize that for any immigrants these basic assumptions of his life should be surprising. . . .

Many a Puerto Rican does not leave the Island with a clear plan of settling on the mainland. How can a man who leaves on the spur of the moment, planning to make a fast dollar in New York and be back as soon as he has enough to buy a store, take roots in New York? I remember one woman who was in despair because her husband had disappeared on his way to the cane-fields, carrying his machete. She thought, of course, that a rival had grabbed him from her. And then, after a week, she got a money-order from Chicago. On the way to the cane-field he had run into a hiring gang and decided to try his luck—and that was the reason he neglected to come home for dinner. In a case like this, in which a man "drops in" on New York, with no intentions of staying but of eventually commuting "home," how can the transient have the same effect on his neighborhood in New York as the old immigrant who came to stay? Yet the statistical curve of emigration from the Island is in exact correlation with the curve of employment on the mainland. If employment is scarce, the reflux increases correspondingly. Many, even after years in New York, feel they got stuck there because of money.

With the arrival of hundreds of thousands from Puerto Rico and the other Central American States (it is estimated that more than one-fourth of N.Y.'s Spanish-American population is not Puerto Rican), not only a new language but a new pattern of living has been added to the city. Instead of the strangers speaking only a foreign tongue who formerly arrived exhausted from the long journey, American citizens, all of whom know some basic English, arrive in airplanes within six hours[1] of leaving their tropical island.

The old immigrants settled in national neighborhoods; the new commuter spreads out all over the city; ten years after the beginning of the mass influx, Spanish has already become ubiquitous in New York. Unlike European immigrants, all Puerto Ricans know some English, and this helped, but there is another factor that has contributed to this spreading to all quarters by South Americans. In former times when a neighborhood became a center for the newest immigrant, it was either a slum or tended to become one. And once a neighborhood had deteriorated it hardly ever was redeemed. The great immigration from Puerto Rico started after World War II, due to such factors as cheap air transportation, acquaintance with the mainland acquired by many during service in the army, rising education under the new political order on the island, and, last but not least, the growing pressure of population which has more than doubled since the beginning of the century. At that same time, the city was embarking on its great slum-clearance program, and the first blocks to be torn down were almost invariably those where the newest immigrant had just settled. As a result, the Puerto Ricans began to be resettled all around town in new projects, and on a non-discriminatory basis.

---

1. By 1971, air time between San Juan and New York was three and one-half hours.

Considering this dispersal and the tendency to commute to the Island, it is no wonder that there are hardly any Puerto Rican national neighborhoods in the traditional sense. One result is that it is difficult for Puerto Ricans to develop local grass-roots leadership within their own group; either their concentration per city block is too thin, or the intention to stick to the neighborhood is absent, or the necessity to organize with their own is weak because all are citizens who at least understand some English and have official "protection" from the government labor office—the first instance of something like a "Consulate for American Nationals." And there is no doubt that another factor contributing to the relative lack of neighborhood leadership is the lack of a tradition in leadership, caused by hundreds of years of colonial administration.

Thus Puerto Ricans in New York find it more difficult than groups which came before them to form their own in-group leadership, if they do not find it completely impossible. This fact gives them a very real advantage over former migrations in one way, because it almost forces them into an active participation in the established community. On the other hand, the sudden challenge of having to participate in a settled New York community proves too arduous for many who might have been able to become leaders in their own cliques . . .

"HISPANOS" AND "MARINE TIGERS"

Throughout the history of U.S. immigration, new groups—Italians, Russians, Greeks, Germans, Poles—have shed their old culture and mannerisms, as one would a ragged suit of clothes, as they eagerly tried to fall in step with "The American Way of Life." The children of Jewish immigrants from Europe, for example, sometimes denied their religion, or changed their surnames; a few even resorted to plastic surgery to straighten their "un-American" noses.

Puerto Ricans have also taken part in this sometimes pathetic process. Many, unable to "pass" as 100 percent Americans, created their own pecking order. They called themselves "Hispanos" or "Latinos." In this way, they tried to associate themselves with Spain or the Latin American republics, and to disassociate themselves from what some U.S. newspapers called "the Puerto Rican problem." The following book excerpt describes the situation in the 1950's, which is far different from today, now that a new concept of ethnic pride has emerged among different racial and national groups.

From Elena Padilla, *Up from Puerto Rico* (New York: Columbia University Press, 1958), pp. 32-35. Reprinted by permission.

Among Puerto Ricans . . . the terms "Hispano" and "Latino" are used and preferred to "Puerto Rican" for self-identification. . . .

In the past, Hispanos or Latinos were a small minority of intellectuals and middle-class professionals from Puerto Rico, Spain, and Latin America who lived in New York. By 1950, the Spanish-speaking socially mobile persons of lower-class origins, who now considered themselves in a higher social position than the recent lower-class migrants from Puerto Rico, were calling themselves Hispanos. More recently, the term has been extended to include all Spanish-speaking persons who reside in New York, regardless of their social and economic class.

In Puerto Rico, a Puerto Rican is someone born on the island, which is his country. He may be a member of the upper, the middle, or the lower class; he may come from either country or city; he may be a farmhand, a farmer, or a banker; he may be a millionaire, a salaried employee, or a wage earner. But whatever else he is, he is Puerto Rican and is not regarded as a member of an ethnic or minority group.

In New York, the terms "Hispano" and "Latino" have been substituted for that of "Puerto Rican," because the latter, in more ways than one, has become a "bad public relations" identification for New York Puerto Ricans. It is associated with unfavorable pictures of the behavior and respectability of Puerto Ricans, which are not necessarily true or real. Even when used in Spanish and by Puerto Ricans themselves, it may convey an assumption of undesirable characteristics of the persons referred to. . . .

When referring to friends, or to persons considered "decent and respectable," the term "Hispano" is preferred by Eastville[1] Puerto Ricans. Recently arrived migrants soon learn that they are to call themselves Hispanos and drop their identification as Puerto Rican. They will probably not deny their country, but will resort to the linguistic subterfuge of Hispano to protect themselves from being characterized in a derogatory manner. They will tend to emphasize their particular home towns and municipalities in Puerto Rico, for to be accepted among Hispanos, it is important to know something specific about one's past and where one came from. . . .

One of the common forms of relating personally . . . is by initiating a conversation in which one identifies oneself as Hispano, in the sense of Puerto Rican, and by establishing this clearly. This particular approach to personal relations suggests three major social features of the Puerto Rican group. First, that being Puerto Rican and referring to oneself as Hispano is an entree for

---

1. Fictitious name used by author to denote a Puerto Rican community in New York City.

social relationships, and second, that the participants in the relationship have to establish the authenticity of their being Puerto Rican by showing some particular knowledge of the island, such as being conversant with a specific *municipio,* town, or city, and then a particular street there. Thus the identification is narrowed down to a level that no foreigner can reach. . . . Third, the identification also calls for establishing that one belongs to a particular family. One's status must be defined and acceptable if a personal relationship of any continuity is to be formed.

Hispanos classify themselves into three major groups with reference to life-experience and time spent in New York City. Those who have lived here for many years *(los que llevan muchos años aquí)* are the first. Those who grew up in this country, including the second generation, *nacidos y criados* (born and brought up), and those born in Puerto Rico who come to New York in early childhood comprise the second. Recent migrants, those who have come in the last several years from Puerto Rico, and who are referred to in derogatory terms . . . as "Marine Tigers" are the third. *(Marine Tiger* was the name of one of the Liberty ships which made a number of trips between San Juan and New York after the war, bringing many thousands of Puerto Ricans to the States. It lent its name to the new "greenhorns," and the name has continued to stick.)

DOWN THESE MEAN STREETS

There are countless tales of horror about Puerto Rican migrant workers who have been misled, cheated, and abused. Some of the worst episodes occurred in the years immediately following World War II, when migrants knew little about the pitfalls of trusting smooth-talking employment agents.

In Chicago, in 1946, the Castle Barton and Associates employment agency imported 362 young Puerto Rican girls to work as housemaids, at about $60 a month. From this low salary, the agency deducted $125 as its fee, at the rate of $10 per month, and held an additional sum in escrow for each girl's air fare home. The girls were little better off than indentured servants. Lonely, underpaid, unable to speak English, a number of the girls were lured into prostitution; others took factory jobs, and others returned home disillusioned.[1]

In another notorious case,[2] sixty Puerto Rican men were promised jobs in

---

From Piri Thomas, *Down These Mean Streets* (New York: Alfred A. Knopf), pp. 98-104. Reprinted by permission.

1. *The New Republic,* April 28, 1947, p. 7.
2. Ibid.

the North Chicago Hardware Foundry. After deductions for room and board, employment agency fees, and compulsory allotments for their dependents back home, the already meager $34.50 weekly pay-check shrank to virtually nothing. The employer was housing the men, during the winter, in unheated railway cars.

Once Puerto Ricans settled permanently on the mainland with their families, some of the obvious abuses ceased. But there were other problems. The Puerto Rican was "the last to be hired, and the first to be fired." A lack of skills made it hard to secure good-paying work. And the color of a man's skin often proved more important than what he could do.

Piri Thomas grew up in Harlem, and, despite extreme poverty, and bouts with narcotics and prison, has become a successful writer. Being a dark-skinned Puerto Rican, while some of his friends and relatives were "white," taught him some hard lessons. He learned quickly that America is a black-white world; there is little tolerance for the polychromatic reality of Puerto Rican culture. This selection, from his first book, describes a job interview in 1945.

YOUNG MEN, 17-30, GREAT OPPORTUNITY
LEARN WHILE WORKING EARN WHILE TRAINING
Door-to-door salesmen in household wares.
Guaranteed by Good Housekeeping. Salary and commission.
603 E. 73 St., 2nd fl.—9 a.m.

"Dig, Louie, this sounds good," I said to my boy. "Let's go over in the morning. Hell, with our gift of *labia* we're a mother-hopping cinch to cop a slave."

"*Chévere,* Piri, man, we got all Harlem and we know plenty people. Bet we can earn a hundred bucks or more on commissions alone."

We went down the next day and walked into the office and a girl handed me and Louie each a paper with a number on it and told us to please have a seat. My number was 16 and Louie's was 17. Man, me and Louie were sparklin'. We had our best togs on; they were pressed like a *razor* and our shoes shone like a bald head with a pound of grease on it.

"Number 16, please?" the girl called out.

I winked at Louie and he gave me the V-for-victory sign.

"Right this way, sir, through the door on your left," the girl said.

I walked into the office and there was this paddy sitting there. He looked up at me and broke out into the friendliest smile I ever saw, like I was a long-lost relative. "Come in, come right in," he said. "Have a chair—that's right, sit right there. Well, sir, you're here bright and early. That's what our organization likes to see. Yes sir, punctuality is the first commandment in a salesman's bible. So you're interested in selling our household wares—guaranteed, of course, by *Good Housekeeping*. Had any experience selling?"

"Well, not exactly, sir, but—er—when I was a kid—I mean, younger, I used to sell shopping bags in the *Marketa.*"

"The what?"

"The *Marketa* on 110th Street and Park Avenue. It, er, runs all the way up to 116th Street."

"Ummm, I see."

"And my mom—er, mother, used to knit fancy things called *tapetes.* I think they're called doilies, and I used to sell them door to door, and I made out pretty good. I know how to talk to people, Mr.—er—"

"Mr. Christian, Mr. Harold Christian. See?" and he pointed a skinny finger at a piece of wood with his name carved on it. "Ha, ha, ha," he added, "just like us followers of our Lord Jesus Christ are called. Are you Christian?"

"Yes, sir."

"A good Catholic, I bet. I never miss a Sunday mass; how about you?"

"No, sir, I try not to." *Whee-eoo!* I thought. *Almost said I was Protestant.*

"Fine, fine, now let's see . . ." Good Catholic Mr. Christian took out some forms. "What's your name?"

"Piri Thomas—P-i-r-i."

"Age?"

"Er, seventeen—born September 30, 1928."

Mr. Christian counted off on the fingers of one hand . . . "twenty-eight, er, thirty-eight, forty-five—ahum, you were just seventeen this September."

"That's right. Paper said from seventeen to thirty."

"Oh, yes—yes, yes, that's correct. Where do you live?"

I couldn't give him the Long Island address; it was too far away. So I said, "109 East 104th Street."

"That's way uptown, isn't it?"

"Yes, sir."

"Isn't that, um, Harlem?"

"Yes, sir, it's split up in different sections, like the Italian section and Irish and Negro and the Puerto Rican section. I live in the Puerto Rican section. It's called the *Barrio.*"

"The *Bar-ree-o*?"

I smiled. "Yes, sir, it's Spanish for 'the place'—er—like a community."

"Oh, I see. But you're not Puerto Rican, are you? You speak fairly good English even though once in a while you use some slang—of course, it's sort of picturesque."

"My parents are Puerto Ricans."

"Is Thomas a Puerto Rican name?"

"Er—well, my mother's family name is Montañez," I said, wondering if that would help prove I was a Puerto Rican. "There are a lot of Puerto Ricans with American names. My father told me that after Spain turned Puerto Rico over to the United States at the end of the Spanish-American War, a lot of Americans were stationed there and got married to Puerto Rican girls." *Probably fucked 'em and forgot 'em, I* thought.

"Oh, I—er, see. How about your education? High school diploma?"

"No, sir, I quit in my second year . . ."

"Tsh, tsh, that was very foolish of you. Education is a wonderful thing, Mr. Thomas. It's really the only way for one to get ahead, especially when—er, uh—why did you leave school?"

My mind shouted out, *On account of you funny paddies and your funny ideas in this funny world,* but I said, very *cara-palo,* "Well, sir, we got a big family and—well, I'm the oldest and I had to help out and—well, I quit." Then, in a sincere fast breath, I added, "But I'm going to study nights. I agree with you that education is the only way to get ahead, especially when—"

"Fine, fine. What's your Social Security number?"

I said quickly: "072-20-2800."

"By memory, eh? Good! A good salesman's second commandment should be a good memory. Got a phone?"

"Yes, sir. Lehigh 3-6050, and ask for Mr. Dandy. He's my uncle. He doesn't speak English very well, but you can leave any message for me with him."

"Very, very good, Mr. Thomas. Well, this will be all for now. We will get in touch with you."

"Uh, how soon, about, Mr. Christian? 'Cause I'd like to start work, or rather, training, as soon as possible."

"I can't definitely say, Mr. Thomas, but it will be in the near future. Right now our designated territory is fully capacitated. But we're opening another soon and we'll need good men to work it."

"You can't work the territory you want?" I asked.

"Oh no! This is scientifically planned," he said.

"I'd like to work in Harlem," I said, "but, uh—I can make it wherever you put me to sell."

"That's the spirit!" Mr. Christian bubbled. "The third commandment of a good salesman is he faces any challenge, wherever it may be."

I took Mr. Christian's friendly outstretched hand and felt the warm, firm grip and thought, *This paddy is gonna be all right to work for.* As I walked out, I turned my head and said, "Thank you very much, sir, for the opportunity."

"Not at all, not at all. We need bright young blood for this growing organization, and those that grow with us will be headed for great things."

"Thank you. So long."

"So long, and don't forget to go to mass."

"No, sir, I sure won't!"

"What church you go to?" he asked suddenly.

"Uh"—I tried to remember the name of the Catholic Church on 106th Street—"Saint Cecilia's!" I finally burst out.

"Oh yes, that's on, er, 106th Street between Park and Lexington. Do you know Father Kresser?"

"Gee, the name sounds sort of familiar," I cooled it. "I can almost place him, but I can't say for sure."

"Well, that's all right. He probably wouldn't remember me, but I was a youngster when he had a parish farther downtown. I used to go there. Well, if you run into him, give him my regards."

"I sure will. So long, and thanks again." I closed the door carefully and walked out to where Louie was still sitting.

"Man, Piri," he said, "you was in there a beau-coup long-ass time."

"Shh, Louie, cool your language."

"Got the job? You were in there long enough for two jobs."

I smiled and made an okay face.

Louie cupped his hand to his mouth and put his head next to mine. "That cat ain't a faggot, is he?" he whispered.

I whispered back with exaggerated disgust, "Man! What a fuckin' dirty mind you got."

"Just asking, man," he said. "Sometimes these guys are *patos* and if you handle them right, you get the best breaks. Well, how'd you make out?"

"In like Flynn, Louie."

"Cool, man, hope I get the same break."

"Number 17," the girl called.

"Here I go," Louie said to me.

"*Suerte,* Louie," I said. I gave him the V-for-victory sign and watched his back disappear and dimly heard Mr. Christian's friendly "Come right in. Have a—" before the door closed behind Louie.

Jesus, I thought. *I hope Louie gets through okay. It'll be great to work in the same job. Maybe we can even work together. He'll cover one side of the street and I'll cover the other. As tight as me and Louie are, we'll pool what we make on commissions and split halfies.*

"Hey Piri," Louie said, "let's go."

"Damn, Louie, you just went in," I said. "You only been in there about five minutes or so. How'd Mr. Christian sound?"

We walked down the stairs.

"Okay, I guess. Real friendly, and he asked me questions, one-two-three."

"And?"

"And I'm in!"

"Cool breeze. What phone did you give?" I asked.

"I ain't got no phone. Hey, there's the bus!"

We started to run. "Fuck running," I said, "let's walk a while and celebrate. Man, you could've gave him Dandy's number like I did. Aw, well, they'll probably send you a telegram or special delivery letter telling you when to start work."

"What for?" Louie asked.

"So's they can tell you when the new territory is opened up and when to come in," I said. "'Cause the other territory—"

"What new territory?"

I opened my mouth to answer and Louie and I knew what was shakin' at the same fuckin' time. The difference between me and Louie was he was white. "That cat Mr. Christian tell you about calling you when some new territory opens up?" Louie said in a low voice.

I nodded, "Yeah."

"Damn! That motherfucker asked me to come and start that training jazz on Monday. Gave me a whole lotta shit about working in a virgin territory that's so big us future salesmen wouldn't give each other competition or something like that." Louie dug that hate feeling in me. He tried to make me feel good by telling me that maybe they got a different program and Mr. Christian was considering me for a special kinda job.

"Le's go back," I said coldly.

"What for, Piri?"

"You see any colored cats up there?"

"Yeah, *panín,* there's a few. Why?"

"Le's wait here in front of the place."

"Por qué?" asked Louie.

I didn't answer. I just watched paddies come down out of that office and make it. "Louie," I said, "ask the next *blanco* that comes down how the job hiring is. There's one now."

Louie walked over to him. "Say, excuse me, Mac," he said. "Are they hiring up there—you know, salesmen?"

"Yes, they are," the guy answered. "I start Monday. Why don't you apply if you're looking for work? It's—"

"Thanks a lot, Mac," Louie said. "I might do that." He came back and started to open his mouth.

"Forget it, *amigo,*" I said. "I heard the chump."

We waited some more and a colored cat came down. "Hey, bruh," I called.

"You callin' me?"

"Yeah. I dug the ad in the paper. How's the hiring? Putting guys on?"

"I don't know, man. I mean I got some highly devoted crap about getting in touch with me when a new turf opens up."

"Thanks, man," I said.

"You're welcome. Going up?"

"Naw, I changed my mind." I nodded to Louie, and he came up to me like he was down for whatever I was down for.

"Let's walk," I said. I didn't feel so much angry as I did sick, like throwing-up sick. Later, when I told this story to my buddy, a colored cat, he said, "Hell, Piri, Ah know stuff like that can sure burn a cat up, but a Negro faces that all the time."

"I know that," I said, "but I wasn't a Negro then. I was still only a Puerto Rican."

"MY PARENTS, THEY CRY WITH JOY"

Like a huge magnet, New York City attracted the vast majority of Puerto Rican migrants until the late 1950's. Today, about 40 per cent of migrants from the island settle outside New York. Most Puerto Rican communities are clustered on the eastern seaboard, in New York, New Jersey, and the New England states. But a substantial number of Puerto Ricans—perhaps 130,000—have settled in the Chicago area. As a Chicago journalist reports, "many have made it here," but "there are serious problems of poverty and alienation." Significantly, Chicago was the spawning ground for the Young Lords, a Puerto Rican street gang that evolved into a militant social activist movement.

From John Adam Moreau, "The Puerto Ricans: Who Are They?", *Midwest Magazine, Chicago Sun-Times,* September 21, 1969. Reprinted by permission.

Many have made it here in Chicago. Many find disappointment and become caught in circles of despondency. How severe their problems are is virtually impossible to express in numbers. The welfare roles and unemployment statistics don't have entries under "Puerto Ricans." No one really knows the extent of Puerto Rican misery in Chicago.

"There aren't any figures," says one Puerto Rican, Mrs. Isabel Collazo, veteran case worker in the Wicker Park office of the Cook County Department of Public Aid. "But naturally since there are more Puerto Ricans than ever, the caseload is up, way up. The problems certainly are bigger. Credit buying is quite a temptation to people who've had little; all those pretty things. Then there's gar-nisheeing of wages. . . . When you dig into why someone is applying for help it so often turns out that the newcomer got in over his head and leaving his family was all he could think to do." . . .

There are serious problems of poverty and alienation here. The Latin American Defense Organization, a largely Puerto Rican group, stormed the Wicker Park headquarters of the Cook County Department of Public Aid in disgust and frustration with the welfare system. . . . Something is clearly the matter in the Puerto Rican community if a former street gang, the Young Lords Organization, declares its contempt for its elders and capitalism and says that it patterns itself after the radical Black Panthers. . . .

It is the Lords who participated in May in the occupation of the administration building of McCormick Theological Seminary to publicize demands that McCormick and the city do more for the poor on the Near North Side where the Young Lords live.

It was the Lords who in June took over the Armitage Ave. United Methodist Church at No. 834 on that street, managed not to be thrown out, and who in August opened a day-care center in the church basement.

And it was the Lords who took over urban renewal land at Armitage and Halsted to make a People's Park, and who used physical force to break up a meeting of the Lincoln Park Community Conservation Council to protest possible use of urban renewal land for a tennis club.

In every instance the Lords argued they acted on behalf of the poor and because the city is not "responsive" to the needs of the poor in its area.

Underlying their fervor and aggressiveness . . . is a conviction that some kind of socialism is the answer to the nation's woes, and that class, not race, is what divides the nation.

The Lords are relatively impotent and have no strength resembling that of some of the black youth gangs. . . . For months there have been abortive talks among the Lords and other gangs about some kind of coalition but there has been little progress. There are, by police count, 13 predominantly Puerto Rican street gangs, a potential but as yet little exploited source of power. . . .

One of the greatest weaknesses of the Puerto Rican community is that it is not organized politically, partly because there are so few professional men— probably no more than 50 in the entire Chicago area.

No Puerto Rican has ever held a major office in Chicago. . . . In short, the Puerto Ricans are the only major ethnic group in this country which has not become a pressure group.

"Whenever you see some Puerto Ricans getting power," says Mike Barreto, a Puerto Rican who is executive director of the Spanish Action Committee, "you see them begin to sell out." . . .

Barreto mentions names like Manuel Toledo, director of the Division St. Urban Progress Center, and Carlos Caribe Ruiz.

"I admit I'm a patronage worker," Toledo replies, "but when we talk the city listens. I push when it is needed. The Puerto Ricans who have gotten some influence with the city got it because they are strong leaders."

Says Caribe Ruiz, executive director of the Puerto Rican Congress:

"Believe me, I understand what groups like these Young Lords feel. I believe they mean well. They want a slice of the pie just like I did when I came here. But you never get anything by marching, like Barreto and his people. . . . These people couldn't have broken the communications barrier with the city, the police, the schools, but we have."

There are few Puerto Rican precinct captains in Chicago and except for a pitifully incompetent and ill-timed effort last March during the special aldermanic race, no Puerto Rican has run for political office. . . .

Says Marcelino Díaz, a prominent real estate man: "You Anglos tried to put Puerto Ricans on a reservation, but they're beginning to get out. . . . We're here only 18 years and the machine overcomes us because of our disunity. . . . We're going to have to fight for a long time."

Shortly after the Division St. riot of 1966, the city fathers planted saplings on that street near Damen, where the trouble broke out. A few of the trees have died, and the rest have grown irregularly. A tiny minority of the Puerto Ricans (and there were non-Puerto Ricans involved, too) took part in the riots. . . .

One wonders . . . whether Puerto Ricans in Chicago are better off in 1969 than they were in 1966. The statistics are not there and the answer depends on to whom you talk. . . .

Marcelino Díaz says:

"I know I'm selling more real estate to Puerto Ricans." . . .

Claudio Flores, successful publisher of the newspaper *El Puertorriqueño,* co-owner of a restaurant in Niles, and owner of travel agencies, sees betterment everywhere.

"I ought to know," he remarked, "because I file a lot of income tax returns for Puerto Ricans." . . .

From the standpoint of Jorge Prieto, a Mexican-American physician who works in Spanish-speaking areas, "things have gotten much worse since '66."

"Malnutrition among the Puerto Ricans is practically universal," he contends. "As a result, the rule—not the exception, but *the rule* —in almost every pregnancy is some kind of abnormality in the prenatal period, during delivery or during the first year. . . . This is because they're too poor to take care of themselves. City health facilities are adequate but under-used because of the language problem. No Puerto Ricans have any influence with the Board of Health, of course."

And James Fernández, of the Chicago office of the Commonwealth of Puerto Rico's Economic Development Administration, says, "You'd have to prove it to me that things are better. A little here, a little there, but it's still mostly a life of factory work and dishwashing. The Puerto Rican still does a lot of your dirty work." . . .

The 1960 census said there were 35,000 Puerto Ricans in Chicago, 25,000 of them born on the island. There are many more today. Luis Machado, of the Chicago office of the commonwealth's Department of Labor, estimates 70,000. Other sources say 80,000 to 100,000. . . .

"In the strong trade unions like plumbing, electrical work, carpentry and bricklaying," says Thomas Pietrantonio, a Puerto Rican born on the mainland who is editor of the National Labor Journal, "The Puerto Rican doesn't stand a chance. They won't let him in. But he's welcome in the machine shops where there's a lot of risk. Take a look sometime when you're down on Division St., and if you don't see a couple of guys within an hour's time with a finger or two missing, I'd be surprised."

"Puerto Ricans don't like to go to classes and union meetings and, of course, they tend to fear recriminations from employers," says Alicea Martínez, a staff representative for the United Steel Workers of America, who came in 1954 intending to make money and go home, but who got a good job as a welder and . . .

And made it.

Like Carlos Caribe Ruiz, 41, executive director of the Congreso Puertorriqueño, an umbrella organization of social and civic groups. In 1947 Caribe Ruiz left his parents and 16 brothers and sisters in Cabo Rojo.

"I sold my bicycle and chickens and took off," Caribe Ruiz recalls, "and I studied for a while at the Juilliard School of Music in New York."

Now Ruiz is a real estate agent.

"In those days," he went on, "it wasn't like now. We were discriminated against everywhere we went. You'd buddy up with a guy for protection. I lived in an 8-by-10 room. It cost me $22 a week."

Things got better for Caribe Ruiz. For $12,000 he bought on contract a house worth $3,000— that's the method whereby you can lose everything if you miss a payment. He is enormously proud of the home at 1901 W. Erie. There he has raised or is raising five children, three already in college.

"I don't think I'm particularly bitter against Anglo society," he says today. "It's been hard but better than I expected. But I remember things, a beating I got once — and the way the Italians treated us when we moved in over on Erie, for example."

And Manuel Toledo, 37.

He is president of the Board of Coordinators of Puerto Rican Affairs, and he holds a patronage job from the Regular Democratic organization: director of the Division St. Urban Progress Center.

Toledo came here from his native Lares in 1951, became a factory worker, eventually rose to foreman, and now owns a house. "If I had stayed in Puerto Rico," he says, "I probably would be ignorant and poor . . . Today I feel like a king."

And Marcelino Díaz, 45.

Díaz had some formal education before he left Cidra and came to Chicago in 1949. He finished his schooling at Valparaiso University. Like his father, he is a real estate man.

And Cayetano Vallejo, 28.

Vallejo couldn't better fit the model for the role of office manager at American Dream Corp. He arrives here in 1959 from San Lorenzo, is befriended by a Polish-American man, works for him, learns cabinetmaking—"I didn't know anything about wood; I had worked in a beauty parlor"—saves $7,000, buys machinery, borrows more money from the Small Business Administration, and opens a factory for making display equipment on S. Wabash.

Many have known first-hand themselves what Vallejo has gone through: 10 to 12 hours of work a day, seven days a week, your heart in your mouth, your future uncertain.

"I was cheated once along the way," Vallejo said one day, "but I got smart after that. Everything legal, in black and white. I have never been more happy."

Vallejo owns a home in Bellwood, where his parents, who were farm people, live. There are five sisters and four brothers, ages 21 to 37. True to the contemporary Puerto Rican pattern, two sisters married Puerto Ricans from here and returned to the island with them to help set up a grocery store and a television repair shop.

These are, of course, the people who have succeeded to the extent of having enough money to live in dignity, the people who can afford to have ever bigger aspirations.

They and Puerto Ricans like them are the newest link in the ethnic chain. They have sat down to the great American banquet. They are the newest newcomers, hankering to become something and somebody, to have cause for a joy like that of Vallejo who, when he recalls setting up in business, says:

"My parents," Vallejo says, "they cry with joy when they hear I open my own place."

"EL BARRIO'S WORST BLOCK"

[As the years pass, old and new generations of Puerto Ricans fan out into other cities of the United States; a growing number, particularly in the New York metropolitan area, have moved to middle-class suburbs. But El Barrio in Spanish Harlem is still a point of reference for Puerto Ricans, just as New York's Lower East Side was for the thousands of Jews who came to America from Eastern Europe. El Barrio is still an impoverished ghetto that holds one of the largest single concentrations of Puerto Ricans; it is a point of entry for many of the poorest newcomers, a trap for those unable to escape, and a home for those who know no other home. This article shows how, in the midst of the most hostile conditions, people struggle to survive—and how some do.]

A block in El Barrio—Spanish Harlem—despite all the speeches and studies and community-action programs of the last years, remains remarkably foreign to most Americans, who have never lived in the crowded, dirty world of aging, six-story tenements, or talked to the people who live there—the parents, the children, the wage-earners, the welfare-takers, the healthy and the sick. Another reason why the area is hard to understand is that most studies of this world have focused on only one of the dark aspects of its

---

From David and Sophy Burnham, "El Barrio's Worst Block is Not All Bad," *New York Times Magazine,* January 5, 1969, pp. 24-25. Reprinted by permission.

life—the lack of family stability, or the drug addicts, or unemployment, or the obviously unsuccessful schools—and failed to portray the stable families, the industrious working fathers, and the teen-agers who have rejected drugs, the large numbers who grow strong and survive. . . .

[One block in El Barrio] has been more completely portrayed. The work was begun four years ago by Dr. Bernard Lander, a New York sociologist, his brother Nathan and Dr. H. P. O'Brien of Notre Dame, and was supported by a series of grants. . . . A rare picture has emerged by now of one period in the life of the block and some changes in the life-styles of its residents.

The 25 tenements facing the 630-foot street are red brick, most of them blackened with grime. They seem to press in on the street. Two buildings have been abandoned, their windows broken, their insides gutted by fire and emptied by thieves. Between some of them are sudden open spaces where a building has been torn down and the empty lot has become filled with rubble and beer cans. In contrast are five freshly painted tenements on one side of the street which are being renovated by a local housing organization, Metro-North.

When the study began, 2,500 people in 640 families lived on the block. Today, after the removal of a few tenements, there are 400 families of 1,750 individuals. Three out of every five residents are Puerto Rican, almost all the rest Negro. The population is far younger than that of the city as a whole; every other person is under 21. . . .

Two of every three families are headed by men; the rest by women. Of these family heads, more than half had not finished school, more than half were unemployed, a quarter were on welfare, a third made less than $60 a week. Rent, compared with the rest of Manhattan, seems low; two-thirds of the families pay between $25 and $45 a month for a three- or four-room apartment.

The block was built in 1906 to accommodate a wave of Jewish immigrants from the lower East Side (upper Manhattan was opened to construction two years earlier with the completion of the first subway). The houses were "new-law" tenements. Among other reforms, every room had to have at least 70 square feet of space. Every room had to have a window.

The Jews were supplanted by the Italians and the Italians by the Puerto Ricans and Negroes, but the housing did not begin to get really bad until 1953, when the city designated the block for public housing, and then did nothing. The landlords, awaiting renewal, stopped making repairs; and during the next 15 years the block gained its reputation as a "bad" block.

Sixty per cent of the people on the block have lived there for 10 years or more, despite the fact they say they want to move, and most look back to a golden past: "It's not the street. It's the people who moved into the street. See,

'cause . . . it was a very good neighborhood. I mean it was quiet. It was, I could-
n't say it was clean, but it was quiet, and they didn't have a lot of burglars and
murders that they have now. It's just the dope and the marijuana that's being
brought into the street that's messing up the street. . . ."

The poorest people tend to remain on the block; and the poorest are also
those with the least education, the least resistance to and the fewest outlets for
frustration, the highest incidence of ill health, mental disturbance and unemployment. The interior of the housing on the block has often been described:
brown hallways with their rotten stairs and the acrid smell of garbage; cold
apartments with overflowing toilets and moist, peeling paint. Housing probably
is the worst problem because it is always with you. . . .

None know this better than the people who live there. About eight years ago
the neighborhood formed Metro-North to do something about housing in a
seven-block area. This organization is completely self-supporting, financing its
two offices, supplies and phone bills with bus outings, dances and private donations. In the last three years it has fought the city bureaucracies, organized
the tenants in rundown buildings, obtained vacate orders from the buildings
department, relocated numerous families from dangerous buildings, and finally
acquired about $12 million in private grants to buy and renovate 17 tene-
ments—an example of concerned citizens' action that would make any middle-class family proud.

Though most of the work of Metro-North is in housing, in 1965 it persuaded
the city to build a vest-pocket park on the block. It is a bare asphalt slab, more
like a parking lot than the usual leafy image of a park, but to the residents of
the block it is an achievement. . . .

But this, of course, is only a beginning; the block's major problems remain.
The fighting gangs are gone now, and apparently there are fewer crimes of
violence, but the street—almost without shops, seemingly deserted on a cold
winter day—is a marketplace for drugs. A bookie hangs out here. A numbers
racketeer. Two pushers. Youths watch for fags to service for $5, money that
immediately will be converted into a bag of heroin. Girls walk the streets. You
can find almost anything here, and the activities permeate the lives of everyone,
whether they participate and approve or not.

The fact is that the majority of the people on the block do not participate
even peripherally in the life of crime, beyond a regular bet on the numbers.
. . . On this block, if there is considerable crime . . . there is also a surprisingly
conservative, even middle-class, morality.

Of the 50 teen-age members of the old fighting gang that was centered on
the block . . . three are now in rackets, eight or ten are addicts; but three are

members of the police force, one is a lieutenant in the Marines and the remaining 30 or 35 have also "gone straight." It seems to be a matter of growing up.

Look at Angelina, the 19-year-old mother of an illegitimate child, who admitted she smoked pot when she was 14, shoplifted, roamed the streets. She doesn't do that anymore.

"It's not lady—it's not for a woman. That's men's stuff. Boys' stuff."

The block is composed of 1,750 individuals as different as characters in a good novel. There is the short, heavy woman, a social worker, with direct brown eyes and a finely arched nose, strong, proud, self-sufficient. She has lived on the block with her husband and four children for 40 years. She sent one son through college. And there is the woman whose two daughters are lesbian—and it is a sad commentary on the neighborhood that the third will probably be one. (There seems to be a lot of lesbianism on the block. Many girls are drawn to it, either from fear of the hit-and-run tactics of the boys, or else because they grew up in state institutions where homosexuality is common. . . .)

A large number of people on the block believe that ability is more important than pull or "who you know." Many of the 25 per cent on welfare are ashamed of receiving it, though others accommodate themselves to it quite cynically. . . .

If some people abuse the welfare agency, the agency sometimes returns the favor. One caseworker, for example, tried to dissuade an ambitious youngster from learning a trade. "He say to me, 'Why don't you just go to work and forget the problem of going to school?' I told him if I go to work . . . I'm going to get a job washing dishes, somewhere, going for 15 dollar. That's what he requested I do." This youth is now working on a B.A. degree at City College.

Perhaps drugs have the most to do with the evil reputation of the block. One-twentieth of all the deaths from overdoses in Manhattan in 1967 (20 out of 400) occurred on this block, and despite continued and frequent arrests, the block has maintained its reputation as a place to get heroin. Cars with Jersey plates cruise down the street, looking for a connection. Yet only a small proportion of the block's population, less than 2 per cent, uses heroin. . . .

While Lander found that during the four-year period of his study one-third of the kids began taking heroin, he also discovered that about one-third of those with a drug history—22 out of 60 addicts and former addicts—had quit. It seems they reached their late 20's and early 30's and simply stopped. On the average they had been off drugs for three years or more. All but three stopped without the assistance of the various government programs. . . .

Many on the block, especially the young people, admit that they commit illegal acts on a fairly regular basis. For the teenagers, for example, the weekly shoplifting trip down to Macy's or up to Incredible Alexander's in the Bronx is a regular Saturday entertainment, like going to a movie.

"Why do you steal?"

"To get what we wanted. Pocketbooks and clothes." . . .

They rarely are caught, partly because they are very adept, partly because the stores find it cheaper to accept a certain amount of shoplifting than to hire enough clerks to wait on each customer. One store detective estimates that his staff catches one of five of the shoplifters, about half of whom are middle-class. When the slum kids are caught, he said, "the Puerto Ricans break down and cry; the Negroes are cool and tough." . . .

If surprisingly small numbers are arrested on the block, an even smaller proportion ever get to court or prison. According to police records, only 11 percent of the boys between 11 and 20, and only 30 per cent of the adults who were arrested ever went on to court. . . . There is an almost unanimous lack of respect for the police there, a widespread belief that they are corrupt and brutal.

"One of my friends got killed by a cop," a pretty young Puerto Rican girl remembered. "The cop was drinking and they say he came out of a bar on 103d Street, and the kid was running and some lady was yelling, and he got shook up and he shot him in the back and got him killed, and he died."

"Had your friend done anything?"

"I don't know. You really don't know what happened 'cause the cop told his story and that's all the story. It was still wrong 'cause he coulda shot him in the leg or something, but he shot to kill."

She added: "Cause you're a Puerto Rican or Negro, they just take you in the car and beat you up and then take you to the precinct and everything." . . .

A young man was asked whether the police accept bribes.

"Oh sure, they do that all the time."

"Have you ever seen it yourself?"

"Giving them money? Oh sure."

"Who would it be?"

"Bookies. All over. Everything."

A runner for the numbers racket was even more definite. "They, you know, they come around the first of every month. There is the cop which you call the captain's man and he comes around and he picks up for the captain and then the cop on duty he gets paid, too."

"Aren't there any honest cops?"

"Yeah. You get an honest cop on Fifth Avenue someplace. You can't have honest guys around a block like this."

NEO-RICAN JETLINER

Jaime Carrero's bilingual "*Jet Neorriqueño*/Neo-Rican Jetliner" was probably the first literary mention of the concept of Neo-Ricanism. "Neo-Rican" has become a term commonly used to describe the "in-between" product of Puerto Rican and North American culture, a hybrid person who speaks and thinks in both languages, sometimes simultaneously, but is a stranger in both lands. There are, today, probably a few hundred thousand Neo-Ricans in America; still others have returned to the island of their birth, or their parents' birth, where their children are being taught Spanish for the first time. Neo-Ricanism involves more than language; it encompasses a complex set of attitudes, set forth in the following poem.

Ticket please
   Me recuerda ese señor
     a Dick Tracy
     a Trucutú
         (Alleyoop *en inglés*)
   Ahí viene otra vez
   con el 'no se ponga de pié
       por favor'

Fasten your seat belt
   Ahí viene esa señorita
   con el 'abróchese el cinturón
     en seguidita please'
     please' por favor
       plis
       plis

No smoking *señor*
   Is this seat taken?
   No. Please.
   Thank you.
   Are you from over here?
   No Sir from New York
   But you look Puerto Rican.
   I'm not I'm not born in New York
      born in New York

No smoking please
   My name is Raúl.
   From Puerto Rico?
   Jes an'now from Noo Jork.
   Muee bieeen senhor
   Raúl is may name *señor.*
   American—you look American blond
     you don't look Puerto Rican:
   Raúl *señor* my name is Raúl.
   R-A-U-L u.u.u.
   Like the U you find in fool?
   Jes. U.U.U. fool.
Fasten your seat belt fasten your seat
Fasten your fasten fast fast fast
F-f-f-f-s-s-s-t-t. . . . .

Vuelo A

New York the center of the world is big the dream my father had when the sugar cane died of drought Sir and bad fertilizing Sir did its job to force his wings open to search for the greatest money on earth the dream my father had.

Conversación I

Hey boy
Le tengo miedo a esa voz.
'We the people of the United States in order to form
Hey boy
I am scared of that voice with the
Hey boy
'a more perfect union,
Hey boy
'establish justice,
Me duele esa voz con el
Hey boy
Me duele esa voz coino un SUR
Hey boy
'insure domestic tranquility'
Me duele el color de esa voz
con
el
Hey boy
and so on
and so on
promote the general welfare,
Hey boy it is it
and so on
and so on
'over the land of the free'
Me duele, me duele esa voz . . .
. . . .
Hey boy did you see
        did you see   ?

Vuelo B

New York Sir the center of the world gave birth to my little kid sister yeah and you know the doctor said and the nurse said when the other doctor and the other nurse showed up with my kid sister Sir that no other baby was as big Sir as my kid sister Sir was.

Conversación II

My friend is big man
a new man man Neo-Rican
a big man man
Big man, my friend is big
Neo-Rican
A Jetliner man
Big man, my friend is big
big as fire man
As big as I can say mountain
    as I can say sky
    my friend is big
    big man big
    as the dry season
    as the rain
    big I say
    my friend is big
    big man big
As big as I can say Manhattan
    my friend is bigger
    the size of God
    The Jetliner
    Neo-Rican
    MAN . . .

Vuelo C

New York the center of the world taught me law-stick ball pool the street money
man—the wings my father saw but forgot to take when he saw them there man
everywhere anyway in the law in the street in the money.

Conversación III

La primera vez que la escuché
    en mi primer viaje
    me sonó poética
        esa frase
        o gráfica
   algo así
S.O.B.

Yes Raol like *CERVEZA*
        the word to me
        is a girl
Oh Raol you're nuts

. . . .
Man you spelled his name bad

. . . .
How?
        R-A-U-L like fool
Jes like foool
Ah Raool sounds like fool
a U like fool
Jes fool U like foool
U U U fool

Vuelo D

New York the center of the world taught me law yes Sir the color of the wings my father found when he came to forget his land yes Sir and decided the wings money can buy were better than the land.

Conversación IV

    A ver mi hermana he venido
    Hace tiempo no la veo
Slow please did you say NANA
    No señora hermana dije hermana
        Sister *dije* sister
That I come to see her
        you see?
    La pobre no se levanta
Is she sick?
    Si señora
Is she old?
        yes yes *no se puede mover*
I am sorry to hear that.
    podía caminar
    la última vez que la ví
Is she sick?
    yes yes
Is she old?
    yes yes
I'm sorry to hear that

LAMENTO 3
This Puerto Rican is silent
This Puerto Rican is sad
    to be silent and sad
      I feel something big
          or low
          or dark
          is going on
          in the back
          of the mind man.
This Puerto Rican is silent and sad.
The color no white man dares to ask.

LAMENTO 2
I was born in New York new blood.
I was born in New York
I'm not a Jones Act Puerto Rican.
yeah?
I'm a Neo-Rican man new flash,
yeah?
I known what I know no
Jones Act man
yeah?
. . . .
what was that   ?

LAMENTO 1
    Hay horas de espalda: sin terminar
Jetliner warned—you're high
    Hay horas de frente: ahí puestas,
    tranquilas
Jetliner cracks
    Hay horas de día: que hay que caminar
Overshoot — too high
    Hay horas de hombre: volar
cracks open
    Hay horas . . .
CRASH   in the dark

LAMENTO 0
On the fringe of trouble if you ask
    ¿por qué señor
      por qué?
On the fringe of trouble I say
    ¿olvida el Jones Act?
On the fringe of trouble I say.
    a chance sir do we have
    a chance sir a chance?
We cannot solve your problems I say
On the fringe of trouble again
On the fringe . . .

PART X

THE DIVIDED NATION

What appears to be taking place . . . is a growing movement of young Puerto Ricans back and forth between the island and the United States. They come back looking for a job, but rarely find one. They had been reminded in the United States that they were Puerto Rican, but here they are told that they speak Spanish with an "English accent," that "you are not really one of us." The young Puerto Rican may well ask himself, not only "Where am I going—" but "Who am I?"

—*A. W. Maldonado,* The Nation, *March 16, 1964*

I am proud of my accent, I don't want to drop it.

—*Carmen Oliveri, a New York-born Puerto Rican student,*
New York Times, *April 23,1968*

After more than a century of United States rule, while substantial progress has been achieved, Puerto Rico is still the poorest community under the American flag. In 1946, former island governor Rexford Guy Tugwell wrote, of Puerto Ricans:

I am ashamed of my country, sometimes, for not having cared enough to do something for them besides hand out relief and use them for political advantage. I am humiliated that, having been Governor for almost five years, I have not been able to make some considerable change in this. . . . Puerto Rico comprises one of those small groups of people, of whom there are many in the world, who are tied by destiny to a larger entity. The process of working out a satisfactory organization of the relationship is a matter in which only a few of us happen to be interested. . . . Something will happen in the case of Puerto Rico, but it seems awfully slow in coming.[1]

---

1. Rexford Guy Tugwell, "In Defense of Puerto Rico," *The New Republic,* April 15, 1946, p. 512.

Since those words were written, more economic and social change has occurred in Puerto Rico than in the previous four centuries. Some of this change
was generated by Mr. Tugwell, the last—and by far the best—American to govern the island. But most of it took place when the federal government relaxed
its colonial leash a few notches, and allowed Puerto Ricans to play a more
active role in running their own affairs.

The same phenomenon is slowly, agonizingly, developing in the *barrios* of
America's cities, where second and third-generation Puerto Ricans are educating and organizing themselves, and starting to demand their fair share of power.

A large question that remains, however, is not how quickly—but *where*—
Puerto Ricans are heading.

A final decision on the island's political status will have far-reaching consequences. Puerto Ricans disagree strongly about the political future of their island. Even if they eventually reach a consensus, they will not be the only ones
to drive the final bargain. U.S. businesses have a $3 billion stake in the island.
The U.S. Army, Navy, and Air Force maintain bases there, and, although modern technology makes these bases less crucial than they were during World War
II, Puerto Rico still occupies a strategic location.

As if matters were not complicated enough, the Puerto Rican population in
the continental United States has soared (4.6 million according to the 2010 census) and now outnumbers the population on the island (3.9 million). Puerto Ricans represent 11.3% of all Hispanics living in the United States, as migrants
flow in from other parts of the Caribbean and Central America. While Puerto
Ricans in the United States were once heavily concentrated in New York, there
are now large communities elsewhere, with especially strong growth in Florida.

The Puerto Rican community has organized itself to represent its interests
in stateside political institutions for close to a century. In New York City, Puerto
Ricans first began running for public office in the 1920s. In 1937, they elected
their first government representative, Oscar Garcia Rivera, to the New York
State Assembly. In 1988, Nelson Merced became the first Hispanic elected to
the Massachusetts House of Representatives. A few decades ago, the most important Puerto Rican political figure in the United States was Congressman
Herman Badillo, who was raised in New York. By 2012 there were four Puerto
Rican members of the United States House of Representatives: Democrats Luis
Gutierrez of Illinois, José Enrique Serrano of New York, and Nydia Velázquez
of New York, and Republican Raúl Labrador of Idaho, complementing the one
Resident Commissioner elected to that body from Puerto Rico. Puerto Ricans
have also been elected mayor of numerous cities, such as Miami, Hartford,
Camden, and Perth Amboy. And Sonia Sotomayor, born in the Bronx to Puerto

Rican parents, sits on the U.S. Supreme Court.

Over the years, the island has become more urban-industrial, and the cultural gap between it and the United States has narrowed. Over a long period of time, it may narrow to such a fine divide that political assimilation may not imply any drastic surrender of cultural values.

On the other hand, the island's leaders may balk at relinquishing their hard-earned control to a centralized government in Washington. Today, at a time when America's minority groups are putting unprecedented emphasis upon ethnic pride, Puerto Ricans in the United States may be the first to protest against full assimilation. They may, instead, relish the fact that there is still a *patria* to which one can return, or of which one can at least dream. Only time will tell.

"NATION AND HOMELAND"

In November, 1968, wealthy industrialist Luis A. Ferré surprised many experts—and himself as well, he admitted—when he won the governorship of Puerto Rico. For 28 years, island politics had been dominated by the Popular Democratic Party, led by Luis Muñoz Marín. But many voters, particularly those in the middle-class suburbs that ring San Juan, were clamoring for change; also, the Popular Democrats were weakened by bitter internal struggles. Ferré took advantage of this, and mounted a vigorous, well-planned campaign. For the first time in Puerto Rican politics, television was employed to market a candidate as one would a household product. The air waves were saturated by spot commercials showing a firm, paternalistic Ferré, promising *La Nueva Vida*, The New Life, to the island's citizens. He barely won, with 44 per cent of the votes, compared with 42 per cent for the Popular Democrats.

Because Ferré had long been identified with the pro-statehood cause, Puerto Rico was polarized into two hostile political camps. Many advocates of the middle-of-the-road Commonwealth status began to sound like *independentistas*, as they warned of the dangers of statehood. Ferré did little to allay the fears of his opponents; in a speech seven months after his election, he supported the presidential vote for Puerto Ricans, a step that would immerse the island in the U.S. political system.

As the rhetoric grew more heated, and violence shook the University of

---

From *Speech Delivered by the Governor of Puerto Rico, Hon. Luis A. Ferré on Heritage Day (Día de la Raza), October 12, 1969.* Commonwealth Department of Education, Santurce. Puerto Rico, 1969. The text is in both Spanish and English.

Puerto Rico campus, Ferré adopted a more conciliatory tone. His New Progressive Party proposed the concept of jíbaro statehood; meaning political, but not cultural, assimilation with the United States.

Ferré's views on how Puerto Rico could join the Union, without surrendering its unique personality, are outlined in a speech given in San Juan on October 12, 1969, to mark Columbus Day. In Puerto Rico, it is known as *Día de la Raza*, Heritage Day; the island also celebrates its discovery by Columbus on November 19, 1493. (Note: In November 1972, Ferré lost in his bid for re-election as governor; the winner was Rafael Hernández Colón of the Popular Democratic Party, which espouses Commonwealth status and increased autonomy.)

Puerto Rico has warmly hailed our New Life, but there are noisy voices hawking that it will result in the cultural disappearance of Puerto Ricans. Those who say so are basing their position on hackneyed arguments. . . .

We are Puerto Ricans. At a glorious moment in the first decade of the 19th Century, the patriot Ramón Power and Bishop Arizmendi managed to congeal the awakening of our conscience as a people. From that moment we move . . . to the Lares Revolt [1868] and to the achievement of the Autonomic Charter [1897]. The people of Puerto Rico slowly achieve a greater conscience of themselves and greater powers of self-government. Then there comes the change in dominion. Puerto Rico is shaken by the impact of the American presence.

In this century, after having overcome a naive and mistaken colonialist policy, our people take up a new struggle to obtain more powers of self-government, a struggle which peaks a half century later with the election of the Governor and with the drafting, by ourselves, of our own Constitution. I feel honored to have been able to make at that Constitution . . . my modest contribution to this process of the definitive quest for our own values and our own governmental powers. But I am further honored to have been able to contribute to this stream of development of our values which set us apart from the other peoples of the world.

There is a simple definition of what it means to be a Puerto Rican. Hostos gave it in his diary and I want to share it with you. The great Teacher told us: "Whence does that come and why is it so? Why do we cling so tenaciously to the native land? I think I have found the answer. I set it down here in order to come back to it and think about it some more. We love our land because it is for us a reference point. Life is a journey; reason would not know how to find the starting point were it not for the piece of earth whose image is before our eyes everywhere."

I tell you that, as it is for Hostos, Puerto Rico is my starting and reference point. It is also yours.

Once the journey of life has begun, we may ask ourselves where we are going. It is also Hostos who can best answer that question. Writing in Paris on the fifth of August in 1868 he speaks of heading immediately for Europe to— and I quote: "free myself from the struggle with shameful hunger and thence take me on to Puerto Rico and grant myself a month of oblivion and hope and place myself in my theatre of operations, in that America to whose future I have pledged my own."

I have come before you, my fellow citizens, young people of Puerto Rico, to extend to you the invitation for us as people and as men, collectively and individually, to follow the example of Hostos and consecrate our future to the future of America.

The American world, the entire hemisphere from Alaska to Tierra del Fuego, must make a superhuman effort so that men in it may unchain themselves from poverty, oppression and hunger so that the children of today's poverty shall not become the parents of tomorrow's poverty. Puerto Rico may very well become the leader in this humanitarian effort. We have established an ever closer union with the United States of America. We want to be a part of the United States forever. But we want to be so not with the attitude of one who seeks admission into another's house, but with the attitude of one who comes home and has something of himself to offer also.

I conceive of our participation in the great task of hemispheric integration as the best contribution which we Puerto Ricans may make to our fellow citizens of the North. A fulcrum of two cultures, a center for change and adaptation of what is best in both, Puerto Rico has in this Hemisphere the paramount task of contributing to the understanding between the United States and Latin America. We have such an ability and we should exercise it. We should offer Puerto Rico as a center of work where the United States of America and our neighbors on the rest of the Continent may learn together how to live in harmony and how to solve without violence their problems and how to work out for themselves a better and more just future.

To bring about this ideal of Latin and North American harmony, Puerto Rico has to make a special effort to understand its own nature and to show, by its everyday life how a people of a great cultural richness can also make use of the most modern concepts of technology. We can show how an essentially Latin people can, at the same time, be perfectly American. We must feel as Puerto Ricans, operate like Americans and dream of a united America where we will have been the home and seat of both cultures.

I now want to address myself most specially to our youth. . . . To be Puerto Rican is the most significant achievement before us as a people. It is precisely that quality of being a culturally united people which gives us the credentials to improve understanding between Latin American culture and North American culture.

But Puerto Rico has also achieved the technical proficiency of the American people and you, the young, are experiencing that. That ability is of great value in this task. Both abilities, the ability to feel as creatures of Hispanic culture and the ability to perform as beings of Anglo-Saxon culture, are the two which permit us to make our mark in the Hemisphere. To do so we must develop ourselves as a people in both directions at once.

We must understand, my dear young fellow citizens, that in order to better serve this purpose of understanding of which Hostos spoke, that we must give a new dimension to progress. During the last 20 years there has been a revolution in the communications media, radar, television, satellites. The world has grown smaller and we men can communicate with each other faster and easier than we ever dreamed. But, in spite of this easier communication, we have made precious little progress in comprehension and understanding. That is the new dimension which we must add to progress. Man must learn to understand himself better and to understand his fellow man better. We need a revolution for understanding. Here, the Puerto Rican, because of his understanding of the two cultures of America, has the ability and also the obligation to serve in achieving the Hostosian dream of a united America, through a greater understanding.

And that is why I conceive as one of the principal duties of the New Life that of preserving, promoting and perpetuating the Puerto Rican being. This is not a new posture in my life. I have always held up and have always defended the values of our land. On July 27, 1963 I pointed out: "To be an American does not mean to speak English or to be the son of a Yankee. The United States, today with a population of 180 million, has received throughout its history more than 40 million immigrants of all races—English, German, Italian, Polish and Jewish. For Puerto Ricans to be Americans, as for millions of the children of other races which today make up the American nation, is to be true to the principles of democracy which are set forth in the Constitution, and to feel one with other American citizens in the protection of our freedoms and our national life."

It is moved by this knowledge and, even more, by that feeling in my soul that I now add: "Nation" is a concept of political, social and human identification. "Homeland" *(patria)* is the heart's affection for the place of birth. Our Nation, the United States. Our homeland, Puerto Rico.

I have had occasion during my life to propitiate and defend the values which make me feel proud to be a Puerto Rican. You will remember that during the deliberations of the Status Commission a prominent U.S. senator took the following position—and I quote: "The people of Puerto Rico represent a rich and old culture. We gladly welcome diversity; therefore, the characteristic culture of Puerto Rico, as such, is no barrier to statehood. However, the unity of our structure of federal states requires a common language. . . . The recognition and acceptance of English as the official language must be a previous condition for statehood." Faced with this absurd position, born of a poor understanding of what the American nation is, I made it clear then that if assimilation was to be made a condition *sine qua non* for statehood, then it would be impossible to accept. . . .

History has proved me right. Sociologists, psychologists, and even the large communication media in the United States recognize that diversity, not *assimilation,* is the nerve and essence of the new American culture. This very week a well-known national magazine says:

> The hard truth is that the celebrated American melting pot has never worked quite so well in life as in nostalgic myth. As Nathan Glazer and Daniel P. Moynihan pointed out six years ago in "Beyond the Melting Pot," Americans tend to maintain their sense of ethnic identity far more tenaciously than was once supposed.

But over and above that, the nation's Supreme Court said:

> Congress could very well have concluded that as a means of promoting the intelligent use of the vote, the ability to read or understand Spanish is as effective as reading English for those who have access to newspapers and programs in Spanish.

The opposite, the demand for assimilation, in the words of the judges of the nation's highest court, would be "an abominable crime."

Fellow citizens . . . this is the moment for diversity within the unity of the great American nation. Let us make our contribution to this precious moment in her history! . . .

I . . . invite you to serve in this noble endeavor: that we come before history to promote two fertilizing and enriching streams of our past and our future which have been the source of our achievements as people. Let us follow the road of Puerto Ricanism. Let us follow the road of unity with the United States. Following these two paths of noble and generous projections which transcend our naturally limiting boundaries as an island and enable us to contribute to the achievement of hemispheric peace, solidarity and progress, we will arrive at our rendezvous with history.

"FROM A JAIL IN PUERTO RICO"

In the preceding article, Governor Luis A. Ferré appeals to Puerto Rico's youth "to feel as creatures of Hispanic culture" and "to perform as beings of Anglo-Saxon culture," which is the essence of his concept of *jíbaro* statehood.

But many of Puerto Rico's young people, particularly those on the college campuses, are attracted to the views of men such as Rubén Berríos Martínez, the youthful president of the Puerto Rican Independence Party.

Berríos was imprisoned for three months during the spring of 1971, for violating a federal injunction that ordered him to leave the U.S. Navy's firing range in Culebra, an offshore municipality of Puerto Rico. Since World War II, the Navy has used Culebra, and some of its surrounding islets, for naval and aerial target practice. In 1971, naval plans to secure more land on Culebra collided with resistance from the island's 600 residents, who claimed that they were being forced to abandon their birthplace.

The issue became an international controversy. Culebrans received support from virtually every political group in Puerto Rico, as well as from sympathetic congressmen, lawyers, and activists in the United States. The Navy phased out its operations in 1975. Berríos and his followers, who adopted a tactic of "militant nonviolence," were among the leaders of the "Save Culebra" movement. Unarmed, they "invaded" the island in a small boat, and erected a Christian chapel right on the very beach that was used as a target for naval cannon. Berríos wrote the following letter while serving his prison sentence; when he emerged from jail, he was greeted by a large crowd, and it was generally conceded that he had gained the sympathy of many persons not formerly identified with the independence cause.

S AN JUAN— I am writing from a jail in Puerto Rico, the last classical colony in Latin America. The slave-master relation, in whatever form, negates that which separates human beings from animals: freedom.

I am writing in an American newspaper because the American people are our potential allies. To become independent, Puerto Ricans must make it more convenient for the United States Government to leave than to stay in our land, and in that endeavor, free Americans can be of great help.

In a country where 13 per cent of its scarce arable land is occupied by foreign armed forces which also make an atomic arsenal of its territory; where its youth is ordered to fight in the wars of a foreign nation, thus making the cry of "tax-

---

From *New York Times,* April 28, 1971, p. 43. Reprinted by permission.

ation without representation is tyranny" a sigh compared to this blood tribute; where the laws of a foreign parliament apply without the consent of the governed, thus making a mockery of the most elementary rules of representative democracy, the fight for national liberation has become the duty of every self-respecting man and woman.

If to these abusive political conditions one adds a 28 per cent unemployment rate, vast squalid slums populated by 25 per cent of our families, prices higher than those in New York with incomes of less than $300 per capita for one-third of our population, an abysmal maldistribution of income whereby 9 per cent of the families receive 40 per cent of the net income and 40 per cent receive 9 per cent of the net income, yearly returns of $450 million for American investors and a $1-billion deficit in the balance of payments in favor of the United States, then the fight for social revolution becomes part of the obligation of every Puerto Rican.

It is not surprising that the Americans are starting to hear about a different Puerto Rico. The widely publicized occurrences, such as the Navy's abusive bombardment of Culebra Island, the university riots, the more than 150 acts of sabotage that have plagued American enterprises in Puerto Rico during the last two years, are the symptoms of a deeper problem. To the institutionalized violence of the colonial system some respond with nonviolence, others with violence, and, sad to say, some still respond with collaboration.

Genuflecting, the collaborators will apologize and reassure Americans that "independentistas" constitute a minority in a community of loyal American citizens. As proof they will submit the thesis of colonialism by consent.

And in a sense, they might have been right. Classical manipulations of colonial masters, division of spoils with local tories, propaganda bombardment through American-controlled television and newspapers, an educational system destined to instill Puerto Ricans with a feeling of inferiority, impotence and dependence, and direct persecution of independence forces have occurred. The United States Government managed in the past to divide Puerto Ricans and confuse and suppress their urge for liberation.

But now the colonizer-colonized contradictions, particularly the incompatibility between social justice and colonial status, have become evident. And the independence forces have directed their energies toward erasing the traditional psychological misconception whereby the mass of the Puerto Rican people, through constant indoctrination, believed the republic to be equivalent to hunger. By uniting the fight for national liberation with the fight for radical social change, by answering the question—why independence?—our fight for freedom has ceased to be an elite movement and is being transformed into a mass movement.

Besides realizing the need for a radical change, Puerto Ricans see the possibility of such a change. This is due, in large part, to the declining prestige of the United States, and to the effective addition to our methodology of nonviolent tactics. These are particularly suited to situations like ours where the balance of physical power is disproportionate and the colonized nation is forced, by internal and international policy considerations, to wear a mask of democratic respectability.

Colonized, exploited, ideologically prepared, and full of hope, our people are on the road to freedom.

"CANCIO AND COMPASSION"

Should a Puerto Rican who believes in independence be required to serve in the U.S. military, which he considers to be a "foreign" army? For that matter, should a resident of Puerto Rico, who considers himself loyal to the United States, be required to serve, if he cannot vote, either for the President, who is Commander-in-Chief of the Armed Forces, or for members of Congress, which has the power to declare war? The issue of the military draft is one of several which remains unsolved, because of Puerto Rico's anomalous Commonwealth relationship with the United States. Here, a Puerto Rican journalist describes how one U.S. federal judge on the island wrestled with his own conscience in deciding the case of a conscientious objector to the draft.

A lmost inevitably, a judge leaves his imprint on the court over which he presides. Some judges are lenient in their interpretation of the law, others are strict. Some judges go about their job in a matter-of-fact way, others like to add a touch of drama. Through their interpretation of the law, either liberally or conservatively, judges sometimes make decisions that change the course of a nation's history. Witness, for example, the 1954 decision of the U.S. Supreme Court, under Chief Justice Earl Warren, outlawing segregation in the public schools.

Federal Judge Hirám Cancio has definitely left his mark on the U.S. District Court over which he presides. Cancio's emphasis on Puerto Rican values, his sometimes unorthodox approach to his job and his flair for the dramatic has

Frank Ramos, *San Juan Star,* January 30, 1970, p. 33. Reprinted with permission.

distinguished his four years as a federal judge. Now, Cancio's dramatic announcement that he was reducing the sentence of convicted draft evader Edwin Feliciano Grafals from one year to one hour has brought him once again into the public spotlight.

Cancio has his admirers but he also has his critics. His outspokenness has sometimes brought charges that he has exceeded the authority vested in him as a judge. For example, in March 1968, Cancio delivered an impassioned plea against the death penalty to a jury which could have ordered Mrs. Carolyn O. Wilkins sentenced to death on a first degree murder charge. Cancio told the jury:

"The vast majority of the people of Puerto Rico do not believe in the death penalty. That is the reason why the Constitution of Puerto Rico clearly prohibits the death penalty. Unfortunately, the Constitution of Puerto Rico does not apply in this jurisdiction. Therefore, you have a great responsibility in your hands. You are to decide whether this lady is going to live or whether this lady is going to die. . . ."

Cancio's plea brought charges that he was interfering with the right of the jury to reach its own conclusions. But it also reflected Cancio's compassion for those persons who are brought before him on trial. People at federal court tell the story of the old man who was brought before Cancio on a charge of capturing and selling canaries and nightingales.

It seemed the old man had violated a long-standing statute that prohibited the capture of migratory birds. When Cancio learned that the old man lived on the verge of poverty and that he depended on the sale of these birds for his livelihood, Cancio persuaded the U.S. attorney to drop the case.

Moreover, when he learned the man had spent his last cent in coming to San Juan for the hearing, Cancio gave him several dollars of his own funds so he could take a público home.

Cancio's compassion was undoubtedly a factor in his decision to reduce the sentence he himself had originally imposed against Feliciano Grafals. He felt that Feliciano Grafals was technically guilty of violating the law but morally innocent. Had he written the law, Cancio said, he would have declared persons like Feliciano Grafas to be true conscientious objectors. Cancio's concern was best expressed by the judge himself in a statement he made to the accused shortly before imposing the original one year sentence. He said:

"Judges often suffer when sentencing human beings, even though those human beings happen to be hardened criminals. In your case, my suffering has been the greatest of all the cases before me. It has been the greatest because I do not believe you are a criminal but a person who for ideas and ideals in which he firmly believes, has chosen to violate a law which he believes unjust, invalid and unconstitutional.

"I know that you love Puerto Rico. I love Puerto Rico as much as you do. The only difference is that we disagree as to what is best for our country. I wish you would have given me the opportunity to avoid this sentence by having accepted probation. I think I know why you would not voluntarily accept any conditions, but I am very sorry not to have been able to avoid sentencing you as I did. Good luck."

Cancio's statement not only reflected his compassion but also his concern for Puerto Rico and its future. The idea that Puerto Rico is a distinct entity, with its own culture and value, is a theme that has emerged time and time again during Cancio's tenure as judge. It was this feeling that led Cancio to deliver a eulogy from the bench praising Puerto Rican composer Rafael Hernández the day after his death. More recently, Cancio's concept of the island's distinct character led him to deliver a speech urging that Spanish should be the preferred language used in the U.S. District Court in San Juan.

In the Feliciano Grafals case, Cancio's concern for the island caused him to dwell at length on Puerto Rico's status dilemma. Although he expressed his belief in the validity of the island's present status, he acknowledged in his ruling that some people might have good reason for thinking otherwise. He said:

"There is today a respectable number of respectable people, some of them to be found even among the defenders of commonwealth status, who honestly believe that the United States governs in Puerto Rico in the limited form allowed it by the Puerto Rico Federal Relations Act without there having really been consent of the people of Puerto Rico."

Cancio's statement on status was intended as a warning light to Congress and the island government to resolve, once and for all, the perennial problem of status. Cancio suggested that the problem could be resolved in three ways: statehood, independence or a clarification of commonwealth status, in which the powers of the U.S. and Puerto Rican government would be clearly defined. In the absence of a new pact clarifying commonwealth status, Cancio said, Congress could approve a law granting that the penal provisions of the Selective Service Act and other federal laws would not apply to the island without the expressed consent of the island's Legislature and Governor. Until the status question is resolved, the judge concluded, there will be persons like Feliciano Grafals who will question the applicability of compulsory military service and other federal laws to the island.

Cancio's plea may or may not stir Congress and the Puerto Rican government to action. In the long run, its possible impact on the U.S. Supreme Court may be even more significant. Should the high court decide to hear an appeal of the Feliciano Grafals case, and most informed people feel there's a strong possibility that it might, then it could provide the high court with its first real opportunity to consider some of the questions concerning the island's political status that are raised by Cancio.

A DAY AT THE BODEGA

The dream of many a hardworking immigrant is to save a little money and open a store. The Spanish-speaking *barrios* of the United States are dotted with *bodegas*, or *colmados*, as they are known in Puerto Rico. The owners of these small grocery stores, caught in the vicious circle of poverty, are often as much victims as their clients. In his exhaustive study of the impact of America's inadequate welfare policies upon the poor, Brooklyn-born writer Richard M. Elman spent a day in one *bodega*. As he observes, many of these small entrepreneurs "are abused and hated by the very people they serve, and in the course of the day's business they will hate and abuse their customers in turn." The *bodega* owners in the slum may perform a "vital function . . . but at what expense to themselves and their lives!"

A ntonio Ubas has been the owner of a . . . *bodega* on Clinton Street for the past six years. In all that time he has still not managed to sell off any of the huge pyramid of canisters of kosher salt that were in his store windows the day he gave $150,00 key money to its former occupant, Mr. Alex Colmar. Antonio has a wife and two children. He lives in a project, considers himself a good manager, and is generally well liked in the neighborhood. To his kosher salt display he quickly added the standard array of Puerto Rican delicacies—chick peas, guava shells, nonalcoholic malt beers, and tamarind juice—and then he ran leaders on such items as rat poison and cockroach powders, which are also staples among the urban poor; but he has never yet been able to do as much business on the register as he can usually show in his little black book. Antonio's is that kind of tiny, close establishment, a storefront deep, with shelves going up to the ceiling. The place gives off a deep, rich smell, and

From Richard M. Elman, *The Poorhouse State: The American Way of Life on Public Assistance* (New York: Pantheon Books, Random House, 1966), pp. 217-30. Reprinted by permission.

you feel you could reach up with his wooden pole hook and pull down exquisite delicacies. Not so! Paying $80.00 a month rent and $20.00 more for his telephone and utilities, Antonio has been in such a tight squeeze over the past six years that most of his top shelves are still crowded with old Mr. Colmar's dusty boxes of Quaker Oats and Oxydol.

As he puts it, "you build up a lot of credit and you hope that people will start repaying you so you can buy more goods and sell more.

Sometimes they just don't. It's hard. I'm not complaining. Some of these people have it worse than me, but it's hard . . .

"When a person comes in and it's not the first time, he don't ask permission," Antonio continued, explaining the rules by which he must do business. "He will take this. He will say he wants something like that. Then he will say, 'Write it down!' Well, Macy's can write it down and the Welfare will say okay, because they have people who make up the bills and it looks good, but all I have is this little book. How do they know whether I am telling the truth? If I say it's not all right to such a person, she will only go to the place down the street, and then maybe when she has a little money she won't come back here. I give people what they want . . . and all month long they give me back a little at a time. It's not so nice because sometimes I can't do that with my jobbers. It just seems like I have to be here for these people, and they are sometimes very inconsiderate. They run up a big bill . . . maybe $25.00 . . . and then they disappear.

"Well, if you go to Welfare about such a person they will say, 'It is your own fault, for being so greedy. We give such people cash so they should buy with cash. If you want to take risks with people like that it is your own fault.'"

It hardly seems fair to call Antonio Ubas a greedy person. Once, a few days before Thanksgiving, I was talking to him when Brownleaf came into the store. Brownleaf nodded to me with the blind side of his face and then went over to browse among the shelves, as if in some lending library.

"Watch this," Antonio winked at me.

When Brownleaf showed up at the counter, he unburdened himself of a large can of turkey, two small cans of cranberries, a frozen turkey TV dinner, a loaf of bread, a bottle of hard cider, and four bananas. Antonio wrote up each item on his pad and added up the total, which came to $2.59, but he wouldn't put anything into the bag.

"And two packs of Salems," Brownleaf added then.

Antonio stared down at his fists which were digging into the sticky counter.

"I'd like those cigarettes," Brownleaf said.

Antonio smiled. "I don't even know your name . . ."

"You know me," Brownleaf said. "My wife is here all the time . . ."

"I don't know you," Antonio insisted. "Tell me your name."

"Come on," Brownleaf said. "You know me."

"What's your name, Mister?"

Brownleaf said, "Are you being funny?"

Antonio did not act as if he were being funny. He was putting all the groceries away under his counter.

"Holy shit," Brownleaf said "You want me to spell it out? It's Brownleaf— B .. r .. o .. w .. n .. l.. e .. a .. f .."

"I still don't know that name," Antonio said "Are you sure I know your lady?"

"You know her. She comes in all the time with the kids."

"You got to do better than that. A lot of people do that." Antonio was smirking as he put the purchases into a bag and handed them across the counter to Brownleaf.

"What about my Salems?"

"I don't like people to go hungry," Antonio smiled. "But I don't see why they got to smoke . . . I don't smoke . . ."

Brownleaf said, "Cocksucker," and he went out the door with the package in his hands.

"So that's what I am," Antonio said. He found a page marked Brownleaf in his little book and wrote down $3.00 next to the date. I asked, "What was all that about?"

"What do you want me to do?" Antonio exclaimed. "Call the police?

"I know that guy. Sure," he added, "he and his wife . . . they're, coming in here all the time just like he says. Look at this!" He showed me the page in his ledger with a long column of scribbles on it. Brownleaf seemed to owe at least $20.00. "He knows I know him. Sure,"

Antonio said then, slamming his book shut. "We just play this little game sometimes. It's just a little thing he's got with me . . ."

"An expensive thing," I said.

"That?" Antonio is blushing. "He doesn't mind that. He's a pretty good guy most of the time and he pays his bills. It's just that I've got to take care of my customers and so they've got to pay a little extra for the service."

"So you two knew each other all the time?"

"You don't understand anything." Antonio said, turning back to his book.

Antonio Ubas is a small, plump, fair-skinned little man with shiny black curly hair and soft brown eyes. He always wears a clean white shirt with sleeves rolled up to the elbows, and his arms are firm and thick but hairless. If Antonio were not so plump, he would be handsome, like his fifteen-year-old son Dickie, who is sometimes pressed into helping out in the store. One Jewish holiday, when school was out, I stayed with them from 8:00 A.M. until closing time to keep a log of the day's business. Here are my notes.

7:51 A.M.: I arrive. Store open. Dickie loading milk in fridge. Antonio sweeping.

8:35 A.M.: Antonio sends Dickie for three containers sweet coffee. First customer arrives. Young bohemian girl in slacks. Buys milk, a box of chocolate doughnuts, Kents. Pays cash.

8:40 A.M.: Man buys Luckies, cash.

8:42 A.M.: Woman buys three oranges, a pound of margarine, a pack of frankfurters, and cigarettes. Asks for credit. Dickie comes back with coffee as Antonio is writing down purchases. Woman is reminded that she needs coffee. Antonio grinds a pound of beans. Woman says, "That's a nice smell."

8:51 A.M.: Boy buys toothbrush, chocolate milk. Pays cash.

9:03 A.M.: Bill collector buys cigarettes. Woman with three children gives Antonio a slip of paper with a big order. They seem to know each other well. She asks if he will send Dickie with the packages. Dickie, who is playing with her kids, looks up frowning but agrees to go. Antonio puts slip with order next to register, asks if she will pay. She hands him $5.00, which he pockets. "I owed you this. Now I'll have to owe you some more."

9:35 A.M.: Antonio completes order, sends Dickie with delivery. Total sale: $6.75. He writes it in the book and then subtracts $4.75. "I want to be able to give Dickie something for his trouble," he explains. Woman comes in, buys sugar. Pays cash.

10:03 A.M.: Antonio is putting away the rest of the milk when Dickie returns. He asks, "Was she all right?"

"I got a dime," Dickie says.

Antonio throws him a quarter. "For school!" He smiles at his son warmly.

Dickie says, "I think that man is back with her—"

"She better watch out," Antonio says. "I can't carry her like that last time."

10:37 A.M.: Antonio has been telling me about his army service in Korea, which he enjoyed, he claimed, because it gave him a chance to see a lot of things.

Dickie is reading *El Diario,* looks up, says, "Tell him about Japan."

Then a customer walks in, Spanish-speaking, asks for Drano. Antonio hasn't got it. Offers to send Dickie down the block. Woman shrugs, walks out. Antonio writes down Drano on a pad next to register and then starts adding up due bills. Man in work clothes comes in, obviously a friend. He and Antonio chatter together in Spanish. Dickie asks if he can take a break. Man goes to counter.

Order a half-pound of bacon, bread, eggs, a chocolate bar, and a large bottle of orange soda. Pays cash—$2.15.

"She got her check today. She'll pay what she owes," the man says in English as he leaves.

11:07 A.M.: No business at all. Antonio working on due bills. Beer truck arrives. Dickie goes to unload cases. Delivery man buys a pack of Camels and some gum, hands Antonio an invoice, which he signs.

"Tomorrow I will have it," he tells the man, who says, "I won't be back until next Monday."

11:23 A.M.: Dickie putting away beer. Goes to lunch. No business for half an hour. Then a sudden flurry: Spanish-speaking woman buys can of beef stew (charges); boy buys rice, can of spaghetti, bread, and a jar of peanut butter (charges $1.39). Boy also wants cigarettes. Antonio says no because he is under age. Negro man buys a large bottle of beer. Pays cash. Fast-speaking woman gives large order in Spanish for bread, milk, rice, beans, fishsticks, condensed milk, teabags, sugar, half pound of butter, hot chocolate, three tomato soups, a pound of hamburger, box of Tide; she says she wants to charge everything, and she adds bananas, Brillo pads, and another container of milk; but when Antonio says no, she finds $3.00, which he pockets, and then he lets her charge the rest. Other women waiting. One wants soap. One wants chocolate doughnuts. Both cash. Delivery man arrives with soda. Antonio asks, "Where the hell is Dickie?"

1:00 P.M.: Dickie has returned. Still busy. Mostly school children. They each buy a different can for lunch . . . corned beef hash, spaghetti, beef stew, baked beans. One kid insists on Franco-American. Antonio doesn't think he has any. Too busy to make sure in the back room. Six children, six different credit sales . . . total $1.46. Antonio sends Dickie out for more coffee, eats a banana and a Drake's cake. Offers me some.

2:15 P.M.: Very, very slow. Antonio turns on radio. We listen to news in Spanish, then he switches and we listen to English-language news. Bohemian girl wants Gauloises. Antonio hasn't got any. Woman buys Tampax and toothpaste. Friend of Dickie's drops by. They go for a walk. Creamery truck arrives. Antonio waiting on customer with thick Jewish accent, wants *Yartzeit* candle. Antonio hasn't got. Creamery man presents bill for $25.00. Antonio looks in the register, gives $15.00 on account. Policeman comes by. They chat about a certain Mr. Box, whom I don't know. Maybe Antonio's landlord? Woman buys Ivory soap, a can of chick peas, a roll of toilet paper. Pays cash. Man buys Mars bar, flips dime against counter. Antonio all out of pennies. I volunteer to go next door . . .

2:50 P.M.: I have come back to busy store. Children buying ice cream; women buying potatoes and chopped meat, onions, fishsticks, detergents. Children pay cash—$.60. Women pay cash—$3.05 and $2.55, but one woman realizes she must charge—$4.50. Afterwards Antonio looks in book. He is very angry! Woman now owes $32.00. Dickie comes back.

"Where the hell you been?"

Dickie shows father that he has bought *El Diario.* Antonio smiles, sends Dickie with order to Mrs. Cabeza.

"Be sure you collect!"

He takes a bag of potato chips and offers me some. I buy a bottle of coke for each of us—$.20 cash sale. Antonio waits on Negro man who wants link sausages and half a dozen eggs. Pays cash—$1.02. Dickie comes back with $9.00. Antonio gives him another quarter. Pleased. Dickie starts to sweep up. Antonio yawns. Man buys Winstons. Woman buys English muffins. Antonio grinds coffee and tells Dickie to take it home to wife.

He says, "You got the rest of the day off. Take your sister to a show."

Dickie runs away. Antonio yawns again. Goes to back of store. Calls a number. His wife. They are talking in Spanish.

Antonio comes back. "You think this is interesting?"

I try to duck his question. Customer walks in wearing big heavy coat. Asks for Carbona. Antonio hasn't got. I look at watch. 4:15 . . .

6:03 P.M.: Very slow. One woman wanting fish balls for cash. A man to whom Antonio won't sell. Mrs. Ubas comes with stew for Antonio's dinner in double boiler. She says children all went to movies. She is going to see her sister. Will Antonio stay open late? He shrugs, starts to eat dinner. Wife wishes me good night. Dark outside now. Man comes in to buy milk. Pays cash. Woman wants a lemon and a bottle of Clorox. Antonio won't charge. Woman puts back Clorox but buys lemon with cash.

Antonio says, "She is a terrible woman."

Won't tell me why. Antonio's sister-in-law calls. Could he lend her a few dollars tomorrow? He says he will give it to his wife in the morning, but she mustn't come to the store. Man wants to know if Antonio can cash Welfare check for $39.00. Antonio hasn't got enough in register. Offers to hold the check and lent him $15.00 on account until tomorrow, when he will give him the rest.

Man says, "You give me $20.00 and the rest is for my wife's bill."

Antonio smiles and looks into register. It's a deal. He hands man $20.00 in singles from register and sticks check in pocket. Only two of three bills now in register. Antonio marks off $19.00 from man's account. Still plenty more on the bill. Man breaks bill to buy Luckies . . .

7:19 P.M.: Very, very slow. Kid wanting correct time. Woman pays for phone call. Buys milk and a square of cream cheese. Antonio's supper cold. Empties out double boiler. Says he has heartburn. Asks if I would go next door for tea. As I leave, he turns on radio again . . .

7:30 P.M.: Antonio too busy to say thank you when I return with tea. Radio blaring. Spanish-speaking man with big order: rice, beans, sardines, anchovies, eggs, bread, canned tomatoes, olive oil, Malamar cookies, Ajax, canned peaches, pineapple cubes, milk, and frankfurters. Also thinks of buying guava shells but decides no when Antonio gives him price. Pays cash—$9.15.

8:05 P.M.: Antonio and I have been talking about all the airplane crashes lately when Drano woman comes back. She has Welfare check for $55.00. Can Antonio cash? He tells her he hasn't got. She becomes angry. Curses. Leaves store. Antonio picks up *El Diario.* His eyes are a little bloodshot, and it looks as if somebody has just dabbed shoe polish underneath the lower lids. I go to get a sandwich . . .

9:12 P.M.: Come back to Antonio's store. Door open. Lights on. No Antonio. Finally he appears from back carrying heavy case marked "Franco-American."

"I just knew I had some . . ."

Sweating and panting, he tears open the case, puts all the cans on the shelf, and asks me to throw the cardboard box in the can outside.

"Any more business?"

"A woman with a nosebleed," Antonio smiles. "I sold her Kleenex."

9:36 P.M.: I feel as if I have been here forever. Antonio is very silent. I don't think he has much patience with my hanging around, although he seemed pleased at first. He asks me when I intend to leave, and I say

whenever he closes down.

Antonio says, "Won't be long now."

He opens up the register and starts to count his money. There is not too much to count, but he knows he has a few dollars in his pocket. Three teenagers come in. Antonio slams register. Boys want cigarettes. Antonio sells a pack of Camels and a pack of Kools for cash. Third boy buys cupcakes. Cash.

Antonio sings *"En mi corazón . . ."* as he goes back to register.

Spanish-speaking man comes in. Very timid. Looks over at me once as he talks, and Antonio finally sells him large box Kotex—man pays cash.

"No me burlas," Antonio starts singing again.

Woman enters store. Buys milk and Easy-Off. Pays cash.

Antonio asks, "You new around here?"

"I just moved in."

She buys cockroach powder and a stick of gum. Goes out and then comes back in. She lives across the street. He name is Helen Dugan. She needs a bed.

"Where is a good place to buy a bed?"

Welfare gave her the money, but they didn't tell her where to go. Antonio says he doesn't know but he will ask his wife if she will come back tomorrow.

She says, "Why not? I live right across the street."

10:45 P.M.: I am getting very groggy. Antonio also seems to be feeling the strain. Once I catch him dozing against the counter. At 10:15, a phone call. A woman wants him to deliver, Antonio says he can't. At 10:25 teenagers. Cigarettes again. A man buys a pound of coffee. A man in work clothes buys cigarettes and a Mounds bar. Another man comes into store.

Antonio says, "I've been waiting for you."

Man hands him check. Antonio takes out book, crosses out column of figures. Writes down balance: $14.00. Goes to register and gives man five singles.

Man says, "My wife will be in tomorrow for a big order."

Antonio nods sleepily. Man breaks single to buy Kents. Antonio goes to center of store and pulls switch on light. Starts sweeping up, but won't lock door. Man drops by. Shows Antonio paper.

"No," he adds, "I don't know of such a family."

Man buys cigarettes and leaves.

Antonio says, "I bet he's from the Welfare . . ."

Negro woman comes in. Buys a can of tuna, a jar of mayonnaise, some onions, and a bar of chocolate Halvah. Pays cash—$1.25.

Antonio says, "Don't you want bread?"

When she doesn't answer, he goes to empty out register. Man comes in. Doesn't seem to know what he wants. Walks from shelf to shelf.

"I'm closing," Antonio says.

Man has hands in pockets. Antonio repeats that he is closing, in Spanish. Man comes over to counter. Buys a loaf of bread. Pays cash. Fat man comes in. Has Antonio got fresh ham?

"I'm closing," he says.

Man buys a pound of frankfurters. Wants to charge. Antonio asks for name and address. Man lives right above store. Produces Welfare card. Antonio okays sale but copies down serial number in book. Man then buys cigarettes and orange soda.

When he leaves Antonio says, "Now I'm really closing." Bolts front door.

"I hope you know why you stayed here," he says, "because I don't."

I offer to buy him a beer but he says that he is just too tired. I buy a pack of cigarettes. Antonio wants me to pay wholesale. We argue. I look at my watch. It's 11:27 . . .

By working nearly a hundred hours a week Antonio Ubas is likely to gross in the neighborhood of $1,400 a month, from which he will net about $350 to $400. About one in ten dollars will go directly to his pocket so he won't have to report them to the government. As much as 20 percent more of his business will consist of credit, on which he will charge a small premium, probably no greater than the inflationary trend. Antonio will carry his people just so long as they continue to pay him back every couple of weeks, and his jobbers will endeavor to carry him in the same way. Twice monthly he will need large sums of cash on hand to redeem Welfare checks that will be proffered as partial repayment on bills. In 1964 he filed a federal income tax return showing $4,160 gross income on which he paid $450 in taxes. There were also state taxes and licensing fees amounting to perhaps $100. He sent $10 a month to his mother in Puerto Rico and supported his family on a budget of approximately $55 weekly, which he earned at a rate of less than $1.00 per hour. Antonio has GI life insurance worth $10,000 and a small savings account, which is used to pay taxes and licensing fees to forestall creditors in a pinch, or to cash Welfare checks. In any week his margin of profit is usually the few extra pennies he can wring out of his clients through credit. This tends to make his attitude toward people on Welfare somewhat ambivalent. On the one hand, he recognizes with a certain bitterness that some people are not working yet are doing nearly as well as he. On the other hand, he sees that his chief *raison d'être* at present is to provide a service that the larger stores refuse to provide. The following morning, after my visit, Antonio was at work by 8:00 A.M. I didn't arrive until 11:00. He looked a little tired but was in good spirits. His sister-in-law's husband had just found work through the State Employment.

"That's a load off my back," he smiled, and began to thumb his way through the pages of his ledger.

It was a school day. Dickie would not be coming to help out. He was going to close early because he wanted to take his wife shopping. How early was early? Antonio scratched his head. He explained that he wasn't quite sure when he would actually be able to close down. This guy owed him a lot of money and he had just gotten his check, but he was in the Bronx and would be there all day. Antonio would just have to wait until the man got downtown after suppertime.

THE YOUNG LORDS

The Young Lords, an organization of street-wise young activists formed in the late 1960's, reflects the growing maturity of the Puerto Rican migrant community on the U.S. mainland—which was once a voiceless appendage of the island, and is now developing its own institutions. Until recently, militant political leaders in the Puerto Rican *barrios* of America belonged either to pro-independence groups in Puerto Rico, or to left-wing U.S. groups. But the Lords emerged from the *barrios* where they were raised; they borrowed some of their original impetus from the Black Panthers, but have since evolved their own style. They have avoided violent conflict and have focused instead on dramatic, issue-oriented ploys: the sudden takeover of a *barrio* church for a free children's breakfast program, or the "hijacking" of a New York City mobile clinic to examine slum children for tuberculosis. The Lords were mainly the children of poor migrants, raised in urban ghettos, and English was their first language. The "official 13-point program and platform," published frequently in *Palante*, the newspaper of the Young Lords, outlines their basic goals. They want "a socialist society" and "oppose capitalists and alliances with traitors." They want "liberation and power in the hands of the people, not Puerto Rican exploiters." They want self-determination and liberation, not only for Puerto Ricans but also for "all Latinos" and "all third world people." Thus, the Lords were not strictly a Puerto Rican party, but a socialist movement that had sprung up from within the poor Puerto Rican working class on the mainland, where blacks, Chicanos, Dominicans, Haitians, and poor whites all suffered together. The thrust of most protest groups in Puerto Rico is nationalistic, and strongly defends traditional Puerto Rican culture; the Young Lords—while demanding "a true education of our creole culture and Spanish language"—are more ideological than nationalistic.

The following excerpt—the story of a Young Lord named Georgie—tells of his upbringing in New York's junglelike *barrio*, and of his growing political awareness.

I think if I would have been raised up upstate, man, in a good community, I would've never become a gangbuster, I would've never shot nobody, I would never have stabbed nobody—but since I was raised up in this community, this is what it, oppression, teaches you—kill, stab, steal, and shoot dope—like, now the thing is dope, mainly. I got a lot of brothers out there, man, that are shooting dope—they used to jitterbug with me. They used to call me Little Man, 'cause I always was really small for my age. But smallness to me didn't mean nothin', because wherever there was a bat, it used to make me always the same size as the other person.

When I was a little kid, around seven years old, they used to have what they called the Lightnings. Later on, they became the Lightning Dragons. You know little kids see those big guys and say, "Wow! Man, when I grow up I wanna be like them." Because that's all there is to do in your neighborhood—like if you don't learn how to be a pimp, you learn how to be a jitterbug. Those were the two big things then, because at that time there wasn't that much drugs around the neighborhood. I always wanted to be a pimp, because the pimps they were always clean, they had shoes, a lot of wing-tips, a lot of sharkskin, mohair suits, and they always had money in their pockets. I always used to say to myself, "Oh, man, when I grow up I want to be a pimp."

I started all my fighting when I was really young. My father used to have a very nasty attitude—anybody that looked at him, he would go up to them and say, "Have I got a monkey in my face or somethin'?" If it was a little kid, he would put me to fight against him. And I got into the habit of always fighting in the block—as a matter of fact, when the older guys wanted to play stickball in the block I used to tell 'em. "No, man, you people ain't gonna play in the block—me and my fellows are playing." And, my fellows were all guys six years old, seven years old, and you know, against guys eighteen. And, since we wanted to be like them we used to, like, put on a show, and we thought we were *bad* 'cause we had stickball bats and shit.

My father and my mother used to give me everything I wanted. Except my father—he always told me, like, the only two things that he wouldn't give me in life was roller skates and bikes, because I might get killed by a car. And, that's where my trouble really started, because when I was around nine years old, like, I wanted a pair of roller skates *so bad,* and my father would never buy them for me. I remember, five of us went to Central Park and we dug these guys rollerskating. I was nine years old and I wanted some skates—and there was five of us, and we seen these guys skating down the thing, and like, we beat 'em up and we took off their skates. Anyway, the pigs came, and me and my brother got busted for the skates and shit, and I went to the Youth House for a few months.

The next year I got busted again—this time for robbing *La Marqueta* and I did five years in Children's Village.

When I came out I was tired. On 111th Street they had the Viceroys and the

Dragons then. At first I really didn't want to join them. I said, "Oh man, if I join one of them, I'm just gonna go back upstate again."

But I used to live in Viceroy turf, right across from where their center was. I was raised up with a lot of those guys and I always wanted to hang out with them. A lot of the debs, the sisters, used to go for me, too. What happened was that the Dragons saw me hangin' out with the Viceroys, and thought I was in the Viceroys—you couldn't blame them, you know.

In P.S. 83, where I was going, they had around two Viceroys, and maybe fifty Dragons—so you know where that was at. One day I was playing dice and all these Dragons surrounded me and asked me, "Hey man, are you a Viceroy?" I told 'em "Look, man, I'm not no Viceroy," and I tried to explain to them that I had just come out of jail, but they thought I was bullshitting them.

I remember they hit me all the way from the schoolyard—for a whole block they were hitting me. And then they got me in this telephone booth and broke a telephone right over my hand. So now I was mad, but I still didn't want to join the Viceroys. Another time I was with this guy named Bimbo—he used to be an old Viceroy, he was from my neighborhood. Anyway, they caught me and Bimbo in the train station and they came over to us, and they told me, "Look, man, this is the second time we catch you—the last time we bust your ass, man, and you tell us you wasn't a Viceroy. And every time we see you, we see you with Viceroys."

What they did was, they waited around a minute before the train came and threw me on the train tracks. And I got up and I ran, you know. I said, "Damn, man, these guys are fuckin' me up every time they see me—so I'm gonna join the Viceroys, man. I might as well join them."

We used to jitterbug, right. Some times we used to go down to 103rd Street and, like, go up to the block and shoot up the candy store or shoot up the guys that were around. Sometimes we used to stab guys, sometimes we used to get stabbed. We wasn't thinkin' about the other guys being Puerto Ricans. Like, now we're political, but at that time Puerto Ricans were Puerto Ricans—if he was your enemy, you kill him.

When you used to go to school, like, the teacher used to tell you, "Oh, man, you dumb—like, you nothing but a little boy," and shit like that. So all the young brothers used to have that complex of the teacher calling them a boy, and they wanted to prove it to themselves they were a man. And they would go to any means to prove it.

When I first started jitterbugging, a brother named King Kong got shot at 117th Street. When he got killed I was hurt—that was my main man, you see, one of my brothers. A week after that, the Dragons came down to 112th Street in a car and they started shooting at us. We had a gun on us, so when they started shooting, one of the brothers was gonna run over to the car to, like, to shoot the Dragons. But the Dragons they shot him in the arm with a .38 and he fell. So this guy named Chico grabbed the gun. This other guy, Nate, opened up the door from the car and Chico shot the Dragon in the head, you know, shot him in the head. He fell against the horn dead, and the car went out of control and went into that store on the corner of 112th Street and Madison. Even though I knew Chico had killed this dude, I felt bad about it. You know, you say, "Ah, fuck it, yeah we killed a motherfucker, man." But inside, you really say, "Man, one of these days they probably come up to me and shoot me. . . ."

Some of us been lucky, that we stabbed a lot of guys, right, but never killed nobody, and we not doin' time. But some of the brothers, like, they're unfortunate—they're doin' life in jail. And right now I feel sorry for a lot of these brothers, even the Dragons, man. I know if they had another chance to live, they would never jitterbug no more to kill another brother. You know, they might turn political, like I did and Bobby did, right—because, like, I cooled down.

I stopped jitterbugging because my enemy became my best friend. Like, they got this guy named Feather, from the Young Dragons—right now, man, he's like my brother—I love that cat, I love him. If anybody would try to hurt me, I know he'll kill for me—if anybody try to hurt him, I know I'd kill for him, man. Me and him were real together in jail. A lot of Dragons that I met there, some of them are more friends of mine than my old, old friends the Viceroys, you know. And you go ask the Dragons, man—Dragons will tell you the same thing.

I guess it's because we got to know each other and that's what the Yong Lords is really about, man—to show you you don't fight against brothers, because you might be angry against your brother today, and tomorrow he might be your best friend. Tomorrow, he might be the guy that saved your own life.

THE FBI DOSSIERS

In the year 2000, the FBI acknowledged that for the past seven decades it had been keeping dossiers on Puerto Rican *independentistas* and other suspected "subversives" on the island. Not only was Nationalist Party Leader Pedro Albizu Campos marked by the federal agency as a threat to the security of both Puerto Rico and the United States, but four-term Governor Luis Muñoz

Marín also came under the Bureau's 70-year scrutiny of the island's political leaders.

In the first year of the new millennium, the FBI began releasing the first few thousand of what it said were 1.8 million documents on Puerto Rico. It pledged to eventually turn over all the documents to island authorities. The Bureau's acknowledgement of its past complicity in the decades-long persecution of independence supporters came as the Puerto Rico government also admitted that over the years it had gathered more than 100,000 dossiers on suspected island subversives.

Washington—FBI Director Louis Freeh on Wednesday turned over to Rep. José Serrano, D-N.Y., agency surveillance files dating back to the 1930s on former Gov. Luis Muñoz Marín and Nationalist Party head Pedro Albizu Campos.

The thousands of pages made available in Serrano's office at a meeting that also included island lawmakers were, Freeh said, the first installment of the 1.8 million agency documents on Puerto Rico that eventually will be delivered by the FBI to island authorities.

He said that he would also attempt to obtain Puerto Rico files from other federal agencies, such as the Central Intelligence and Naval Intelligence agencies. The newly released FBI documents, the agency chief said, would contain "99 percent less blackouts" than those that had been released in the 1970s and 1980s.

He noted that the Puerto Rico Police Department has agreed to waive any blotted out information of its activities. This means that past FBI informants on the island could become public record.

While it could not be determined how much new information was contained in the files, a quick perusal of the Muñoz Marín documents held some surprises, such as allegations of a plot in 1961 apparently instigated by Dominican Dictator Rafael Trujillo to assassinate Muñoz, Cuban President Fidel Castro and Venezuelan President Rómulo Betancourt.

The documents also contain FBI accusations in 1941 that Muñoz was not only the "communist leader for Puerto Rico, but the entire Caribbean Sea area."

After Muñoz was elected governor in 1948, the FBI appeared to change its perception of him and become mostly involved in his security.

The Puerto Rico Senate will use the documents in its investigation of the in-

---

Robert Friedman, "FBI Chief Hands Over Surveillance Files," *San Juan Star,* May 29, 2000. Reprinted with permission.

volvement of federal agencies in the compilation of more than 100,000 dossiers on suspected island subversives, said Sen. Kenneth McClintock, NPP-at large, who chairs the Governmental and Federal Affairs Committee in the island's upper chamber.

McClintock said the investigation would not go past 1975 or 1980 to avoid it becoming a current political issue, rather than an historical process.

Island and federal officials have acknowledged that the dossiers, as well as FBI documents already released, show a pattern of persecution against Puerto Rico independence supporters. The commonwealth established a fund to compensate those targeted in the dossiers.

McClintock attended the meeting with Freeh along with Senate President Charlie Rodríguez and Sens. Eduardo Bhatia of the Popular Democratic Party and Manuel Rodríguez Orellana of the Puerto Rican Independence Party.

Serrano, who was instrumental in getting Freeh to pledge during a House hearing in March that the FBI will examine its role in any unsavory, illegal and possibly criminal activity on the island, called Wednesday's meeting "historic, dramatic and important."

"Just seeing representatives from each party in Puerto Rico agreeing that we have to know who was hurt and how, and to make sure that it never happens again, and to hear the FBI director telling you he wants to get to the truth and let everyone know about it, that was much more than I expected," Serrano said.

PIP Sen Rodríguez Orellana agreed on the historic nature of the day's events.

Four boxes of documents were released Wednesday, two of the cartons containing 4,500 pages on Albizu, one holding 1,700 pages about Muñoz and a fourth box with 2,100 pages of material gathered by the FBI's Counter Intelligence Program.

Freeh said 17 agents are gathering the Puerto Rico material. The agency also is expected to give answers to specific questions posed by Serrano, such as charges that authorities carried out radiation experiments on Albizu when he was in La Princesa prison.

McClintock said that the most significant documents would be placed on the Internet, after his committee has a chance to review them, probably starting in June. The documents eventually will be given to the University of Puerto Rico for historical reference, he said.

Bhatia of the PDP said the April 26, 1941 document identifying Muñoz, the island's first elected governor, as the Caribbean's leading communist shows the "horrible mentality that the United States had at the time. Not only was Albizu persecuted, but Muñoz also."

The former governor apparently lost that stigma in the FBI's eyes as the years rolled on. In a May 1, 1952 memorandum he was referred to as "the honorable Luis Muñoz Marín."

The FBI reported to bureau chief J. Edgar Hoover on Oct. 2, 1961 that Muñoz said he would avoid commercial planes between the island and the mainland and try to travel either by military or chartered aircraft because he believed a commercial flight could be hijacked to Cuba, "and that Castro would offer a political exchange" of Muñoz for the imprisoned Albizu Campos.

Washington—"[Luis] Muñoz Marín is the rather Bohemian elected governor of Puerto Rico. . . . He is something of a poet, a fabulous orator in both languages, a man of singular intellectual attainments, but a dilettante about everything, probably including politics, in which he is certainly a gifted amateur, if not an absolute genius."

That was the assessment, on May 4, 1953, of L.B. Nichols of the FBI's San Juan office, which was sent to Clyde Tolson, FBI chief J. Edgar Hoover's right-hand at the bureau. The brief bio was drawn up in anticipation of a Muñoz visit to Hoover's office. It illustrates in part the rocky relationship through the years between the island's first elected governor and the FBI.

The bureau saw fit to keep at least 1,700 pages worth of dossiers on Muñoz, most dating from 1941 to 1978. A good deal of the documents were concerned with Muñoz's security during his four terms as governor—he was subject to what seems like an incredible number of death threats and rumors of assassinations cited over 33 years, from 1945 to 1978, including a purported plot in which Nationalists were set to contract an underworld hit on him.

Also noted in September 1961 was a supposed plan instigated by Dominican dictator Rafael Trujillo to assassinate Muñoz, Cuban President Fidel Castro and Venezuelan President Rómulo Betancourt. Trujillo, himself, was knocked off that year.

But other documents were also concerned with Muñoz's "threat"— especially in his early political years—to the security of the U.S.A., as perceived by the FBI.

The Muñoz file was recently turned over by FBI chief Louis Freeh to Rep. José Serrano, D-N.Y., as a show of good bureau faith. Freeh has pledged to eventually give up 1.8 million documents from the bureau on Puerto Ricans kept under surveillance over the years.

In 1941, the FBI was sure that Muñoz was not only the top communist in

---

Robert Friedman, "Dossiers Trace the LMM, FBI Relationship," *San Juan Star,* May 18, 2000. Reprinted with permission.

Puerto Rico, but also for "the entire Caribbean Sea area." To offer a little hindsight humor, an FBI agent named—believe it or not— Nixon Butt, Jr. filed a surveillance report in 1943 on "José Luis Munozo Martin."

By the following year, when Muñoz was elected Senate president, the bureau seemed to be softening somewhat in its take on him. It was noted that even though Muñoz still wanted independence for the island, he believed it should be accomplished by "legal and pacific means."

Attitudes seemed to be further turning in 1950, after the Nationalists' attempt to assassinate President Truman in Washington and Muñoz in San Juan. Special agent H.H. Clegg told Hoover in a memo that he made a visit to Muñoz to express his "appreciation for the cooperation given the San Juan [FBI] office" by the governor and the local police. Clegg said Muñoz responded that he was the one who owed thanks to Hoover "for the excellent cooperation he has received from the FBI."

Clegg further told Hoover that Muñoz had asked the FBI for suggestions on search-and-seizure legislation, in which the governor said he would ask the Legislature "to go as far as they can . . . and yet keep within the bounds of the Constitution." Muñoz supposedly said he would make any FBI suggestions "in his own name without disclosing from whom the suggestion came."

Muñoz and Hoover exchanged then a series of "love letters" each complimenting the other on his cooperation, gratitude, etc. The governor sent new friend J. Edgar a thick book of photos on various aspects of life in Puerto Rico. He even asked Hoover to drop by and spend several days with him as a guest at La Fortaleza. Unfortunately, said the FBI chief, he was very busy, but would take a rain check.

The FBI seemed to come to the aid of Muñoz in 1954 when a possibly witch-hunting congressmen, John Taber, R-N.Y., wanted the bureau to give him all its data that would show the attitude and position of Muñoz with respect to the "independent movement," the Nationalist Party and "any other anti-American or subversive groups in that country."

While it was not clear from the documents whether the FBI complied, it seemed to be drawing up a favorable profile of the governor as a former independence supporter who had since seen the light. The FBI reported that in interviews with 45 professional and prominent Puerto Ricans on the island "all . . . agreed that Muñoz was a good administrator and has outstanding qualities of leadership, resourcefulness and integrity."

The FBI memo said: "Since becoming governor of Puerto Rico, Muñoz has been extremely friendly with the Bureau and has worked very closely with the Bureau's office in San Juan," which may be less than surprising since he was, according to the files, such a frequent target for assassination plots.

Nevertheless, the friendship appeared to be unraveling by 1961, after an article appeared in the Miami Herald with the headline: "Red Peril Report Hit by Muñoz." The governor, it seemed, had the temerity to suggest that an FBI report on all the "red" menaces in the nation may have been overblown. He particularly objected to the bureau's belief that the Nationalist Party was a real threat to overthrow not only the Puerto Rico government, but perhaps the U.S. government as well.

Several memos on what the FBI saw as a big to-do appear in the file, which noted that "the director [Hoover] said the San Juan office should tactfully but firmly pin Marín down on this matter . . ."

In a subsequent interview, Muñoz apparently tried to placate the bureau, by acknowledging to them that the Nationalists were a threat, at least as possible assassins of himself and President Kennedy. At the bottom of the report on the interview was a hand-written comment by Hoover: "Just another expedient politician caught up with."

In April 1964, the San Juan chief told Hoover that Muñoz tried to get him, probably for upcoming election purposes, to issue a statement that communism was not a threat in Puerto Rico. "I will continue to be most circumspect in all my dealings with Gov. Muñoz," the agent-in-charge told his boss. Another hand-written Hoover note: "Right, as Muñoz is an expedient politician."

PUERTO RICANS: CITIZENS YET FOREIGNERS

Marcantonio lost the election. They're jumping every Spic they can find.
—New York Cty cop, 1950

Until World War II, Mexican farmworkers were the most familiar Latin Americans in this country. True, a Latino might occasionally turn up in a Hollywood film role, or leading a band in a New York nightclub, or as the fancy fielder of some professional baseball team, but outside the Southwest, Anglo Americans rarely saw Hispanics in everyday life and knew almost nothing about them.

Then the Puerto Ricans came.

More than 40,000 migrated from the Caribbean to New York City in 1946 alone. Actually, a small Puerto Rican enclave had existed in that city since World War I, and that *colonia* grew to 135,000 by the end of World War II, but the year 1946 saw an astonishing explosion in Puerto Rican arrivals, one that continued without letup for the next fifteen years. By 1960, more than 1 million were in the country, part of what one sociologist dubbed "the greatest airborne migration in history." Today, almost as many Puerto Ricans live in the fifty states, 2.8 million, as on the island, 3.8 million.

My family was part of that 1946 wave. My parents, Juan and Florinda González, arrived on one of the first regular Pan American Airline flights from San Juan. Along with the Mexican *braceros* out West, they were pioneers of the modern Latino diaspora.

Puerto Ricans were uniquely suited for a pioneer role. To this day, only we among all Latin Americans arrive here as U.S. citizens, without the need of a visa or resident alien card. But this unique advantage, a direct result of Puerto Rico's colonial status, has also led to unexpected obstacles. Despite our de jure citizenship the average North American, whether white or black, continues to regard Puerto Ricans as de facto foreigners. Even the Supreme Court, as we have seen, has had difficulty explaining the Puerto Rican condition. The contradiction of being at once citizens and foreigners, when joined with the reality that ours was a racially mixed population, has made the Puerto Rican migrant experience in America profoundly schizophrenic, more similar in some ways to that of African Americans or Native Americans than to any other Latino group.

To comprehend that schizophrenia, we would do well to examine the forces that shaped the Puerto Rican worldview: Why did the migrants leave their homeland in such numbers? What happened when they arrived here? How did others regard them? How did they cope with and survive in their new conditions? Why did so many get stuck in poverty, unable to climb the immigrant ladder? Hopefully, my family's story, one very typical of that early migration, will provide some insight.

Why We Came

One morning in May 1932, road workers found chief engineer Teofilo González, my grandfather, feverish and delirious at their work camp on Puerto Rico's southwest coast. He died a few days later of pneumonia, and his death immediately plunged his young wife, María González Toledo, and their six children into abject poverty.

My grandmother had married Teofilo in 1914 in the mountain town of Lares. She was sixteen at the time, an orphan, illiterate, and desperate to escape from her Spanish-born godmother, who had raised her as a virtual servant. Her new husband was thirty-four, well educated, and the eldest son of a prosperous coffee grower whose own parents had migrated to Lares from the Spanish island of Majorca in the late 1850s.

Puerto Rican *criollos* resented the Majorcan *peninsulares* who quickly bought up most of the businesses in Lares and rarely employed the town's native-born residents. The Majorcans were loyal to the Spanish Crown, while Lares was a hotbed of separatist and abolitionist sentiment. On September 23, 1868, El Grito de Lares erupted. It was the most significant independence revolt in island history. My grandfather's parents, Teofilo González, Sr., and Aurelia Levi, were only teenagers then, but they cheered the Spanish soldiers who quickly crushed the rebellion. To quell further unrest, Spain's Cortes abolished slavery on the island in 1873, but my great-grandparents, like many of the small coffee farmers in the region, circumvented the emancipation decree and illegally kept a few black laborers on their farm as semislaves. This infuriated their youngest son, Onofre, who soon turned into a political dissident opposed to Spanish rule.

According to family legend, my great-grandparents scoffed at Onofre and called him a crazed idealist. They were still ridiculing him when the Spanish-American War erupted and U.S. soldiers landed at Guánica. Soon after, Onofre stole several of his father's horses and rode south to volunteer his services to the Yankee invaders. He returned after a few weeks, proudly galloping into Lares as the lead scout for a column of U.S. soldiers.

That early military occupation, as we have seen, quickly disillusioned even its Puerto Rican supporters. It wrecked the small coffee and tobacco growers who were the backbone of the island's economy. U.S. sugar companies gobbled up the land and created a vast agricultural proletariat whose members only worked a few months of the year. For the multitudes of poor, life became unbearable. "I have stopped at farm after farm, where lean, underfed women and sickly men repeated again and again the same story—little food and no opportunity to get more." Theodore Roosevelt, Jr., governor of the island for a time, wrote in 1929.

During those desperate years, María and Teofilo González lost five of their eleven children to disease. Still, they were in better shape than most, thanks to his job building roads for the government. After her husband's death in 1932, though, the family's fortunes plummeted. María sold the big house they owned in the southern coastal city of Ponce and moved to a squalid shack in El Ligao, the worst section of the Mayor Cantera slum high in the hills of town. She found work as an aide in Ponce's Tricoche Hospital and occasionally as a coffee bean picker in the fields near Lares.

But the odd jobs could not provide enough money to support a large family, so she reluctantly gave several of her children away to friends in hopes of saving them from starvation. Her oldest daughter, my aunt Graciela, she placed with neighbors who owned a local store, and there the girl worked behind the counter in return for food and board. She sent another girl, my aunt Ana, to live with a neighbor as a housekeeper. She dispatched one son, my uncle Sergio, to live with a childless schoolteacher.

But her two youngest, my aunt Pura and my father, Pepe, were too young to be useful to anyone, so she placed six-year-old Pepe in an orphanage. The day she left him with the nuns at the orphanage, his terrified wails almost crushed her heart. Her guilt was so great that after a few years, she reclaimed him from the nuns and sent him to live with another childless teacher. But the teacher sexually abused Pepe for years, turning him into a sullen and explosive alcoholic. Throughout the rest of his life there was such aimless rage buried inside him that whenever he drank heavily, he would always recite the story of how his mother had abandoned him.

Pura, the only one left at home, became her mother's constant companion—the other children were permitted to visit their mother only a few Sundays a month. María dragged the little girl with her everywhere. She hid her under the sink in the hospital whenever the supervisors appeared; in the fields, she would tie a can around Pura's neck and show her how to pluck the coffee beans with her tiny fingers. The psychological scars left in all of them by their long childhood separation were so deep that decades later, after they'd all been reunited and the family had moved to New York City, the González brothers and sisters never spoke openly of those times.

The 1930s were the most turbulent in Puerto Rico's modern history, and Ponce, where my family had settled, was the center of the storm. The Depression turned the island into a social inferno even more wretched than Haiti today. As one visitor described it:

> Slow, and sometimes rapid, starvation was found everywhere. If one drove a car over the country roads, one was delayed again and again by sorrowing funeral processions carrying the caskets of dead infants.
>
> Most of the cities were infested by "wolf gangs" of children ranging in ages from six to sixteen, many of whom had no idea who their parents were. They pilfered and robbed; they "protected" parked automobiles, and if the drivers didn't want to pay for such protection, they siphoned gasoline out of the tanks, stole hub caps, slashed tires. They slept where they could—in parks, in hallways, in alleys . . .

Ponce's hilltop El Ligao was notorious for its violence and crime. Neighbors often feuded and brutal killings in machete or knife fights were commonplace. One day, Pura González watched in horror as a young resident named Saro, who sold ice in a small pushcart, was dragged bleeding through the dirt streets in front of her house by four men who brazenly hanged him from a tree, stabbed and castrated him. Saro, she discovered, was a numbers runner. An important town official had placed a bet with him, but when the number hit and the official came to collect his money, he discovered Saro had blown it all on liquor. As a lesson to El Ligao, the official ordered Saro's public execution.

Ponce was, at the same time, Puerto Rico's most prosperous and cultured city. It was the center of the island's Nationalist movement, whose president was Pedro Albizu Campos. Albizu graduated from Harvard in 1916, served in the U.S. Navy, and spent years traveling throughout Latin America. In 1932, he returned to his homeland and assumed the party's leadership. A charismatic speaker and devout Catholic, Albizu wasted no time tapping into the country's long-felt frustration over U.S. control, and soon took to propagating an almost mystical brand of anti-Yankee, anti-Protestant nationalism.

By the time of Albizu's return from abroad, the greed of the U.S. sugar plantations had created a social tinderbox. Wages for cane cutters, which had been 63 cents for a twelve-hour day in 1917, were down to 50 cents by 1932. Forty percent of the workforce was unemployed, yet company profits remained high. During the last six months of 1933 alone, eighty-five strikes and protests erupted, several of them directed against the colonial government. In one of those strikes, thousands of sugar workers demanding an eight-hour day rebuffed their own ineffectual leaders and called on Albizu Campos and the Nationalists for help. For the first time, the Nationalists and the labor movement were becoming united. In other parts of the country, picket line violence during walkouts by needle-workers in Lares and Mayagüez left two dead and seventy injured.

To stem the anti-Yankee violence, federal agents arrested Albizu and several of the party's leaders on sedition charges in 1936. While they were in jail, the youth brigade of the party, the Cadets, scheduled a peaceful march in Ponce to press for their release. Governor Blanton Winship refused at the last moment to issue them a permit, but the Nationalists decided to march anyway.

The day was Palm Sunday, March 21, 1937. My aunt Graciela was sixteen and caught up in the Nationalist fervor at the time. Luckily, she decided to skip the march that day and go on a picnic with her sisters, Ana and Pura. They all trekked up to El Vigía, the magnificent hilltop estate of the Serralles family, owners of the Don Q rum distillery. From the rolling castle grounds you can look down on all of Ponce. Pura, who was a child at the time, recalls that shortly after the Nationalists gathered, the church bells began to ring, and when she looked down the mountain toward the plaza she saw people scattering in all directions. A young woman they knew ran up to them, screaming. "There's a massacre in town. The Nationalists and the soldiers are fighting. The hospital is full of wounded." When the smoke had cleared, 21 people were dead and 150 were wounded. A human rights commission would later report that all had been gunned down by police. It was the biggest massacre in Puerto Rican history.

After the Palm Sunday Massacre, hysteria and near civil war swept the island. Nationalists were hunted and arrested on sight. Some headed for exile in New York City or Havana. Graciela, our family's only Nationalist Party member, decided that nothing could be won by righting the Americans. With Albizu Campos in jail and the Nationalist ranks decimated, she abandoned the party.

By the early 1940s, my grandmother María managed to reunite the family. Her children were grown up by then, and the outbreak of World War II had made jobs more plentiful. My father, Pepe, enlisted in the all-Puerto Rican Sixty-Fifth Infantry and served with the regiment in North Africa, France, and Germany. His brothers, Sergio and Tomás, were drafted a year later.

The Puerto Ricans of the Sixty-Fifth were segregated from the other American soldiers throughout the war and assigned largely to support work for combat units. Their officers were all North Americans, and the Puerto Ricans, who spoke no English, were frequently ridiculed by their fellow GIs. Beyond the prejudice they faced, they were deeply shaken by the devastated countryside of southern France and Germany, which reminded them of the lush green hills of Puerto Rico. Displaced French farmers became haunting reminders of their own destitute *jíbaro* countrymen. The war transformed not only the González brothers, but also every Puerto Rican who participated in it. For the first time, a large group of Puerto Ricans had left home and traveled the world. Many of them were exposed to ethnic prejudice for the first time. And for the first time they had fought in defense of a country they knew nothing about. Nonetheless, the veterans returned home, like their Mexican American counterparts, believing they had earned a place at the American table; for the first time, they felt like citizens.

While María González's three sons were away at war, their army pay-checks pulled the family out of poverty. But the returning González brothers found the island nearly as poor as they'd left it. As soon as he got back, Pepe married my mother, Florinda, an orphan whose own mother had died giving birth to her, and whose father had gone off one day to work in the sugar plantations of the Dominican Republic and never returned, leaving her and her older brothers to be raised by their grandmother.

The postwar period, however, brought rapid change. In 1946, President Truman appointed the first Puerto Rican governor of the island, Jesús Piñero. Soon afterward, on December 15, 1947, Pedro Albizu Campos returned home after serving ten years in federal custody for his sedition conviction. Thousands of Nationalists greeted him at the airport as a returning hero. "The hour of decision has arrived," Albizu Campos warned his followers. As the Nationalist Party and the U.S. government hurried toward a final bloody confrontation, the González family and thousands of others packed their bags and headed for New York.

Early Life in New York City's El Barrio

They settled in the tenements of El Barrio in northern Manhattan, and there they encountered both helping hands and hostility. My uncle Tomás was the first to arrive in 1946. A fellow migrant found him a job serving coffee at the Copacabana, the most famous nightclub in New York at the time. Tomás immediately sent for his brothers, Sergio and Pepe, and landed them jobs at the Copa as dishwashers. Even though mobster Frank Costello ran the place then, politicians and police inspectors, high-priced lawyers, and professional ballplayers all flocked to the club to listen to performances by the era's biggest entertainers. The Filipino waiters and Puerto Rican kitchen workers reveled in the club's glamour and intrigue and enjoyed boasting about the famous people they routinely served.

My parents settled in a cold-water tenement flat on East 112th Street near First Avenue. The block was part of East Harlem's Italian section. The neighborhood's Sicilian elders would gather each day inside unmarked storefront social clubs. At night, the men, most of them garment workers and many of them members of the anarchist or social movements, would play dominoes outdoors while they debated the future of the union movement. By the late 1940s, many of the Italian immigrants' sons were joining neighborhood street gangs. The gang members, who were determined to keep their tidy ghetto off-limits to outsiders, would patrol the big city-owned Jefferson Pool and the string of bars along First and Second Avenues, chasing off any blacks or Puerto Ricans who wandered into the neighborhood.

Ethnic tensions stayed under control as long as Vito Marcantonio was the local congressman. Marcantonio, an old-style socialist, managed to fashion a unique coalition of East Harlem's ethnic and racial groups, one that had kept him in the House of Representatives from 1934 to 1950. Marcantonio could always be found advocating for the poor, whether it was unemployed workers being evicted from their homes or families with no food to eat. For years, he was the lone critic in Washington of U.S. rule in Puerto Rico. In 1937, he helped elect this country's first Puerto Rican to political office. His protégé, Oscar Rivera García, won an assembly seat that year as the candidate of both the Republican and American Labor parties. The city's political establishment, on the other hand, abhorred Marcantonio and his radical notions. In 1950, his enemies finally beat him in an election and ousted him from Congress, but even then it took an unprecedented alliance of the Republican, Democratic, and Liberal Party bosses to unite behind one candidate.

With Marcantonio gone, East Harlem lost its main voice for working-class unity. Racial tensions flared up immediately, with some Italians blaming Puerto Ricans for his defeat. The elders of our family still recall the terrible election night in November 1950 when the ethnic war began. That night, Eugenio Morales, a onetime neighbor from Ponce's El Ligao, was visiting my grandmother, María, and her grown daughters, Graciela and Pura. A handsome, dark-skinned, humorous man, Morales delighted the women with a stream of hilarious reminiscences about life in Puerto Rico. Around 10:00 P.M., as Morales got up to leave, Pura heard the radio blaring the news about Marcantonio's losing his election, but no one was paying much attention.

"Be careful out on those streets," my grandmother told him. "The Italians on this block know us, but you're a stranger—" She didn't say what she was thinking, that the González family was so light-skinned most of us could easily pass for Italian, but not Eugenio with his chocolate complexion.

"Don't worry, Doña María," he said with a shrug and a smile, "I can take care of myself." Then he walked out. A few minutes later, there was a loud banging at the door. Graciela rushed to open it and Eugenio collapsed at the entrance, blood spurting from his head, mouth, and chest. The bones on one side of his face had collapsed and fragments were piercing the skin. An ambulance rushed him to Metropolitan Hospital, where a few minutes later medics wheeled in a bloodied man named Casanova, a Puerto Rican amateur boxer. Casanova, Eugenio later learned, had been beaten and stabbed by Italians. Half an hour later, another battered Puerto Rican was admitted. Eugenio overheard a young Irish cop whisper to one of the nurses in the emergency room, "Marcantonio lost the election. They're jumping every Spic they can find." Eugenio Morales never visited our family in East Harlem again, nor did any other of our dark-skinned relatives or friends. To keep from being run out of the neighborhood by the racist attacks, Puerto Ricans started organizing their own street gangs, groups like the Viceroys and Dragons, and soon the city's major newspapers were depicting a city terrorized by Puerto Rican and black gangs. As the years passed, however, the new migrants became too numerous to frighten off and the street gangs faded in importance.

Despite that bitter 1950s gang war era, common work experiences and the bond of the Catholic religion gradually drew Puerto Ricans, Italians and Irish together—as neighbors, as friends, sometimes even as family. My aunt Pura, for instance, married Bing Morrone, whose parents owned the only grocery store on our block, and their children, my cousins Anthony, María, and Julie, all grew up as both Puerto Rican and Italian.

This was still the era when working with your hands was considered the most honorable of professions, when downtown white-collar office workers were few in number. It was the era before the welfare system turned into an economic crutch, chaining countless Puerto Rican families into dependence on government. Jobs were still plentiful, mostly the kind that threatened to puncture or amputate your limbs with needles, presses, or blades, those mechanical contraptions of some entrepreneur who'd already made your dream of wealth his reality, but those jobs in postwar America, the chance to provide something better for your kids with enough ten- and twelve-hour sweat-filled days, made it possible to endure everything else.

My mother and aunts had their pick of employers when they arrived. Aunt Graciela, who had been a skilled seamstress in garment plants in Puerto Rico, could command a salary as high as $30 a week, a tidy sum in those days. "Sometimes we would go out and in one day try out three or four different factories until we found one that we liked," she recalled.

The González brothers moved on from the Copa to better-paying union jobs in the meat-packing, restaurant, and taxi industries. By the mid-1950s, our family, along with many other Puerto Ricans, started moving into public housing projects the federal government was building all over the city for the working poor. As we left East Harlem, however, we said good-bye to that close-knit network of Puerto Rican pioneers.

Meanwhile, new Puerto Rican communities were cropping up in Chicago, Philadelphia, and sections of Ohio, as both the U.S. and Puerto Rican governments encouraged emigration as a safety valve to prevent further social unrest on the island. Labor recruiters wound through the poorest neighborhoods, loudspeakers mounted atop their cars, offering jobs in the United States and the travel fare to get there. In Lorain, Ohio, for instance, the National Tube Company, a U.S. Steel subsidiary booming with military contracts, recruited 500 Puerto Ricans from the island to work in the company's steel mill in 1947-1948. Carnegie-Illinois Steel of Gary, Indiana, recruited 500 to work in its mill in 1948. And, in 1951, the Ohio Employment Service brought 1,524 Puerto Ricans to Youngstown and Cleveland.

Much of the hiring was contracted to the Philadelphia-based H.G. Friedman Labor Agency. (The president of the agency was the son of a Spanish-American War veteran who settled in Puerto Rico and organized the island's police department.) Once the migrants arrived in the mills, they sent for their families, while others came on their own after hearing stories about all the jobs in the steel, rubber, and auto industries of the Midwest.

More than a million Puerto Ricans were living in the United States by the mid-1960s, most of them in New York City. But they were still largely invisible to Anglo society. They quietly pushed carts in the city's garment center, cleaned bedpans in the hospitals, washed dishes in hotels and restaurants, performed maintenance for the big apartment buildings, or they worked on factory assembly lines, or drove gypsy cabs, or operated *bodegas*. By then, however, the migration had spilled all over the Northeast and Midwest. Farms in Connecticut, eastern Pennsylvania, upstate New York, Ohio, and South Jersey recruited Puerto Ricans to pick the crops. When the harvest ended, the migrants settled in nearby towns, and thus sprouted the Puerto Rican *barrios* of Haverstraw, New York; Vineland, New Jersey; Hartford, Connecticut; and Kennett Square, Pennsylvania.

The Second Generation

As the children of those migrants started attending public schools in the 1950s, they—I should say, we—entered a society accustomed to thinking only in black and white. It didn't take long for the white English-speaking majority to start casting uneasy glances at the growing number of brown-skinned, Spanish-speaking teenagers who didn't seem to fit into any established racial group. New York tabloids took to portraying young Puerto Rican criminals as savages. The most notorious of them were Salvador "Cape Man" Agron and Frank Santana. Despite the clear working-class character of the Puerto Rican migration, Hollywood created the enduring image of Puerto Ricans as knife wielders, prone to violence and addicted to drugs, in such films as *Cry Tough* (1959), *The Young Savages* (1961), and *West Side Story (1961)*.

Most of us became products of a sink-or-swim public school philosophy, immersed in English-language instruction from our first day in class and actively discouraged from retaining our native tongue. "Your name isn't Juan," the young teacher told me in first grade at P.S. 87 in East Harlem. "In this country it's John. Shall I call you John?" Confused and afraid, but sensing this as some fateful decision, I timidly said no. But most children could not summon the courage, so school officials routinely anglicized their names. Though I had spoken only Spanish before I entered kindergarten, the teachers were amazed at how quickly I mastered English. From then on, each time a new child from Puerto Rico was placed in any of my classes, the teachers would sit him beside me so I could interpret the lessons. Bewildered, terrified and ashamed, the new kids grappled with my clumsy attempts to decipher the teacher's strange words. Inevitably, when the school year ended, they were forced to repeat the grade, sometimes more than once, all because they hadn't mastered English. Even now, forty years later, the faces of those children are still fresh in my mind. They make today's debates on bilingual education so much more poignant, and the current push toward total English immersion so much more frightening.

Our parents' generation rarely protested the way we were treated in school, which is understandable. After the terrible poverty they'd faced in Puerto Rico, they believed that an education—any education—was their children's only hope for progress. And if that meant putting up with a few psychological scars from Americanization, then so be it. My grandmother, who was illiterate, drove that into my father, who was barely literate himself, and he pushed my sister, Elena, and me to study with a frenzy that bordered on cruelty. It was not unusual for him to beat us mercilessly with a leather strap for bringing home a poor report card. These days, he'd probably be thrown in jail for child abuse.

As time passed, the González family became a melting-pot success story by anyone's measure. One by one, each of us completed high school and joined the first college-educated generation in the family's history. My uncle Sergio and aunt Catin produced a college instructor in Greek and Latin, another son who rose to be an official in the Nixon and Reagan administrations and a South Bronx social worker. I went to Ivy League Columbia College and eventually on to a career in journalism; my sister became a public school and later a college instructor; another cousin became a doctor; another a psychiatric social worker; another a police detective.

But we in that second generation—smart, urban, English-dominant—remained acutely aware that the broader Anglo society still regarded Puerto Ricans as less than full Americans. We studied the history and culture of Europe in our classes, but nothing about Puerto Rico or Latin America, not even an inkling that our tiny homeland possessed any history and culture worthy of study. After the Vatican II reforms ushered in vernacular Catholic Masses, even the Church relegated Puerto Ricans and Latinos to the basements of most parishes, despite our being its fastest-growing membership.

The country's ingrained racial traditions meant that black or dark-skinned Puerto Ricans faced even greater prejudice. The lighter-skinned among us tended to settle in more stable Italian or Irish neighborhoods, and to pass for white. The darker-skinned ones, unable to find housing in the white neighbor-hoods, formed all-Puerto Rican enclaves or moved into black neighborhoods. In many cities, our communities emerged as buffer zones between blacks and whites. In Philadelphia, for instance, the Puerto Rican community evolved into a narrow north-south corridor on either side of Fifth Street, which ran almost the entire length of the city, separating the white eastern neighborhoods of town from the black western ones.

While de facto segregation has been a pernicious part of this society since the end of slavery, in our case, it became an unbearable assault on our family bonds. *¿Y tu abuela, dónde esta?* ("And your grandmother, where is she?") is a familiar Puerto Rican refrain and the title of a popular poem by Fortunate Vizcarrondo. The phrase reminds us that black blood runs through all Puerto Rican families. Puerto Ricans resisted the sharp racial demarcations so preva-lent in this country, and their implicit diminishment of our human worth. But gradually, almost imperceptibly, I watched my aunts and uncles begin to adopt antiblack attitudes, as if this were some rite of passage to becoming authentic Americans. "A hostile posture toward resident blacks must be struck at the Americanizing door before it will open," is how writer Toni Morrison so aptly describes it.

The social imperative to *choose a racial identity,* and then only in purely black-and-white terms, impelled those of us in the second generation at first to jettison our native language and culture, to assimilate into either the white or the black world. My uncle Sergio and aunt Catin were my family's exception. They were the only ones who never left East Harlem. There, they fiercely clung to the culture of the island. In their home, *aguinaldos,* the music of Puerto Rican *jíbaros,* could always be heard, a dominoes hand was always in the offing, weekend family *fiestas* were routine, and the neighbors, whether Puerto Rican or Anglo, black or white, were always welcome.

Not surprisingly, one of the first expressions of community organization in the 1950s was an event that celebrated cultural pride—the annual Puerto Rican Day Parade. As the Puerto Rican population grew, the parade became the largest of the city's many ethnic celebrations. By the 1990s, more than a million people attended it.

In the midst of the high tide of Puerto Rican migration, something else hap-pened—African Americans rose up against racial segregation, unmasking the chasm that still existed between black and white society. We Puerto Ricans found ourselves having common ground with both sides, yet fitting in with neither. We simply had not been a part of the congenital birth defect of this country, the Anglo-Saxon slave system and its Jim Crow aftermath.

In 1964, the Reverend Milton Galamison, Malcolm X, and other black leaders led a boycott of New York City public school parents against racial discrimination. A handful of Puerto Rican community leaders from the prewar migrant
generation joined the boycott. Among them were Frank Espada, Evelina Antonetty and Gilberto Gerena Valentin. Espada, a community organizer before
joining Republican mayor John Lindsay's administration, would later develop
a career as a brilliant photographer chronicling the Puerto Rican diaspora.
Antonetty went on to found United Bronx Parents, the seminal parent advocacy
group for Puerto Ricans in education. And Gerena Valentin, a nationalist, onetime Communist Party member, and labor union organizer, would later create
an influential federation of Puerto Rican hometown clubs. Those clubs formed
the political base with which he captured a city council seat in the 1970s. They,
and others like them, comprised the first postwar leadership of the emerging
Puerto Rican community in New York.

That wave of leaders, however, was soon eclipsed by an even more radical
group. The assassinations of Malcolm X (1965) and Martin Luther King (1968)
sparked mass urban riots among blacks and polarized the civil rights movement,
and many of us who were influenced by those events found greater affinity to
the black power movement than to the integration movement. That identification intensified as thousands of Puerto Ricans went off to fight in the Vietnam
War, only to return, like the veterans of World War II, to a country that still
misunderstood and mistrusted them as foreigners.

As we came of age, we responded to that mistrust and misunderstanding
with open rebellion. A slew of new nationalist and left-wing organizations
sprang up among Puerto Ricans. Some were inspired by the old Nationalist
Party in Puerto Rico or by the Black Panther Party here. The most influential
was the Young Lords, an organization I helped to found in 1969. During its
apogee (1969-1972), the Lords galvanized thousands of young Latinos into
radical politics, and an amazing portion of the group's members later became
influential leaders of the community.

Fueled by that political awakening, a cultural renaissance emerged among
Puerto Rican artists. Writers Piri Thomas and Nicolasa Mohr, poets Pedro Pietri
and José Angel Figueroa, playwrights Miguel Piñeiro and Miguel Algarín
caught the public's attention as vibrant voices of the Puerto Rican migrant experience. Even Latin music experienced a resurgence as Eddie and Charlie
Palmieri, Ray Barretto, and Willie Colón began producing politically charged
lyrics that celebrated the new sense of emerging Puerto Rican power.

The essence of that new movement was a sudden realization of who we were,
economic refugees from the last major colony of the United States. That real-

ization caused us to reject the path of our immigrant predecessors from Europe; the first generation accepting decades of second-class status while it established a foothold, the second securing an education and assimilating quietly, and the third emerging as 100 percent melting-pot Americans.

Puerto Ricans, we concluded, were in a different position from Italians or Swedes or Poles. Our homeland was invaded and permanently occupied, its wealth exploited, its patriots persecuted and jailed, by the very country to which we had migrated. Our experience was closer to Algerians in France before independence, or to Irish Catholics in England today. For decades, textbooks made in the United States had taught island schoolchildren our homeland was incapable of self-government and would perish economically without Uncle Sam. But in the early 1970s a new generation of independent Puerto Rican scholars arose to challenge that premise. They confirmed for the second generation that Puerto Rico was as capable of being a prosperous independent nation as Israel or Taiwan or Switzerland, but that its history had been consciously distorted to encourage a sense of dependence.

Our parents instinctively sympathized with this new awakening. Unlike white America, where New Left activism divided father and son, mother and daughter, the new nationalism brought the two Puerto Rican generations closer together. It inspired the young to reclaim and study our language. It helped us understand the suffering our parents had endured. And it transformed our psychological outlook. Never again would a Puerto Rican quietly accept an Anglo's barking, "Speak English, you're in America now!" or the rote admonition, "If you don't like it here, go back where you came from."

By the mid-1970s, however, economic recession struck, and new groups of Latinos began arriving in the nation's cities. Competition soared for a diminishing number of unskilled jobs, and the class nature of the Puerto Rican migration radically changed. Many college graduates and professionals from the island, unable to find jobs there, relocated to the United States, as did many of the poorest and least skilled urban slum dwellers. At the same time, the first generation of migrants, the former factory workers and *bodega* owners, having accumulated substantial savings, started returning to the island to retire or to fill jobs in the booming tourist industry, where a good command of English was required. So many Puerto Ricans left this country that the decade witnessed net migration back to the island.

Thus the Puerto Rican migrant community became dominated during the 1980s by two very different social classes, both highly dependent on government. At the top was a small but growing number of intelligentsia and white-collar professionals, many employed in social programs or the educational system, and at the bottom a large and fast-growing caste of low-paid, unskilled workers, alongside an underclass of long-term unemployed and welfare recipients. Missing in any significant numbers were two critical groups: the private business class whose members provide any ethnic group's capital formation and self-reliant outlook, and the skilled technical workers who provide stability and role models for those on the bottom to emulate.

Meanwhile, life in America's inner cities by the early 1980s was verging on chaos. A dwindling tax base, brought about by the flight of industry and skilled white workers to the suburbs, massive disinvestment by government in public schools and infrastructure, and the epidemics of drug and alcohol abuse, all tore at the quality of city life. As might be expected, the chaos took its heaviest toll on the African American and Puerto Rican migrant communities of the inner cities.

The third generation of Puerto Ricans, those who came of age in the late 1980s and early 1990s, found themselves crippled by inferior schools, a lack of jobs, and underfunded social services. They found their neighborhoods inundated with drugs and violence. They grew up devoid, for the most part, of self-image, national identity, or cultural awareness. They became the lost generation.

But the schism over identity and the quandary over language and heritage soon turned into problems not just for the Puerto Ricans. As Latin American immigration exploded, many Anglos started to worry that America's social fabric was disintegrating. The biggest source of that worry, as we shall see, was the nation's growing Mexican population.

THE VIEQUES CONTROVERSY

On the evening of April 19, 1999, a U.S. Marine pilot mistook his target on Vieques and launched from his FA-18 jet two five-hundred-pound live bombs that exploded at an observation post, killing civilian David Sanes Rodriguez, who was employed by the Navy as a guard, and injuring four others. The accident re-ignited the smoldering resentment on Puerto Rico of the 60 years of bombing and shelling of the small offshore island and reverberated all the way up to the Pentagon and the White House.

Robert Friedman, "Study: Vieques death rate 34% higher than P.R. over last 4 years," *The San Juan Star,* May 25, 2000. Reprinted with permission.

Puerto Ricans of all political stripes demanded that the Navy halt its training exercises on the 21-mile-long island municipality, located six miles off the eastern coast of the main island. Two-thirds of Vieques has been under Navy occupation since the military started buying up land there in 1941, and began exercises on a 900-acre target range in the east of the island and in surrounding waters. Although there had been protests dating back to the 1960s and 1970s, the bombing accident gave new impetus to complaints by Vieques residents.

The residents charged that the constant bombing and shelling was causing serious health problems, damaging the environment, impeding economic growth and renting the social fabric. New studies showed higher rates of cancer, heart ailments and infant mortality among the 9,400 Viequenses than in the rest of Puerto Rico. A few days after the death of Sanes, protesters occupied the target range and held up the resumption of exercises for more than a year.

In January 2000, Puerto Rico Governor Pedro Rosselló entered into an agreement with the federal government allowing the Navy to continue exercises with inert ordinance and setting a referendum, in which the residents of Vieques would decide the Navy's future on their island. On November 6, 2001, the voters would decide whether the Navy leaves Vieques by May, 2003, or stays indefinitely and resumes live-fire exercises. If they chose the latter, the federal government would invest $50 million into the Vieques economy, on top of the $40 million pledged as part of the Vieques Agreement. Under the accord, the Navy transferred some 8,000 acres in the west of the island back to the municipal government and to federal and local environmental entities.

Gov. Sila Calderon, who took office on Jan. 2, 2001, insisted, however, that the health ailments of the residents required the Navy to permanently end its exercises before 2003. In April 2001, the Commonwealth took the Navy and the Department of Defense to court, asking for a permanent injunction to the exercises.

Washington—A "highly significant" study of Puerto Rico Department of Health death certificates over the past four years has shown that the mortality rate in Vieques is 34 percent higher than in the rest of Puerto Rico, a doctor investigating health concerns on the island municipality said here Wednesday.

The mortality rate is based on a comparison between the ratio of deaths to population. Each year, more people in Vieques, on a per capita basis, die than in mainland Puerto Rico, according to the study.

The study also revealed that Viequenses have a 50 percent higher cancer mortality rate and a 40 percent higher rate of death due to heart disease than their counterparts on the main island of Puerto Rico, according to Dr. Carmen Ortiz Roque, an obstetrician and gynecologist, who practices on the island and in stateside hospitals.

Ortiz Roque said the study was highly significant because evidence showed that the findings were not a chance occurrence. She said some 120,000 death certificates were looked at and called the study "very powerful" in its objectivity since all the data came from the certificates on which doctors listed causes of death.

Because of its war-game activities on the island, "the Navy is the main suspect, until proven otherwise" for the causes of the higher death and disease rates, Ortiz Roque said.

With the aid of graphs and charts, environmentalist Neftalí García Martínez pointed to studies showing that Vieques residents have been contaminated with heavy metals from exploded Navy ordnance. The contamination has been carried by dust to the island's residential areas and has entered the food chain, García Martínez said.

Ortiz Roque's finding and other medical evidence allegedly proving "the Navy is killing American citizens in Vieques," according to attorney John Arthur Eaves, Jr., were delivered Wednesday to Navy Secretary Richard Danzig as part of a class-action claim that could precede a multimillion-dollar federal court suit.

Eaves said at a news conference at the National Press Club Wednesday that he is representing some 2,000 Vieques residents, of which 110 are cancer victims, who are asking compensation from the Navy for their health care costs and suffering.

Individual claims, he said, could range from $200,000 to $5 million or $10 million. A similar class-action claim had been filed in San Juan last December, but had to be withdrawn because it was not accompanied by medical evidence, Eaves said.

Under law, the Navy Secretary has six months to respond to the compensation claims. If no settlement is reached in that time, then the claimants have the right to go to court, and will do so, said Eaves, who is a member of his father's office, the John Arthur Eaves Law Firm, in Jackson, Miss. The firm specializes in asbestos and tobacco damage cases, as well as accident liabilities, and recently settled a suit on behalf of the families of the 20 people who died when a Marine jet severed a cable car at an Italian ski resort in 1998.

A call to Danzig's press office for comment on the claims filing was not returned. Navy officials have previously denied that military training on Vieques is harming the environment or is a threat to the residents' health.

Capturing the most attention at the press conference was Vieques-born Milivy Adams, who has suffered various forms of cancer in her less than three years of life. Accompanied by her parents, José and Zulayka Adams Calderón, the young girl, despite the scar cut clear across her shaved scalp from the removal of a brain tumor, smiled often and was playful as her father related his daughter's ordeal.

"Seven months ago we started our battle with cancer," Adams said. "The doctors found a tumor on her brain and said she needed an immediate operation to avoid brain damage. Then they gave her a bone scan and found a tumor in her kidney and one on her left arm and left leg and on three of her ribs.

"We proceeded with chemotherapy for three months, then she was given more studies and they found the cancer had advanced. The doctors told me my daughter would not be able to endure more treatment."

Adams said he moved the family to Camden, N.J., and took the child to the Children's Hospital of Philadelphia. "She was given more chemotherapy and now, thank God, she has responded," the father said. "She's had more surgery and radiation therapy. We just hope she has no more cancer," he said.

"I'm disgusted with the Navy," said Adams. "We have a right to live in good health and in peace."

SOCIAL STRUGGLE AGAINST THE U.S. NAVY IN VIEQUES, PUERTO RICO: TWO MOVEMENTS IN HISTORY

[In May 2003 the U.S. Navy shut down its live-fire training ground on the Puerto Rican island municipality of Vieques. The base closure marked the victory of a grassroots movement against the world's most powerful military. Since World War II the navy had maintained a major training installation on this 51-square-mile island, located six miles off the southeast coast of Puerto Rico. Its retreat came after four years of mass mobilization, thousands of arrests for civil disobedience, and international media attention to the struggle to halt live bombing exercises on the island. While Vieques was the site of one of the navy's key military installations in the Western Hemisphere, it was also home to 10,000 American citizens, who lived sandwiched between an ammunition depot and

From Katherine T. McCaffrey, *Latin American Perspectives* Issue 146, XXXIII, No. 1 (January 2006), 83-101. Reprinted with permission.

a maneuver area. The expansion of the base and the intensification of weapons testing and maneuvers had created an environment that was incompatible with a viable residential community. This article examines the way the grassroots struggle against the navy overcame highly divisive colonial politics to build unprecedented political solidarity in Puerto Rico. It analyzes the success of the Vieques movement in relation to a less successful grassroots struggle that unfolded on the island in the late 1970s and focuses on the framing of opposition to the U.S. military at different historic moments.

The catalyst for the recent protest was the accidental death of a civilian employee on the base. On April 19, 1999, during a routine training mission, two navy jets missed their mark by a mile and a half. Flying between 500 and 1,300 miles per hour, they dropped two 500-pound bombs not on the live-impact range but on the barbed-wire-ringed observation post from which the navy surveyed the shelling. The navy's range control officer and three security guards inside the observation post were injured by fragments of shattered glass and concrete. David Sanes Rodríguez, a thirty-five-year-old civilian security guard on patrol outside, was knocked unconscious by the explosion and bled to death from his injuries.

Within days of Sanes's death, waves of protesters positioned themselves as human shields on the bombing range, bringing military maneuvers to a halt. Scaling fences or arriving by fishing boat, activists poured onto the bombing range, building over a dozen encampments on the target zone. Thousands of supporters from Vieques, Puerto Rico, and the United States visited the campsites to express their solidarity. Puerto Rico's governor, Pedro Rosselló, a loyal ally of the U.S. government and military, called for an immediate halt to the bombing. The support from Puerto Ricans on the main island, the diaspora, and international allies helped to create a powerful movement that eventually caused the navy to abandon its "crown jewel" in the Western Hemisphere.

The Vieques movement points to the power of locally based social movements that are linked to broader goals, visions, and alliances. In the past two decades theorists have analyzed and debated the significance of small-scale popular movements in Latin America (Alvarez, Dagnino, and Escobar, 1998; Eckstein, 1989; Escobar and Alvarez, 1992; Fox and Starn, 1997). Rather than seeking total social transformation, these small movements focus on more specific, concrete, everyday concerns and grievances. Hellman (1997) cautions, however, that unless locally based social movements are connected to broad-based visions and goals and forge wider alliances, they risk political insignificance. In Vieques, a key aspect of expanding the struggle was finding a meaningful framework that would build wider solidarity while sidestepping the volatile issue of Puerto Rican sovereignty.

In the late 1970s, cold-war politics impeded activists from forging the alliances and formulating the vision that might advance their cause. A focus on local fishermen and their grievances against the navy appealed to the economic and cultural nationalist dimensions of the struggle, but it ultimately narrowed the movement, which succumbed to political pressure and navy strong-arm tactics. In the 1990s, the political climate beyond Vieques's snores shifted dramatically after the collapse of the Soviet Union and the end of the cold war. The threat of communism in Latin America that had justified U.S. military actions in Vieques suddenly disappeared. The changed political context opened up a new space for protest to develop. Activists' new focus on peace was crucial to strengthening, expanding, and internationalizing the Vieques movement.

The article first considers the way material grievances in Vieques are complicated by broader political forces emanating from Puerto Rico's colonial status. It then outlines the roots of the conflict in the history of military control over the island. Its central concern is to examine the mobilizations against the navy in the 1970s and the 1990s through historical analysis and comparison of their politics and discourse.]

Colonial Citizens

Much recent analysis of conflict around military bases assumes that nationalist ideology is a central motivating factor (Smith, 2000). In Vieques, however, conflict had its foundation in the material conditions of everyday life. Vieques is the poorest municipality in Puerto Rico, with 73 percent of the population living below the poverty line. It has among the highest rates of unemployment, with almost half the adult population lacking work, according to the 1990 census. It has among the highest infant mortality rates in Puerto Rico and a growing rate of cancer and other health problems that residents believe are caused by weapons testing. Although military bases are commonly assumed to provide jobs and economic growth for surrounding communities, the military's legacy in Vieques has been poverty and stagnation. What the recent mobilization in Vieques made clear was that the material harm caused by the military—the destruction of the ecology, the health effects of weapons testing, the squelching of economic development, the dislocation of civilians and the navy's antagonism toward them—was the basis of protest.

Vieques's local grievances became enmeshed, however, in broader political controversies connected to the geopolitical interests of the U.S. military and the colonial relationship between Puerto Rico and the United States. Vieques is a municipality of Puerto Rico, a nonsovereign territory of the United States. Its residents are U.S. citizens who serve in the U.S. armed forces and can be drafted to fight in times of war but who have neither political representation in Congress nor the right to vote for president. As Ayala (2003) notes, U.S. colonialism in Puerto Rico operates through a combination of coercion and consent.

The predicament of Vieques, an inhabited bombing range, illustrates the more naked forms of domination: the usurpation of national territory and the exercise of power in the face of widespread discontent. But colonialism is also maintained through consent. The extension of U.S. citizenship in 1917 to Puerto Ricans effectively silenced more vigorous protest by offering individuals the rights of citizenship even while denying Puerto Rico a place in the American polity. Puerto Rican citizens have freedom of movement to the United States and privileged access to the labor market denied their Latin American neighbors. They have high rates of participation in the U.S. military and live on an island with a strong presence of U.S. armed forces and bases. Political debate in Puerto Rico is shaped primarily by autonomism, the struggle to advance local interests within the colonial framework. A vocal minority advocates independence, radicalizing political discourse, and tapping into widespread cultural nationalism (Ayala, 2003: 217), but the large majority of the Puerto Rican population is politically moderate, preferring continued political and economic ties to the United States even while maintaining a profound sense of Puerto Rican identity (Dávila, 1997; Duany, 2000, 2002; Morris, 1995).

Conflict with the military exposes the ambivalence about citizenship, sovereignty, and national identity that are at the heart of Puerto Rican society (see Flores, 2000; Negrón-Muntaner and Grosfoguel, 1997). As both a potent symbol of American influence and a powerful actor in island affairs, the U.S. military evokes charged debates over loyalty and identity. In general, opposition to the military is viewed as part of the anticolonial movement. What is peculiar about Vasquez's struggle is the way residents have strived to assert specific material grievances that are a fundamental consequence of Puerto Rico's political domination by the United States and its armed forces while avoiding the delicate issue of sovereignty.

Historical Background

The U.S. Navy usurped three-quarters of Vieques Island in a series of land expropriations during and after World War II.[1] The rise of German fascism and the outbreak of war in Europe had raised American anxiety about the security of the Caribbean region and the Panama Canal. Declaring a national emergency, the navy expropriated 6,680 acres of land in eastern Puerto Rico and 21,020 acres of Vieques, two-thirds of that island's land, to build the Roosevelt Roads

---

1. Data in this section are drawn from McCaffrey (2002) and are the product of ethnographic, documentary, and archival research.

Naval Station, which was intended to rival Pearl Harbor in scale and significance.

At the time of the military occupation in the early 1940s, Vieques Island was devoted to sugarcane cultivation. Two large estates, one U.S.-controlled and the other Puerto Rican-owned, dominated the local economy and controlled most of the land. Stark social inequality and overwhelming poverty facilitated the military takeover. The landless majority who lived on the expropriated acres had little political clout, and thousands were evicted from their homes and deposited in razed cane fields that the navy declared "resettlement tracts."

Initially, the base created a construction boom that provided employment and filled residents with hope. The construction of the base, however, stopped almost as quickly as it had begun. Military priorities shifted to the Pacific when the United States entered the war, and the navy scaled back its original plans. The devastation at Pearl Harbor challenged the wisdom of concentrating a fleet at one massive installation (Tugwell, 1976: 68). The construction of the massive stone and cement breakwater from Puerto Rico to Vieques was suspended, and work on Roosevelt Roads slowed because of a shortage of supplies. The abrupt halt of construction had a disastrous effect on Vieques's economy.

In 1947 the navy drew up new strategic plans for Vieques. It re-designated Roosevelt Roads as a naval training installation and fuel depot (Langley, 1985: 273). Vieques was to be used for firing practice and amphibious landings by tens of thousands of sailors and marines. Because this new vision of the base required more land, the navy expropriated over 4,000 acres from eastern Vieques, displacing 130 families. With three-quarters of its land usurped, Vieques found its quality of life severely debased and its economy crippled.

Although the United States was officially at peace, Vieques became a hostage of the cold war. Despite growing social tensions and repeated calls for the return of the land, the military remained entrenched on the island. After the Korean War, U.S. rivalry with the Soviet Union intensified. The Soviets' testing of the guided missile gave the United States new impetus to compete for technological superiority. Roosevelt Roads assumed new strategic significance as a place to test missiles, and Vieques was the perfect bull's-eye (Langley, 1985). The Cuban Revolution of 1959 jolted the U.S. military, which feared the rise of communism in a crucial strategic position in the region. That year the navy activated on Vieques a marine base, Camp García. With the fear of a "communist menace" in Latin America, Vieques took on an increasing importance as a staging ground for interventions, as in, for example, Guatemala in 1954 and the Dominican Republic in 1965. When the Bay of Pigs invasion failed in 1961, the surviving forces gathered in Vieques.

Although the navy maintained no formal jurisdiction over the civilian sector, in reality it controlled the fate of the entire island. It controlled the majority of the land, water, and air surrounding Vieques. It controlled nautical routes, flight paths, aquifers, and zoning laws in civilian territory. It blocked developers from establishing a resort on the island. It held title to the resettlement tracts in the civilian sector, where the majority of the island's population lived under constant threat of eviction. In 1961 it drafted secret plans to remove the entire civilian population of 8,000 from the island; even the dead were to be dug up and removed from their graves (Fernández, 1996). The plan would have allowed the navy to expand the base without interference. Governor Luis Muñoz Marín intervened and a presidential order from President John F. Kennedy eventually blocked the navy from carrying out its plans, but the tension between the military and civilian population persisted.

Vieques's plight dramatically exposed Puerto Rico's lack of sovereignty and subordinate status within the U.S. orbit of power. Although President Harry Truman had proclaimed Puerto Rico's colonial status resolved in 1952 with the conferral of "commonwealth status," its newly conceived political relationship with the United States did not confer self-determination. Ultimate power lay not in the hands of islanders but in the U.S. Congress. Puerto Ricans continued to hold U.S. citizenship but had no representation in federal government. They paid no federal taxes but were subject to the military draft. Foreign policy matters were in the hands of the United States. Nowhere was the contradiction between internal autonomy and external control over "foreign policy" so vividly expressed as in Vieques, where U.S. national security directly impinged upon the community's internal affairs.

Despite Puerto Rico's heralded commonwealth status, the U.S. navy continued to function as a colonial power in Vieques. Nationalists and advocates of Puerto Rican independence long viewed Vieques as a rallying point for opposition to U.S. imperialism. In the 1940s, the nationalist leader Pedro Albizu Campos denounced the U.S. occupation of Vieques as the "vivisection of the Puerto Rican nation." Despite the apparent clarity of the injustice—the virtual stranglehold the navy held on the island and its antagonism toward the resident civilian population—residents' understanding of the navy and the nature of their dilemma was ambivalent and divided. This ambivalence expressed itself in the protest movement that unfolded in 1978.

Cold War Social Struggles

In the late 1970s, protest erupted in Vieques in response to the intensification of maneuvers and live-fire exercises on the island. When a militant anticolonial movement opposing live-fire exercises emerged on the neighboring island of Culebra, the navy transferred bombing to Vieques, and the heightened bombing and stepped-up maneuvers pushed Vieques's conflict over the edge.[2] For approximately five years, 1978-1983, fishermen led a dramatic grassroots struggle against the military presence in Vieques. Positioning themselves in the direct line of missile fire, local fishermen succeeded in interrupting international military maneuvers. Pickets, demonstrations, and a campaign of civil disobedience put Vieques's grievances on an international stage. The U.S. Congress held hearings on naval activities on the island and recommended that the navy leave Vieques (U.S. House, 1981). Geraldo Rivera traveled to the island with his film crew. The fisherman leader Carlos Zenón spoke before the UN decolonization committee on Vieques's crisis. Daily papers in Puerto Rico tracked the conflict. Thousands of islanders and supporters were mobilized in Vieques, Puerto Rico, and the United States.

Despite winning several important concessions from the navy and broadcasting Vieques's plight to the world, the movement was ultimately unsuccessful in its goal of evicting the navy and recovering land. Three major factors were responsible for its failure. First, activists emphasized local economic grievances rather than the broader political or human rights aspects of the case. Second, they were ambivalent in the alliances they formed with a broader network of supporters, emphasizing a hierarchical structure with local leadership and control of the movement. Finally, they contested the navy at a moment of increased military entrenchment.

Both the fisherman-led movement of the 1970s and the more recent mobilization emerged from the grass roots in response to military incursions. Both evoked discourse that sidestepped charged debates over Puerto Rican sovereignty. The earlier movement, however, erupted at a time of heightened cold-war tensions that constrained its effectiveness. In 1979 Soviet tanks rolled into Afghanistan, a wave of revolutionary movements swept Central America and the Caribbean basin, and the U.S. public consciousness was shaped by grim images of hostages in Iran. The United States dramatically expanded its economic and military presence in the Caribbean, intervening in regional conflicts and arming and training security forces in the basin. This polarized political climate shaped the movement's expression and, ultimately, its outcome.

Vieques activists resisted framing their grievances in broad political terms that would confront the issue of Puerto Rican sovereignty and thus raise

---

2. For further discussion of the Culebra movement, see McCaffrey (2002) and Delgado Cintrón (1989).

potentially divisive questions of loyalty, patriotism, and national identity. Although the movement emerged in direct response to the intensification of maneuvers and the shifting of bombing exercises from Culebra to Vieques, activists did not address the broader human rights aspects of the conflict. Instead, they emphasized that the local movement was not about politics but about the "authentic" problems of the Vieques people—the concrete, material needs of the people that seemed to be ignored by the maneuverings of politicians and activists with broader agendas. Discourse focused on the struggle of the fishermen: the destruction of traps and fishing gear by navy boats on maneuvers and the restrictions on the use of prime fishing grounds. There were several motivations for narrowing the focus. First, compared with the recent Culebra mobilization, which was spearheaded and sustained by the Puerto Rican Independence Party, the Vieques movement emerged from a community with a pro-statehood majority and mayor. A focus on local grievances was effective in building consensus in a politically conservative populace. It was also a way of keeping Viequense leadership at the helm and preventing the movement from becoming merely a platform for the cause of Puerto Rican independence or a tool of political interests. Fishermen were important to the success of the movement because they characterized it as based on issues of quality of life and economic opportunity as opposed to broader anticolonial concerns.

The fisherman-led mobilization fused highly confrontational tactics with moderate politics. Fishermen in 18-foot boats positioned themselves in the direct line of missile fire, halting warfare training at sea. They became key protagonists on an island where residents were vehemently opposed to military practices that stifled the economy and impinged upon their freedom. Fishermen, furthermore, talked not about imperialism but about the damage that ships caused to their traps. They argued not for Puerto Rican independence but for their individual rights as U.S. citizens to make a living. They served as cultural icons evocative of the island's rural past and harnessed cultural nationalist sentiment and a strong local identity for resistance against the military.

There were strategic weaknesses, however, in framing grievances in local economic terms and in emphasizing the fishermen's leadership of the grassroots movement. The David-and-Goliath imagery of fishermen in wooden boats confronting battleships at sea was evocative and built international sympathy for Vieques's cause, but the movement's failure to highlight the live bombing of an inhabited island was a lost opportunity for building broader support. The Vieques solidarity network in Puerto Rico and the United States, while militant and committed, emanated almost entirely from the political left (McCaffrey, 1998). This contrasted significantly with the more recent movement, in which solidarity was extremely broad and cut across class, religion, and political affiliation. Puerto Rico- and U.S.-based supporters perceived the anticolonial dimensions of the case but were discouraged by local activists from developing the political dimensions of the struggle. Tensions erupted over questions of leadership, with local Viequense activists asserting the right to frame the terms and direction of the struggle. When Puerto Rico-based supporters burned an American flag at a demonstration at the Roosevelt Roads Naval Station in Ceiba, fractures developed in the movement, with some members arguing that outside forces were attempting to hijack the struggle as a platform for the independence movement.

On a local level, the focus on fishermen and male leadership limited women's participation in the movement. Vieques women were involved in the mobilization, but their participation was often auxiliary. They picketed, demonstrated, wrote pamphlets, and cooked rice and beans for protesters but did not give press conferences, travel on lecture circuits, or rise to leadership positions. Circumscribing the participation of half of the population limited potential sources of creativity and solidarity. Women often play instrumental roles in community-based mobilizations, especially when they perceive threats to their internalized domestic or caretaking roles (Kaplan, 1982; 1990). The focus on fishing traps rather than live bombing exercises, however, inhibited the growth of what Temma Kaplan (1982) has called "female consciousness."

The movement's failure can in large part be attributed to a broader political context that was hostile to Vieques's cause. The navy made clear its determination to hold onto Vieques and sought to squelch the movement by dividing it.[3] The military attempted to build a civilian constituency on the island by hiring 100 residents to work on the base as civilian security guards. It hired a community-relations official to organize a militant pro-navy support group that held pro-military counterdemonstrations calling the protesters' patriotism into question. By focusing the debate on politics, the group aimed to drive a wedge between local residents and Puerto Rican leftist supporters. Increasingly, the navy and its support group sought to undermine the movement by depicting it as a communist insurgency run by outside agitators. It arrested demonstrators for

---

3. Vice Admiral G.E.R. Kinnear II testified that Vieques was crucial to maintaining the U.S. edge in the balance of power with the Soviet Union: "The essential element that provides the U.S. navy its advantage over the Soviets is our ability to deploy high performance aircraft, that is, carrier aviation. They have us outnumbered in submarines and surface ships. Only in the area of high performance aircraft at sea do we have the edge. The Roosevelt Roads training complex, of which Vieques is an integral part, is absolutely essential in enabling us to maintain that margin" (quoted in Langley, 1985: 274).

trespassing on navy land and moved the conflict into the federal court system, which was largely sympathetic to its position. In court, protest was treated as a threat to national security and, again, the protesters' patriotism was called into question.

One particular case marked a turning point for the movement. When a Puerto Rican social activist arrested for trespassing on federal property died under suspicious circumstances in a federal prison, a veil of violence and terror descended upon Vieques's struggle.[4] The following month, clandestine factions of the Puerto Rican independence movement issued a response. On December 4, 1979, gunmen ambushed a busload of navy personnel in Sabana Seca, killing two sailors and wounding ten others. Several radical groups claimed responsibility for the attack, calling it retaliation for the death of David Sanes Rodríguez and two young *independentistas* murdered at Cerro Maravilla. The incident sent shock waves across Puerto Rico and the United States and caused horror in Vieques.[5]

Under the shadow of this violence, and with deep divisions within the Vieques movement, Governor Carlos Romero Barceló intervened, signing a good-neighbor agreement with the navy (the Fortín accord of 1983) that effectively diffused protest.

Formation of a New Movement

For five decades Vieques languished as a cold-war hostage. The island suffered direct material harm as a consequence of U.S. military expansion and rivalry with the Soviets. To protest these conditions, however, was deemed anti-American and subversive. The collapse of the Soviet Union in 1991 changed the contours of debate. The end of the cold war changed the political climate in Puerto Rico, diminishing the intensity of the anticommunist sentiment that had long constrained political expression. Geopolitical shifts triggered a reevaluation and restructuring of the U.S. military. In this context, local activists launched new grassroots efforts to build consensus for a withdrawal of the military from Vieques. The military's resistance to moderate efforts at political change was the catalyst for protest.

---

4. Angel Rodríguez Cristóbal was found dead in his prison cell two months into a six-month jail term on trespassing charges. Prison officials declared his death a suicide, but an independent autopsy concluded that he had been beaten to death.
5. The incident and the subsequent government cover-up shook the foundations of the Puerto Rican political system. For further discussion, see Aponte Pérez (1995) and Suárez (1987).

Because the United States was reassessing its military installations after the cold war, activists initially sought to have Vieques included on the federal list of military facilities to be closed. By drawing in a mix of citizens of different ages, classes, partisan political affiliation, and history of participation, they aimed to form a new group that would lobby for change. After collecting hundreds of signatures and traveling to Washington to advance their cause, activists were dismayed when Carlos Romero Barceló, now Puerto Rican resident commissioner in Washington, intervened with compromise legislation. Romero proposed leaving the eastern bombing range under military control but recovering 8,000 acres of land in the west that was being used for ammunition storage and was of questionable value for national defense. While activists were skeptical of Romero's motives, his intervention suggested a shifting political context. The advocacy of a member of the Partido Nuevo Progresista (PNP, pro-statehood party), which was widely regarded in Puerto Rico as the most pro-U.S. party, conferred legitimacy on the new movement.

The navy moved to thwart Romero's proposal. In the midst of efforts to reclaim land, it announced plans to erect a "relocatable-over-the-horizon-radar" (ROTHR) station on some of the western land under consideration for civilian use. Developed by the Raytheon Company during the cold war to monitor Soviet fleets in the Pacific Northwest, this sophisticated radar system now had a new purpose: to scan the Caribbean and Latin America for aircraft carrying drugs to and from the United States. Governor Pedro Rosselló hailed it as an important contribution to the war against drug trafficking, and it gave the navy a new reason to hold onto 8,000 acres of land.

In Vieques, the perceived health threat of the radar became a rallying point for new opposition to the navy. Residents were increasingly concerned about contamination from military explosives and reports of high levels of certain kinds of cancer in the community. The secretive nature of military activity and the community's lack of access to information intensified fear and suspicion. The navy's determination to build the cluster of 34 towers, ranging in height from 71 to 125 feet, despite local health concerns and the uncertainty of scientific evidence, inflamed passions. The movement against the radar system expanded to Puerto Rico, where a sister station was to be erected in Lajas.

The opposition developed into a coalition movement with fronts in Vieques and Lajas. While in Vieques the focus was mainly on the health and environmental consequences of the radar facility, in Lajas protesters resisted the seizure of agricultural land in the Puerto Rican heartland. The emphasis on defending the land was reminiscent of struggles against strip mining and the privatization of Puerto Rican beaches in the 1960s (Nieves Falcón, García Rodríguez, and Ojeda Reyes, 1971). By 1995 there was mass support for the struggle. In

October tens of thousands of demonstrators converged on the streets of San Juan in one of the largest mobilizations in Puerto Rico in years. Delegations from Lajas and Vieques had effectively mobilized both cultural nationalist sentiment about the land and fear of electromagnetic radiation. Confrontation over military expansion and encroachment had been channeled into discussion about the environment and health.

The coalition that Vieques and Lajas activists forged was a fundamental aspect of the broad-based anti-navy movement that emerged in Vieques in 1999. The radar mobilization renewed the solidarity network between activists in Vieques and in Puerto Rico. In contrast to the 1970s movement, in which Viequenses were wary of losing control of the movement to outsiders, the radar struggle was waged as a common struggle against military imposition. Significantly, the Catholic Church lent its support to the Viequenses' struggle for health.

The antiradar mobilization pointed to a shifting political climate in Puerto Rico as a whole. Three years later, the island was gripped by a massive general strike in response to the Rosselló administration's plan to sell the state-owned telephone company to the U.S.-based GTE Corporation. The battle over the telephone company evolved into a broader struggle against privatization and U.S. imposition. For 48 hours in early July 1998, more than half a million workers and students shut down most government offices, universities, the ports, public buses, taxis, and numerous private businesses (González, 1998). With a broad coalition of labor, student, environmental, community, cultural, political, and religious groups standing behind the telephone workers' unions, the strike was christened "the People's Strike." All over the island, thousands of Puerto Rican flags symbolized support for the telephone company and the nation. The struggle signaled a new militancy and consensus on the island and became an important precedent for the struggle that unfolded in Vieques.

Mobilizing for Peace

David Sanes Rodríguez's death opened a new chapter in a decades-long story of conflict between the U.S. Navy and the residents of Vieques Island. From a short-term perspective, the movement was built on six years of grassroots organizing and coalition building. Viewed more broadly, however, it was an expression of a shift in the Puerto Rican political landscape. Hundreds of thousands of Puerto Ricans throughout Puerto Rico and the diaspora put aside political and religious differences to rally behind the cause of Vieques. Puerto Rican celebrities such as Ricky Martin spoke out on behalf of the island's cause. In New York, the Puerto Rican Day parade, long a symbol of ethnic pride that shied away from politics, embraced the cause of Vieques. U.S.-based politicians traveled to Vieques, viewing their support of the struggle there as important to their electoral ambitions back home. Vieques not only captured the daily headlines of Puerto Rican newspapers but entered the mainstream debate in the United States, with President Bill Clinton publicly expressing regret over David Sanes's death.

The Vieques movement evolved from a local struggle over military encroachment into a mass mobilization with international support. A key factor in the movement's expansion was the strategic decision to frame grievances in more universal terms, as a struggle for peace. The framework of peace appealed to a wide constituency. While in North America and Europe pacifism has been viewed as morally suspect, in Puerto Rico peace offered a broad discourse that sidestepped partisan debate over colonialism. The discourse initially emanated from the Catholic Church and drew on both traditional religious ideology and more progressive notions of social justice. The struggle for peace, however, also linked Vieques's cause to the international peace movement, nonviolent resistance, and opposition to militarism. The broad discourse drew in a multi-class constituency of veteran activists, women, youth, the elderly, and the formerly unaffiliated in Vieques. In Puerto Rico and the United States, it attracted university students, the labor movement, the religious sector, the political left, and the average citizen.

Peace functioned as a broad ideology that was interpreted in different ways by the coalition movement. From the earliest days of the mobilization, mainstream religious institutions supported Vieques's cause as a struggle against militarism, war, and violence. The Catholic Bishop of Caguas, Alvaro Corrado del Río, traveled to Vieques to officiate at Sanes's funeral mass, signaling concern for the case at the very highest level of the Catholic Church in Puerto Rico. Corrado called for the immediate exit of the navy, the liberation of Puerto Rico from military domination, and the practice of civil disobedience to stop the bombing (El Nuevo Din, May 23, 1999). He was backed by the archbishop of San Juan, Roberto González Nieves, who traveled to New York calling for peace and justice for Vieques. Corrado launched a campaign of "white flags for peace," and Vieques was soon awash in white flags hung from doorposts, clotheslines, windowboxes, and car antennas all over the island.

The newly formed Vieques Women's Alliance also decided to adopt the symbolism of peace in its organizing efforts. Despite initial organizational meetings in which Vieques women expressed concern about cancer and health, activists elected to emphasize women's concerns for peace in their rhetoric and imagery. It was hard to prove that the navy caused cancer on the island, one activist explained, whereas peace was a universally recognized basic human right.

The Women's Alliance attached white ribbons to the chain-link fence of Camp García as a testament to Viequenses' desire for peace and encouraged supporters to wear white ribbons as a symbol of that desire. "Everyone loves the ribbons," noted a leading activist. "We in Puerto Rico operate on symbols. On the surface, the white ribbon seems so innocent, feminine and nice. It's appealing. Everyone says, 'Give me a ribbon. I'll wear that.' But the more people see the ribbons, the more they think of Vieques. It raises consciousness."

Activists from the political left used peace as a discourse to internationalize their claims—to link Vieques's struggle to global problems of inequality, war, and militarism. They traveled to peace conferences in India, Hawaii, Okinawa, and Korea. Nobel Peace Prizewinners—the Dalai Lama and Rigoberta Menchú —spoke out on behalf of peace for Vieques, while Oscar Arias traveled to Vieques from Costa Rica. In New York, where organized support for the Vieques cause emanated from the political left, activists combined the call for peace with more militant rhetoric. The Puerto Rican Day parade of 2000 was devoted both to the struggle for peace in Vieques and to the memory of the nationalist hero Pedro Albizu Campos.

Peace informed not only discourse but tactics. The movement was strongly committed to nonviolence, a reflection of the moral support and ideological influence of religious actors in defining and directing the struggle. Protestant and Catholic leaders emphasized peace and nonviolence not only through sermons and prayers but through training programs in civil disobedience. All of the participants in the Catholic encampment on the bombing range, for example, received training in nonviolence and catechism. Activists took their protest directly to the bombing range to block naval exercises. They chained the gates of the base shut and blocked access with church pews on which elderly protesters sat vigil and said the rosary. They marched, picketed, and clanged pots and pans in the street. Their militancy was tempered, however, by the commitment to nonviolence that gave discipline and focus to the movement.

The solid backing of the religious sector gave Vieques's struggle a new legitimacy and moral authority.[6] Church involvement helped change the cold-

---

6. The Catholic Church's advocacy for social justice and an end to the bombing in Vieques marked a new development in Puerto Rico. Historically, the Church has acted as a conservative force in Puerto Rican society. In the 1960s, when liberation theology swept across Latin America, it remained focused on doctrine, protesting not social injustice but birth control. Protestant churches as well shied away from political involvement. During Vieques's movement in the 1970s, the Catholic Church and the religious sector in general were absent from the struggle with two exceptions: Bishop Antulio Parrilla was a strong supporter of efforts to remove the navy and participated in civil disobedience on the island, and the U.S.-based American Friends Service Committee also supported the movement in the 1970s.

war framework that depicted protest as anti-American or communist-inspired. With priests and ministers throughout Vieques and Puerto Rico celebrating its work for peace, the movement expanded. Conservative denominations such as the Baptist church in Vieques spoke out against the "sinful" naval bombing exercises. Individuals who had never felt comfortable participating in demonstrations joined prayer vigils for peace. What was particularly interesting was Catholics' ability to form a coalition with mainline Protestant and Pentecostal churches. Tensions between Catholicism and Protestantism in Puerto Rico extended back to the U.S. occupation of 1898, when the United States encouraged Protestant missionaries to convert, "civilize," and "Americanize" the largely Roman Catholic island. The arrival of Pentecostalism in 1916 with its fundamentalism and socially conservative morality further polarized the religious denominations on the island (McGrath, 2000). The struggle to halt the bombing in Vieques brought together Catholics, Baptists, Disciples of Christ, Episcopalians, Lutherans, Methodists, Presbyterians, United Evangelicals, and even Pentecostals.

The unity of the religious sector was important on two levels. First, it formed a very dramatic model of consensus building on an island deeply divided along religious and political lines. Second, the coalition formed by the different religious denominations emerged as a powerful alternative to the government when the Rosselló administration retreated from Vieques's cause. In the days after Sanes's death, Governor Rosselló had called for a halt to bombing in Vieques. His willingness to oppose the navy was a dramatic departure from a position of seemingly unconditional support for all things American and military.[7] He championed Vieques for a period of nine months, convening commissions on the impact of live bombing exercises on the island that called for an immediate end to the bombing, cleanup of the contaminated land, the withdrawal of the navy, and the return of the land to the islanders. Ultimately, however, he gave in to a plan pressed on Puerto Rico by the Clinton administration that would allow for continued bombing of the island, and his doing so threatened to fragment the unprecedented consensus.

The ecumenical coalition played a crucial role in maintaining the movement's momentum. Leaders rejected the compromise, upset that the pact did not include an option to halt all bombing immediately, and that the navy would be allowed to resume bombing exercises at least temporarily. They denounced

---

7. During Rosselló's administration, the National Guard took over public housing complexes as part of a very visible, militarized campaign against drug trafficking. Rosselló supported the ROTHR program and opposed Romero's efforts to return empty land in western Vieques to civilian control.

as immoral cash incentives to continue the bombing. Bishop Corrado del Río declared that "there is no bomb sufficiently small to be morally acceptable." In the face of angry denunciations by the governor, religious leaders convened the *Marcha, para la Paz de Vieques,* and on February 21, 2000, 150,000 demonstrators carrying white flags and demanding peace for Vieques massed in the streets of San Juan. The silent march of tens of thousands of white-clad demonstrators, arguably the largest mass demonstration in Puerto Rican history, marked a public repudiation of the compromise agreement. Organized with the help of *Coordinadora Todo Puerto Rico con Vieques,* a civic group connected to labor and activist networks, the demonstration asserted the public will when the weak colonial state faltered. The massive march infused the Vieques movement with energy and foreshadowed the movement's ultimate success.

Conclusion

In the 1990s, in the aftermath of the cold war, there was a wave of mass demonstrations in Puerto Rico that marked a rise in activism, militancy, and unprecedented political consensus building on the island. The struggle to halt the installation of the radar system in Vieques and Lajas, the telephone strike, and the Vieques movement demonstrated successful coalition building across party, class, religious, and territorial lines in a new political climate. A key aspect of the recent Vieques movement's success was the broad framework of peace that activists employed to advance their cause. Compared with the more circumscribed ideology developed in the 1970s, the discourse of peace allowed local activists to build a broad coalition and cultivate consensus and international solidarity. The movement's victory can be viewed as the product not only of different strategies but of new political possibilities in the post-cold-war world.

Vieques can be understood in relation to the recent wave of mobilizations that pursue radical social change without seeking state power. Like the Zapatista uprising and the Seattle demonstrations against the World Trade Organization, the Vieques movement can be seen as part of a more widespread effort to block intrusions of state power and capitalism (see Falk, 1993; Holloway, 2002). By focusing on a concrete, achievable objective—the halt to live bombing exercises—the Vieques movement was able to achieve measurable success. As in the International Campaign to Ban Landmines, activists connected a vision of world peace to a specific, winnable battle.

After more than 100 years of domination by the U.S. military, in Vieques Puerto Ricans for the first time exercised veto power (Rodríguez Beruff, 2001). By mobilizing to stop the naval bombing exercises, they challenged the structures of power that had long controlled their island. Victor Rodríguez

Domínguez (2000) notes that in the history of U.S.-Puerto Rico relations all of the major milestones have been set by the United States. The Vieques mobilization marks a "refusal to accept" (Holloway, 2002) injustices of state power.

References

Alvarez, Sonia E., Evelina Dagnino, and Arturo Escobar (eds.). 1998 *Cultures of Politics, Politics of Cultures: Re-Visioning Latin American Social Movements.* Boulder, CO: Westview Press.

Aponte Pérez, Francisco. 1995 *Las víctimas del Cerro Maravilla.* San Juan, Puerto Rico: Centro de Estudios Legales y Sociales.

Ayala, César. 2003 "Recent works on Vieques, colonialism, and fishermen." *Centro* 15 (1): 212-225.

Dávila, Arlene. 1997 *Sponsored Identities: Cultural Politics in Puerto Rico.* Philadelphia: Temple University Press.

Delgado Cintrón, Carmelo. 1989 *Culebra y la Marina de Estados Unidos.* Río Piedras, Puerto Rico: Editorial Edil.

Duany, Jorgé. 2000 Nation on the move: the construction of cultural identities in Puerto Rico and the Diaspora." *American Ethnologist 27:* 5-30.

Duany, Jorgé. 2002 *The Puerto Rican Nation on the Move: Identities on the Island and the United States.* Chapel Hill: University of North Carolina Press.

Eckstein, Susan (ed.). 1989 *Power and Popular Protest: Latin American Social Movements.* Berkeley: University of California Press.

Escobar, Arturo, and Sonia E. Alvarez (eds.). 1992 *The Making of Social Move ments in Latin America: Identity, Strategy, and Democracy.* Boulder, CO: Westview Press.

Falk, R. 1993 "The making of global citizenship." Pp. 39-50 in J.B. Childs, J. Brecher, J. Cutler (eds.), *Global Visions: Beyond the New World Order.* Boston: South End Press.

Fernández, Ronald. 1996 *The Disenchanted Island: Puerto Rico and the United States in the Twentieth Century.* New York: Praeger.

Flores, Juan. 2000 *From Bomba to Hip-Hop.* New York: Columbia University Press. Fox, R. and O. Starn (eds.). 1997 *Between Resistance and Revolution: Cultural Politics and Social Protest.* New Brunswick: Rutgers University Press.

González, Juan. 1998 "'Puerto Rico had never seen anything like it.'" *Progressive 62* (9): 24-27'.

Hellman, Judith Adler. 1997 "Social movements: revolution, reform and reaction." *NACLA* 30 (6):13-18.

Holloway, John. 2002 *Change the World without Taking Power: The Meaning of Revolution Today.* London: Pluto Press.

Kaplan, Temma. 1982 "Female consciousness and collective action: the case of Barcelona, 1910-1918." *Signs?:* 545-560.

Kaplan, Temma. 1990 "Community and resistance in women's political cultures." *Dialectical Anthropology'*15: 259-264.

Langley, Lester. 1985 "Roosevelt Roads, Puerto Rico, U.S. Naval Base 1941-," in Paolo E. Coletta with K. Jack Bauer (eds.), *United States Navy and Marine Corps Bases, Overseas.* Westport, CT: Greenwood Press.

McCaffrey, Katherine T. 1998 "Forging solidarity: politics, protest, and the Vieques support network." In Andres Torres and José Velázquez (eds.), *The Puerto Rican Movement: Voices from the Diaspora.* Philadelphia: Temple University Press.

McCaffrey, Katherine T. 2002 *Military Power and Popular Protest: The U.S. Navy in Vieques, Puerto Rico.* New Brunswick: Rutgers University Press.

McGrath Andino, Lester. 2000 "The American intifada: the United States Navy and the Puerto

Rican civil disobedience campaign in Vieques (a case in church-state conflict)." Paper presented at the interdisciplinary conference "Hispanic Churches in American Public Life," Santa Barbara, CA, September 1-2. Morris, Nancy. 1995 *Puerto Rico: Culture, Politics, and Identity.* Westport, CT: Praeger.

Negrón-Muntaner, Frances, and Ramón Grosfoguel (eds.). 1997 *Puerto Rican Jam: Essays on Culture and Politics.* Minneapolis: University of Minnesota Press.

Nieves Falcón, Luis, Pablo García Rodríguez, and Félix Ojeda Reyes. 1971 *Puerto Rico: Grito y Mordaza.* Río Piedras, Puerto Rico: Ediciones Libreria Internacional.

Rodríguez Beruff, Jorge. 2001 "Vieques and Puerto Rican politics." Paper presented at the symposium "None of the Above: Puerto Rican Politics and Culture in the New Millennium," New Brunswick, NJ.

Rodríguez Domínguez, Victor M. 2000 (September) "Vieques movement redefines U.S./Puerto Rico relations." *Politico Magazine* 3 (22). (www.politicomagazine .com).

Smith, Daniel. 2000 "The disappearing welcome mat." *Weekly Defense Monitor* (Center for Defense Information) 4 (38). (www.cdi.org).

Suárez, Manuel. 1987 *Requiem on Cerro Maravilla: The Police Murders in Puerto Rico and U.S. Government Cover-Up.* Maplewood, NJ: Waterfront Press..

Tugwell, Rexford G. 1976 *The Stricken Land: The Story of Puerto Rico.* New York: Greenwood Press.

U.S. House of Representatives. 1981 Committee on Armed Services, Report of the Panel to Review the Status of Navy Training Activities on the Island of Vieques, Puerto Rico. 96th Congress, 2d session, no. 31.

THE DIASPORA FACTOR: STATESIDE *BORICUAS* AND THE FUTURE OF PUERTO RICO

The role of the more than 4 million stateside Puerto Ricans in determining the future political status of Puerto Rico has been a recurring theme since at least the 1960s. This question has become more significant in the twenty-first century; according to census figures and documented in the report *Atlas of Stateside Puerto Ricans* (2004), since 2003, the number of Puerto Ricans living stateside exceeded those on the island for the first time. In 2010, the U.S. Census counted 4.2 million Puerto Ricans living stateside and 3.8 million in Puerto Rico. This pattern has continued, with the stateside Puerto Rican population growing faster than that on the island; indeed, from 2000 to 2010, Puerto Rico's population actually decreased.

Despite the so-called "Serrano Amendment," sponsored by Bronx Congressman José Serrano, recent proposals to the U.S. Congress to sponsor status plebiscites, while consistently failing to gain support, have included

From Angelo Falcón, *NACLA Report on the Americas.* Copyright © 2007 by the North American Congress on Latin America, 38 Greene Street, New York, NY 10013. Reprinted with permission.

provisions to provide island-born Puerto Ricans living stateside the right to participate in those votes. However, in 2011, Puerto Rico Governor Luis Fortuño proposed a local status plebiscite to the Puerto Rico legislature that, to the surprise of many, did not include the participation of stateside Puerto Ricans. This, therefore, remains an unresolved issue, as does the future political status of Puerto Rico.

Puerto Rican migration patterns in the past two decades have undergone significant changes that have had profound effects on Puerto Rican politics stateside and in Puerto Rico itself. As noted above, the 2010 census found that from 2000 to 2010, Puerto Rico experienced a net population decline of 300,000. Traditional Puerto Rican migration patterns in this period changed dramatically as the main stateside destination shifted from New York to Florida. This shift was characterized by many as largely a "brain drain" from Puerto Rico, as many professionals left the island for these new destinations. The result is a new geographical polarization in the stateside Puerto Rican population, with poorer Puerto Ricans still residing in the northeast and midwest and more affluent Puerto Ricans living in the southern and southwestern United States.

The proposed plebiscite discussed below ultimately failed to get the support of the U.S. Congress. This article attempts to provide some historical perspective on the issues involved. —Angelo Falcón

The debate over the future political status of Puerto Rico has appeared once again in the U.S. Congress, raising the question of what role the nearly four million Puerto Ricans living stateside will play in this debate. Two competing House bills, both proposed by Puerto Rican representatives, call for Puerto Ricans to express their preference for statehood, commonwealth, independence, or even for an associated republic in a new plebiscite. The Puerto Rico Democracy Act, proposed in February [2007] by Representative José Serrano (D-NY), calls for a two-stage referendum in which voters would first be asked whether they prefer to maintain Puerto Rico's current commonwealth status or pursue a permanent solution. If the status quo option prevailed, the plebiscite would be repeated every eight years until a permanent option was chosen. If a permanent solution won, a second plebiscite would ask voters to choose between statehood and independence.

The bill mirrors the recommendations of a report released in December 2005 by the White House Task Force on the Status of Puerto Rico; the task force was commissioned by President Clinton, and continued by the Bush administration, to reach a permanent solution following the results of the last plebiscite in 1998. A majority of voters in that vote, 50.3%, chose "none of the above," a result of a boycott of the vote by the pro-commonwealth party, the Popular Democratic

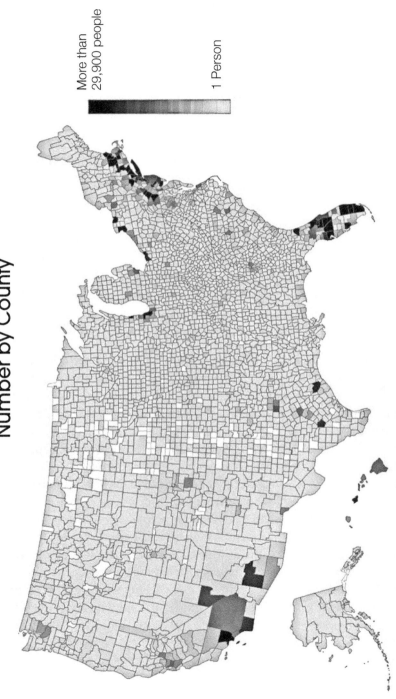

Puerto Ricans in the United States, 2010
Number by County

More than
29,900 people

1 Person

Party (PPD), which objected to how its status option was defined on the ballot.

Meanwhile, Representative Nydia Velázquez (D-NY), who criticized the presidential task force for failing to include Puerto Ricans, introduced the Puerto Rico Self-Determination Act, which calls for the formation of a constitutional convention to elect local representatives who would themselves draft the plebiscite to choose among statehood, independence, and a new "enhanced commonwealth" option. The outcome of that plebiscite would then be presented to Congress for approval.

Both bills are viewed by opposing island political parties as biased—Serrano's toward statehood and Velázquez's toward a commonwealth victory. This perceived difference in perspective between two Puerto Rican politicians from the same party and the same state highlights new complications in the island's diaspora with regard to the status question, complications that make forging a common agenda difficult. Indeed, the stateside Puerto Rican population has always had a problematic relationship with Puerto Rico. Especially since the post–World War II great migration, this has been a movement of people tied to the failure of Puerto Rico's economy and symbolizing a colonial dilemma magnified by the population's concentration for so many decades of the twentieth century in the international city of New York.[1]

The diaspora has always been a bit of a mystery in terms of its attitudes toward its homeland. Because they were now participants in the world's most advanced economy, were they now supporters of statehood for Puerto Rico? Because they left during the long-term regime of the pro-Commonwealth political party, did they support the status quo? Or did their racialization in the United States make them support independence?[2] And, in the end, does this matter to the future of Puerto Rico?

* * *

One of the most striking recent developments in the Puerto Rican experience was the realization that in 2003 the size of the stateside Puerto Rican community exceeded that of the island for the first time.[3] The latest census figures

---

1. Gabriel Haslip-Viera, Angelo Falcón, and Félix Matos-Rodríguez, eds., *Boricuas in Gotham: Puerto Ricans in the Making of Modern New York City* (Princeton, NJ: Markus Wiener Publishers, 2005).

2. Ramón Grosfoguel, *Colonial Subjects: Puerto Ricans in a Global Perspective* (Berkeley: University of California Press, 2003).

3. Angelo Falcón, *Atlas of Stateside Puerto Ricans* (Puerto Rico Federal Affairs Administration, 2004). The figure for Puerto Rico indicates the number of residents who identified as Puerto Rican in the census's so-called Hispanic question.

.

estimate that in 2005 there were about 3,780,000 Puerto Ricans living in the States compared with about 3,670,000 in Puerto Rico.[4] This has generated considerable discussion in Puerto Rico and in the diaspora, signaling that the stateside Puerto Rican community may now be in a position to redefine its relationship to the island.

While there have always been strong connections between Puerto Rico and the stateside Puerto Rican community through family ties and migration, it wasn't until the 1990s that this relationship took on an increasingly political nature. It was then that the stateside Puerto Rican community increased its representation in the U.S. House of Representatives from one to three—two members from New York and one from Chicago, all Democrats. This increased representation resulted from the growth of the Puerto Rican population and its ability to more effectively use the federal Voting Rights Act in redistricting. Puerto Rico, on the other hand, continues to elect only one nonvoting resident commissioner to Congress (currently Luis Fortuño, a Republican).

During this period, political elites and activists in Puerto Rico increasingly turned to the stateside Puerto Rican leadership for support on local issues. Whether it was securing favorable U.S. federal policies toward Puerto Rico in terms of tax policy or social welfare expenditures or the campaign to get the U.S. Navy out of Vieques, the three stateside Puerto Rican congressional representatives became invaluable and reliable allies, along with many Puerto Rican officials at the state and local levels.

Supporting this relationship was the strong nationalist identity of many stateside Puerto Ricans manifesting itself in myriad parades, festivals, and cultural events throughout the United States. Culminating in early June every year with the massive National Puerto Rican Day Parade in New York City, Puerto Rican nationalism and interest in Puerto Rico remain high. This nationalism has been buttressed by the "Latin music explosion" starting at the end of the 1990s in which Puerto Rican entertainers have played a major role. The successful campaigns to free Puerto Rican political prisoners, which led to pardons and clemency under presidents Carter and Clinton, demonstrated a level of nationalism that many in the United States found confounding.

But new socioeconomic and political developments both stateside and in Puerto Rico have complicated this relationship in ways that make building a common agenda difficult. The model for some is the powerful U.S. Israeli lobby, but this model has proved hard to emulate in the Puerto Rican case. First,

---

4. U.S. Bureau of the Census, American Community Survey, 2005.

.

the stateside members of the Puerto Rican congressional delegation don't always agree on central issues, especially as their seniority increases and their ties to different political sectors in Puerto Rico deepen.

Second, while historically concentrated in the Northeast, especially New York City, and the Midwest, the U.S. Puerto Rican population has not only increased but become more dispersed during the last two decades.[5] In the 1990s, the Puerto Rican population in Florida dramatically increased, making it the state with the second largest concentration. Puerto Rican populations are also growing fast in other parts of the South, in smaller cities, and in suburban and ex-urban areas where a Puerto Rican presence is new. This new geographical distribution has been accompanied by new patterns of migration from Puerto Rico and new professional and middle classes moving to these new areas, prompting the potential for a new north-south economic polarization whose political implications have yet to become fully clear. These demographic changes trigger challenges to the more traditional stateside Puerto Rican political and economic narratives—those of a Northeast urban population loyal to the Democratic Party and New Deal policies.

Third, in Puerto Rico the traditional status-based colonial political party system has become increasingly difficult to manage, with political deadlock among the parties and the loss of the tax incentives that formerly attracted U.S. capital, along with ineffective economic management and multiple corruption scandals. With the U.S. Congress now considering proposals for resolving Puerto Rico's status in the midst of a presidential election, this polarization will only intensify.

* * *

Although Puerto Ricans have been migrating to the United States since the mid-1800s, it wasn't until after World War II that the size of this migration became enormous and subject to efforts to manage it from both the colony and the metropolis. The out-migration from Puerto Rico as an integral part of its economic development planning, which was based on neo-Malthusian principles, led in 1948 to the establishment of New York City's Migration Division of Puerto Rico's Department of Labor. This became the mechanism by which the government of Puerto Rico tried to steer Puerto Rican labor flows and negotiate on workers' behalf with U.S. local, state, and federal authorities.

---

5. Carmen Teresa Whalen and Víctor Vázquez-Hernández, eds., *The Puerto Rican Diaspora: Historical Perspectives* (Philadelphia: Temple University Press, 2005).

In 1986, this division, which now had offices in several states, was seen as a way to create a U.S. Israeli lobby–type operation, and the then pro-commonwealth governor elevated it to the status of the cabinet-level Department of Puerto Rican Affairs in the United States. This status was short-lived when, in 1992, the statehood party candidate was elected to the governorship, which resulted in the new department's being replaced by a lobbying operation called the Puerto Rican Federal Affairs Administration (PRFAA).[6]

Depending on which political party was in power, this new office's relationship to the stateside Puerto Rican community changed in dramatic ways. Generally similar in function to foreign consulates, PRFAA differs in technically being a part of the U.S. government and in representing people who are all already U.S. citizens. Under the commonwealth party, this office collaborated closely with the stateside Puerto Rican political leadership, but under the statehood party the relationship was less friendly and often hostile. With the current divided government, the pro-commonwealth governor, Aníbal Acevedo Vilá, has turned the office into a Washington, D.C.–focused lobbying and public relations operation whose relationship to the stateside Puerto Rican community has focused on narrowly partisan concerns. Pressure to change the mission of this agency in this way was prompted in large part because the divided government in Puerto Rico replicated itself in Washington, D.C., where Resident Commissioner Fortuño [now Governor of Puerto Rico—ed.] is a pro-statehood Republican, while the governor is pro-commonwealth and identified with the Democratic Party.

One reason for this uncertainty about how Puerto Rico political elites related to the stateside Puerto Rican community was the lack of information about the political status preferences of the diaspora. This became a practical political problem for these colonial politicians as the stateside population grew larger and more politically engaged and began in the mid-1960s to demand a voice in determining Puerto Rico's future status. After a 1967 plebiscite held on the island, the stateside community demanded, with increasing intensity, the right to participate in these votes. Today, the major bills before Congress make some provisions for the stateside Puerto Rican community to directly participate in this status-definition process.

But knowledge on how stateside Puerto Ricans would vote on the future political status of Puerto Rico remains a problem because they have not been

---

6. Jorge Duany, *The Puerto Rican Nation on the Move: Identities on the Island and in the United States* (Chapel Hill: University of North Carolina Press, 2002), chapter 7.

recently polled on this issue, despite extensive such polling on the status issue in Puerto Rico. The most reliable survey conducted on the subject was the Latino National Political Survey (LNPS), conducted in 1989–1990.[7] It found that more than two thirds (69%) of stateside Puerto Ricans supported commonwealth status. But since then there have been major changes in the social, geographical, and political composition of this community; it is not at all clear what its status preferences are today. One further complication is that most stateside Puerto Rican leaders and activists support independence. In a national Web survey conducted of this elite group in 2006, it was found that 45% supported independence, while in the 1989–1990 LNPS, fewer than 4% of stateside Puerto Rican adults did.[8] It is doubtful that there has been a large pro-independence surge in the stateside community since then and more likely that pro-statehood sentiment has grown, as has been the case in Puerto Rico. The status preferences of the stateside community may now be similar to those of Puerto Rico, but this is only speculation.

The pro-independence preference of a plurality of the stateside leadership and activists has complicated the process in interesting ways. It has made the stateside Puerto Rican more open to controversial issues like freeing Puerto Rican political prisoners and supporting the ouster of the U.S. Navy from Vieques. It has also made it easier for the pro-commonwealth party to deal politically with the those leaders, while the pro-statehood party finds itself at odds with this large sector of the stateside Puerto Rican political leadership. This characteristic of the diaspora community's political experience has been little studied or understood, but it continues to have a major impact on that community's relationship to the politics of its homeland.

The role of the stateside Puerto Rican community in determining the future political status of Puerto Rico becomes further complicated by new socioeconomic changes and the changing narrative of race in the United States. Stateside Puerto Ricans, once the poster children for the urban underclass, have developed a more layered economic reality over the past couple of decades. Whereas once the major policy agenda for the stateside leadership was the issue of persistent poverty, there are now more voices joining the U.S. left in focusing the political agenda on the plight of the middle class. But while the community's

---

7. Rodolfo O. de la Garza, Louis DeSipio, F. Chris Garcia, John Garcia, and Angelo Falcón, eds., *Latino Voices: Mexican, Puerto Rican, and Cuban Perspectives on American Politics* (Boulder, CO: Westview Press, 1992), p. 104.
8. Angelo Falcón, *Stateside Puerto Rican Activist Findings* (unpublished manuscript, National Institute for Latino Policy, August 2006).

poverty rate has dropped significantly over the past 30 years, in 2005 it stood at 23%, compared with 8% for non-Latino whites. (For further comparison, in 2006, the poverty rate in Puerto Rico stood at an appalling 45%.[9])

* * *

While experiencing a persistently high poverty rate, the stateside Puerto Rican community finds itself challenged to reframe its agenda in ways that may undermine its economic base. Poverty remains a serious problem in the stateside communities of the Northeast and Midwest, but less of a problem in the newer ones in the South and Southwest. How can the stateside Puerto Rican community recast its policy priorities as it also experiences such a potential economic polarization along regional lines? And how will this affect its relationship to the politics of Puerto Rico and the status question?

The stateside Puerto Rican community has been formally a part of the United States since the annexation of Puerto Rico in 1898, has had U.S. citizenship since the 1917 Jones Act, and has even had a presence within the states well before then. But along with second- and later-generation Latinos, Puerto Rican issues have become less visible because of the growing attention to the controversial problem of immigration. Although Puerto Ricans have been negatively impacted by the racist backlash from this immigration debate, policy makers at all levels of government and in the private sector have difficulty focusing on the specificities of the Puerto Rican condition and how it differs from those of new immigrants and noncitizens.

With its policy and political agendas at one of those messy crossroads, it is not particularly clear which road the stateside Puerto Rican community will be taking, now that the issue of its formal participation in resolving the status question is no longer a matter of debate. But whether the diaspora will come down on the side of statehood, commonwealth, or associated republic is not at all clear. Independence? Well, that's another story about the failure of a movement and the power of the United States' new imperialism.

---

9. Edna Acosta-Belén and Carlos E. Santiago, eds., *Puerto Ricans in the United States: A Contemporary Portrait* (Boulder, CO: Lynne Rienner Publishers, 2006), chapter 5.

PART XI

PUERTO RICO IN CRISIS

INTRODUCTION

By Luis Martínez-Fernández

T he first two decades of the twenty first century have been disastrous for Puerto Rico. The-thirteen readings and documents included in this part of the book tell the story of a compounding series of developments that have brought the island to a seemingly insurmountable economic, social, and political crisis: the termination of Section 936 of the US Internal Revenue Service Code, the erosion of political autonomy and sovereignty under the Commonwealth status, the debt crisis that exploded in 2015, the deadly and destructive impact of Hurricane Maria in 2017, and the political crisis and mass popular mobilization culminating in the disgraceful resignation of Governor Ricardo "Ricky" Roselló in the summer of 2019.

In 1996, President Bill Clinton signed into law a bill that began the 10-year phase out of Section 936, which since 1976 provided tax exemptions or reductions for US corporate profits as long as they were reinvested in Puerto Rico. This began a decade-long count down that ended in 2006. Precisely that year, the government ran out of operating funds and temporarily furloughed all nonessential public employees. Beginning in 2005, Puerto Rico entered a prolonged—still running—streak of consecutive years of falling (or stagnant) GDP growth rates.

While some scholars and observers of Puerto Rican reality question the extent of the impact of the demise of Section 936 (see report by Arthur MacEwan), it is a fact that Puerto Rico's manufacturing sector fell sharply from around 150,000 manufacturing jobs in 1997 to around 100,000 in 2007. Puerto Rico's recession was compounded by the US and worldwide recessions that erupted two years later but the island did not join in their recovery.

From the moment the United States gained colonial domination over Puerto Rico in 1899, the island's economy has depended on—and has been limited by—US legislation. The resulting balance has included some beneficial provisions such as including Puerto Rico's exports within the US tariffs system and some harmful restrictions such as limiting the transportation of goods between Puerto Rico and the United States to the US Merchant Marine, the most expensive in the world. The Commonwealth status in place since 1952, seemed to offer, as pro-Commonwealth 1996 Resident Commissioner candidate Celeste Benítez repeatedly said, "the best of both worlds": the benefits of association with the United States (i.e., Section 936) without the tax burdens levied upon residents of the fifty states (i.e., Federal Income Tax).

In recent years, the political status debate has become more complex and has intensified. Pro-Statehood Governor Pedro Rosselló (Ricardo's father) pushed through a referendum in 1993 in which none of the three traditional formulas (Commonwealth, Statehood, Independence) received a majority of the votes but a substantial percentage of the electorate (46.3) came out in support of Statehood. Re-elected in 1996, Roselló led another referendum in 1998 but this time the consultation included two other options: Free Association (a sort of Commonwealth with expanded autonomy) and "None of the Above,"—the latter of which received 50.3 percent of the votes (46.5 % voted for Statehood).

Since its creation in 2000, the President's Task Force on Puerto Rico's Status has produced reports in 2005, 2007, and 2011. The first and second reports outlined the three traditional options; differentiated the "territorial" Commonwealth status from the non-territorial (sovereign) options of Statehood and Independence; and recommended a two-phase consultation: first, for voters to express their preference for either remaining under the status quo or changing it; and second, if they favored a change of status, to select one of the two non-territorial options. Included in this part are excerpts of the 2011 Report by the President's Task Force on Puerto Rico's Status. Its recommendations include adding a fourth status option, "Free Association," and several pages of specific economic development and social improvement recommendations. The following year, Puerto Rico held yet another status plebiscite. It followed the two-phase consultation model and included the four options outlined in the 2011 report. A sample ballot is reproduced here.

Pro-Statehood leaders spinned the plebiscite's results as a victory for Statehood but others have challenged that interpretation. In response to the question "will Puerto Rico become the 51st US State?" historian Luis Martínez-Fernández offers a different reading of those results.

More recently in 2016, the US Supreme Court, while opining on a Double Jeopardy Clause case, held that Puerto Rico and the United States were not separate sovereignties, that the Commonwealth's sovereignty was subordinate to federal sovereignty where it has its origins, and that someone prosecuted in a federal court cannot be prosecuted for the same crime in a Commonwealth court.

After ten years of uncontained economic bleeding, the island's long-mounting public debt reached a critical point in the summer of 2015, when Governor Alejandro García Padilla declared the obvious, that the Commonwealth's 73-billion-dollar debt was unrepayable.

Articles by Chandler Foust and Ed Muñoz, published just a few days after Governor García Padilla's somber announcement, look into the manifold factors behind the fiscal crisis. They stress the importance of structural causes, concluding that any chance of recovery requires structural transformations, namely changes in political and economic relations with the United States.

Faust argues that savings from austerity measures were minimal and would barely make a dent on the budget deficit, let alone the crushing debt. Like many—perhaps most—observers he saw a solution in bankruptcy declaration. Because it is not a state of the Union, however, Puerto Rico cannot benefit from Chapter 9 bankruptcy protection which leads Faust to the conclusion that Statehood offered the possibility of a way out.

Muñoz, meanwhile, explores the origins of the debt crisis and finds blame in yet another Commonwealth tax concession: the triple (local, state, federal) exemption on profits from Puerto Rico's municipal bonds, which were downgraded to junk rating in 2014. Muñoz comments on the unlikelihood of Statehood and highlights the political mainstream's preferred option, the long-heralded strategy of lobbying Congress, this time for a special provision to allow the island to declare bankruptcy.

Short of giving the Commonwealth the right to declare bankruptcy, in April 2016, Congress delivered a bill to create an oversight board composed of seven presidential appointees to "achieve fiscal responsibility and access to the capital markets." Segments of the actual bill, 114th Congress, 2nd Session, H. R. 4900, are reproduced in this section. The resulting Puerto Rico Oversight, Management and Economic Stability Act (PROMESA) created the Financial Oversight and Management Board of Puerto Rico, tasked with working with the insular government toward balancing its budget and creating a fiscal plan with the primary goal of paying off the public debt.

The provisions of the law that created PROMESA expose the vulnerability of the Commonwealth status and make evident the fact that Puerto Ricans are second-class citizens who are not protected by some federal laws such as the minimum wage and are not entitled to the same levels of Medicare and other federal social programs. Could it be that the Commonwealth status now offers "the worst of both worlds?"

The economic crisis perfect storm was aggravated by yet another perfect storm: Hurricane Maria. On September 20, 2017, just two weeks after the ravaging Hurricane Irma passed close to the island's northeastern coast, Hurricane Maria struck as a category 4 hurricane with 155 mph winds. With an estimated 90 billion dollars-worth of damages, it is the most destructive hurricane to ever hit Puerto Rico. Up to that date, the deadliest hurricane had been San Ciriaco (1899) with an official estimated death toll of 3,369. For several months following Maria's destructive path, the government of Puerto Rico maintained an official death toll of 64. Widely regarded as an undercount, a team of scientists from Harvard University's T.H. Chan School of Public Health, Carlos Albizu University in Puerto Rico and the University of Colorado School of Medicine published the first scientific estimate of deaths attributable to Hurricane Maria. Included among this section's readings, "Puerto Rico: How Do We Know 3,000 People Died as a Result of Hurricane Maria?" concludes that Maria produced a death toll of about 3,000.

Hurricane Maria prompted a wave of emigration to the United States that expanded the already massive exodus that had been growing for decades. The ongoing wave had begun in the early 1980s during the world recession stemming from the period's severe oil crisis. The US Census estimated in 2000 that 3.4 million Puerto Ricans lived in the United States, a number that grew to 4.7 million in 2010. Around 2005, the Puerto Rican population residing in the 50 states surpassed the island's population. The latest census estimates (2018) include 5.68 million, 1.19 million of them in the state of Florida.

Damayra I. Figueroa's "Puerto Ricans in Florida: 2010-2017," originally published by the Center for Puerto Rican Studies in 2019, discusses the latest US Census estimate of Puerto Ricans in Florida and their demographic, educational, and economic characteristics.

The last three readings of this new part chronicle the political crisis that broke out in July 2019 and the unremitting and creative ways in which over one million Puerto Ricans responded. Luis Martínez-Fernández's essay explores the manifold long-term tensions clashing along a web of political, racial, gender, and class fault lines. Articles written by journalist Charo Henríquez and political anthropologist Yarimar Bonilla provide a silver lining to an otherwise catastrophic period by highlighting the protagonist role played by women during the protests that forced Ricardo Roselló out of office and the energy, passion, and creativity that protesters displayed.

THE EFFECT OF 936

In the late 1500s, *Situado* funds earmarked for troop salaries and the costs of fortifying San Juan began to flow into Puerto Rico. Those early allotments of silver from Mexico laid the groundwork for the island's economy's structural dependence on external subsidies, special trade concessions, and tax exemptions. Four centuries later, the United States Congress granted Puerto Rico its latest fiscal concession, known as the Section 936 of the US Internal Revenue Service Code which granted federal tax exemptions for US corporate profits that were reinvested on the island.

Dr. Hexner, founder and director of the Science Initiative Group at the Institute of Advanced Study in Princeton and Dr. Arthur MacEwan, Professor Emeritus of Economics at the University of Massachusetts in Boston, produced this report for the Congressional Task Force on Economic Growth in Puerto Rico.

Dr. Hexner and Dr. MacEwan challenge the long-hailed popular notion that Section 936 provisions were key to the island's economic performance, and that its final demise in 2006 is largely responsible for the crisis that exploded in 2016.

From the era when Rexford Tugwell governed Puerto Rico in the early 1940s, Puerto Rico has sought provisions in the U.S. tax code that provide special incentives for U.S.-based firms to operate on the island. These provisions, according to Tugwell and later Puerto Rican governments, would create a basis for Puerto Rico to catch up economically with the states. Special tax incentives have thus long been a central element in governments' economic development programs, and they are touted as promoting economic growth and increased employment.

The principal such provision was Section 936 of the federal tax code, which allowed subsidiaries of U.S. firms operating in Puerto Rico to pay no federal

J. Thomas Hexner and Arthur MacEwan, "The 936 Effect," included in Congressional Task Force on Economic Growth in Puerto Rico Report to the House and Senate, 114th Cong., December 20, 2016.

taxes on their Puerto Rican profits, even if those profits were returned to the United States (i.e., to the parent company in the states). However, the Puerto Rican government, with the concurrence of the federal government, established a 10% tax on profits that were returned to the states—a so-called "tollgate tax." But the tollgate tax would be reduced substantially (to 4% or less) if the funds were held in Puerto Rican financial institutions for a specified period. In the early 1990s, when the federal government began to consider the termination of Section 936, there was a general outcry from Puerto Rican officials. This outcry continued when the ten year phase out of 936 was set in place to begin in 1996, and the severe recession that began in 2006 is often attributed, at least in large part, to the termination of this federal tax incentive.

The phase out and termination of 936, whatever its impact on the overall Puerto Rican economy (about which more shortly), undercut a substantial gain that had accrued to the financial sector. The tollgate tax worked to the extent that 936 firms deposited a large amount of funds in Puerto Rican banks. In 1980, 936 funds amounted to 33% of all deposits in Puerto Rican commercial banks. By 1985, the figure had risen to 42%. Although the relative share of 936 deposits in the banks' total deposits dropped off in subsequent years, the role of 936 funds initiated a substantial expansion of the role of finance in the economy. Whereas in 1975, finance had accounted for 13.6% of total income, by 2000 it had risen to accounting for 23.9%.

However, the rising role of the banks did not mean that they were playing a driving role in financing productive investment. Instead, their activity was concentrated in securities trading and mortgages. It seems that the banks did relatively little to use 936 funds to support economic development and build a local basis for business activity, but they did gain a strong interest in the perpetuation of 936.

. . . .

The gains to the financial sector notwithstanding, the "conventional wisdom" in Puerto Rico regarding 936 is a myth with little connection to reality. Section 936 and similar provisions have not been a favorable, driving force of the Puerto Rican economy. Equally, the current recession cannot be attributed in significant part to the termination of 936.

Furthermore, while 936 was failing to drive the Puerto Rican economy forward, it was quite costly for the U.S. Treasury. According to a U.S. Treasury Department report, in 1987 it cost the U.S. government on average at least $1.51 in lost tax revenue for each $1.00 in wages paid in Puerto Rico by firms operating under the provisions of Section 936. Or, put another way, on average it cost at least $26,725 each year to maintain a job that was paying an annual salary of $17,725. For the pharmaceutical industry, the figures were $3.08 per $1.00 in wages, or $81,483 to maintain a job paying $26,471.

In the late 1980s and early 1990s, when the program was at the center of economic policy in Puerto Rico, annual costs (in terms of lost revenue to the U.S. Treasury) were running between $2 billion and $2.5 billion. In terms of 2016 dollars, this would amount to between $3.7 billion and $4.5 billion. This figure far exceeds the costs to the Treasury of alternative policies that would stimulate growth of the Puerto Rican economy.

The Era of 936: No Great Growth Impact

In the 1950s and 1960s, the era of Operation Bootstrap, federal (as well as local) tax incentives may have played a role in the rapid growth of the Puerto Rican economy. While 936 did not exist in those years, similar provisions were put in place, implementing Tugwell's concept that Puerto Rico needed special tax treatment to attract investment to the island. In this early period, however, the major factors pushing the expansion of output and employment were low-wage labor and privileged access to the U.S. market. As wages rose and privileged access largely disappeared (as many lower-wage parts of the world obtained virtually equal access), the tax incentives remained but economic growth faltered. Since 1980, economic growth in Puerto Rico has lagged substantially behind that in the states.

During the twenty years from the implementation of 936 in 1976 to the initiation of its phase out in 1996, real (i.e., inflation adjusted) GNP in Puerto Rico grew at an annual average rate of 2.5%, while the U.S. economy grew by 3.0% annually. That is, over this 20 year period, the U.S. economy grew 17% more than the Puerto Rican economy. In the twenty year 936 era, then, Puerto Rico was falling further and further behind the states.

The association of 936 with years of relatively poor economic performance is often obscured by the fact that growth of gross domestic product (GDP) was fairly strong in the 1970 to 2000 period. GDP growth, after all, is the standard by which a country's or a region's economic expansion is usually gauged, and between 1970 and 2000 GDP (inflation adjusted) grew at a 3.8% annual rate. Gross national product (GNP), however, expanded at an annual rate of only 2.7% in this thirty year period. By 2000, GDP was almost 50% greater than GNP. This difference was largely, if not entirely, accounted for by the profits of firms based outside of Puerto Rico—mostly in the states. The growth of GNP is a much better measure of the improvement of the Puerto Rican economy— of the well-being of the Puerto Rican people and the condition of firms based in Puerto Rico—than is GDP. This is especially the case because much of the earnings of the firms based outside of Puerto Rico has been a result of the ownership of their patents being located in Puerto Rico and of transfer pricing, both designed to locate profits, but not real activity, in Puerto Rico....

By the GNP measure, during these decades when 936 was in force, the Puerto Rican economy grew relatively slowly. In particular, by comparison with the U.S. economy in this 30 year period, Puerto Rican GNP was diverging downward, with its 2.7% annual growth rate well below the U.S. rate of 3.3%. The experience of these years is, then, hardly a brief for the success of 936 as driving the Puerto Rican economy forward.

The Decline in Manufacturing Employment

Yet manufacturing has played a large role in the Puerto Rican economy for many years, and this large role is usually attributed in large part to 936. When, from the mid-1990s onward, employment in manufacturing dropped off sharply, this was widely seen as evidence that the impending termination of this favorable tax treatment was a cause of decline. (Section 936 was phased out over the ten year period from the beginning of 1996.)

It was only after the recession began in 2006 that employment in these four sectors followed the same downward path as did manufacturing overall. Furthermore... while employment in all manufacturing fell by 28% between 1995 and 2005, employment in pharmaceuticals and medicines and in chemicals rose in that decade, by 13% and 10%, respectively. These two sectors accounted for 36% of manufacturing employment in 1995 and 53% in 2005.

Also, it is useful to compare manufacturing employment in Puerto Rico to manufacturing employment in the states.... Between 1990 and 2010, when recovery from the Great Recession began in the United States, manufacturing employment fell by 35%. In Puerto Rico, for this same period, manufacturing fell by 45%, and no recovery is yet apparent. While the decline in Puerto Rico is somewhat greater, the similar experience in the states suggests that the decline is not primarily explained by factors particular to Puerto Rico—i.e., by the termination of 936. It is more likely that import competition from low-wage areas of the world and technological change account for most of the employment decline in both Puerto Rico and the United States.

After 2006

One of the reasons that the termination of 936 is not accountable for Puerto Rico's current economic difficulties is that the advantages that U.S.-based corporations obtained from 936 did not end when this section of the federal tax code was terminated. By obtaining Controlled Foreign Corporation (CFC) status, firms were able to retain virtually all of the federal tax advantages they had had with 936. CFC status allowed the U.S.-based firms to continue to avoid U.S. taxes on their Puerto Rican operations as long as they did not return those profits to the parent corporation in the states.

Nonetheless, employment in the group of four 936 sectors . . . dropped off substantially from 2005 (except in medical supplies and equipment). Some of the employment decline can be attributed to the Great Recession in the United States, which is the principal market for the products of these firms. Something else, however, was going on, and here the switch from 936 to CFC status appears to have made a difference.

. . . .

Conclusion

The evidence does not support the claim that Section 936 was an important foundation for favorable economic expansion in Puerto Rico when it was in force or that the termination of 936 was an important factor bringing about the severe recession, which began in 2006. There is limited evidence that firms' switch from Section 936 to CFC status contributed to some extent to the employment decline of the recession. The firms themselves, however, have remained in good condition, as indicated by their post-2006 exports, and plant closings in recent years do not appear to have any substantial relation to the termination of 936 or other tax factors. The 936 myth should be abandoned.

Although manufacturing has played a major role in the Puerto Rican economy for several decades, it has not driven the economy forward nearly to the extent that has been widely believed. The role that manufacturing has played can be explained by the favorable tax advantages that have been supplied by Section 936 and CFC status, but also by tax incentives provided by the Puerto Rican government. There is no reason to believe that, absent these tax factors, Puerto Rico would have a comparative advantage that would generate a substantial role for manufacturing. While labor costs are lower in Puerto Rico than in the states, other factors raise costs—e.g., energy prices, regulations, and transportation. Moreover, labor costs are probably partly accompanied by lower levels of productivity. Consequently, it would seem reasonable to view the heavy reliance on manufacturing—a reliance that has not produced very positive results—as an artificial distortion of the Puerto Rican economy.

Rather than yearning for the return of 936, Puerto Rico would do well to abandon of the 936 myth. This recognition of reality could be one important step in laying the foundation for a new era of economic development for Puerto Rico.

PRESIDENT'S TASK FORCE REPORT

While Puerto Rican's overwhelmingly voted in the referendum of 1952 in favor of the Commonwealth Constitution, the new political status formula was not universally welcomed: 18 percent of the electorate voted to reject it. Since its inception, the Commonwealth status has been the subject of criticism from partisans of Statehood and Independence, as well as Autonomists, seeking to expand Puerto Rico's self-rule. The first of four status plebiscites/referendums took place in 1967; it was followed by similar consultations in 1993, 1998, and 2012, none of which have produced a majority preference, let alone a national consensus. Through an Executive Order, in 2000, Bill Clinton created the President's Task Force on Puerto Rico's Status. It has since produced reports in 2005, 2007 and 2011, the last of which is partially reproduced below.

Executive Summary

The President's Task Force on Puerto Rico's Status (Task Force) was created by President Clinton in 2000. The Task Force's sole focus at that time was to examine proposals for Puerto Rico's future status and for a process by which Puerto Ricans could choose a status option. President Bush continued the Task Force's sole focus on the issue of political status. The Bush Administration's Task Force issued reports in 2005 and 2007.

On October 30, 2009, President Obama signed Executive Order 13517, which directed the Task Force to maintain its focus on the status question, but added to the Task Force's responsibilities by seeking advice and recommendations on policies that promote job creation, education, health care, clean energy, and economic development on the Island.

Report of the President's Task Force on Puerto Rico's Status (2011) (excerpts)

Status Recommendations

The Task Force's public hearings and meetings revealed that status remains of overwhelming importance to the people of Puerto Rico. This Task Force committed to taking a fresh look at issues related to status without being bound by prior analyses or limited in the issues on which it focused.

Recommendation # 1: The Task Force recommends that all relevant parties— the President, Congress, and the leadership and people of Puerto Rico—work to ensure that Puerto Ricans are able to express their will about status options and have that will acted upon by the end of 2012 or soon thereafter.

The government of Puerto Rico has discussed the possibility of holding a plebiscite this summer that would seek to ascertain the will of the people of Puerto Rico concerning status. Without taking a position on the particular details of this proposal, the Task Force recommends that the President and Congress support any fair, transparent, and swift effort that is consistent with and reflects the will of the people of Puerto Rico. If the process produces a clear result, Congress should act on it quickly with the President's support.

Recommendation # 2: The Task Force recommends that the permissible status options include Statehood, Independence, Free Association, and Commonwealth. The Report provides descriptions of these options.

Recommendation # 3: Although the Task Force supports any fair method for determining the will of the people of Puerto Rico, it has a marginal preference for a system involving two plebiscites. This two plebiscite system would allow the people of Puerto Rico first to vote on the question of whether they wish to be part of the United States or wish to be independent, and then to choose between the available status options, as limited by the outcome of the first vote.

Recommendation # 4: If a plebiscite is chosen, only residents of Puerto Rico should be eligible to vote. This issue is a difficult one. But on balance, those who have committed to the Island by residing there have strong arguments that only they should vote on its future. In addition, the complexities of determining who is eligible to vote among those of Puerto Rican descent and managing a vote among a population dispersed throughout the United States and elsewhere would be daunting.

Recommendation # 5: The President and Congress should commit to preserving US citizenship for Puerto Rican residents who are US citizens at the time of any transition to Independence, if the people of Puerto Rico choose a status option that results in Puerto Rico's Independence.

Recommendation # 6: The President and Congress should ensure that Puerto Rico controls its own cultural and linguistic identity. The Task Force recognizes that, if Puerto Rico were admitted as a State, the English language would need to play—as it does today—a central role in the daily life of the Island.

Recommendation # 7: If efforts on the Island do not provide a clear result in the short term, the President should support, and Congress should enact, self-executing legislation that specifies in advance for the people of Puerto Rico a set of acceptable status options that the United States is politically committed to fulfilling.

This legislation should commit the United States to honor the choice of the people of Puerto Rico (provided it is one of the status options specified in the legislation) and should specify the means by which such a choice would be made. The Task Force recommends that, by the end of 2012, the Administration develop, draft, and work with Congress to enact the proposed legislation.

Task Force's Status Recommendations

Recommendation # 2: The Task Force recommends that the permissible status options include Statehood, Independence, Free Association, and Commonwealth.

Prior Task Force reports have identified and discussed constitutionally permissible status options. As discussed above, the Task Force took a fresh look at the issues, including the constitutional questions central to prior reports, and concluded that the permissible status options include Statehood, Independence, Free Association, and Commonwealth.

Each status option is discussed below, along with a brief mention of some of the issues that would be raised by a choice of that option.

Statehood

Statehood would result in several significant consequences for Puerto Rico and the United States, only a few of which are laid out here. If Puerto Rico became a State, citizens of Puerto Rico would be entitled to full representation in Congress, would be permitted to participate in Presidential elections, and would be eligible to receive Federal economic assistance identical to that granted to citizens of other States. This economic benefit would be offset, to some degree, by the impact of the Tax Uniformity Clause of the US Constitution, which would prevent Congress from treating Puerto Rico differently for purposes of Federal income taxes. Currently, Puerto Rican residents do not pay Federal taxes on income generated in Puerto Rico.

Congress has the ultimate authority over admission of States, and it could impose requirements on Puerto Rico prior to admission. Among other things, Congress could establish a transition period during which, for example, Federal funding could increase incrementally until parity with other States was reached and the Federal income tax could be phased in for Puerto Rican residents. Finally, including Puerto Rico as a State would affect the composition of Congress, as the new State would be entitled to two Senators as well as representation in the House of Representatives to accommodate Puerto Rico's representation in the House, Congress could increase the size of the House, reapportion the 435 representatives to include Puerto Rico, or temporarily increase the size of the House until reapportionment at the next census.

Independence

For purposes of this Report, the Task Force has assumed that Independence refers to full Independence from the United States with the prospect of government-to-government negotiation of a treaty between the United States and a new independent nation of Puerto Rico with all issues on the table Congress would need to pass specific legislation to allow the creation of a fully independent nation of Puerto Rico.

As discussed below, a key issue with respect to Independence as a status option is the impact on Puerto Ricans' US citizenship at the time of Independence. Citizenship is not, however, the only question raised by Independence. A host of issues, such as restrictions (or lack thereof) on travel to the mainland, immigration regulation, security arrangements, and economic aid would need to be specified in enabling legislation or negotiated by a subsequent treaty. It is likely that a significant transition period from the Island's current status to its future as an independent nation would be needed.

Free Association

Free Association is a type of independence. A compact of Free Association would establish a mutual agreement that would recognize that the United States and Puerto Rico are closely linked in specific ways as detailed in the compact. Compacts of this sort are based on the national sovereignty of each country, and either nation can unilaterally terminate the association.

Free Association would provide for an independent Puerto Rico with a close relationship to the United States, similar in status to the Republic of the Marshall Islands, the Federated States of Micronesia, and the Republic of Palau. The United States provides defense and various forms of economic aid to these countries and exercises control over their defense and security policy. Their citizens may work and attend schools in the United States, but they are not US citizens. As noted below, the Task Force recommends that at the time of any transition to a freely associated state, all Puerto Rican US citizens retain their US citizenship.

As with other options, Free Association could be accompanied by a transition period in which the United States would continue to administer certain services and provide economic assistance for a period of time. This option would require the Administration to consider border security and other security implications

Commonwealth

The Commonwealth option was the subject of much debate before the Task Force. The Commonwealth is commonly referred to as the "status quo" option. At the same time, however, advocates have argued for the possibility of an "enhanced" Commonwealth that would give greater political autonomy to the Island, including, in some instances, a form of autonomy bordering on Independence.

Prior Task Force reports have focused their constitutional analyses on the Commonwealth option, in particular on whether some version of "enhanced" Commonwealth was consistent with the US Constitution. The results of those reports have been embraced by some and decried by others, The Task Force and the Administration committed to taking a fresh look at status, including the question of enhanced Commonwealth. The Task Force's review has led it to a number of conclusions, which both reaffirm and depart from past Task Force reports. First, there has been confusion about what the Commonwealth option is, and is not. The use of terms like "status quo" and "enhanced Commonwealth" do not provide a complete picture for the people of Puerto Rico. Some have commented that the notion of "status quo" suggests that the laws affecting Puerto Rico cannot or will not be changed but that is not the case; indeed, Congress enacts laws every year that have profound effects throughout the country, including on the Island.

Under the Commonwealth option, Puerto Rico would remain, as it is today, subject to the Territory Clause of the US Constitution. The present Common-wealth government system in Puerto Rico has its genesis in a set of legislative enactments (whether characterized as legislation or a compact). Currently, Puerto Rico has significant local political autonomy. The Task Force believes that such autonomy should never be reduced or threatened.

Second, while some have argued that Commonwealth is not an appropriate option because it is said to be "territorial" or "temporary" in nature, the Task Force believes that it must be an available option for the people of Puerto Rico. Although prior plebiscites have been unclear in many respects, there can be no doubt that a substantial percentage of the population has indicated support for some version of Commonwealth. The Task Force recognizes that some have criticized those prior plebiscites because of the lack of clarity about the defini-tion of the Commonwealth option. The Task Force believes the remedy for this concern is to make the options as clear as possible before the next vote by the people of Puerto Rico but removing the Commonwealth option would raise real questions about the vote's legitimacy.

Third, consistent with the legal conclusions reached by prior Task Force reports, one aspect of some proposals for enhanced Commonwealth remains constitutionally problematic—proposals that would establish a relationship be-tween Puerto Rico and the Federal Government that could not be altered except by mutual consent. This was a focus of past Task Force reports. The Obama Administration has taken a fresh look at the issue of such mutual consent provisions, and it has concluded that such provisions would not be en-forceable because a future Congress could choose to alter that relationship uni-laterally (Congress similarly could elect to enact legislation violating a treaty with a foreign country or to legislate over the opposition of one or more States.)

SAMPLE BALLOT 2012 PLEBISCITE

The following document is a sample of the bilingual ballot used in the status plebiscite of November 6, 2012. It was created by New Progressive Party legislators without input from other parties. The leadership of the Popular Democratic Party opposed its use and advised its members to abstain from voting on the second question.

PAPELETA OFICIAL
OFFICIAL BALLOT

COMISIÓN ESTATAL DE ELECCIONES
STATE ELECTIONS COMMISSION
MARTES, 6 DE NOVIEMBRE DE 2012
TUESDAY, NOVEMBER 6, 2012

CONSULTA
PLEBISCITE

MODELO

SAMPLE

CONSULTA SOBRE EL ESTATUS POLÍTICO DE PUERTO RICO
PLEBISCITE ON PUERTO RICO POLITICAL STATUS

Instrucciones: Marque la opción de su preferencia. La papeleta con más de una (1) opción marcada en esta sección no será contabilizada.
Instructions: Mark your option of preference. Those ballots with more than one (1) mark in this section shall not be tallied.

¿Está usted de acuerdo con mantener la condición política territorial actual?
Do you agree that Puerto Rico should continue to have its present form of territorial status?

Sí / *Yes* | ## No / *No*

Instrucciones: Irrespectivamente de su contestación a la primera pregunta, **conteste cuál de las siguientes opciones no territoriales usted prefiere.**
Instructions: Regardless of your selection in the first question, please mark which of the following non-territorial options would you prefer.

La consulta con más de una (1) opción marcada en esta sección no será contabilizada.
Those ballots with more than one (1) mark in this Section shall not be tallied.

Estadidad:
Prefiero que Puerto Rico sea un estado de Estados Unidos de América, para que todos los ciudadanos americanos residentes en Puerto Rico tengan iguales derechos, beneficios y responsabilidades que los demás ciudadanos de los estados de la Unión, incluyendo derecho a la plena representación en el Congreso y participación en las elecciones presidenciales, y que se requiera al Congreso Federal que promulgue la legislación necesaria para iniciar la transición hacia la estadidad. Si está de acuerdo marque aquí:

Statehood:
Puerto Rico should be admitted as a state of the United States of America so that all United States citizens residing in Puerto Rico may have rights, benefits, and responsibilities equal to those enjoyed by all other citizens of the states of the Union, and be entitled to full representation in Congress and to participate in the Presidential elections, and the United States Congress would be required to pass any necessary legislation to begin the transition into Statehood. If you agree, mark here:

Independencia:
Prefiero que Puerto Rico sea una nación soberana y totalmente independiente de Estados Unidos y que se requiera al Congreso Federal que promulgue la legislación necesaria para iniciar la transición hacia la nación independiente de Puerto Rico. Si está de acuerdo marque aquí:

Independence:
Puerto Rico should become a sovereign nation, fully independent from the United States and the United States Congress would be required to pass any necessary legislation to begin the transition into independent nation of Puerto Rico. If you agree, mark here:

Estado Libre Asociado Soberano:
Prefiero que Puerto Rico adopte un estatus fuera de la Cláusula Territorial de la Constitución de Estados Unidos, que reconozca la soberanía del Pueblo de Puerto Rico. El Estado Libre Asociado Soberano se basaría en una asociación política libre y voluntaria, cuyos términos específicos se acordarían entre Estados Unidos y Puerto Rico como naciones soberanas. Dicho acuerdo dispondría el alcance de los poderes jurisdiccionales que el pueblo de Puerto Rico autorice dejar en manos de Estados Unidos retendría los restantes poderes o autoridades jurisdiccionales. Si está de acuerdo, marque aquí:

Sovereign Free Associated State
Puerto Rico should adopt a status outside of the Territory Clause of the Constitution of the United States that recognizes the sovereignty of the People of Puerto Rico. The Sovereign Free Associated State would be based on a free and voluntary political association, the specific terms of which shall be agreed upon between the United States and Puerto Rico as sovereign nations. Such agreement would provide the scope of the jurisdictional powers that the People of Puerto Rico agree to confer to the United States and retain all other jurisdictional powers and authorities. If you agree, mark here:

WILL PUERTO RICO
BECOME THE 51st US STATE

Leaders of the New Progressive Party spinned the 2012 plebiscite results as a victory for Statehood. The following reply by Luis Martínez-Fernández to the editors of the *Latin American Advisor* challenges that assertion.

Question:

In a nonbinding plebiscite on Nov. 6, Puerto Ricans endorsed statehood for the U.S. territory. At the same time, they voted out the commonwealth's pro-statehood governor, Luis Fortuño, and replaced him with Alejandro García Padilla, whose party supports the island's current status. Why did a majority of voters back statehood, yet oust the pro-statehood governor? What are the benefits and downsides to Puerto Rico becoming the 51st U.S. state? What would it take for the U.S. Congress to advance statehood for Puerto Rico?

Answer:

The results of the referendum are being portrayed as a surprising watershed in which, for the first time ever, a majority of Puerto Ricans expressed support for statehood. What appears to be an unprecedented, overwhelming preference for that status formula, when closely analyzed, reflects that in reality statehood failed to receive even a simple majority of the votes.

This distortion responds, in part, to the compounded two-question format ballot drafted by the New Progressive Party (PNP)-dominated legislature. On the first question, 54 percent of the voters responded "no" when asked if they wished to retain the current commonwealth status. Forty-six percent of voters preferred the commonwealth status.

The second question adds to the level of distortion. In this case, voters were asked to express their preference for one particular "non territorial" option. The results were Statehood (61 percent), the sovereign free associated state (33 percent), and slightly over 5 percent for independence. These percentages are misrepresentations for a couple of reasons. First, the second question left out the commonwealth option. Second, only 809,652 voters selected statehood, which is very close to the 803,407 who voted for the commonwealth in the first question. Seen this way, both options were virtually tied. Any analysis of these results must also take into consideration that the pro-commonwealth Popular Democratic Party (PPD) had called for its members to abstain from selecting any of the three options included in the second question and 472,674 voters heeded that advice.

In conclusion, the plebiscite reflected neither change nor growth in support of statehood. As far as the status issue goes, Puerto Rico is back to square one.

U.S. SUPREME COURT REINTERPRETS PUERTO RICO'S SOVEREIGNTY

In recent years, the limits of Puerto Rico's autonomy and sovereignty have been tested by all three branches of the Federal government through legislation, executive branch actions and court decisions. The Supreme Court majority decision in *Commonwealth of Puerto Rico v. Sánchez Valle et. al.* (2016) while dealing specifically with a Double Jeopardy matter, has broader implications on issues of sovereignty and autonomy. While recognizing Puerto Rico's "distinctive, indeed exceptional, status as a self-governing Commonwealth," the Court's majority opined that unlike the Union's fifty states, Puerto Rico does not have the benefit of the dual-sovereignty doctrine. Below are excerpts of the Supreme Court's majority decisions penned by Justice Elena Kagan.

SUPREME COURT OF THE UNITED STATES
Syllabus
COMMONWEALTH OF PUERTO RICO v. SANCHEZ VALLE ET AL.
CERTIORARI TO THE SUPREME COURT OF PUERTO RICO
No. 15–108. Argued January 13, 2016—Decided June 9, 2016

Respondents Luis Sánchez Valle and Jaime Gómez Vázquez each sold a gun to an undercover police officer. Puerto Rican prosecutors indicted them for illegally selling firearms in violation of the Puerto Rico Arms Act of 2000. While those charges were pending, federal grand juries also indicted them, based on the same transactions, for violations of analogous U. S. gun trafficking statutes. Both defendants pleaded guilty to the federal charges and moved to dismiss the pending Commonwealth charges on double jeopardy grounds. The trial court in each case dismissed the charges, rejecting prosecutors' arguments that Puerto

---

US Supreme Court Decision on Puerto Rico's Sovereignty as It Relates to the Double Jeopardy Clause (2016)

Rico and the United States are separate sovereigns for double jeopardy purposes and so could bring successive prosecutions against each defendant. The Puerto Rico Court of Appeals consolidated the cases and reversed. The Supreme Court of Puerto Rico granted review and held, in line with the trial court, that Puerto Rico's gun sale prosecutions violated the Double Jeopardy Clause.

. . . .

KAGAN, J., delivered the opinion of the Court, in which ROBERTS, C. J., and KENNEDY, GINSBURG, and ALITO, JJ., joined. GINSBURG, J., filed a concurring opinion, in which THOMAS, J., joined. THOMAS, J., filed an opinion concurring in part and concurring in the judgment. BREYER, J., filed a dissenting opinion, in which SOTOMAYOR, J., joined. _____ 1 Cite as: 579 U. S. ____ (2016)

SUPREME COURT OF THE UNITED STATES
No. 15–108
COMMONWEALTH OF PUERTO RICO, PETITIONER v.
LUIS M. SANCHEZ VALLE, ET AL. ON WRIT OF CERTIORARI
TO THE SUPREME COURT OF PUERTO RICO
[June 9, 2016]
JUSTICE KAGAN delivered the opinion of the Court.

In this case, we must decide if, under that test, Puerto Rico and the United States may successively prosecute a single defendant for the same criminal conduct. We hold they may not, because the oldest roots of Puerto Rico's power to prosecute lie in federal soil.

Following their pleas, Sánchez Valle and Gómez Vázquez moved to dismiss the pending Commonwealth charges on double jeopardy grounds. The prosecutors in both cases opposed those motions, arguing that Puerto Rico and the United States are different sovereigns for double jeopardy purposes, and so could bring successive prosecutions against each of the two defendants. The trial courts rejected that view and dismissed the charges. See App. to Pet. for Cert. 307a–352a. But the Puerto Rico Court of Appeals, after consolidating the two cases, reversed those decisions. See id., at 243a–306a.

The Supreme Court of Puerto Rico granted review and held that Puerto Rico's gun sale prosecutions violated the Double Jeopardy Clause. See id., at 1a–70a. The majority reasoned that, under this Court's dual-sovereignty doctrine, "what is crucial" is "[t]he ultimate source" of Puerto Rico's power to prosecute. Id., at 19a; see id., at 20a ("The use of the word 'sovereignty' in other contexts and for other purposes is irrelevant"). Because that power originally "derived from the United States Congress"—i.e., the same source on which federal prosecutors rely—the Commonwealth could not retry Sánchez Valle and Gómez Vázquez for unlawfully selling firearms. Id., at 66a. Three justices disagreed, believing that the Commonwealth and the United States are separate sovereigns. See id., at 71a–242a.

We granted certiorari, 576 U. S. ___ (2015), to determine whether the Double Jeopardy Clause bars the Federal Government and Puerto Rico from successively prosecuting a defendant on like charges for the same conduct. We hold that it does, and so affirm.

. . . .

With that background established, we turn to the question presented: Do the prosecutorial powers belonging to Puerto Rico and the Federal Government derive from wholly independent sources? See Brief for Petitioner 26–28 (agreeing with that framing of the issue). If so, the criminal charges at issue here can go forward; but if not, not. In addressing that inquiry, we do not view our decisions in Grafton and Shell Co. as, in and of themselves, controlling. Following 1952, Puerto Rico became a new kind of political entity, still closely associated with the United States but governed in accordance with, and exercising self-rule through, a popularly ratified constitution. The magnitude of that change requires us to consider the dual-sovereignty question anew. And yet the result we reach, given the legal test we apply, ends up the same. Puerto Rico today has a distinctive, indeed exceptional, status as a self-governing Commonwealth. But our approach is historical. And if we go back as far as our doctrine demands—to the "ultimate source" of Puerto Rico's prosecutorial power, Wheeler, 435 U. S., at 320—we once again discover the U. S. Congress.

Recall here the events of the mid-20th century—when Puerto Rico, just as petitioner contends, underwent a profound change in its political system. See Brief for Petitioner 1–2 ("[T]he people of Puerto Rico[] engaged in an exercise of popular sovereignty . . . by adopting their own Constitution establishing their own government to enact their own laws"); supra, at 3–4. At that time, Congress enacted Public Law 600 to authorize Puerto Rico's adoption of a constitution, designed to replace the federal statute that then structured the island's governance. The people of Puerto Rico capitalized on that opportunity, calling a constitutional convention and overwhelmingly approving the charter it drafted. Once Congress approved that proposal—subject to several important conditions accepted by the convention—the Commonwealth, a new political entity, came into being.

Those constitutional developments were of great significance—and, indeed, made Puerto Rico "sovereign" in one commonly understood sense of that term. As this Court has recognized, Congress in 1952 "relinquished its control over [the Commonwealth's] local affairs[,] grant[ing] Puerto Rico a measure of autonomy comparable to that possessed by the States." Examining Bd. of Engineers, Architects and Surveyors v. Flores de Otero, 426 U. S. 572, 597 (1976); see id., at 594 ("[T]he purpose of Congress in the 1950 and 1952 legislation was to accord to Puerto Rico the degree of autonomy and independence normally associated with States of the Union"); Rodriguez v. Popular Democratic Party, 457 U. S. 1, 8 (1982) ("Puerto Rico, like a state, is an autonomous political entity, sovereign over matters not ruled by the [Federal] Constitution" (internal quotation marks omitted)). That newfound authority, including over local criminal laws, brought mutual benefit to the Puerto Rican people and the entire United States.

. . . .

And contrary to petitioner's claim, Puerto Rico's transformative constitutional moment does not lead to a different conclusion. True enough, that the Commonwealth's power to enact and enforce criminal law now proceeds, just as petitioner says, from the Puerto Rico Constitution as "ordain[ed] and establish[ed]" by "the people." P. R. Const., Preamble; see Brief for Petitioner 28–30. But that makes the Puerto Rican populace only the most immediate source of such authority—and that is not what our dual-sovereignty decisions make relevant. Back of the Puerto Rican people and their Constitution, the "ultimate" source of prosecutorial power remains the U. S. Congress, just as back of a city's charter lies a state government. Wheeler, 435 U. S., at 320. Congress, in Public Law 600, authorized Puerto Rico's constitution-making process in the first instance; the people of a territory could not legally have initiated that process on their own. See, e.g., Simms v. Simms, 175 U. S. 162, 168 (1899).

. . . .

Puerto Rico boasts "a relationship to the United States that has no parallel in our history." Examining Bd., 426 U. S., at 596. And since the events of the early 1950's, an integral aspect of that association has been the Commonwealth's wide-ranging self-rule, exercised under its own Constitution. As a result of that charter, Puerto Rico today can avail itself of a wide variety of futures. But for purposes of the Double Jeopardy Clause, the future is not what matters—and there is no getting away from the past. Because the ultimate source of Puerto Rico's prosecutorial power is the Federal Government—because when we trace that authority all the way back, we arrive at the doorstep of the U. S. Capitol—the Commonwealth and the United States are not separate sovereigns. That means the two governments cannot "twice put" respondents Sánchez Valle and Gómez Vázquez "in jeopardy" for the "same offence." U. S. Const., Amdt. 5. We accordingly affirm the judgment of the Supreme Court of Puerto Rico.

It is so ordered. ____ 1 Cite as: 579 U. S. ____ (2016)

CAPITAL OVER PEOPLE?

The roots of Puerto Rico's massive public debt run deep and far; there is plenty of blame to go around: Puerto Rican Politician's irresponsible public spending, lack of clarity and inaction on the part of Congress, and bond speculators, who saw an opportunity for profit when the island's bonds dropped to junk. In this comprehensive essay, Chandler Foust examines the roots of the debt crisis, the failure of austerity measures to make a dent on that debt, and the structural changes required to bring the economy afloat.

Foust wrote this essay in 2015, while working as research associate at COHA (Council of Hemispheric Affairs). He later volunteered in the Peace Corps, and since 2018 is pursuing a law degree at Washington University in St. Louis.

On Monday August 4, Puerto Rico's Public Finance Corporation failed to pay the $58 million USD it owed creditors, making only a $628,000 USD payment. In addition, the island owes $5 billion USD over the next twelve months. Monday marked the first day in the island's history where it failed to make a payment.

The current debt crisis in Puerto Rico not only illustrates a need for a complete restructuring of the island's economy, but a closer look taken toward its further political union with the United States. In addition, the current crisis shows the flawed way that politicians respond to debt crises, and how the people who end up getting hurt are usually not the ones who started the crisis. Lastly, the current political debate between debtors and creditors, harsh austerity measures, and further concessions to capital has shown that these lessons have yet to sink in for many.

What Happened

On June 28, 2015 Puerto Rican Governor Alejandro García Padilla declared the commonwealth's massive debt not payable. Likening the island's economic trajectory to a "death spiral", Padilla concluded that Puerto Rico's creditors must take part in the island's attempt to rid itself of its debt problem. He claimed that without debt restructuring, Puerto Rico's economy would not grow, and

---

Chandler Foust, "Capital Over People? Puerto Rican Debt Crisis Explained," COHA, August 3, 2015.Reprinted with permission.

added that lack of growth would, in turn, make it increasingly unlikely that Puerto Rico would be able to pay off its debt in the foreseeable future. In addition to this statement, Governor Padilla passed an executive order that created the Working Group for Economic Recovery, and commissioned a report on the island's economy by former International Monetary Fund Economist Anne Krueger. The group is tasked with crafting legislation by August 30, which includes a five-year fiscal plan, cuts in government spending, privatization of certain services, and establishing a Fiscal Council to ensure that the proposed changes are implemented in good faith. The group consists of Governor Padilla's Chief of Staff Víctor Suárez, President of the islands' Government Development Bank (GDB) Melba Acosta, Senate President Eduardo Bhatia, and House President Jaime Porello. The group met for the first time at the GDB, on July 7, to begin forming its recommendations for future economic reforms. Whatever the final recommendations, the legislature is required to approve the plan.

Thus far, Puerto Rico has managed to pay off its debts and avoid default, but with so many deadlines in the near future, it will get no easier from here. Recently, the commonwealth's Electrical Power Authority (PREPA) staved off default on its $9 billion USD debt with a $415 million USD payment. The GDB paid $300 million USD on July 10, while the Public Finance Corporation was not able to pay the $94 million USD it owed on July 15. By August 1 Puerto Rico will owe another $169.6 million USD to service its sales tax-backed bonds as well. On top of this, the commonwealth is constitutionally bound to pay off its General Obligation Bonds before all other debt, which necessitates Puerto Rico setting aside $93 million USD each month.

To put Governor Padilla's comments about the impossibility of paying off its debt in perspective, the Puerto Rican government, under Padilla, has implemented massive austerity reforms, yet has little to show for it. In fact, cuts in government spending and increases in taxes have further constricted the Puerto Rican economy, making it increasingly difficult for the island to pay off its outstanding debt: the "death spiral" Governor Padilla has referred to. Just to show how serious Puerto Rico's economic situation is and how little continued austerity will help, simply look at the government's response to its performance over the past decade.

Since 2006, the Puerto Rican economy has contracted every year except for one. The unemployment rate of 14 percent is over double that of the United States and 45 percent of the population lives below the federal poverty line. A seven percent drop in population in the last decade accompanies the sheer size of the island's debt, $73.5 billion USD with $38 billion USD in unfunded pensions and public health care liabilities. Since the United States has made it clear that no bailout will be given, Puerto Rico has fended for itself, which is reflected in this year's budget. On May 14, the island's government submitted a budget request for $9.8 billion USD, which entails a $674 million USD cut in spending. The budget proposed raising the sales tax from seven percent to 11 percent and increasing the value-added tax four percent. The budget set aside $1.5 billion USD for debt repayment but also plans to close 95 schools and 20 public agencies. This piles on top of continuous cuts since 2013.

The current trend is unsustainable. For instance, even while cutting spending and raising taxes, Puerto Rico is only expected to bring in $825 million USD in 2015, despite needing $1.2 billion USD to run the government. What Puerto Rico needs isn't more austerity; it needs structural reforms to put the economy on a sustainable path so it can pay off its debt without irreparably damaging itself in the process. This means Congress giving Puerto Rico the ability to declare Chapter 9 bankruptcy, which will in no way forgive all of Puerto Rico's debt, but will help some. This means creditors forgiving debt or at least allowing the postponement of debt payment for a period of time until Puerto Rico is in a position to pay. This means guilt falls on both sides of the mainland, the U.S. for propping up a noncompetitive and inefficient economy with tax-breaks for most of its history while incentivizing the continued buying up of unsustainable debt, and Puerto Rico for spending money it simply did not have, even before its economy began to contract. As Governor Padilla said, "sacrifices must be made by all."

How U.S. and Puerto Rican Policy Has Contributed to the Debt Crisis

Placing all the blame on U.S. policy would be disingenuous at best, but concentrating all ire on the Puerto Rican government is irresponsible. Throughout Puerto Rico's history as a U.S. possession, and eventual Commonwealth, its economic fortunes have not only been tied to a strong U.S. economy, but have been propped up by tax breaks and bond exemptions. These tax breaks go all the way back to 1921 when Congress passed the Revenue Act. Later in 1948, when Puerto Rico changed its tax policy through the Industrial Incentives Act, U.S. subsidiaries became tax exempt from both Puerto Rican taxes and from the U.S. Income Tax. Section 936, which has generated substantial publicity in explanations of the island's current debt crisis, only began in 1976. Section 936 fully exempted profits and passive investments made by U.S. subsidiaries in Puerto Rico from federal corporate income taxes. By 1993, around $3.9 billion USD in tax revenue had been forgone due to the tax credit.

On top of the huge benefits US companies received from the Section 936 tax credit, Puerto Rican tax law allowed a subsidiary that was at least 80 percent foreign owned to deduct 100 percent of dividends paid to the parent company. This means that US subsidiaries in Puerto Rico could pay all their revenue to parent companies in dividends and pay no taxes whatsoever on their profits. Even with the high input costs of doing business on the island, these tax breaks made Puerto Rico an attractive place for investment and business by US companies. At least as long as the tax breaks were left intact. In 1996, President Clinton passed legislation that began a ten-year phase-out of the Section 936 tax credit, which ended in the same year that the Puerto Rican economy began to contract in 2006. By phasing out the Section 936 tax credit, US subsidiaries were forced to pay the same corporate tax rate as all other foreign companies, which added to the high input costs of doing business on the island, contributed to the whittling away of the island's manufacturing base, and many companies leaving the island.

In addition, the U.S. government effectively subsidizes Puerto Rico's debt through its legal treatment of the purchase of the island's bonds. Ever since 1917, the US government has exempted the purchase of Puerto Rican bonds from local, state or federal taxes. They are referred to as "triple-exempt" bonds and have remained popular even as the island's debt climbed up to 100 percent of GNP in 2014. The amount of debt held by US mutual funds, hedge funds, and individuals has led to major investor concern over the thought of Puerto Rico restructuring its debt. Currently, $11.3 billion USD of the island's debt is held by mutual funds, $15 billion USD is held by hedge funds, while largely Puerto Ricans and "mainland Americans" hold the rest of the debt. This cycle ended, in June 2014, when Puerto Rico's bonds were demoted to junk status by various rating agencies. High yield bond funds, in turn, began buying up more of the Puerto Rican debt, due to the lower quality but higher possibility of return given high interest rates. Many of the largest holders, run by Oppenheimer Funds and Franklin Templeton Investments, have made it clear that they will seek litigation if Puerto Rico does not pay.

Krueger Report

The pure amount of debt, the number of Puerto Rican debt holders who are gearing up for litigation, and the lack of money brought in from austerity measures illustrates the need for structural reform of the Island's economy, as well as Congress allowing Puerto Rico to declare Chapter 9 bankruptcy. Anne Krueger, a former economist at the International Monetary Fund, stated in her report commissioned by Governor Padilla that the debt cannot be paid if the economy doesn't grow. She then states that the economy will not grow if structural reform is not implemented and if questions about the future of the heavy debt burden are left unanswered. In the report, Krueger documents many reasons for how Puerto Rico got to this perilous situation.

The first and most important factor is what Krueger calls the creditors' "Crisis of Confidence." Basically, Puerto Rico's debt burden is due to the eleven consecutive years of economic contraction and mounting public debt, which fed each other. As stated in the previous section, due to the "triple-exempt" status of Puerto Rican bonds, investors continued to buy up debt even as it mounted to over 100 percent of Puerto Rico's GDP in Fiscal year 2014. While the continued purchase of bonds temporarily kept Puerto Rico afloat, when risk premiums started to rise on Puerto Rico's bonds, with their eventual decline to junk status, the situation couldn't be sustained. Due to the much lower ratings and growing fear of the debt's sustainability, investors "demanded higher risk premiums, shorter maturities, and greater securities." The decline in ratings exposed the island's precarious fiscal position and effectively cut it off from continuing on its current trend.

With the economy set to shrink another percentage point in 2015, structural reform must be made if creditors want to get their money back. On the supply side, Krueger suggests that labor, energy, and transportation be reformed. For instance, in Puerto Rico only 40 percent of the population is either employed or looking for work, compared to 63 percent in the U.S. One major contributor to this is the high labor costs and generous social benefits on the island. The minimum wage is 77 percent of the average per capita income, compared to 28 percent on the mainland. On the benefits side, those receiving unemployment benefits generally make more than those earning the minimum wage. For example, a family of 3 that receives food stamps, AFDC, Medicaid, and utility subsidies makes $1,743 USD a month, while a minimum wage earner makes $1,159 USD. These generous benefits incentivize many not to search for work, while the relatively high minimum wage encourages employers not to hire more workers, which helps to explain the massive migration out of Puerto Rico. In addition to the high costs of energy on the island, coupled with the Jones Act, which doubles the costs of imports by forcing all shipments to the island to be made by US crews and vessels, Puerto Rico is not in a position to grow.

Lastly, Krueger states that a complete restructuring of Puerto Rico's fiscal regime is necessary to prevent this dire fiscal situation from occurring again. The Puerto Rican government has been running deficits since 2000, six years before the economy began to contract. The main drivers of this debt are the public sector agencies such as PRASA, PREPA, and HTA. From 2004 to 2014, the expected revenue was $1.5 billion USD above the amount collected. While debt was increasing, tax revenue was shrinking, from 15 percent of GNP to 12 percent during this time period. In addition to the growing debt burden, the true amount of debt is much larger than expected because Puerto Rico's General Fund does not properly account for its expenditures. Krueger asserts that the General Fund does not include the deficits run by 150 government agencies, including the GDB, which paid creditors $300 million USD on July 10. In her own calculation, which includes the "full public sector," Krueger estimates that from 2013 to 2014 the public sector ran a deficit that was five percent of GNP.

Political Union, Bankruptcy, and Bye to Austerity

The question of Puerto Rico's political status and the Commonwealth's ability to declare Chapter 9 bankruptcy are connected and must be resolved to help ensure that this debt crisis is ended and never occurs again. For instance, Puerto Rico is home to 3.5 million American citizens but is not represented by a voting member in Congress. This political deficit undeniably leaves the island at a disadvantage when it comes to U.S. policy. This disadvantage is shown in Puerto Rico not being able to declare Chapter 9 bankruptcy, unlike the other 50 states.

Until 1984 Puerto Rican municipalities and public corporations were able to declare bankruptcy, but in that year Congress changed the law and excluded Puerto Rico. This exclusion is critical, because its public corporations and municipalities hold around a third of Puerto Rico's debt. Recently, Democrats Richard Blumenthal and Chuck Schumer introduced a bill in the Senate that would rectify this. Puerto Rico's non-voting representative, Pedro Pierluisi, introduced a similar bill in the house back in February, but as it stands nothing has been done. In fact, the bills have gained little traction and can be expected to remain there; in the meantime Puerto Rico's economic future hangs in the balance.

The lack of political will further highlights Puerto Rico's current second-class status. The only answer to a lack of political will and political space to end the mounting debt crisis is further representation. The only way to achieve this is statehood. In 2012, Puerto Rico held a referendum on their political status, and 54 percent voted "no" on retaining their current status. In addition, 61 percent voted "yes" on becoming the 51st state. Becoming a state would grant Puerto Rico access to an additional $20 billion USD in funds, and ensure that the US federal tax code applies to Puerto Rico. The additional federal funds are sorely needed, but, more importantly, applying the US federal tax code would help the Puerto Rican government to raise revenue and better combat tax avoidance.

While it remains unlikely that Puerto Rico will be admitted as a state in the near future, its current debt crisis must be put into perspective. Paul Krugman writes that as a territory in the US Federalist System Puerto Rico benefits from receiving increased amounts of federal social benefits even as its payments to the federal government decline, which helps to cushion the blows. While mentioning that he is in no way minimizing the human suffering on the Island, he then shows that the unemployment rate has only risen four percent and that consumption per capita has actually risen. On top of this, even though the Puerto Rican economy has steadily contracted since 2006, its "drop per working age adult is less," because of the 7 percent decline in population in the last decade. In other words, Puerto Rico is a region that has lost its comparative advantage, for a variety of reasons, which means "large scale-emigration" of its working age population and receiving an increasing amount of federal funds is expected. Since states such as West Virginia that lose comparative advantage in producing goods are not expected to reduce minimum wage levels in order to compete, Puerto Rico should not be expected to either.

This leads to a larger point. Puerto Rico, when viewed in this context, must be put back on a track towards growth. Further attempts by creditors to squeeze more payments out of the Island will only make the situation worse, and further hazard the lives of millions of American citizens. A recent report commissioned by "38 investment managers" that hold 5.2 billion of the island's debt shows this implication. The report states that Puerto Rico can pay back its massive debt by further increasing taxes, selling off some of the $4 billion USD in government real estate, and cutting government spending. One major area the report focuses on is education, saying "education expenditures increased 39 percent or $1.4 billion USD in the past decade while total school enrollment declined 25 percent."

This ignores, as the *Guardian* noted, that 56 percent of Puerto Rican children live in poverty, and the spending per pupil is $8,400 USD compared to $10,667 USD on the mainland. The island's debt crisis is only a surface level problem; the Puerto Rican people need investment. Continued austerity will only exacerbate the crisis and lead to further economic contraction, not only harming the lives of millions of American citizens, but also destroying the US budget. Not only does it not make sense for the Puerto Rican people, it does not make sense for the US budget.

Conclusion

With its massive debt and the failure of austerity measures to stop the increasing debt load, Puerto Rico needs help. Help, not in the sense of completely forgiving the debt, but help to implement structural reforms so that this situation can be prevented in the future and so that the economy can grow. Without growth it seems increasingly unlikely that the debt will be paid. Currently, a bill is in both houses of Congress that would give Puerto Rico the same right as states to declare Chapter 9 bankruptcy. While it remains unlikely that anything will be passed soon, Hillary Clinton and Jeb Bush, both front-runners for their party's presidential nominations, have come out in favor of allowing Puerto Rico to declare Chapter 9 bankruptcy. Lastly, Puerto Rico's economic problems, and the limits it faces in fixing them are directly tied to its lack of political representation. Any structural reforms must be accompanied by soul-searching and further deliberation on its future political status.

THE ROOTS OF PUERTO RICO'S DEBT CRISIS

Puerto Rico's crushing debt has been mounting exponentially since the 1970s but most scholars and policy makers agree that the crisis' roots run deeper, dating to the US acquisition of Puerto Rico in 1899, and that the crisis is structural, rather than junctural. On June 28, 2015, Governor Alejandro García Padilla somberly announced that Puerto Rico's public debt of over 73 billion was "not repayable." His words and Puerto Rico's first default five weeks later brought increasing attention to the seemingly insurmountable debt crisis. The following document is an article by journalist, author and university lecturer Ed Morales published in *The Nation* (July 8, 2015).

R iding through the hills of Canóvanas last weekend with Prima, a vacationing 65-year-old Brooklynite who was born and raised in the Puerto Rican countryside, I got a brief lesson on the island's history and political economy. "This land was all *cañaverales*," she said, meaning rough acres of sugarcane, which has now been replaced by mile after mile of suburban tract housing. "When that ended, some people worked in factories and construction. Now, I don't know what's going to happen. I think the empire is collapsing."

Today that history has caught up with the island. Puerto Rico—an unincorporated territory of the United States with 3.5 million US citizen residents who do not have the right to vote for president or representation in Congress—is

Ed Morales, "The Roots of Puerto Rico's Debt Crisis—and Why Austerity Will Not Solve It," *The Nation*, July 8, 2015. Reprinted with permission of *The Nation*.

making headlines these days because of its inability to pay a $72 billion debt owed to holders of its devalued bonds, often issued through such entities as the infamous PREPA, the electrical power authority. The threat of default was signaled by Governor Alejandro García Padilla's admission last week to *The New York Times* that the debt was "not payable."

The debt crisis, which has spurred comparisons to Argentina, Detroit, and, of course, the recent tumultuous events in Greece, occurs at the climax of a local recession that began in 2006, two years before the Great Recession, and is accompanied by other bad news. Because of the government's shrinking tax base and huge debt-service expense, a sales tax of 11.5 percent—higher than in any state in the Union—has been imposed. Hundreds of schools are closing, and more than 31,000 jobs have been lost since García Padilla took office two and a half years ago. A healthcare crisis is looming because of a proposed cut of $150 million in Medicare Advantage reimbursements. The unemployment rate, now more than 13 percent, is bad, but it pales in comparison to a dismal workforce participation rate of around 40 percent—far worse than the US rate, which is itself at a 38-year low of 62.6 percent. As a result, the island is in the throes of a persistent depopulation, with about 200,000 migrating to the mainland over the past decade.

What Puerto Rico has in common with Greece is that it is a peripheral economy that has been invaded by hedge funds and pushed, by speculation and ballooning debt-service payments, to its limits. But since Puerto Rico's banks are tied to the US Federal Reserve and not its own government, there is no bank panic. What it has in common with Detroit is a history of inefficient administrations that borrowed to pay for pension payments and services, but, unlike municipalities in the 50 states, Puerto Rico cannot declare bankruptcy. Its territorial status also made its bonds triple-tax-exempt for any buyer, adding to the lure of their high yield and fueling the desires of an erratic muni bond market for paper that would quickly become junk.

García Padilla's announcement came about a year after he passed a law to restructure the debt, which was struck down in court in February (on Tuesday the Court of Appeals for the First Circuit in Boston upheld the decision on appeal, citing a 1984 decision by Congress that excludes US territories from Chapter 9 bankruptcy protection). He simply came to the conclusion that with zero economic growth and a debt-to-GNP ratio of about 100 percent, the situation was untenable. "This is not politics, this is math," he said. The moderate mainstream holds that the island's only recourse—a path that is supported by presidential candidates like Democrats Hillary Clinton and Martin O'Malley, independent Bernie Sanders, and Republican Jeb Bush—is to petition Congress to change the bankruptcy laws so that Puerto Rico would be allowed to file.

But even if bankruptcy protection were granted, it would most likely entail painful austerity measures. The recommendations of last week's Krueger Report, "Puerto Rico: A Way Forward," commissioned by Puerto Rico's government and put together by several current and former IMF employees, are clearly along those lines. Among other things, the report recommended shrinking the size of the government, lowering the minimum wage, and trimming federal entitlements—including Medicaid and Medicare, which would be a particularly dire step, since 2 million people, or roughly 60 percent of Puerto Rico's residents, depend on those programs. The report also recommended making it more difficult to get overtime pay—on the same week that President Obama expanded it for US mainland workers. For its part, the Obama administration is saying that no bailout is being contemplated, although it is urging Congress to consider changing the law to allow Puerto Rico to declare bankruptcy. Last February, Pedro Pierluisi, the resident commissioner of Puerto Rico, who is the island's non-voting representative in Congress and a member of both the pro-statehood party and the US Democratic Party, introduced HR 870, which would accomplish that. The bill has not made much progress, however; the latest action was in March, when it was referred to the Subcommittee on Regulatory Reform, Commercial and Antitrust Law. Most House Republicans are against the measure, considering it a bailout, despite the fact that most of Puerto Rico's pro-statehood party is affiliated with the GOP, most notably Alaska's Don Young.

In his telecast speech on June 30, García Padilla said he was not in favor of lowering wages, but he also said he would push for "legislation to make our laws more competitive" to promote job creation, which is code for doing just that. What many left-leaning Puerto Rican economists and political theorists are saying is that they agree, as the Krueger Report says, that the island's economy has deep structural problems. It's the report's remedy that they disagree with, especially when it's been shown that austerity in times of recession tends to depress economies further.

Working People's Party spokesperson and University of Puerto Rico professor Rafael Bernabe supports a recent legislative proposal to audit the debt, as was done in Greece, where that process called the imposition of the debt "premeditated" and "immoral." In fact, Puerto Rico has become the victim of a high-stakes game of hedge-fund casino gambling, with about 43 percent of the debt held by so-called vulture funds and Wall Street banks and lawyers charging over $1.4 billion in a seven-year period between 2006 and 2013 for charges like swap termination fees. "We want to study the general conditions that led to the creation of the debt, the terms of the contracts, the role of intermediaries," said Bernabe in an interview with *The Nation*.

For the most part, the debt crisis has been portrayed as something that arose after the advent of the current ten-year recession. But in fact, Puerto Rico's government has been borrowing to finance its expenses since the 1970s, when the limited success of the post–World War II Operation Bootstrap, which transformed its economy from an agricultural one to a light manufacturing one, lost its luster. The resulting cure, Section 936 of the IRS code, exempted US and multinational corporations from paying taxes on profits, but that spur to investment was phased out between 1996 and 2006. Meanwhile, NAFTA had already depressed wages in nearby Mexico, making Puerto Rican workers too high-priced, and a construction and infrastructure building boom that was partly financed by bond-selling had burst, driving the island's economy into its current death spiral.

Herein lies the Puerto Rican economy's "structural problem": It's not about workers having salaries and benefits that are too high; it's about the fact that the island's territorial status means that since the days of the 19th-century sugar growers, whose drive to avoid tariffs were an early manifestation of hemispheric free trade, capital has fled the island at a steady rate, without interruption. "The economy of Puerto Rico is mainly controlled by US corporations, which generate a tremendous amount of profit that is not reinvested and does not create economic growth," said Bernabe. "It's a cycle of dependency that reproduces itself."

It's reasonable to ask whether the US government is at least partially responsible for the crisis—both through creation of the nebulous commonwealth status and the actions of its financial institutions—and whether it has a moral obligation to help resolve it through financial support. In 2004, legal scholar Pedro Malavet suggested that it was the social construction of Puerto Ricans as a non-white race that made them "unassimilable as Americans," cementing their colonized status, and that they were therefore owed reparations.

While the idea of asking for reparations may have lost its feasibility after the Great Recession, both the United States and the ruling party of Puerto Rico should begin to view the debt crisis as a human problem affecting millions of what are effectively second-class US citizens, and not a matter of business mathematics. If mainstream politics on the mainland refuses to consider a restructuring of the US economy away from a blind profit motive, it should at least have the intelligence and decency to help Puerto Rico restructure its own economy to create new modes of capital reinvestment on the island, just as it would anywhere on the mainland.

Some argue that a change in political status is necessary to effect real change in the economy. Statehooders push for entrance to the union—highly unlikely, given the Republican-controlled Congress bent on reducing spending, which statehood would sharply increase, not to mention the probability that Puerto Rican voters would send Democratic representatives and senators to Congress. On June 22, the UN Special Committee on Decolonization called once again for the United States to "expedite a process that would allow Puerto Ricans to fully exercise their inalienable right to self-determination and independence."

Any movement for independence, which might choose to lobby for reparations, needs to highlight class, race, and gender marginalization, as well as environmental reform, as part of its agenda. New parties that do not prioritize status change, such as All Puerto Ricans for Puerto Rico, the Sovereign Unity Movement, and the Working People's Party have tried to enter the arena, but according to political scientist Manuel Almeida, "the rules of the game" in the island's political structure have hindered their emergence. Puerto Rico's ruling party has used technical challenges to delay the Working People's Party's re-certification for elections, despite electoral reform that had allowed the new parties to field candidates for the 2012 elections.

With an overly moralistic tone directed at the island's mostly Catholic residents, Governor García Padilla spoke of "shared sacrifices," in which the community, supposedly complicit in the actions of an irresponsible government, would share the pain with the bondholders. But many Puerto Ricans I've spoken with, from academia to the working class, agree that they've sacrificed enough, and that it's time for those most responsible for creating this mess to own up to their transgressions.

BILL ESTABLISHING THE OVERSIGHT BOARD

In 2016, this House bill became law, creating the Financial Oversight and Management Board of Puerto Rico, whose primary task is to work with the Commonwealth of Puerto Rico toward a debt restructuring plan to ensure payment to holders of Puerto Rican bonds. PROMESA granted the Oversight Board broad powers that sharply limit the insular government's authority over fiscal and budget matters and reduces Federal protections such as the minimum salary and Medicare and Medicaid allocations.

H. R. 4900, 114th Congress, 2nd Session, April 12, 2016, "A Bill to Establish and Oversight Board to Assist the Government of Puerto Rico, Including Instrumentalities, in Managing its Public Finances, and for other Purposes (excerpts)

114TH CONGRESS, 2D SESSION **H. R. 4900**
To establish an Oversight Board to assist the Government of Puerto Rico, including instrumentalities, in managing its public finances, and for other purposes.

IN THE HOUSE OF REPRESENTATIVES, APRIL 12, 2016

Mr. DUFFY introduced the following bill; which was referred to the Committee on Natural Resources, and in addition to the Committees on the Judiciary and Education and the Workforce, for a period to be subsequently determined by the Speaker, in each case for consideration of such provisions as fall within the jurisdiction of the committee concerned

A BILL To establish an Oversight Board to assist the Government of Puerto Rico, including instrumentalities, in managing its public finances, and for other purposes.

Be it enacted by the Senate and House of Representatives of the United States of America in Congress assembled,

TITLE I—ESTABLISHMENT AND ORGANIZATION OF OVERSIGHT BOARD

SEC. 101. TERRITORY FINANCIAL OVERSIGHT AND MANAGEMENT BOARD.

(a) PURPOSE.—The purpose of the Oversight Board is to provide a method to achieve fiscal responsibility and access to the capital markets.
. . . .

(c) TREATMENT.—An Oversight Board established under this section—
(1) shall be created as an entity within the territorial government for which it is established in accordance with this title; and
(2) shall not be considered to be a department, agency, establishment, or instrumentality of the Federal Government.
(d) OVERSIGHT OF TERRITORIAL INSTRUMENTALITIES.—
(1) DESIGNATION
(A) IN GENERAL.—The Oversight Board shall consist of 7 members appointed by the President who meet the qualifications described in subsection (e), except that the Oversight Board may take any action under this Act (or any amendments made by this Act) at any time after the President has appointed 3 of its members.
. . . .

(e) MEMBERSHIP.—
. . . .

(2) APPOINTED MEMBERS.—The President shall appoint the individual members of the Oversight Board, of which two individuals should be selected from a list of individuals submitted by the Speaker of the House of Representatives; two should be selected from a list submitted by the Majority Leader of the Senate; one should be selected from a list submitted by the Minority Leader of the House of Representatives; and one should be selected from a list submitted by the Minority Leader of the Senate. Of the two individuals to be selected from a list of individuals submitted by the Speaker of the House of Representatives, one shall maintain a primary residence in the territory or have a primary place of business in the territory.
(3) EX OFFICIO MEMBERS.—The Governor, or the Governor's designee, shall be an ex officio member of the Oversight Board without voting rights.
. . . .

SEC. 104. POWERS OF OVERSIGHT BOARD.

. . . .

(e) SUBPOENA POWER.—

(1) IN GENERAL.—The Oversight Board may issue subpoenas requiring the attendance and testimony of witnesses and the production of books, records, correspondence, memoranda, papers, documents, electronic files, metadata, tapes, and materials of any nature relating to any matter under investigation by the Oversight Board.

. . . .

(k) CIVIL ACTIONS TO ENFORCE POWERS.—The Oversight Board may seek judicial enforcement of its authority to carry out its responsibilities under this Act.

. . . .

SEC. 108. AUTONOMY OF THE OVERSIGHT BOARD.

(a) IN GENERAL.—Neither the Governor nor the Legislature may exercise

(1) any control, supervision, oversight, or review over the Oversight Board or its activities; or

(2) enact, implement, or enforce any statute, resolution, policy, or rule with respect to the Oversight Board or its activities.

. . . .

TITLE II—RESPONSIBILITIES OF OVERSIGHT BOARD

SEC. 201. APPROVAL OF FISCAL PLANS.

. . . .

(c) DEVELOPMENT, REVIEW, APPROVAL, AND CERTIFICATION OF FISCAL PLAN.—

. . . .

(2) FISCAL PLAN DEVELOPED BY GOVERNOR.—The Governor shall submit to the Oversight Board any proposed Fiscal Plan required by the Oversight Board by the time specified in the notice delivered under subsection (a).

(3) REVIEW BY THE OVERSIGHT BOARD.—The Oversight Board shall review the proposed Fiscal Plan to determine whether it satisfies the requirements set forth in subsection (b) and, if the Oversight Board determines in its sole discretion that the proposed Fiscal Plan—

(A) satisfies such requirements, the Oversight Board shall approve the proposed Fiscal Plan; or

(B) does not satisfy such requirements, the Oversight Board shall provide to the Governor—

(i) a notice of violation that includes recommendations for revisions to the applicable Fiscal Plan; and

(ii) an opportunity to correct the violation in accordance with subsection (d)(1).

. . . .

(c) BUDGETS DEVELOPED BY GOVERNOR.—

(1) GOVERNOR'S PROPOSED BUDGETS.—The Governor shall submit to the Oversight Board proposed Budgets by the time specified in the notice delivered under subsection (a). section (a). The Oversight Board shall determine whether the adopted Territory Budget is a compliant budget and—

(A) if the adopted Territory Budget is a compliant budget, the Oversight Board shall

(i) approve the Budget; and

(ii) if the Budget is a Territory Budget, submit the Territory Budget to the Legislature; or

(B) if the Oversight Board determines that the Budget is not a compliant budget, the Oversight Board shall provide to the Governor—

(i) a notice of violation that includes a description of any necessary corrective action; and

(ii) an opportunity to correct the violation in accordance with paragraph (2).

. . . .

SEC. 203. EFFECT OF FINDING OF NONCOMPLIANCE WITH BUDGET.

(a) SUBMISSION OF REPORTS.—Not later than 15 days after the last day of each quarter of a fiscal year (beginning with the fiscal year determined by the Oversight Board), the Governor shall submit to the Oversight Board a report, in such form as the Oversight Board may require, describing—

(1) the actual cash revenues, cash expenditures, and cash flows of the territorial government for the preceding quarter, as compared to the projected revenues, expenditures, and cash flows contained in the certified Budget for such preceding quarter; and

(2) any other information requested by the Oversight Board, which may include a balance sheet or a requirement that the Governor provide information for each covered territorial instrumentality separately.

. . . .

(d) BUDGET REDUCTIONS BY OVERSIGHT BOARD.—

. . . .

(2) with respect to covered territorial instrumentalities at the sole discretion of the Oversight Board—

(A) make reductions in nondebt expenditures to ensure that the actual quarterly revenues and expenses for the covered territorial instrumentality are in compliance with the applicable certified Budget or, in the case of the fiscal year in which the Oversight Board is established, the budget adopted by the Governor and the Legislature or the covered territorial instrumentality, as applicable; or

(B)(i) institute automatic hiring freezes at the covered territorial instrumentality; and

(ii) prohibit the covered territorial instrumentality from entering into any contract in excess of $100,000, or engaging in any financial or other transactions, unless the contract or transaction was previously approved by the Oversight Board.

. . . .

SEC. 204. REVIEW OF ACTIVITIES TO ENSURE COMPLIANCE WITH FISCAL PLAN.

(a) SUBMISSION OF LEGISLATIVE ACTS TO OVERSIGHT BOARD.—

(1) SUBMISSION OF ACTS.—Except to the extent that the Oversight Board may provide otherwise in its bylaws, rules, and procedures, not later than 7 business days after a territorial government duly enacts any law during any fiscal year in which the Oversight Board is in operation, the Governor shall submit the law to the Oversight Board.

(2) COST ESTIMATE; CERTIFICATION OF COMPLIANCE OR NONCOMPLIANCE.—The Governor shall include with each law submitted to the Oversight Board under paragraph (1) the following:

(A) A formal estimate prepared by an appropriate entity of the territorial government with expertise in budgets and financial management of the impact, if any, that the law will have on expenditures and revenues.

(B) If the appropriate entity described in subparagraph (A) finds that the law is not significantly inconsistent with the Fiscal Plan for the fiscal year, it shall issue a certification of such finding.

(C) If the appropriate entity described in subparagraph (A) finds that the law is significantly inconsistent with the Fiscal Plan for the fiscal year, it shall issue a certification of such finding, together with the entity's reasons for such finding.

. . . .

(5) FAILURE TO COMPLY.—If the territorial government fails to comply with a direction given by the Oversight Board under paragraph (4) with respect to a law, the Oversight Board may take such actions as it considers necessary, consistent with this Act, to ensure that the enactment or enforcement of the law will not adversely affect the territorial government's compliance with the Fiscal Plan, including preventing the enforcement or application of the law.

. . . .

(b) EFFECT OF APPROVED FISCAL PLAN ON CONTRACTS, RULES, AND REGU-LATIONS.—

(1) TRANSPARENCY IN CONTRACTING.—The Oversight Board shall work with a covered territory's office of the comptroller or any functionally equivalent entity to promote compliance with the applicable law of any covered territory that requires agencies and instrumentalities of the territorial government to maintain a registry of all contracts executed, including amendments thereto, and to remit a copy to the office of the comptroller for inclusion in a comprehensive database available to the public;

. . . .

SEC. 207. OVERSIGHT BOARD AUTHORITY RELATED TO DEBT ISSUANCE.

For so long as the Oversight Board remains in operation, no territorial government may, without the prior approval of the Oversight Board, issue debt or guarantee, exchange, modify, repurchase, redeem, or enter into similar transactions with respect to its debt.

. . . .

SEC. 211. ANALYSIS OF PENSIONS.

DETERMINATION.—If the Oversight Board determines, in its sole discretion, that a pension system of the territorial government is materially underfunded, the Oversight Board shall conduct an analysis prepared by an independent actuary of such pension system to assist the Oversight Board in evaluating the fiscal and economic impact of the pension cash flows.

. . . .

TITLE III—ADJUSTMENTS OF DEBTS

. . . .

SEC. 303. RESERVATION OF TERRITORIAL POWER TO CONTROL TERRITORY AND TERRITORIAL INSTRUMENTALITIES.

Subject to the limitations set forth in titles I and II of this Act, this title does not limit or impair the power of a territory to control, by legislation or otherwise, the territory or any territorial instrumentality thereof in the exercise of the political or governmental powers of the territory or territorial instrumentality, including expenditures for such exercise, but—

(1) a territory law prescribing a method of composition or moratorium of indebtedness of the territory or any territorial instrumentality thereof may not bind any creditor that does not consent to the composition or moratorium; and

(2) a judgment entered under a law described in paragraph (1) may not bind a creditor that does not consent to the composition.
. . . .

TITLE IV—MISCELLANEOUS PROVISIONS
. . . .

SEC. 402. RIGHT OF PUERTO RICO TO DETERMINE ITS FUTURE POLITICAL STATUS.

Nothing in this Act shall be interpreted to restrict Puerto Rico's right to determine its future political status, including by conducting the plebiscite as authorized by Public Law 113–76.

SEC. 403. FIRST MINIMUM WAGE IN PUERTO RICO.
Section 6(g) of the Fair Labor Standards Act of 1938 (29 U.S.C. 206(g)) is amended
. . . .

by adding at the end the following: "(B) the Governor of Puerto Rico, subject to the approval of the Financial Oversight and Management Board established pursuant to section 101 of the Puerto Rico Oversight, Management, and Economic Stability Act, may designate a time period not to exceed five years during which employers in Puerto Rico may pay employees who are initially employed after the date of enactment of such Act a wage which is not less than $4.25 an hour."
. . . .

(l) FINDINGS.—Congress finds the following:
(1) A combination of severe economic decline, accumulated operating deficits, lack of financial transparency, management inefficiencies, and excessive borrowing has created a fiscal emergency in Puerto Rico.
(2) As a result of its fiscal emergency, the Government of Puerto Rico has been unable to provide its citizens with effective services.
(3) The current fiscal emergency has also affected the long-term economic stability of Puerto Rico by contributing to the accelerated outmigration of residents and businesses.
(4) A comprehensive approach to fiscal, management, and structural problems and adjustments that exempts no part of the Government of Puerto Rico is necessary, involving independent oversight and a Federal statutory authority for the Government of Puerto Rico to restructure debts in a fair and orderly process.

PUERTO RICO: HOW DO WE KNOW 3,000 PEOPLE DIED AS A RESULT OF HURRICANE MARIA?

After months of speculation and misinformation, it became evident that the government's estimate of Puerto Rico's death toll from Hurricane Maria—64 people—was a gross undercount. More studies followed, including one by the Milken Institute of Public Health and another published in the *New England Journal of Medicine* by a group of scientists from Harvard's T.H. Chan School of Public Health, Carlos Albizu University in Puerto Rico and the University of Colorado School of Medicine. Both placed Hurricane Maria among the five deadliest hurricanes on US soil and the deadliest ever to strike Puerto Rico. A September 2018 article by Sheri Fink in the *New York Times* is reprinted below.

It assesses previous studies and includes new data from *New York Times* researchers.

Sheri Fink is a correspondent for the *New York Times*, where her co-authored articles on the West Africa Ebola crisis were awarded the 2015 Pulitzer Prize for international reporting. Dr. Fink is the author of the *New York Times* bestseller *Five Days at Memorial: Life and Death in a Storm-Ravaged Hospital* (Crown, 2013), about choices made in the aftermath of Hurricane Katrina.

When Hurricane Maria struck Puerto Rico a year ago, it was clear that the storm had left a fatal imprint on the island—and that the magnitude might take months to fully assess.

That has proved to be the case. While the government in the early weeks reported that 64 people had died in the storm, a number of assessments in the ensuing months have demonstrated that the toll was much higher.

Recently, the Puerto Rican government revised its official death estimate to 2,975, reflecting the fatalities that occurred during Hurricane Irma and Maria, as well as after—deaths that were because of the storms' brutal and lingering impact.

This week, President Trump raised new questions about the death toll. He said on Twitter that "3000 people did not die in the two hurricanes that hit Puerto Rico." It was only later, well after the storms, he said, that the numbers started to go up.

3000 people did not die in the two hurricanes that hit Puerto Rico. When I left the Island, AFTER the storm had hit, they had anywhere from 6 to 18 deaths. As time went by it did not go up by much. Then, a long time later, they started to report really large numbers, like 3000...

"This was done by the Democrats in order to make me look as bad as possible when I was successfully raising Billions of Dollars to help rebuild Puerto Rico," Mr. Trump said "If a person died for any reason, like old age, just add them onto the list. Bad politics."

Was it bad science?

Experts who study the health impacts of natural disasters say no.

Sheri Fink, "Puerto Rico: How Do We Know 3,000 People Died as a Result of Hurricane Maria?" *The New York Times*. September 13, 2018. Reprinted by permission. A version of this article appears in print on June 3, 2018, Section A, Page 21 of the New York edition with the headline: A Guide to Differing Hurricane Death Tolls. Reprinted with permission of *The New York Times*.

What was the basis for the 2,975 death toll?

Shortly after the storm in September 2017, the official death toll stood at 64. That number included only people whose death certificates listed Hurricane Maria as a contributor, as certified by the Puerto Rico Forensic Sciences Institute in San Juan.

But under pressure from a skeptical public, the Puerto Rican government announced in December that all deaths that had occurred in the months after Hurricane Maria would be reviewed, and that people who had died either directly or indirectly as a result of the storm would be included in a revised tally.

The authorities commissioned researchers at George Washington University's Milken Institute of Public Health to do this work, which has not yet been completed. However, the researchers came back with an initial report in August, which compared the total number of deaths that occurred in the months after the hurricanes with the number that would normally have been expected.

This provided the scientific foundation upon which the territorial government immediately announced that it was revising its death toll estimate upward, to match the numbers in the new report.

Is it legitimate to count both direct and indirect deaths?

The federal government says yes. In relation to hurricane deaths, the term "direct" means those that occurred from drowning or other effects of the storm itself. "Indirect" deaths include those in which related factors, such as difficulty reaching a hospital for care, or trouble refilling medical prescriptions, played a role.

George Washington researchers said they found that doctors in Puerto Rico at the time of the storm were not aware of new guidelines from the federal Centers for Disease Control and Prevention, released the month after the hurricane, which recommend that doctors also consider a natural disaster's indirect impacts in assessing how to tally deaths.

What was The New York Times's estimate?

In December, The New York Times analyzed vital statistics from the Puerto Rican government. They showed that in the 42 days after Hurricane Maria made landfall on Sept. 20, 2017, 1,052 more people than usual died in Puerto Rico.

That figure was particularly striking because thousands of people had left the island, including many with chronic medical conditions. Based on the likelihood that the population there was smaller in the fall of 2017, we would have expected the number of deaths per day to decrease, not increase.

To obtain our figure of 1,052, we compared the number of deaths for each day in 2017 with the average of the number of deaths for the same days in 2015 and 2016. The figures came from the Puerto Rican government, which provided us with tables showing the number of deaths per day and deaths broken down by cause. The 2017 numbers were preliminary, so we limited our analysis to September and October.

But then new information suggested even more deaths?

On June 8, the health department released updated figures to The Times, which showed an even more pronounced trend toward increased deaths in certain categories, lasting into at least October as utility failures persisted. The figures for September 2017 exceed those provided at the time of the Times study, and the department had provided only preliminary data for October until June.

In September and October of 2017, 197 people died of sepsis—a complication of severe infection. That was a 55 percent increase from the average for the same months in 2015 and 2016. Those changes could be explained by delayed medical treatment or poor conditions in homes and hospitals.

The number of diabetes deaths in September and October 2017, at 666, was 46 percent higher than the average for the same period in the two previous years. Many people with diabetes had difficulty keeping insulin refrigerated, and some had trouble maintaining special diets.

Deaths from chronic respiratory diseases and Alzheimer's also appeared to be increased. As for suicide deaths, 49 people took their lives in September and October of 2017, whereas in the same months of 2015 and 2016, an average of 33 people died by suicide.

Where did earlier estimates of over 4,000 deaths come from?

A study published in The New England Journal of Medicine, one of the most highly regarded peer-reviewed medical journals, analyzed a longer period than we did. It also used completely different methods.

Researchers visited more than 3,000 residences across the island and interviewed their occupants, asking whether anyone in their households had died, and whether the storm and its aftermath might have contributed. Residents reported that 38 people living in their households had died between Sept. 20, 2017, when Hurricane Maria struck, and the end of that year.

That toll, converted into a mortality rate, was extrapolated to the larger population and compared with official statistics from the same period in 2016. Researchers arrived at an estimate of roughly 4,600.

Was that the most accurate estimate?

At the time, it was probably a good estimate—although the fine print was important. Because the number of households surveyed was relatively small in comparison to the population's size, there was a large margin of error. The true number of deaths beyond what was expected could range from nearly 800 to close to 8,500 people, the researchers' calculations showed. The widely reported figure of 4,645 was simply the midpoint of that statistical window, known as a 95 percent confidence interval. Including a midpoint figure in such a report is standard academic practice.

The study's main finding was that residents of Puerto Rico died at a significantly higher rate during the three months after the hurricane than they did during the same period in the previous year, and that roughly a third of those deaths resulted from delayed medical care. The researchers said in the report that their conclusions were consistent with the analyses of The Times and others.

Why did it take the G.W.U. study to change the official death estimate?

For one thing, this was the study that the government had commissioned itself—the one it said would answer any remaining questions.

It would have been difficult for territorial leaders to ignore the findings. But there were several factors that gave it significant credibility.

Researchers looked at deaths for a longer time period, from September when Irma and Maria hit until this past February. Deaths, they found, continued to be elevated throughout this period.

The researchers also adjusted their calculations for what they estimated to be an 8 percent drop in the population after the storm and prolonged power failures, when thousands of people fled for the mainland. That exodus made it even more significant that deaths had increased compared with previous years.

All told, they found, there was a total "excess mortality" of 2,975 in the months after the storm that could reasonably be attributable to Maria's effects.

This was not people dying of "old age," as Mr. Trump put it. Average life expectancies tend to be relatively constant. This was a spike in mortality that was almost certainly because of the prolonged impacts—lack of access to health care, infections, long-term injuries—of the storm and its aftermath.

Is this the final word?

No. George Washington researchers hope to continue their work over the course of the next year to examine individual death certificates and conduct detailed, in-person interviews to continue refining their findings.

PUERTO RICANS IN FLORIDA: 2010-2017

Puerto Ricans have migrated to the United States even before the island became a formal colony of the United States. Early waves between 1900 and the 1920s included labor migration to New York, and other northeastern and midwestern urban centers, to pineapple and sugarcane plantations in Hawaii, and even an ill-starred migration project to cottonfields in Arizona. During the two decades that followed WWII, with the encouragement of Puerto Rico's government, an estimated one million Puerto Ricans resettled in the United States. The latest census estimates (2018) include 5.68 million, 1.19 of them in the state of Florida. The following document is a report published by the Center for Puerto Rican Studies which is based at Hunter College, New York City. Center researcher Damayra I. Figueroa's 2019 report discusses the latest US Census estimates of the Puerto Rican population in Florida.

According to the U.S. Census Bureau, in 2017, Florida had the largest concentration of Puerto Ricans in the United States (1,128,225). Florida and New York (1,113,123) were the only states with more than one million Puerto Ricans during this year. Puerto Ricans accounted for 5.4 percent of the total population in Florida, and 21 percent of the state's Hispanic or Latino population in 2017. Therefore, one in every five Latinos in Florida was Puerto Rican as was one in twenty Floridians. The state of Florida has one of the most diverse Latino populations in the country. As of 2017, the Puerto Rican population was the second largest group of Latinos in Florida after Cubans (28.5%), and together they comprised almost half the state's Latino population. The other half of the Latino population was comprised of South Americans (17.9%), Mexicans (13.5%), Central Americans (10.7%), Dominicans (4.8%), and lastly other Latinos (3.6%).

Damayra I. Figueroa, "Puerto Ricans in Florida: 2010-2017," Center for Puerto Rican Studies, Data Sheet, April 2019 (excerpts). Reprinted with permission.

Between 2010 and 2017, the Puerto Rican population in Florida grew by 30.5 percent. This rate of growth was more than twice as high as the state's overall population (11.4%) and more than four times as high as that of all non-Latinos in the state (7.0%).

The data shows that, overall, Puerto Ricans in Florida had lower educational levels, median household income, mean earnings, and homeownership rates, and higher employment and poverty rates compared to Florida's overall population. Relative to stateside Puerto Ricans and Puerto Ricans in Puerto Rico, Puerto Ricans in Florida had better employment opportunities, higher median household incomes, and lower poverty rates.

Education

As of 2017, Florida's educational attainment profile among those aged 25 years and older was as follows: 14.3 percent of Puerto Ricans, aged 25 and older, had an educational attainment of less than a high school diploma; followed by 28.9 percent with a high school diploma; 35.9 percent with some college experience or an associate's degree; and lastly, 20.8 percent who had earned a bachelor's degree or higher. Overall, educational attainment among Puerto Ricans has slowly improved between 2010 and 2017.

Despite this increase in educational attainment, compared to Florida's overall population, Puerto Ricans in Florida exhibit relatively lower educational levels. This is driven by an overrepresentation among those without a high school diploma and an underrepresentation among those with a college degree or higher. In 2017, the proportion of Puerto Ricans in Florida that did not have a high school diploma (14.3%) was higher than that of the state's overall population (11.6%). The proportion of Puerto Ricans in Florida with a high school diploma (28.9%) was virtually equal to the state's proportion (28.8%). In addition, among those with some college experience or an associate's degree, Puerto Ricans in Florida (35.9%) had a higher proportion compared to Florida's population overall (29.9%). However, a lower proportion of Puerto Ricans in Florida had a bachelor's degree or higher (20.8%) compared to the state's population as a whole (29.7%).

The most pronounced difference in educational attainment among Puerto Ricans in Florida was found along the gender lines. Overall, Puerto Rican females had a higher proportion of those with a bachelor's degree or higher compared to their male counterparts across the board. In 2017, Puerto Rican females in Florida (22%) were more likely to have a bachelor's degree or higher compared to Puerto Rican males (19.6%). However, the proportions of Puerto Rican females in Florida with a bachelor's degree or higher (19.6%), although increased from 19.9 percent in 2010 to 22 percent in 2017, were lower than the rate of change for Puerto Rican males in Florida (16%); which also increased from 16.9% in 2010 to 19.6% in 2017. Thus, the proportion of Puerto Rican males in Florida earning a bachelor's degree or higher grew at a faster rate than for Puerto Rican females.

The 2017 U.S. Census Bureau data also revealed that stateside Puerto Rican females were more likely to have a bachelor's degree or higher (21.4%) than stateside Puerto Rican males (17.3%). However, these numbers were slightly lower than those of Puerto Rican females (22%) and males (19.6%) in Florida. Relative to Puerto Ricans in Florida, the proportion of Puerto Ricans with a bachelor's degree or higher among Puerto Ricans in Puerto Rico was notably higher for both females (30.1%) and males (20%). The rate of change in obtaining a bachelor's degree or higher among Puerto Rican females in Florida (10.6%) was strikingly lower than the rate of change for stateside Puerto Rican females (18.9%) and in females in Puerto Rico (18%). On the other hand, the rate of change among Puerto Rican males in Florida (16%) with a bachelor's degree or higher was higher than that of males in Puerto Rico (11.1%) but lower compared to stateside Puerto Rican males (21%).

Employment Status

Labor force participation includes all people, 16 years and older, in the civilian labor force and the population serving in the Armed Forces. As of 2017, the civilian labor force participation rate for Puerto Ricans in Florida was 62 percent. This rate fluctuated over the previous seven years, but ultimately settled in 2017 below its 2010 rate. Overall, the civilian labor force participation of Puerto Ricans in Florida has decreased from 63.4 percent in 2010 to 62 percent in 2017 (-2.2%). Civilian labor force participation is divided into two groups: those who are employed and those unemployed. In 2017, the percentages of Puerto Ricans 16 years and older in Florida who were employed was 58 percent, while those unemployed was 4 percent. Overall, the rate of change in employment among Puerto Ricans in Florida increased from 53.5 percent in 2010 to 58 percent (8.4%). Correspondingly, the change among Puerto Ricans in Florida who were unemployed decreased by more than half (-59.6%), from 9.9 percent in 2010 to 4.0 percent in 2017.

Income and Earnings

Household incomes are vital indicators of economic well-being. In 2017, the median household income among Puerto Ricans in Florida was $46,735. This was an increase from $38,807 in 2010. Overall, median household income among Puerto Ricans in Florida increased 20.4 percent between 2010 and 2017.

Puerto Rican households in Florida commanded a lower income than Florida households overall. In 2017, the median household income among Puerto Ricans in Florida was lower than that of the state's population overall ($52,594). Similarly to Puerto Ricans in Florida, the median household income of the state's population increased between 2010 and 2017, but at a slower rate. The rate of change among Puerto Ricans in Florida was higher than the state's median household income rate of growth (18.4%).

In 2017, Puerto Ricans in Florida had a slightly higher median household income ($46,735) when compared to stateside Puerto Ricans ($44,731), but a strikingly higher median household income than Puerto Ricans in Puerto Rico ($19,229). All in all, the continuous increase in median household income over the seven years since 2010 may prove to be an incentive for other Puerto Ricans to move to Florida. On the other hand, the rate of change between 2010 and 2017 in median household income among Puerto Ricans in Florida (20.4%) was slightly lower than that of stateside Puerto Ricans (22.4%). Yet while, the median household income for Puerto Ricans in Puerto Rico increased from 2010 and 2017 at 3.2 percent, it did so at a significantly lower rate than that of Puerto Ricans in Florida.

Housing

Homeownership rates are used as indicators to determine not only the health of the housing markets within a particular area but also of financial stability. Overall, owning a home is considered as an essential step towards economic self-sufficient and upward mobility. However, the effects of the recession of 2008 still persist in homeownership rates. In 2017, 49.5 percent of Puerto Ricans in Florida owned their homes while 50.5 percent rented their homes. Renter-occupied housing units for the Puerto Rican population in Florida increased steadily from 46.7 percent in 2010 to 50.5 percent in 2017. Correspondingly, from 2010 to 2017 the number of homes owned by Puerto Ricans in Florida decreased from 53.3 percent in 2010 to 49.5 percent in 2017. While the rate of change in renter-occupied housing units for Puerto Ricans in Florida increased by 8.1 percent between 2010 and 2017, the rate of change for owner-occupied housing units decreased 7.1 percent.

In 2017, the proportion of Puerto Rican owner-occupied housing units in Florida (49.5%) was lower than that of the state's overall population (65.2%). Between 2010 and 2017, the proportion of all owner-occupied housing units in Florida decreased (-4.3%) while the proportion of renter-occupied housing units increased (9.1%). Furthermore, the proportion of owner-occupied housing units among Puerto Ricans in Florida declined at a faster rate (-7.1%) than for the state's overall population (-4.3%). It is evident that the effect of the Great Recession lingered in the housing market through 2015, when the homeownership rate in the state overall and for Puerto Ricans, specifically, reached its nadir. Since 2015, the rate of homeownership has begun to increase for all Floridians and for Puerto Ricans in Florida.

PUERTO RICO'S DEMOCRATIC REVOLT

I arrived in Puerto Rico for a family visit on July 16, 2019; shortly after landing, a *Time* magazine reporter reached me for comments on the political scandal that had exploded three days earlier when embarrassing profane chats among Governor Ricky Roselló and his closest political allies were leaked to the public. My four decades studying and teaching Puerto Rican history and my historian's intuition moved me to comment that the ongoing protests and scheduled massive mobilizations were unprecedented, were provoked by unprecedented political malfeasance, and did not bode well of the boyish governor's political future. "The most damaging thing is their behavior," I told the reporter. "That idea that they're superior to the common Puerto Rican. They have these privileges and spend the government money the way they wish. What has really triggered protest is this chat, the language really crossed a line." As the days and nights of peaceful protest continued, it became obvious that Roselló would have to do something equally unprecedented: resign in disgrace. This essay, published by *The Globe Post* on July 26, 2019, connects the massive protests to long-active tectonic tensions along a web of fault lines of politics, race, gender, and class.

Puerto Rico is undergoing its most dramatic political transformation since it became a U.S. territory in 1898-1899. Late Wednesday night (July 25), after two weeks of unprecedented popular mobilization and massive

Luis Martínez-Fernández, "Puerto Rico's Democratic Revolt Result of Decades of Mounting Tectonic Pressure," *The Globe Post*, July 26, 2019. Reprinted with permission by *The Globe Post*.

protests, Governor Ricardo Roselló reluctantly and unapologetically announced his resignation effective August 2.

During the first half of the 20th century, Puerto Rico experienced a gradual expansion of self-rule and civil rights that culminated in the 1952 formation of a democratic Commonwealth, neither independent nor a state of the Union but freely associated with the United States.

Under the leadership of progressive politician Luis Muñoz Marín and his selfless think tank and followers, and with the support of the Franklin D. Roosevelt administrations and others that followed, Puerto Rico experienced miraculous economic and social development. Measuring only 3,515 square miles, the island became America's "showcase of Democracy" and model for successful capitalist economic prosperity.

Tax Benefits and Recession

These extraordinary developments, however, were underpinned by structural dependency on the United States and special concessions by the insular government to U.S. corporations and investors. Among them stands out Section 936 of the U.S. Internal Revenue Service Code that freed corporations from tax payments as long as they reinvested their profits on the island.

Fast forward to 1996. For decades, leaders of the pro-Commonwealth Popular Democratic Party claimed that their status preference was the best guarantee for economic prosperity because it allowed the continuation of Section 936, a provision that states of the Union did not enjoy. In an effort to kill the 936 argument, Governor Pedro Roselló – Ricardo's father – argued for the elimination of that provision and did not raise a finger to defend it. The result was a ten-year gradual phase out that ended in 2005. Two years later, the economy entered a deep recession from which it has not yet recovered.

The crisis that exploded in the middle of the century's first decade is complex and has had multiple reverberations that feed off of each other. Factories that enjoyed tax exemptions closed, thus eliminating some of the best paying jobs; mass emigration of Puerto Ricans to the United States (mainly to Central Florida) increased dramatically, ridding the island of hundreds of Puerto Ricans in productive ages; house prices plummeted, and the tax base shrank.

Attempts to Save Puerto Rico's Economy

Beginning in 1973, Puerto Rico, its municipalities, and the state's public corporations issued millions of dollars' worth of bonds to balance their budgets.

In 2014, many of those bonds were downgraded to "junk" status, and a few months later, the unpopular pro-Commonwealth Governor Alejandro García Padilla declared that the 73 billion-dollar debt was unrepayable.

The United States government, in defense of U.S. bondholders, established the Puerto Rico Oversight Management and Economic Stability Act (PROMESA) Board and gave it broad powers that impinged on the island's traditional fiscal and political autonomy, including final say on insular budgets.

Governor Ricardo Roselló, a promoter of statehood, has proven supine. He has imposed austerity measures with detrimental effects on the masses: higher taxes, public utility fee hikes, reduction of public services, and the systematic defunding of the state university system. More alarming yet, are plans to slash retiree pensions, eliminate federal minimum wage protections for younger workers, and sell off, wholesale, state properties.

Hurricane Maria and Corruption

In the wee hours of September 20, 2017, Hurricane Maria struck the island, causing unprecedented damage and the death of over 4,000 residents. The Roselló administration stubbornly maintained for months that the actual death toll was 64. To add insult to injury, President Donald J. Trump visited the island and tossed rolls of paper towel at a gathering of Puerto Ricans. Since then, the Trump administration has withheld the bulk of fund transfers allotted for disaster relief and reconstruction.

In the meantime, members of the island's governing party have engaged in horrendous acts of corruption that included not distributing food and water for hurricane victims because keeping those provisions in truck containers generated enormous profits to well-connected contractors. Two weeks ago, federal authorities arrested several high-ranking administration officials on corruption charges, including the former secretary of education.

Popular indignation with the insular government had already reached a feverish peak when the Center for Investigative Journalism released 900 pages of chats exchanged between the governor and several of his cabinet members and closest political associates. Long familiar with the government's ineffectiveness, abuse of power, and corruption, the people of Puerto Rico read the atrocious chat statements that included misogynistic, homophobic, and other insulting comments.

Chat group members bragged about their own corrupt acts, applauded the fact that they had successfully pushed thousands of Puerto Ricans out of the island, denigrated political opponents, and worse yet, made sick jokes about those killed by the hurricane. The publication of those infamous chats was the crisis' let-them-eat-cake moment. The masses mobilized like never before and charged against the island's tropical bastille.

Social and Political Earthquake

The ongoing protests are the "Big One:" a social and political earthquake resulting from decades of mounting tectonic pressure along the manifold fissures that divide society: rich versus poor, men versus women, light-skinned versus darker-hued, the old versus the young, and those in favor and against gay rights.

The island will continue to shake after Roselló steps down. We can expect thunderous aftershocks for months and years: pressures to clean up all government institutions, fights against the indignities perpetrated by PROMESA, the auditing of the public debt, and the abolition, for once and for all, of the fraud of the island's status-preference-based party system. The Commonwealth is a cadaver: statehood is not an option – now less than ever – and independence will continue to be a unicorn aspiration.

This 100 x 35-miles island, in a peaceful way, has lectured the world on the meaning of true democracy.

PUERTO RICO'S PROTESTORS GOT CREATIVE; DANCING, SINGING, DIVING

Looking back into Puerto Rico's history, one is hard-pressed to find anything that approximates the level of unity that the people of Puerto Rico have displayed since Hurricane Maria struck on September 20, 2017. President Trump's mishandling of the crisis, including the retention of federal disaster funds, his insulting treatment toward Puerto Rican politicians, and his offensive act of tossing paper towels during his only public appearance in the hurricane's aftermath, united Puerto Ricans in a virtually universal repudiation of Trump. That unity became evident during the massive protests against Governor Roselló in July 2019. Charo Henríquez's *New York Times* article, published just hours before Roselló announced his resignation, reflects the unity and diversity of the protesters as manifested through the manifold creative ways in which they expressed their trenchant indignation. Charo Henríquez is a digital media executive based in New York City. She works with the *New York Times* as Senior Editor of Digital Transition Strategy.

Charo Henríquez, "Puerto Rico Protesters Got Creative: Dancing, Singing, Diving…" *The New York Times*, July 24, 2019. Reprinted with permission by *The New York Times*.

The protests in Puerto Rico that besieged the island's embattled governor, Ricardo A. Rosselló, before he announced on Wednesday [July 25] that he was resigning, were unlike any San Juan had seen before. Hundreds of thousands of people from all corners of the island jammed highways and surrounded the governor's mansion.

But they did not just march and shout slogans. They applied pressure in a host of other ways, from singing and dancing to yoga and horseback riding. Activists and celebrities used social media extensively, popularizing hashtags like #RickyRenuncia, #RickyTeBote, #TelegramGate, #RickyLeaks and #PuertoRicoMarcha to amplify their message and inspire more protests.

Here are some especially creative ways Puerto Ricans made their feelings known....

They went scuba diving. For this group of divers, marching on dry land wasn't enough of a statement, so they decided to take their message underwater, where they were documented in a video posted on Twitter.

They performed acrobatics. On July 22, these two protesters dangled from street signs above the Expreso Las Américas, one of San Juan's main highways, and performed in silks as a large crowd marched below.

They danced the electric slide. The four-wall line dance was puzzling and fascinating to some non-islanders on Twitter, but it is fairly common at parties, weddings and *quinceañero* celebrations. Here protesters were dancing to the beat of protest chants. The Electric Slide also spread to protests in New York and Washington in support of the island.

They drove bicycles, motorcycles and ATVs. On Tuesday night, hundreds of cyclists rode through the streets of Old San Juan to join protesters in La Fortaleza, the governor's official residence. Misael González Trinidad, an activist known in Puerto Rico as "Rey Charlie," organized motorcycle protests from the Cantera sector in San Juan through several housing projects and neighborhoods, gathering supporters along the way, before arriving in Old San Juan.

They boarded kayaks and water scooters. On July 21, a group organized by Ángel Jiménez set out from Colorado lagoon in kayaks and small boats and on water scooters, paddleboards and surfboards, and made their way to the stretch of San Juan Bay that the governor's mansion overlooks.

They expressed themselves through music. Well-known musicians like Ricky Martin, Residente and Bad Bunny combined their efforts to energize the protest movement. Ordinary Puerto Ricans also expressed themselves in ways as diverse as the island's culture, with songs played on traditional instruments with rhythms like plena and bomba, as well as more contemporary musical genres like urbano and trap. Protesters have vogued in a square in Old San Juan, and there were calls for a big gathering in front of the governor's mansions for *perreo*, a reggaeton dance style. Crowds have broken out in spontaneous rendition of Puerto Rican standards from the 1940s and 1950s, like "En Mi Viejo San Juan" and "Precisosa," considered unofficial anthems on the island.

They took to the saddle. A cabalgata, or cavalcade, is a mass procession on horseback—often staged to mark a ceremonial occasion, but sometimes as a form of protest. A group of mounted demonstrators rode from Puerto Rico Convention Center to the Capitol of Puerto Rico, just outside of Old San Juan.

They banged pots and pans. Many Puerto Ricans have taken to emulating the *cacerolazo*, a popular South American form of protest that originated in the 1970s in Chile. People could participate wherever they were, even at home, by banging cookware and kitchen utensils at a set time, with the noise calling attention to their grievances. In Puerto Rico, people have been banging pots and pans for one minute every day at 8 p.m.

They practiced yoga. The protests in Puerto Rico have ranged in noise level from clamor of the cacerolazo to the serenity of yoga. On the morning of July 21, a group led by Nicole Bernier, Paola Romo and Manuel Oria, did downward dog and other yoga positions near the governor's mansion and raised donations for a local legal defense fund and the local chapter of the American Civil Liberties Union.

They prayed. Members of some religious communities held gatherings across the island to pray as a form of peaceful protest.

A couple protested on their wedding day. As they exited the cathedral in Old San Juan after their wedding ceremony, a newlywed couple carried a protest sign with a message for the governor, whose official residence is nearby: "Because of you I almost didn't get married. Resign already!"

They accessorized. Another popular avenue of expression at the protests has run though the clothing, accessories and make-up worn by the demonstrators. Some people have worn body paint, slogan-emblazoned shirts and even earrings depicting and mocking Mr. Rosselló.

They put their cause where their mouths are. Food and beverages have also become the stuff of protest. Businesses have advertised special dishes and drinks with names alluding to the political situation. One example came from Luis A. Miranda Jr., the father of the broadway star Lin-Manuel Miranda. The elder Mr. Miranda posted an image on Twitter from La Placita de Güisín, the family's coffee shop in Vega Alta, P.R., where the barista had written the hashtag #RickyRenunica in the foam on a customer's drink.

AT THE HEART OF THE MOVEMENT: PUERTO RICAN WOMEN AND THE TOPPLING OF GOVERNOR ROSELLÓ

Women have increasingly assumed protagonist roles in almost every sector and aspect of Puerto Rican life, including the professions, government, business, and specially in non-governmental organizations and activist groups. Paradoxically, or perhaps not, Puerto Rican women are enduring alarming rates of domestic violence and death at the hands of their domestic partners and other men. It is widely recognized that violence against women has reached epidemic proportions. Political anthropologist Yarimar Bonilla's essay discusses the leading roles played by women (journalists, artists, university students, even school-aged girls) during the popular peaceful uprising that forced Governor Roselló to resign. She connects the political crisis of July 2019 with broader problems affecting the island and places the recent mobilizations within a context of longer-term activism against gender violence, political corruption and the government's shameful handling of the Hurricane Maria disaster. Bonilla is a professor at the City University of New York and is currently working on a book on the political, economic, and social aftermath of hurricane Maria in Puerto Rico.

After nearly two weeks of sustained protests by local residents, Puerto Rico's governor resigned from public office via Facebook Live on July 25, 2019. His unprecedented resignation was the result of massive public pressure from broad sectors of civil society, including international celebrities like Ricky Martin, Bad Bunny, iLe, and Residente, but at the heart of the movement, from beginning to end, were women of all ages and walks of life.

The Whistleblowers

The protests in Puerto Rico were sparked when 11 pages of messages sent by Governor Ricardo Rosselló and some of his cabinet members and top aides using the messaging app Telegram were leaked to the public by several journalists. Among the journalists was Sandra Rodríguez Cotto who focused her reporting on the officials' misogynistic language and the threat of violence

Yarimar Bonilla, "At the Heart of the Movement: Puerto Rican Women and the Toppling of Governor Roselló." Copyright 2019 by Yarimar Bonilla, written for this book, printed by permission.

towards women. As she and others reported, the governor repeatedly referred to women in the opposition as *putas* (the Spanish slur for prostitute), and one of his advisors made crude comments about gunning down Carmen Yulín Cruz, the mayor of San Juan.

According to a report by the American Civil Liberties Union (ACLU), Puerto Rico has the highest per capita rate of femicides, specifically of women killed by their partners, in the world. Local feminists groups have long been requesting greater governmental attention and action toward these issues. One group, la *Colectiva Feminista en Construcción,* has been particularly active in the battle against gender violence both before and after Hurricane Maria. La Colectiva was directly targeted in the governor's chats for extensive protests and efforts to hold the government accountable for the crisis in gender-based violence. It was La Colectiva that first called for a massive march in response to the leaked chats on Wednesday, July 17. La Colectiva was also the first to stage *cacerolazos* (protests with pots and pans) and to camp out outside the governor's mansion, in what they called a *plantón,* demanding the governor declare a state of emergency around gender violence, thus turning the governor's mansion into a site of resistance long before the current protests.

In addition to misogynistic and homophobic content, the chats also mocked the victims and survivors of Hurricane Maria, fueling the anger of many. The governor joked about the cadavers piling up at the public morgue during and after the storm. To this day, neither the U.S. government nor the government of Puerto Rico has publicly acknowledged that over 3,000 people died as a result of the storm or the systemic failures after the hurricane to help people in need.

Even when the government was not working for Puerto Ricans, journalists like Sandra Rodríguez Cotto were; Rodríguez Cotto served as one of the main sources of information on the island for WAPA Radio. When residents found themselves with no electricity or cell phone service, they often used her platform to tell their stories. Women who were deeply affected by the storm, particularly those who were victims of domestic violence and who found themselves doubly vulnerable in the midst of the disaster, benefited from Rodríguez Cotto and WAPA Radio.

In the case of the Telegram scandal, it was another group of women-led journalists who pushed the story to the next level. After the original 11 pages circulated in the press, Governor Rosselló stated there were no illegalities revealed in the chat messages. He also claimed that the rest of the chats had been deleted, leaving out what he considered the necessary context for interpreting the offensive remarks.

The next day, the Center for Investigative Journalism, known by its Spanish acronym CPI, shocked Puerto Ricans by publishing nearly a thousand additional pages of the chats. This women-led organization has earned a reputation in Puerto Rico for its in-depth reporting and unveiling of government mismanagement. CPI led the charge in the wake of Hurricane Maria to counter the official cover-up that claimed a death toll of only 16 for months. Many could tell from their own personal experience that the truth was exponentially larger. CPI eventually created an interactive website where individual stories of hurricane victims have been preserved. To this day, the local government refuses to do a full accounting of those that were lost to the storm. All that exists are statistical analyses suggesting that thousands more Puerto Ricans died the year of Hurricane Maria than would have died in a normal year. The names and individual stories of those who were lost remain preserved only through the efforts of the CPI and other independent journalists.

CPI had received the initial leak of 11 pages, but they held back from publishing until they could see the full context, explained Omaya Sosa Pascual, one of the CPI's founding directors. Unlike other news outlets, their interest was not on the insulting and degrading language but on what they saw as potential illegalities and unethical activity regarding possible corruption. Once they received the full text, CPI executive director Carla Minet decided that they would not just publish snippets as other venues had done but release the text online for all to read along with their own investigation into government corruption.

The Mothers and Daughters of the Crisis

The release of the full chats showed Lourdes Muriente, a practicing attorney in San Juan, that the governor had made light of the death of her former husband, Carlos Gallisá, a prominent activist and political leader on the island who died of cancer in 2018. In response, she and two other women marched into government buildings and began taking the official portrait of the governor off the wall. Videos of their actions soon went viral, inspiring cartoons and copycat actions.

One of the women who joined Muriente was 70-year-old Abigail Ramos, who explained that the chats had affected her emotionally and even physically. When she read the news, all the pain and suffering of Hurricane Maria came rushing back. She had flashbacks of those she had met who had struggled caring for sick loved ones without electricity or basic infrastructure, and of friends who were struggling with reduced pensions due to the island's long-standing financial crisis. The idea of the governor laughing and making light of the events from the safety of his mansion while many Puerto Ricans struggled to survive in the storm-ravaged island was too much for her to bear.

The persistent silence around the people who were lost to Hurricane Maria, the insurmountable challenge of mourning them properly, and the blatant disrespect from their governmental officials were all sore points for islands residents. At the rallies, many carried pictures of those they had lost along with personal stories of friends and family who did not survive the storm. The indignation felt over the dead was key to mobilizing the protestors and ignited a fire within a younger generation of Puerto Ricans.

One of these was Aliana Bigio, a 21-year-old student at the University of Puerto Rico who, immediately after the first information leak, gathered a group of young women outside the governor's mansion to protest. The group, which took on the name *Mujeres en Resistencia* (Women in Resistance), placed duct tape on their mouths as symbols of repression and staged a peaceful protest to demand the governor's removal. They also brought published copies of the governor's chats with them so that visitors to Old San Juan, many of whom were unaware of the actual content of the conversations, could read the messages for themselves.

Bigio was already politically active, running a Facebook and Instagram site called *Con-Sentimiento* (a double entendre in Spanish which means consent but also "with sentiment"). She began the site to launch conversations about feminism, gender binaries, and hot button issues such as abortion. However, many other women who were not already involved in political groups were also moved to action by the chats.

One group of 20-year-old women turned to make-up and body paint to express their discontent, essentially turning their bodies into a political canvas. They drew international attention for their work and soon became known as *las hijas de la crisis* (the daughters of the crisis), a name that captures how the current movement spans beyond the governor's chats and even the crisis of Maria. It tunnels through to a deeper nerve among young Puerto Ricans who are struggling to make the island a place where they can live, dream, and create a new future.

The body painters began with Anamar Pérez-Green, the canvas for makeup artist Melanie Rodríguez Rosado, who painted her subject as a Puerto Rican flag lit up in flames. Rodríguez Rosado placed tape covered in drawings of barbed wire across Pérez-Green's mouth and paired it with smeared black eye makeup streaming down her face. Pérez-Green also wrote the word *'puta'* scribbled across her buttocks and used her back as a message board so that protestors could write their own messages to the governor. Participants filled her back with messages such as "No more abuse!" "Resign!" and other choice words borrowed from the chats. The final look served as a symbol for the pain and emotion felt by protestors and Puerto Ricans at large.

Images and videos of Pérez-Green taken by photographer Valeria Martínez-Marrero quickly went viral. Days later, an iconic image began to circulate of eight girls who together symbolized various aspects of the protests. One was dressed as a white and black Puerto Rican flag, the symbol of resistance; another was painted as a rainbow flag to symbolize inclusivity. A girl painted as a skeleton represented Maria's dead, who were ever-present in the protest, while other girls bore insults from the infamous leaked chats. Together they looked like a band of superheroes fighting for Puerto Rico's future.

As Bigio explained in a recent podcast interview, this new generation of girls are a product of Puerto Rico's crisis: "I don't remember, ever since I was a kid, living in a period not characterized by crisis." "We have inherited a debt that we did not create, and we live carrying a weight that should not be our responsibility," she added in a recently penned post for the feminist website *Todas*. "We do not rest because of the anxiety of what will or will not be our 'future.'"

"It is important that my generation become informed and express themselves politically starting now," explained 14-year-old Lorena Isabel Torres Negrón, an accomplished ballet dancer who attended the protests with her parents and two brothers. She felt that it was important for teens like her to become involved now, even if it will take a few more election cycles for them to be able to cast their ballots. "We are the future, but we have to start becoming informed now. If we wait until we are old enough to vote, they will deceive us and everything will be worse," she added. "We are not only here for ourselves but also for our parents, who pay taxes ... it's not just about us but about defending our country."

Bigio agrees that Puerto Rico's future is in the hands of this new generation. She worries that young people are being forced into greater and greater debt as the university becomes less accessible—due to budget cuts and decreased financial aid in the wake of the financial crisis. But she insists that given all these hardships, Puerto Rican young people have nothing to lose. "We have to go out and take back the country they tried to destroy, always remembering that the resignation of former Governor Ricardo Rosselló is not the end of this fight, but only the beginning," she wrote in *Todas*. "We have a lot that needs cleaning up, and the young people of this country are ready with a broom and dustpan in hand. In the streets, at the polls, in the university, in our homes, and on social media, we will continue to create our homeland (*hacer patria*) and demand a better Puerto Rico for us all."

As Torres Negrón sees it, the chats were not entirely bad. After all, it served to shed light and to help young Puerto Ricans wake up to Puerto Rico's realities and to the next generation's political duties.

INDEX

ABOUT THE EDITORS

Olga Jiménez de Wagenheim is Professor Emerita in History, Rutgers University. She has published several books on Puerto Rico, including *Puerto Rico: An Interpretive History from Pre-Columbian Times to 1900*, *Puerto Rico's Revolt for Independence: El Grito de Lares*, and *Nationalist Heroines: Puerto Rican Women History Forgot, 1930s-1950s*.

Kal Wagenheim is a former New York Times reporter and has taught journalism and creative writing at Columbia University and the State Prison in Trenton, NJ. He is the author of several books and plays including *Clemente! The Enduring Legacy* and the novel *The Secret Life of Walter Mott*.

Luis Martínez-Fernández is Professor of History at the University of Central Florida in Orlando. His research and publications have focused on Cuba, the Hispanic Caribbean, and the Cuban and Puerto Rican diasporas in Florida. He is the author of several books including *Frontiers, Plantations, and Walled Cities and Key to the New World*.

CPSIA information can be obtained
at www.ICGtesting.com
Printed in the USA
LVHW101947131222
735141LV00001B/93